AF522522

PAKISTAN'S OTHER STORY

The 1968-9 Revolution

Lal Khan

Pakistan's Other Story: The 1968-9 Revolution
Lal Khan

Published with permission from
The Struggle Publications, Lahore

First Indian Edition, 2009

ISBN 978-93-5002-000-5 (Hb)

Published by
AAKAR BOOKS
28 E Pocket IV, Mayur Vihar Phase I, Delhi-110 091
Phone : 011-2279 5505 Telefax : 011-2279 5641
aakarbooks@gmail.com; www.aakarbooks.com

Printed at
Arpit Printographers, Delhi-110 032
e-mail : arpitprinto@yahoo.com

To,

The generation of the workers, peasants and youth of 1968-9, who dared to prove to history that revolutionary socialism was possible on this land.

CONTENTS

Acknowledgements		*vii*
***Foreword* by Achin Vanaik**		*ix*
Preface		*xiii*
Pakistan: The Revolution Betrayed	An **introduction** to Pakistan's Other Story—The 1968-9 Revolution **By Alan Woods**	1
One	**A Revolutionary Epoch** Revolutionary Ferment across the Planet	11
Two	**Bloody Partition of The Subcontinent** Birth Pangs of Pakistan	53
Three	**A Failed Start—The Failure of Bourgeois Democracy** Military Rule and the Gathering Storm	92
Four	**The Mass Revolt** When Socialist Victory was on the Agenda	128
Five	**Witnesses to Revolution** Veterans of the 1968-9 Upheaval	164
Six	**War, Repression and Reforms** Lessons of a Derailed Revolution	217
Seven	**Crisis of the Left Leadership** Rise of the Pakistan People's Party	253
Eight	**Dictatorship and Democracy** Regimes Changed, the Masses Continue to Suffer	305
Nine	**Redeeming the 1968-9 Uprising** Perspectives of Revolutionary Socialism	370
Appendix I	**The Role of the Pakistan Army**	413
Appendix II	**Pakistan's Richest List of 2007**	429
Appendix III	**PPP Manifesto 1970 Salient Features**	445
Bibliography		453

ACKNOWLEDGEMENTS
for the Indian Edition

Mr. K.K. Saxena of Aakar Books, without whose strenuous efforts this edition may not have seen the light of the day. A few years ago he published my book *Partition—Can It Be Undone* on his own initiative. I am highly indebted to him for his affection and zeal with which he has published my works. Special thanks are due to Mr. Tanvir Ahmad for his meticulous proofreading and corrections that made this book more comprehensible and easy to read. I have also to thank my dear friend Achin Vanaik for writing the foreword of this edition. I am grateful to Satish Kumar, my dear friend and comrade for 27 years, who introduced me to the dynamics of the movements of the Indian proletariat and helped me attain a deeper understanding of the history of the oppressed toilers of the subcontinent. Last, but not the least I have to express my gratitude for my lifelong friend Vinod Malik, whose compassionate inspiration has always encouraged me to embark upon writing on rather sensitive issues in the subcontinent. He has always ensured that I feel at home whenever I am in India.

FOREWORD

The heroes of this book by Lal Khan are the ordinary working people and students of Pakistan. This was so in that remarkable upsurge of 1968-9 that is still the closest that Pakistan has ever come to the possibility of a socialist revolution. Today, it is again the people of Pakistan who are the heroes of yet another mass movement and struggle even as its basic thrust is different from that of 1968-69. The current struggle is to establish in a more enduring way than ever before the structures appropriate to a liberal democratic polity.

Consider what has happened in the last two years. Despite the military coup of General Pervez Musharraf and his subsequent ascent to President of Pakistan, he was pressured to abandon his uniform and status as Chief of the Armed Forces in November 2007. Three months later, whatever his and the army's reservations and unease, basically free national elections were held and the result was a resounding defeat for Musharraf's party. In August 2008, the opposition parties backed by the public ensured the removal of Musharraf as President. This was the first time that a military leader ensconced in power gave it up to civilian rule without having to be first killed (General Zia-ul-Haq) or after having provoked a civil war (General Yahya Khan).

To update the story, mass anger and the threat of carrying out huge popular demonstrations and of long marches from all parts of the country to eventually converge on the capital, Islamabad, was enough to force the newly installed Zardari Pakistan People's Party (PPP) government to restore Iftikhar Chaudhury as Chief Justice of the Supreme Court and to suspend the earlier dismissal of the Punjab provincial government ruled by the opposition party, the Pakistan Muslim League-Nawaz Sharif or PML(N). Not just the Zardari government but the US government and the armed forces headed by General Kayani had to accept and endorse this turn of events and even to try and claim credit for it, such was the impact of mass anger and resistance.

What has happened of course is far less dangerous for the ruling classes than the turmoil of 1968-69. But a new space for mass political activity has opened up and the recent changes are a tribute to what the people of Pakistan can accomplish in the face of seemingly great odds. These obstacles should not, however, be underestimated despite their current retreat. There is a motley of civilian political parties riding on mass anger but ever willing to betray the hopes and aspirations of ordinary people. There are a variety of reactionary Islamist forces wielding significant influence which are burrowing into the pores of Pakistan civil society. There is still united and powerful army whose lower ranks and higher ranks are being Islamised. There is a US more determined than ever to control the Pakistan establishment as part of its overall imperialist project of dominating West and Central Asia.

Indeed, the appearance of this book by Lal Khan could not have come at a more opportune time. This is a work of panoramic sweep operating at different levels. It situates the 1968-69 upheaval in the wider global context of that time when there was a unique convergence in time of powerful anti-capitalist, anti-imperialist and anti-Stalinist/authoritarian mass movements in the first, second and third worlds symbolized most strongly by the struggles over and in Vietnam, in France, in Czechoslovakia. These were accompanied by a whole range of old and new progressive and democratic movements ranging from the fight against racism, for civil rights to the second wave of feminism.

This book does not just provide a historical narrative of how the '1968-9 Revolution', the sub-title of the book, unfolded and what directions it took. It also offers the testimonials of important actors and leaders who recount their attitudes, beliefs, hopes and expectations of what that great upheaval might have achieved. That was a time when a labour leader could and did walk up to Robert MacNamara, the US secretary of state, and publicly slap him in the face shouting "Down with Imperialism". That was a time when a revered Muslim fundamentalist leader and preacher at a mass meeting of the faithful would ask whether his flock wanted the Koran or mere materialist matters such as bread and receive the unexpected public outcry "We have the Koran at home, but we don't have bread".

Finally, this is a book that by weaving together history with socialist theory and thought offers a vision of both what is needed and possible. May it serve as a source of inspiration and education to those today who by their actions and commitments are seeking to create a new history in Pakistan and elsewhere!

March 22, 2009 **Achin Vanaik**
New Delhi

PREFACE

The greatest of ideas in history have always been put to the test by real life events. The truth and correctness of the theory and ideology of Marxism needed the victory of the great Bolshevik revolution in the land of October to attain its worldwide recognition. After the fall of the Berlin Wall and the collapse of the Soviet Union, the present world crisis of capitalism and the financial meltdown have once again drawn the attention of the world towards the ideas of revolutionary Marxism. In ordinary times, the social political and cultural psyche of society is dominated and shaped by the reactionary ethics and norms of the ruling classes. All conflicts, developments, events, thoughts, societies and countries are defined in accordance with the interests of the elite and the domination of the financial oligarchy.

Pakistan, its history, its character and its role as a country has been portrayed with a similar intention on the world arena. History, as written by most local and foreign historians, and the analysis of society produced in the international and national media by the so-called 'experts' that dominate bourgeois intellectual circles have all been from the point of view and intentions of the ruling classes. Some of the more significant aspects have been downplayed or even ignored, while the most insignificant issues have been blown out of proportion.

The greatest victim of these distortions in the media which so-called left liberal historians and experts have also contributed to, has been that mighty revolution of 1968-9 in Pakistan. Some have described it as an anti-Ayub agitation, some as mere strikes for workers' demands and others as a struggle for democracy against dictatorship.

It was in fact none of these. It was a mass upheaval that created a revolutionary situation, the character of which was socialist. This movement not only challenged the existing order, the dictatorship, the political superstructure, but above all the existing property relations. The revolution had instilled a will and determination, a consciousness of collectivism that dared to move forward and demand workers' ownership and democratic control of industry, the economy and the whole of society.

In this work we will endeavour to highlight all this and pass it on to the present generation of workers and youth in Pakistan and their brethren across the planet. Some other authors have also tried to bring out the revolutionary aspects of that uprising. This work is devoted to the revolutionary character of the movement and the socialist victory it was so close to achieving. Many comrades and friends over the last three decades have encouraged me and suggested I embark on such a work. Due to many commitments the work never started, but now the present precarious situation and the intense crisis and suffering of the working classes in Pakistan at such a crucial juncture, necessitated the writing and publishing of this work.

Pakistan today is portrayed as a bastion of fundamentalism, terrorism and extremism. Its creation as a theocratic state, the long periods of Martial Law, repression, lawlessness, crime, fraud, corruption and instability are the elements that are highlighted to the world. A large section of the new generations within Pakistan have a similar appraisal of the situation. The Islamic fundamentalists' 'solution' is to go back to the dark pre-medieval ages. The imperialists and their stooges in Pakistan claim that liberal democracy and 'good governance' is the solution.

However, the masses in Pakistan have suffered both of these 'solutions'. And all they have experienced has been more exploitation, violence, devastation and misery. That explains why there have been several movements of workers, peasants and the youth. All in their own way have been trying to get rid of capitalist exploitation, feudal drudgery, obscurantist terror and imperialist repression. The 1968-9 movement stands out above all these uprisings, as it came close to winning a socialist victory.

The toiling masses of Pakistan have endured long periods of oppression and exploitation. Time and again they have risen in revolt with fierce volcanic eruptions. The official tale of Pakistani society—from politics to culture, to all aspects of society has been that of the ruling classes and their toadies. It is time to unravel the truth.

The oppressed in Pakistan have a mission to accomplish, that of their own emancipation. They have a historic pledge to redeem. The task of a victorious socialist revolution has to be undertaken. They have fought ferocious battles in this class war. They have made enormous sacrifices. Innumerable silent soldiers have fought to win this war; for generations they have suffered, but they rise again and again to overthrow this yoke of slavery and exploitation. They shall rise once more. This is the verdict of history. They have their own story to tell, that is *Pakistan's Other Story*.

Lahore **Lal Khan**
30 October 2008

Pakistan: The Revolution Betrayed

An **introduction** to *Pakistan's Other Story—The 1968-9 Revolution*

Alan Woods

The publication of a book by Lal Khan on the Pakistan revolution of 1968-9, *Pakistan's Other Story*, is a most important addition to the theoretical arsenal of international Marxism. In 1968 the attention of most people in Europe was absorbed by the revolutionary events in France. But I can vividly remember the marvellous movement in Pakistan, which made a deep impression on me. In fact I wrote an article about it at the time. It was published in our journal *Perspectives* under the title 'Pakistan—The revolution betrayed'. The present introduction is largely based on what I wrote at the time.

At the beginning of 1968 the military dictatorship of Ayub Khan appeared on the surface as one of the most stable regimes in all Asia. For ten years he had ruled the country posing as the 'strong man' who had saved society from 'anarchy'. In classic Bonapartist style, he balanced internationally between the rival great powers of East and West, now taking aid from Britain or America, now from Russia or China. In particular, his close relationship with China paid dividends, not only economically, in terms of massive aid and trade, but also politically, by granting the regime the semblance of a 'progressive' face.

The Chinese bureaucracy supported the dictator Ayub Khan. Chou En-lai congratulated Ayub Khan on his success in rigged elections in 1965. When war broke out between India and Pakistan in the same year, Beijing gave full support to Pakistan, describing it as a 'people's war'. All this was dictated purely by cynical reasons, mainly in response to Moscow's support for India, on the principle that "the enemy of my enemy is my friend".

The successes of the Ayub regime in the international arena concealed the depths of the economic and social crisis of Pakistan. True, the economy had gone forward at a rate of more than five per cent per annum. But this growth was confined mainly to West Pakistan. East Pakistan (now Bangladesh) remained in a state of hopeless, semi-feudal backwardness. In fact it declined. The province was dependent upon two crops: rice (subject to flooding) and jute, which was rapidly being ousted on the international market by the use of plastics and other synthetic material.

In the more industrialized province of West Pakistan, the polarization of wealth was chronic. On the one hand, the notorious twenty-two families owned 66 per cent of industrial assets, 79 per cent of insurance and 80 per cent of banking. On the other, the average income in West Pakistan was a mere £35 per annum: in East Pakistan, the figure was even worse—an abysmal £15.

The misery and chronic backwardness of the population created an explosive situation, which only needed a single spark to ignite. Towards the end of 1967, a series of riots occurred in various regions. These were renewed the following January. The basic issue was the fake elections, which Ayub had called under his system of 'basic democracy', a fraudulent scheme designed to place the power of elections into the hands of 80,000 so-called basic democrats, stooges of the regime.

Revolution

In the first months of 1968, Pakistan was shaken by a series of massive revolutionary movements involving every section of society. The bourgeois press described this as "mob rule". Naturally! For the idle parasites that rule society, the people the workers and peasants who produce all the wealth of society are nothing more than a 'mob'. In reality, the revolution of 1968-9 had been prepared well in advance. Beneath the surface of apparent stability, the unbearable contradictions in Pakistan society were building up slowly but surely.

On January 17 police opened fire on demonstrators in Dacca, killing several. On 24 January, the city was paralyzed by a general strike and student riots and troops were called in. There was even a 24-hour strike of journalists, gagged by the regime's 'emergency laws' (introduced during the Indo-Pakistan war and retained for use against the 'enemy within'). Fearing a general conflagration, the Ayub regime hastily began to throw out concessions aimed, in the first instance, to placate the students. The ban on political organizations in universities was lifted.

Ayub's concessions had come too late: instead of placating the movement, they added fuel to the flames. A freak impetus was given by the victory in India's mid-term elections, of the United Front Government in West Bengal, the effects of which spilled over the borders into East Pakistan. Alarmed at the prospect of new upheavals, Ayub hastily released from prison the leader of the secessionist opposition in East Pakistan, Sheikh Mujib-ur Rahman. In a desperate attempt to stave off the crisis, Ayub agreed to meet the leaders of the opposition parties, which in 1965 he had mocked as "five cats tied together by their tails". The offer, however, did not extend to the left-wing opposition parties.

Throughout the entire crisis, the bourgeois opposition (the DAC) showed itself to be utterly worthless. Their imperious demands for "constitutional rule" which echoed around the cocktail parties of Karachi were unheard in the streets, where the mass movement was growing rapidly in strength and breadth. The movement, which had hitherto been dominated by the students, gave way to the might of the working class. The serious capitalist journals of the West looked on in dismay. The victory of the United Front in West Bengal and the mass movements in Pakistan caused *The Economist* to remark that "If anywhere in Asia is ripe for an attempt at urban revolution it is Calcutta, and the cities of East Pakistan are not far behind".

In February and March, a sweeping wave of strikes engulfed the country. On 13 February, for the first time in ten years, the red flag was hauled up in Lahore, as more than 25,000 rail workers marched along the main street chanting: "Solidarity with the Chinese people: Destroy capitalism." This showed the will of the workers and peasants to change society. Unfortunately, there was no mass Marxist Party to provide the necessary leadership.

The pro-Beijing National Awami Party had the support of a large section of the Pakistani workers and peasants. But it did not have a revolutionary programme. Instead of mobilizing the working masses on a programme of the seizure of power, the pro-Chinese Stalinists called for a bloc with the right-wing Moslem Party, Jamaat-e-Islami. The Maoist peasant leader Maulana Bashani made demagogic speeches, threatening the ruling classes with civil war ("We will burn the houses of those who take part in elections"). But these were just words without any real content.

At this time the peasants in East Pakistan were already seizing the land and executing the criminal elements, village chiefs and rent collectors who made up the ranks of Ayub's so-called 'basic democrats'. The mood of the masses can be gauged by the fact that even the bourgeois Sheikh Mujib-ur Rahman was obliged to accept the programme worked out by the Dacca students for nationalization of industry and withdrawal from imperialist backed CENTO (Central Treaty Organization) and SEATO (South East Asian Treaty Organization).

A magnificent movement

The bourgeoisie was convinced that Pakistan was on the verge of revolution. And they were not wrong. Businessmen inside Pakistan paid large sums to get their money out of the country. The black market rate for sterling shot up from 21 rupees to 30 in two weeks; the price of gold rose by 40 per cent. The British capitalist press also understood the gravity of the situation and the impossibility of the old regime maintaining itself.

'Authority' had broken down. Power was in the hands of the workers and peasants who, like their counterparts in Spain in 1936, realized the whole 'election programme' of democracy and more in a few days. What the cliques and coteries of bourgeois politicians had vainly struggled to obtain for ten years was carried through by the revolutionary action of the masses in an instant. Then what role was left to the 'democratic' bourgeoisie? The answer is: *None, except that which the 'leaders' of the proletariat and peasantry were prepared to hand over to it.*

On 24 February, the *Financial Times* reported: "In Karachi junior army officers were being court-martialled for refusing to fire on demonstrators." *The Times*, in March, described the situation where "... strikers from every profession, trade and occupation from doctors to railway workers and state engineers, parade through the streets almost every hour demanding better working conditions and more pay ... a police uniform has not been seen in the streets of Dacca for a fortnight."

The situation in Pakistan had "got out of hand" from the bourgeois point of view. The government had lost its nerve; the ruling clique was suspended in mid-air; the police force was demoralized and sections of the armed forces wavering; the mass movement, affecting all sections of the populace, had set about a transformation of society. All the elements of a classical revolutionary situation were present, except one: the revolutionary leadership.

Under those conditions, if a clear lead had been given, a *peaceful* transition could have been affected. But if the magnificent movement of the Pakistani workers and peasants were worthy to be placed on a par with the movement of their class brothers in France and Italy, the cowardice, shortsightedness and cynicism of the leadership was not far behind that of its European counterparts. *The betrayal of the Pakistani Stalinists, who refused to mobilize the masses for the seizure of power, inevitably prepared the way for reaction.*

The truly magnificent struggles of the Pakistani workers and peasants at this time are worthy to be put on a par with the great movement of their French and Italian class brothers. The movement in Pakistan, given a correct leadership, could have led to a peaceful seizure of power. But just as in France and Italy in 1968-9, the weakness was in the leadership. Neither Bhutto nor the National Awami Party was prepared to take power. This was what paved the way for the military coup.

The PPP

The Pakistan People's Party (PPP) was formed on 1 December, 1967. Its programme was socialist and its founding manifesto called for nationalization of the productive forces and a people's militia. Zulfiqar Ali Bhutto (the father of Benazir Bhutto) appeared to challenge the Ayub dictatorship, while both the pro-Moscow Stalinists and Maoists were supporting the 'progressive' Ayub Khan. Bhutto therefore became a symbol of resistance, although he himself was a feudal lord from Sindh, and had been foreign minister in Ayub's cabinet. Nevertheless, he raised the slogan of socialism and acquired considerable popularity. The PPP rose to prominence on the wave of the 1968-9 revolutionary movement.

Bhutto claimed to stand for socialism and some regarded him as a "dangerous revolutionary". But the most perspicacious bourgeois did not share this view. *The Times*, anxious to soothe the jangling nerves of its readers, sent a reporter to interview Bhutto, who reported as follows: "Tagging at his cigar in his Karachi home, Mr. Bhutto now says that his concept of socialism is more akin to Scandinavia's than Peking's, Pakistan's ties with China are close enough." (*The Times*, 26 February, 1968) *The Economist* wrote of Bhutto: "It is worth remembering that everything said about him was once said (reading 'Russian' for 'Chinese') about Nehru."

Many of the mass leaders of the 1968 movement joined the PPP. In 1970, the masses in West Pakistan voted massively for this party because they desired a fundamental change in society and were attracted by its socialist programme. They were faced with a stark alternative: either carry out the socialist transformation of society, or else obey the dictates of Capital. There was every possibility of carrying out the socialist transformation of society. But Bhutto and the Right-wing leaders of the PPP failed to do this. Although they carried out some radical reforms they did not carry out fundamental change. They compromised with the feudals and capitalists and allowed the army to regain control.

In every revolution there is a stage when the masses feel cheated and try to take action to regain the initiative. Such a period was the July Days in Russia in 1917 or the Spartakist uprising in Berlin in January 1919. The proletariat took to the streets to press their demands during the period May–September 1972. The movement was especially militant in

Karachi, the Petrograd of the Pakistan proletariat. The government moved to crush the movement. A demonstration of workers was fired on in Landhi, Karachi, leaving dozens dead. This disillusioned the working class and prepared the way for reaction. Having turned against the Left, the PPP government allowed the pendulum to swing to the right.

It is significant that at the height of the crisis, Bhutto's People's Party split. The difference, as always, was on the question of independence for East Pakistan. Bhutto's refusal to deal with this question indicated his subordination to the interests and wishes of the Pakistani bourgeoisie and the military. The result was a terrible tragedy. It led, first to the break-up of Pakistan and then to war with India. Then, inevitably, having played into the hands of the military and reactionary forces, Bhutto was overthrown and hanged in 1979. He was a victim of the reactionary Pakistan oligarchy. But he was also the victim of his own attempts to conciliate the forces of reaction. As a result, the people of Pakistan were thrown down once more into the black abyss of military dictatorship.

The Heritage of 1968

The dictatorship of Zia-al-Huq was a thousand times worse than that of Ayub Khan or Yahya Khan. Backed by American imperialism, this monstrous regime represented an appalling regression, in which ruthless dictatorship and disgusting corruption was combined with religious obscurantism and barbarism. The rich cultural life of Lahore was extinguished and fanaticism suffocated intellectual life. It was at this time that US imperialism became the real Master of Pakistan, which it dragged into its military adventure in Afghanistan. The peoples of both countries have been paying the price ever since.

The plane crash that killed military dictator General Zia was probably an assassination prepared by the CIA and elements within the ISI. The elections of 1988 led to the second government of the PPP under Benazir Bhutto. But she carried out a policy of conciliation with the ruling class and the army, which again disillusioned the working class and ended in new defeats. The policies of the 'free market' adopted by the PPP leaders have led to more downsizing, privatizations, unemployment and a deepening of poverty for the masses. The experiment in 'democracy' ended inevitably in the dictatorship of Musharraf.

Pakistan has been reduced to a desperate position. Its economy, despite its enormous potential, has been ruined. The country's finances are bankrupt and it is on the verge of default. There is mass unemployment and poverty. The counter-revolutionary policies of US imperialism aided and abetted by the corrupt and degenerate Pakistan ruling class have conspired to produce the rise of fundamentalism and black reaction. The symptoms of barbarism are present and threaten to engulf society.

The horrors that threaten the people of Pakistan were shown by the brutal assassination of Benazir Bhutto on 27 December, 2007. This was intended to halt the mass movement that was stimulated by the return of the leader of the PPP. The masses were looking to the PPP for a way out of the crisis, for a change in the miserable conditions of their lives, for *roti, kapra aur makan* (bread, clothing and shelter). The reactionaries, and the imperialists who stand behind them, will stop at nothing to destroy the movement of the workers and peasants.

The present leaders of the PPP would prefer to forget the mass revolutionary struggles of the workers and peasants of Pakistan in 1968-9, although it was the workers and peasants and their revolutionary struggle which created the PPP and propelled it to power. They have forgotten everything and learned nothing. They have turned their backs on the socialist traditions of the PPP. They act as if the PPP's founding Manifesto never existed. They are trying to administer capitalism in a situation where the global crisis of capitalism renders this impossible. As a result, they will be compelled to carry out deep cuts in living standards. This will create the conditions for a new defeat of the PPP and the return of the Right wing. Under these circumstances an explosion of the masses and a new 1968 is entirely possible in the next period.

The American philosopher George Santayana wrote: "He who does not learn from history will be condemned to repeat it." My comrade and teacher, the late Ted Grant, was very fond of this quotation. Today it is more necessary than ever that we study history, especially the history of revolutions. The Pakistan Revolution of 1968-9 was one of the greatest revolutionary movements of the 20th century. It is rich in lessons and Lal Khan's book *Pakistan's Other Story* is an outstanding summing-up of these lessons. It deserves the most careful study by every revolutionary.

Today the traditions of 1968-9 are upheld by the Marxist tendency, *Jeddojuhd* (*The Struggle*). Beginning as a small group of exiled revolutionaries in 1980 in the Netherlands, *The Struggle* has grown in strength and influence, especially in the last ten years, when it has established itself as the only genuinely revolutionary tendency in Pakistan with a mass base. Under the leadership of Lal Khan, who I am proud to call my comrade and friend, *The Struggle* has maintained a firm stand on revolutionary principles, waging an implacable struggle against both ultra-left sectarianism and unprincipled opportunism.

There are only two possibilities before the people of Pakistan: socialism or barbarism. *The Struggle,* in collaboration with the International Marxist Tendency, is fighting for socialism, in Pakistan and the whole subcontinent and on a world scale. The best way to pay tribute to those courageous workers and peasants who fought for socialism in 1968-9 is to continue their struggle and carry it to a victorious conclusion. We pledge ourselves to this end.

London, October 20, 2008.

One

A REVOLUTIONARY EPOCH

Revolutionary Ferment across the Planet

All the factors making for an unprecedented boom were the same factors preparing the way for economic catastrophes and social upheavals.

—Ted Grant (1913–2006)[1]

Bliss was it, to be alive in that dawn, But to be young was very heaven.

—William Wordsworth, in Paris during the great French Revolution of 1789

Revolutionary periods are historical exceptions. They don't occur every day. The period around the years 1968-9 was such a historical exception. It was not just in Pakistan that the torrent of mass revolutionary upheaval swept across the country from 7 November, 1968 till the fall of the formidable dictatorship of Ayub Khan on 26 March, 1969. The mass movement had challenged the state and victory of a socialist revolution seemed to be the inevitable conclusion. Across the planet there were revolutionary uprisings in almost all the continents.

In the aftermath of the Second World War there were huge revolutionary movements. It was the betrayal of these movements, mainly through the treaties in Yalta, Tehran and Potsdam between Stalin, Churchill and US Presidents Roosevelt and Truman, that the communist leaderships of these workers' movement betrayed these revolutions and capitalism retained its stranglehold over these societies.

India, Greece, Italy and France are some of the major examples. However, the post-war upswing of world capitalism and the rise of US imperialism as its bulwark, alongside the rapid growth in the Stalinized Soviet Union, all had a pacifying effect both in Eastern and Western Europe and in most of the advanced capitalist countries. At the same time, imperialist exploitation was so intense and the local bourgeois leaders were so corrupt that the revolutionary tide continued to rise in the so-called 'third world' or the semi- or neo-colonial countries. This led to the overthrow of capitalism and feudalism in a number of these countries.

The most important was the Chinese Revolution of 1949. From a Marxist point of view, it was the second most important event in human history after the October Revolution of 1917 in Russia. However it was not carried out according to classical Marxist lines as was the case with the socialist revolution that started the process of creating the USSR under the leadership of Lenin, Trotsky and the Bolshevik party. The Chinese Revolution of October 1949 under the peasant Red Army led to a caricature of socialism where the working class did not play a leading democratic role in the running of the planned economy, as was the case in the Soviet Union, at least in the first five to seven years of its existence. The new regime in Peking was based not on the lines of Moscow of 1917 but on the deformed Stalinist model of Moscow of 1949.

Many other countries, mainly in Asia, Africa and Latin America where capitalism and landlordism were overthrown in the 1950s and early 1960s, also modelled themselves on Stalinist Moscow and Maoist China, and the social transformations were carried through by guerrilla armies or military coups of the radical officers. They took the form of what is described as Proletarian Bonapartist states. The countries in which such historically peculiar forms of states emerged included China, Cuba, Vietnam, Laos, Cambodia, Syria, Yemen, Ethiopia, Mozambique, Angola, Somalia, Afghanistan and some others who went some distance in this direction.

Although terribly bureaucratically deformed, these regimes were progressive in nature as they were instrumental in the overthrow of landlordism and capitalism. They at least ended the rule of capital, of private ownership of the commanding heights of the economy and the landed estates, along with putting an end to the scourge of imperialist plunder. However, the lack of a soviet/workers' democracy and with a narrow nationalist outlook based on the ideology of "socialism in one country" and their heavy dependence on the Soviet Union and China led to their collapse once Stalinism fell in Eastern Europe and Russia.

In spite of all this, the tidal waves of the colonial revolution surged relentlessly throughout the post-war upswing. In most cases these movements broke through the constraints of national liberation. They went beyond the stage of "national democratic revolution" in most countries of the colonial and neo-colonial world. This was perhaps the largest movement of humanity ever seen since the fall of Rome. Such was the colossal size and ferocity of these movements that imperialist domination was challenged as never before.

In relatively large countries, where either the prevailing pro-Moscow or pro-China Communist parties were small or where they had become an impediment to these movements, stubbornly trying to restrict them to the bourgeois democratic stage, a new phenomenon developed. This was the phenomenon of populism.

From Argentina to Egypt and from Indonesia to Pakistan populism spread like wildfire. It reflected the failure of the traditional Left leadership to pass on to the socialist stage in order to complete the basic tasks of the national democratic revolution on the one hand, and the total incapacity of the local national bourgeoisie to carry out these tasks on the other, while there was a burning desire of the masses to emancipate themselves from exploitation and impoverishment under capitalist rule and the yoke of imperialism.

Most of the individual leaders who became the icons of these populist tides came from within the military elite. At least they had the ability—more than the Stalinist leaders—to understand the nature of these upheavals and had a greater feel of the pulse of the mass revolts emerging from below, than the traditional Left leaders. On the other hand, these populist leaders had little or no understanding of Marxism and revolutionary socialism. They were prompted more by the dynamics of the mass struggles and the sheer intensity of the movements.

In spite of their lack of any basic Marxist training, they proclaimed to be socialist and raised radical revolutionary slogans and put forward programmes that connected with the revolutionary moods and sentiments of the masses that were entering the arena of history to transform society radically. The pressures from below forced these leaders to take radical steps, such as large-scale nationalizations, serious land reform and other radical policies that shook capitalism to its very foundations, without actually overthrowing capitalism.

Egypt

Some of them did indeed wish to go the whole hog and finish off capitalism altogether. This was especially the case in Egypt where Colonel Gamal Abdel Nasser after nationalizing the Suez Canal in 1956 and defeating the joint aggression of Britain, France and Israel wanted to move forward and nationalize the whole economy and join the Warsaw Pact. In the Suez War the imperialists received a stunning blow from the Egyptian army led by the populist Nasser on the back of a rising mass movement. That war broke out on 29 October, 1956 when Israel, Britain and France launched a joint effort against Egypt with the aim of instituting what today would be described as 'regime change' and the deposition of Nasser, but the imperialists failed abysmally to achieve their objectives. Gone were the days when they could march into any colonial country and dictate to the people of that country.

Between 1955 and 1957, Nasser nationalized all foreign-owned banks and insurance companies and many other foreign-owned companies. From this position of strength, Nasser could have completed the revolution. The problem was that when he sent his emissary to Moscow in the early 1960s seeking approval and endorsement, he was rebuffed by Brezhnev, the leader of the Soviet Union at that time. Brezhnev claimed that to move towards a complete abolition of capitalism and landlordism (even in a distorted Stalinist manner) would disturb the balance of forces in the Middle East and disrupt détente and the mutual relations of coexistence during the cold war between the USA and USSR.

The Stalinist leaders both in Moscow and Peking played a similar role in several other countries during this rising tide of the colonial revolution. Egypt was and is probably the most important country in the Middle East, from the point of view of the size of its proletariat and its economy. An overthrow of capitalism and the implementation of a planned economy, even with the drawbacks of doing it from above, would have had a big impact on the region and far beyond. Here again the Stalinist idea of a "national road to socialism" played a disastrous role. The survival of capitalism not only exacerbated the social crisis in Egypt, but in the decaying conditions of Egyptian capitalism Nasser began to lose the initial mass support and social base that he had. He was thus pushed towards Arab nationalism or pan-Arabism, as it was known.

However, Arab nationalism was no solution to the socio-economic problems faced by workers and toiling masses of Egypt and the Middle East. Reaction started to gain force and the social and political weaknesses of Nasser were also reflected on the external front. In the 1967 war Egypt suffered a humiliating defeat at the hands of the reactionary Israeli state, an ironic revenge for the defeat in 1956.

Nasser's response to the humiliating defeat at the hands of the Israeli army was to offer his resignation, which was broadcast on radio and TV. But the reserves of support among the masses were still huge and millions poured out on to the streets, not only in Egypt but across the Arab world, and as a result Nasser withdrew his resignation.

However, it is also true to say that in the period 1962 to 1967 there was growing opposition to Nasser within Egypt itself. From the initial huge economic successes the economy started to slow down. Part of the opposition was expressed through the Islamic clergy and this pushed Nasser into taking measures to limit the powers of this clergy. By 1969 he was also in conflict with the judiciary which he also clamped down on.

Nasser died in 1970 and was succeeded by Anwar Al Sadat. Although formally continuing with the same regime, Sadat moved to radically dismantle the economic policies of Nasser and also purged many leaders from the Nasser era, and subsequently pulled the country back under the sphere of influence of US imperialism, thus unravelling all the gains of the Nasserite revolution. This is a lesson for today, especially for the Venezuelan revolution.

Ever since then the government has been in the hands of pro-Western elements that collaborate with US imperialism and have a good working relationship with the hated Zionist regime in Israel. The main opposition they have been facing has been from the Akhwan-ul-Muslimeen (Muslim Brotherhood), the Islamic fundamentalist reactionary movement. Ironically this movement was set up by US imperialism after the Suez War to destabilize Nasser and other Left-wing leaders of the Arab and Muslim world. Forty years on, however, there are new stirrings of the class struggle in Egypt and Left forces are coming to the fore.

Indonesia

Another traumatic and disastrous outcome of the policies of Stalinism was the bloody massacre of about 1.5 million members of the Communist Party of Indonesia (PKI). In the late 1950s and early 1960s the PKI was the largest communist party in the world outside the Stalinist bloc. Such was the strength of the PKI in those times that in 1958 it had the support of 73% of the soldiers in the Indonesian Army. But here again the Chinese Stalinist bureaucracy instructed the PKI to join and dissolve its forces into the PNI (Nationalist Party of Indonesia) led by the populist Bonaparte, General Soekarno.

The demagogue Soekarno—who had also relations with Mao and the Chinese bureaucracy—in spite of his fiery anti-imperialist rhetoric, aimed to keep capitalism intact. But with the rising strength of the PKI there were revolutionary tremors in Indonesia. With a programme of socialist revolution the PKI could have overthrown capitalism through a revolutionary insurrection in a short span of time. But as a result of the amalgamation into the PNI under the dictates from Peking (Beijing), the PKI leadership had exposed its internal structures, cadres and membership. This was to prove fatal when a CIA-sponsored coup against Soekarno, headed by the treasurer of the PNI General Suharto, led to the setting up of a vicious dictatorship.

It was in 1965, that in connivance with the CIA and its sponsored Islamic fundamentalist vigilantes, Suharto carried out one of the most brutal and massive genocides in recent history. This was another result of this disastrous two-stage theory which the Stalinists, through the respective leaders of the various communist parties, forced on the rising movements throughout the colonial world. Such was the brutality and the bloodshed, such was the defeat, that it took the Indonesian youth and workers 34 long tormented years to rise once again and overthrow the corrupt and brutal dictatorship of General Suharto in 1998.

It is not a historical accident or a coincidence that in many of the proletarian Bonapartist revolutions the Moscow or pro-Peking communist parties actually played a reactionary role in trying to hold back the movement and keeping it within the so-called 'democratic stage', i.e. a stage where capitalism is kept intact. This stubbornness of the Stalinist left to cling on to this historically obsolete and redundant Menshevik "theory of two stages" left a vacuum. And both history and nature abhor vacuums. That explains, as we have seen, why in that period of history the vacuum was filled by populist leaders such as Juan Peron in Argentina or Nassser in Egypt, or Zulfiqar Ali Bhutto in Pakistan. And in fact, the history of the 1968-9 revolution in Pakistan and the events that followed help to explain the phenomenon of populism in great detail.

Impact of Revolution on Advanced Countries

The historical importance of the period around 1968-9 was that the revolutions that had been unfolding in the former colonial world were finding their echo in mass movements of the workers and youth in the advanced capitalist countries. This was still the peak of the post-war boom, the biggest expansion that capitalism had ever witnessed, but that boom was about to slow down dramatically.

After more than two decades of a continual boom and growth in the industrialized world there were mass movements of the youth and workers in countries like Italy and France, of revolutionary dimensions. There was the explosion of the civil rights movement in Ireland, the movement of the youth in the United States. Britain was affected with a massive outbreak of strikes and even countries like West Germany and Sweden were affected. In fact in all the advanced countries there was some degree of mobilizations. A few years later Spain, Portugal and Greece were also affected, which led to the fall of the dictatorships in those countries. Mexico witnessed dramatic events also. Stalinism in Eastern Europe was also shaken by the dramatic events in Czechoslovakia.

But above all the revolutionary upheavals in France of May 1968 became the epicentre of this revolutionary tidal wave that was sweeping across the planet. The events of those tumultuous years have been described as "student revolts", "agitations against military dictatorships", "movements of democratic and human rights" by the traditional bourgeois analysts and even most Left-wing intellectuals.

It is true that most of these revolutionary upheavals were initiated and triggered off by the students. Initially the campuses became the centre of revolutionary ferment. This confirms the fact that student movements are often barometers of the rising temperature and change in mood of the masses and of society as a whole. They are like the leaves of the treetops who are the first to move as the storm begins to rise. They are like the heat lightening that precedes a storm.

But all these movements gained real momentum and force only once the workers and the toiling masses entered the arena of struggle and revolt. In spite of the different shades and intensities of these movements in different countries, the fundamental psychology of the masses in revolt was that of a deep desire for radical change and in many cases for the overthrow of this rotten exploitative system and for a socialist transformation of society. We shall try to prove and substantiate this assertion with the facts, with the events as they actually unfolded on the ground, as the mass movements burst into action. The most advanced and striking examples are France, Italy and Pakistan itself.

France, May 1968—the Greatest Revolutionary General Strike in History

Such was the intensity and ferocity of the French event of 1968 that it not only rattled the French state and the ruling class but sent shock waves throughout the echelons of power around the world. At the same time this revolutionary upheaval with its epicentre in Paris was a huge inspiration to the revolutionaries and the toiling masses around the world. These events brought to the fore the real revolutionary force and the socio-economic and political power of the working class when awakened into action by historic events. Ted Grant, founder of the Marxist Tendency in Britain produced a pamphlet in the white heat of the May 1968 revolutionary upheaval in France, which it is worth quoting at length.

> Not a nut or bolt turns in hundreds of occupied factories: not a wheel moves in public transport. The reactionary newspapers' lies are "censored" by the printers and so are those of the radio and television. The French working class in its millions cocks its little finger, and the vast complex of French capitalism grinds to a halt.
>
> What a mighty demonstration of the invincible power of the working class, when it begins to move! How crushing a refutation this is of all those cynics and sceptics who have written off the working class as "bought off", "apathetic" etc! How clear it should be to even the most politically uneducated workers that their French brothers would now be firmly in power, but for the craven, cowardly policies of the French Labour and Trade Union leaders. This is the essence of the events which have shaken the French ruling class and terrified the exploiters of the world![2]

Here again the role of the students as an initial spark igniting the flames of revolution was graphically demonstrated.

The wave of revolt culminating in the mass sit-in strikes and occupation of the factories began with the students. The pitched battles between them and the police were ignited by the vicious police attacks on a students' meeting in the Sorbonne University: it was the first time that the police had intervened in the university since the German occupation.

The Daily Express (London) reported that 80% of the population of Paris was for the students. Senior secondary school students came out and teachers were forced to lock 13-

year-olds in their classrooms to stop them from joining the strike. Even this restraining hand had been stayed as the teachers and pupils together joined the workers. More important was the fact that the students lifted the lid off the boiling pot of working class grievances. The façade of the French equivalent of the "never had it so good" society has been pierced.

But it was the young factory workers, emboldened and electrified by the success of the students and making contact with them on the million-strong demonstration of 13th May, who took the initiative in organizing the sit-in strikes in the Renault factories and elsewhere.

The general strike of 13th May marked a qualitative turning point. Hundreds of thousands of students and workers poured on to the streets of Paris. Some idea of this is conveyed by the following description of the mighty demonstration of a million, which took over the streets of Paris on the 13th of May:

> Endlessly they filed past. There were whole sections of hospital personnel in white coats, some carrying posters saying 'Où sont les disparus des hôpitaux?' ('Where are the missing injured?'). Every factory, every major workplace seemed to be represented. There were numerous groups of railwaymen, postmen, printers, Metro personnel, metal workers, airport workers, market men, electricians, lawyers, sewer men, bank employees, building workers, glass and chemical workers, waiters, municipal employees, painters and decorators, gas workers, shop girls, insurance clerks, road sweepers, film studio operators, busmen, teachers, workers from the new plastic industries, row upon row upon row of them, the flesh and blood of modern capitalist society, an unending mass, a power that could sweep everything before it, if it but decided to do so.[3]

The leaders of the unions hoped that this would be sufficient to halt the movement. The leaders did not intend the general strike to continue and spread. They saw the demonstration as a means of blowing off steam. But once it started, the movement soon acquired a life of its own. The call for a general strike was like a heavy rock thrown into a tranquil lake. Although there were only about three and a half million workers organized in the unions, ten million went on strike and a wave of factory occupations began all over France.

A gigantic wave had swept from one end of France to the

other. Not only the industrial workers but also the bank employees, white-collar workers, and the catering workers responded to the call to strike. While only 30% were unionized, over 50% of the labour forces was involved which is incontestable proof of the revolutionary energy and determination that had been unleashed. As in all revolutions, from the cracks and depths of society the formerly politically backward workers, the sweating and impoverished, the demoralized and cynical, had been brought to their feet. The poor farmers set up barricades round the city of Nantes and other cities "in support of the workers and students"[4]. Exemplary order was maintained and, as even the capitalist press had been forced to admit, the workers "check and grease factory machines that are lying idle".

All this and yet the leadership of the Communist Party and the CGT, along with the Catholic unions and 'socialist' Force Ouvrière, refused to carry through what the workers had begun: the seizure of power. Gratified, the *Observer* remarked, "the Communist unions and the Gaullist Government they appear to be challenging are really on the same side of the barricades". The reactionary Le Figaro also praised the statesman-like posture of the CP leaders.

Workers took control of petrol supplies in Nantes, refusing entry to all petrol tankers, which did not carry authorization from the strike committee. A picket was placed on the only functioning petrol pump in the town, which made sure that petrol was only issued to doctors. Contact was made with the peasant organizations in the surrounding areas, and food supplies were arranged, with prices fixed by the workers and peasants. To prevent profiteering, shops had to display a sticker in the window with the words: "This shop is authorised to open. Its prices are under permanent supervision by the unions." The sticker was signed by the CGT, CFDT and FO. A litre of milk was sold for 50 centimes compared to the normal 80. A kilo of potatoes was cut from 70 centimes to 12; a kilo of carrots from 80 to 50, and so on.

The students, teachers, professional people, peasants, scientists, footballers, even the girls of the Follies Bergères were all drawn into the struggle. In Paris students occupied the Sorbonne. The Theatre del'Odéon was occupied by 2,500 students and the school students occupied the schools.

Since the schools were closed, teachers and students organized nurseries, playgroups, free meals and activities for the strikers' children. Committees of strikers' wives were set up and played a leading role organizing food supplies. Not only the students, but also the professional layers were infected with the bug of revolution. The astronomers occupied an observatory. There was a strike at the nuclear research centre at Saclay, where the majority of the 10,000 employees were researchers, technicians, engineers or graduate scientists. Even the Church was affected. In the Latin Quarter, young Catholics occupied a church and demanded a debate instead of mass.

The rioting in Paris continued, with workers and students braving tear gas and baton charges. In a single night there were 795 arrests, and 456 injured. Demonstrators attempted to torch the Paris Bourse (Stock Exchange) the hated symbol of capitalism. A Commissaire de Police was killed in Lyons by a truck.

Once in struggle the workers began to take initiatives, which went far beyond the limits of a normal strike. A key element in the equation was the means of mass communication. Formally these were powerful weapons in the hands of the state. But they also depended on the workers who were operating the radio and television stations. On 25 May state radio and television—the ORTF—went on strike. The TV news at 8 p.m. was blacked out. The printers and journalists imposed a kind of workers' control of the press. Bourgeois papers had to submit their editorials for scrutiny, and had to publish the declarations of the workers' committees.

The National Assembly discussed the university crisis and the battles of the Latin Quarter. But the debates in the chambers of the Assembly were already an irrelevance. Power had slipped from the hands of the legislators and was lying in the streets. On 24 May President De Gaulle announced a referendum on radio and television. His plan to hold a referendum was frustrated by the action of the workers. The general was unable even to get ballot sheets for a referendum printed because of the strike of the French printing workers and the refusal of their Belgian colleagues to scab. This was not the only example of international solidarity. German and Belgian train drivers halted their trains on the French border in order not to break the strike.

> Every serious political commentator stressed the revolutionary fervour that existed. 'The waves of protests sweeping France are not merely genuine grievances, but also represent a diffuse and generalised protest against the regime as a whole. The workers are not merely asking for financial compensation, for shorter working hours, but like the students are also talking vaguely of revolutionary committees'.[5]

Peaceful Transformation of Society

Even the mouthpiece of the conservative British bourgeoisie, *The Times* London, had to accept the revolutionary character of the events taking place in France.

"All the conditions for a successful overturn are there; the workers are determined to go the whole hog. The middle class, particularly its lower layers, look with profound sympathy on the strike wave and in many cases join in, e.g. on the ships 'even the officers have joined the sit-ins begun by the crews'."[6]

The Times had to accept the shifting of power to the working classes who had risen to transform the system.

> It is the working class which has the effective power in the factories, the ports, the mines, and the streets. A classic situation of dual power exists. Even the televising of the debate in the National Assembly was done only by permission of the workers' organisations, as even a Gaullist MP was forced to admit. Those vestiges of the Government, the police and the army are completely unreliable. The police themselves have been touched by the hot flames of revolt. Their union issued a warning to the Government that "the police officers thoroughly appreciated the reasons which inspired the striking wage-earners and deplored the fact that they could not by law take part in the same way in the present labour movement ... the public authorities will not systematically set the police against the present labour struggles"[7].

In the event of a clash, many "serious wards, many sections, if not the majority, would go over to the workers. The Army also would be split from top to bottom if the officer caste sought to intervene. This is shown by the comments of a National Serviceman when he was asked if he would fire on the students and workers and replied 'Never. I think their methods may be a bit rough but I am a worker's son myself'."[8] If ever there was a time when the working class could take power peacefully, that time is now, wrote Ted.

Reaction was very weak at this stage but if the fascists and the army elite would seek to whip up gangs of thugs to oppose the workers, they would be silenced first of all by the setting up of workers' defence guards and eventually by an armed people.

The Government and its puppet National Assembly was left suspended in mid-air. If the CP leaders had one ounce of the heroic courage and energy of its own rank and file or the working class generally, it would have broadened and organized the instinctive desire of the masses for their own instruments of power, the workers' councils.

In his sympathetic biography *'The Last Great Frenchman—A Life of General De Gaulle'*, the author C. William wrote:

> But De Gaulle's mood on the morning of 25th had turned for the worse. He was in the words of one of his minister's prostate stooped and aged! Another minister found an old man who had no 'feel' for the future ... from 25 to 28 May De Gaulle remained in a state of profound gloom ... the council of ministers met at 3.00 pm on 27th May. The general presided, but was noted that his heart and mind were elsewhere. He stared at his ministers without seeing them, his arms flat on the table in front of him, his shoulders hunched, seemingly totally indifferent, to what was going on around him. ... according to the US ambassador De Gaulle told him that, 'the game's up'. In a few days the communists will be in power.[9]

In its editorial, *The Times* asked the key question: "Can De Gaulle use the army?" and answered its own question, saying that he could perhaps use it once. In other words, a single bloody clash would be sufficient to break the army in pieces. That was the appraisal of the hardest headed strategists of international capital at the time. There is no reason to doubt their word on this occasion.

But how was it that this gigantic revolutionary movement

failed to overthrow capitalism? Why did the socialist victory slip out of the hands of the mighty proletariat that had so forcibly risen to transform society?

In the entry in May 1968 in the *Encyclopaedia Britannica,* we find an answer:

> De Gaulle seemed incapable of grappling with the crisis or even understanding its nature. The Communist and Trade Union leaders, however, provided him with a breathing space; they opposed further upheaval, evidently fearing the loss of their followers to their most extremist and anarchist rivals.

In his prolific article on the 40th anniversary of those dramatic events, Alan Woods wrote in May 1st, 2008 :

> A general strike is different from a normal strike because it poses the question of power. The question at stake is not this or that wage increase but who is master of the house? In the course of struggle the workers' consciousness increased at a vertiginous speed. They came to understand that this was not a normal strike for economic demands but something far greater. They became conscious of the power in their hands and saw the weakness of those who were supposed to represent all the power of the state. All that was necessary was for every workplace to elect delegates and to link up the strike committees in every town and region, culminating in the formation of a National Committee, which could take power into its hands, consigning the old state power to the dustbin of history.
>
> But none of this was done, and the enormous revolutionary potential of the movement was dissipated, just as steam is harmlessly dissipated in the air unless it is concentrated in a piston-box. In the end, the workers returned to work and the ruling class concentrated power back into its hands. Once the movement began to ebb, the state began to take its revenge.
>
> The marvellous movement of the French workers thus ended in defeat. But the traditions of May 1968 remain in the consciousness of the workers of France and the whole world. Today, after a long period of economic boom, the capitalist system is again entering into a crisis in which all the contradictions that have been building up for the last 20 years will come to the fore. Big class battles are on the order of the day all over Europe.[10]

Revolutionary Ferment in Europe

The stormy events in France had a massive impact, especially on the neighbouring and other European countries. The bursting of the accumulated discontent, even in the most advanced countries of Europe and where reformist ideas had become embedded within the leadership of the labour movement, exposed the contradictions that had built up under the surface. Even at the height of the unprecedented economic boom that followed the Second World War, and with the many concessions granted mostly by the Social Democracy, the class contradictions, which are inevitable under a capitalist mode of production, could not be removed.

Having said that, even those concessions that were given to the European proletariat were not charity granted to the workers by the ruling classes. They were won by serious struggles of the working class. As Marx puts it, "When there is a revolution from below the ruling class resorts to reform from above."

The rapid industrial and economic growth in Europe had expanded and advanced the economy and industry; at the same this changed the balance of forces between the classes. With the growth of the economy came the growth and strengthening of the proletariat. This newly emerged and strengthened proletariat was to reveal its strength, energy and power during the revolts of the 1968 period, and after the powerful movement in France in May 1968 came the massive upsurge of labour struggles in Italy.

The Italian 'Hot Autumn'

Italy too was affected by the generalized situation of revolt affecting many countries at the time. In 1968 it was mainly a student-based movement with some important labour struggles. But it was in 1969 that the Italian proletariat rose up and began to challenge the very existence of capitalism itself.

Throughout the 1950s and early 1960s Italy had undergone a radical economic and social transformation, known at the time as the 'Italian miracle'. From a relatively backward economy with industry concentrated mainly in the northwest, the country became one of the major advanced capitalist countries. This meant that millions of peasants, mainly from the South, were sucked into the cities, into the factories, to swell the ranks of the Italian proletariat.

By 1968 Italy was no longer the predominantly peasant country of 1948. Its cities grew rapidly and with this came a series of new social problems. The first signs of the coming storm were seen in the period 1958–63 with a series of very militant strikes, but the movement that reached its high point in 1969 started in 1966 with the engineering workers strike that was followed by a whole series of other sectors coming out. With this movement came the formation of the first rank and file factory committees in the engineering industry.

In 1967 there were the first stirrings of the student movement, with university occupations in several universities, and this naturally gravitated towards the labour movement. There was an instinctive coming together of workers and students in this period, an indication of what was to come.

What was to bring the situation to a head was a longstanding dispute with the government and the bosses over pensions. In December 1967 the trade union called off a strike over the question, thinking they could calm the movement down, but they were about to receive a shock. The year 1968 opened up with a series of strikes, during which the trade unions put a compromise deal to a ballot, but the workers rejected the proposal. This was the first clear signal that a conflict between the ranks of the unions and the leaders was brewing. The mood was so militant that the unions had to call a general strike which proved to be hugely successful; something the trade union leaders had not expected!

The next big battle was over regional wage differentials. After the Second World War the bosses had managed to impose a wage system where workers in the south received less than workers in the north. In 1968 the workers set about struggling for the abolition of these differentials. The two issues of pensions and wage differentials led to a powerful general strike in November 1968 and in March 1969 the bosses' confederation was forced to abolish the differentials.

With each mobilization of the working class the bosses and the government were forced to retreat and make concessions. With each concession grew the confidence of the working class that then became even more determined to ask for more. The working class became conscious of its power and strength.

It was in the midst of this process that the French events erupted in May 1968, further radicalizing and strengthening the will to struggle of the Italian workers. Throughout the whole year new layers of previously 'dormant' workers started coming out in struggle. Factories in traditionally 'backward' areas came out on strike spontaneously. Women started taking part in big numbers, often outdoing their male colleagues in militancy and determination.

With this radicalization came the building of the Factory Councils, which represented a radical break from the previous trade union structures. These were committees elected by all the workers in a factory, with right of recall. In the autumn of 1969 these committees coordinated the struggle from below and challenged the bureaucracy that dominated the official unions, with an unprecedented wave of strikes.

Initially the sectarian Left meant this was the beginning of the end for the official unions, but they were very mistaken. In the period 1968–77 the membership of the unions almost doubled! Faced with such a radical movement from below the trade union tops were forced to come out and officialize what had been an unofficial movement. They were forced to make radical-sounding speeches to satisfy their own ranks. They were forced to move to the left in words and actions.

This radicalization of the leadership attracted millions of workers into the unions, who were joining because they wanted to fight. This further radicalized the whole trade union movement. The trade union bureaucrats were riding a tiger that they found difficult to dismount!

The difference between the Italian situation and the French was this. In France the movement developed into an all-out general strike with factory occupations. The workers went as far as they could go without actually overthrowing capitalism. It was an extremely intense battle to the end. It lasted a few weeks and then from the great heights it had reached, the French working class was betrayed by its own leaders.

In Italy, although it never reached a May 1968 situation, the movement lasted for years, for ten years in fact! It was an unprecedented situation that only really ended in 1979 with the first electoral setback of the Italian Communist Party after it had openly supported the Christian Democrat government. It took the Italian bourgeoisie many years of manoeuvring, of collaboration with the trade union tops, of many concessions, before they could get the situation under control.

What all this expressed was the immense power of the working class. In fact the Italian workers could have taken power not once but ten times. All that was missing was a leadership up to the task. Tragically there was no such leadership and eventually the movement was defeated and a new period was opened up, one of constant attacks on all the gains of the previous period. The 1970s and 1980s were years of falling strike figures and falling trade union membership.

Only in the recent period have we seen the beginnings of a recovery with a series of very militant strikes and even general strikes. The wheel of history has come full circle and a new opportunity is facing the Italian working class to change society. Now, it is necessary to learn from the mistakes of the past in order not to repeat them!

Ireland

The revolutionary fervour that spread across the globe was also to have a dramatic impact on the North of Ireland. In periods of revolutionary upheavals movements in different countries can inspire and reinvigorate long-standing struggles at a rapid pace. The struggles against different forms of oppression get new infusions of energy from these struggles. This was the case with the Civil Rights movement in Ireland.

Alan Woods explains in detail how things developed.

> The Civil Rights movement was really a reflection of the international situation and especially the revolutionary movement in France in May 1968. This was entirely in line with Irish history. The revolt of the United Irishmen was inspired by the French revolution of 1789–93. The Easter Rising of 1916 was a direct result of the first imperialist World War. The students of the north of Ireland were no different to their counterparts in Paris. The Civil Rights movement began with a march of 2,500 demonstrators from Coal Island to Dungannon on Saturday, 24 August, 1968. Protestant bigots staged vicious attacks against the demonstrators. When the marchers attempted to cross

Craigavon Bridge, the police made a baton charge. Riot equipment was used, stones thrown and 88 people were injured—77 civilians and 11 police.

It is important to note that the IRA had little or nothing to do with the Civil Rights movement, which was influenced by Marxism and revolutionary ideas. The movement contained both Catholics and Protestants. In particular the Derry Young Socialists played a key role, fighting the bigots on the barricades. On 19th April there was a ferocious battle in Derry in which the people fought back against their tormentors. The figures tell their own story. This time 209 police were injured, against 79 civilians. Faced with a barrage of petrol bombs, the authorities were forced to use armoured cars. The next day, O'Neill resigned and the whole reform programme was consigned to the dustbin.

"(...) On 18th March, the Civil Rights Association announced that it would continue and intensify its campaign of civil disobedience. It put forward a programme of transitional demands, including: One person, one vote in local government elections; votes at eighteen; an independent Boundaries Commission to determine electoral boundaries; a fair housing allocation system; anti-discrimination laws for employment; a review of the Special powers Act and disbandment of the B-Specials.

In fact 1966 had been a turning point and as Alan Woods continues:

A number of young people began to join the movement. They were radical in outlook and looking for the revolutionary road. However this did not fit in with the schemes of the then leadership of the Republican Movement. The latter did not have a revolutionary perspective and consequently were taken by surprise by the events of 1969, when the North was moving fast in the direction of civil war. On 12th August in the Catholic Bogside district of Derry the barricades went up in response to attacks by the combined forces of the RUC (Royal Ulster Constablery) and Protestant mobs. Having fought off the forces of reaction, the revolutionary youth raised Republican flags and proclaimed the Bogside Free Derry.

(...) The revolutionary potential was clearly present, but the revolution was not armed. What was needed was an armed workers defence force, based on the trade unions, on the lines of Connolly's Irish Citizen Army (ICA).

(...) When there was no revolutionary force ready and able to take over the leadership, the forces of reaction raised their head. Fearing the development of a revolutionary movement in the North, the Irish bourgeoisie took steps to divert it along nationalist lines. As a key part of this strategy they deliberately split the IRA, which was too left wing for their liking. Large amounts of money were supplied to the right wing, conservative, militaristic elements to set up a rival organization, the Provisional IRA, in opposition to the "Officials", as they became known.

(...) When the population of the Six Counties defiantly resisted the Stormont repression and fought the local forces of "law and order" to a standstill, the Stormont government had to call in the British army to suppress the insurgents. But they were not the only ones who wanted such an intervention. The truth is that both the British and Irish ruling classes were terrified of the prospect of social revolution in the Six Counties that could easily spread to the South and to Britain. They conspired together to crush the revolution at all costs.

In Derry, thanks in no small measure to the Marxist leadership of the Young Socialists, the Bogside district was under the control of the Derry Citizens Defence Committee. Following a stone-throwing incident, the RUC began to attack. There was an imminent danger of a pogrom. As a result, the people of the Bogside and Creggan rose up to defend their areas, setting up barricades. Despite fierce fighting, the forces of the state were unable to penetrate their defences and enter the Bogside. Jack Lynch, the Fianna Fail prime minister in Dublin, made a broadcast in which he informed the people of Ireland that he was asking Britain to apply for a United Nations peacekeeping force, since Stormont was "no longer in control". This was a direct instigation to Britain to intervene in the North to re-establish order.

The British government promptly took its cue from Dublin. On 14th August 1969 British troops were ordered into Derry by Labour Prime Minister James Callaghan. The next day they entered Belfast. By the end of that week there were 6,000 British troops in the Six Counties. The excuse—accepted by many, including it must be stated the so called Lefts. But nothing was solved. In the five years of the O'Neill government only three people had died in sectarian incidents. In the summer of 1969 nine people were killed, 150 were wounded by gunfire, 500 houses were destroyed and over 2,000 people were made homeless. And that was nothing compared to the horrors that lay ahead.

At first the British troops had been welcomed by many Catholics. But soon the real nature of the forces of British imperialism became clear. Their main purpose was to destroy the revolutionary movement that was developing in the North. Their main target was the "Communists", as they made clear. This aim was shared by the bourgeois rulers in the South, who used the Provisional IRA for this purpose. Nowadays it has been forgotten or is not known by many,

> but the Provos were viciously anti-Communist. Their activities included the burning of Marxist books. (...) To imagine that it was possible to defeat the might of the British army in single combat was madness, as subsequently became only too clear.
>
> (...) Yet the only hope for defeating reaction was to cut across the sectarian divide. This was possible, on condition that the correct policies and tactics had been pursued. Without any leadership there were many local initiatives to combat sectarianism. In August 1969 a meeting of 9,000 workers at the big Harland and Wolff shipyard declared their opposition to the sectarian intimidation of Catholics. Joint patrols of Catholic and Protestant workers were established in the Ardoyne and several other areas.
>
> By the summer of 1969 local defence groups—almost all of them non-sectarian—had been formed in Ballymurphy, Springhill, Turf Lodge, New Barnsley, Springmartin, Highfield and Clonard. If this tendency had been encouraged, and the patrols had been armed, an entirely different perspective would have opened up. Instead, the sectarian paramilitary organizations of both sides launched a vicious campaign of intimidation to drive people of the other religion from their homes and create separate enclaves. Families were burned out of their houses just on the basis of their supposed religious affiliation. This systematic criminal activity was intended to reinforce the sectarian divide and turn it into an abyss. It succeeded only too well.[11]

As we can see from Alan Woods' analysis, initially the Civil Rights movement in Ireland in 1968 had all the potential to become a revolutionary movement of the Irish proletariat. What was lacking was a mass revolutionary party of the working class, capable of offering a way out. Lacking this, the ruling class was able to whip up sectarianism, pitting Catholic against Protestant, and thus cutting across the developing revolutionary movement.

Mexico

The stormy tides of the 1968-9 revolution did not need much time to reach the shores of Latin America. For almost 500 years of European colonialism there were relentless struggles of the peoples of this region against it. In the 20th century due to the socio-economic patterns of combined and uneven development under imperialist rule sharpened the contradictions in most countries of Central and Latin America. These have been the victims of some of the most vicious and brutal military dictatorships. These despotic regimes crushed the revolutionary uprisings against imperialist stranglehold, capitalist exploitation and Military rule. US imperialism had been instrumental in setting up, patronizing and imposing these brutal repressive military regimes. Not for nothing is there an ironic and legendary joke in this continent that goes like this: "Question: Why are there no military coups in USA? Answer: because there is no US embassy in the USA."

Historically the most well known movement—and its most barbaric repression—that took place in the year 1968 was in Mexico. In the backyard of US imperialism, with a common border of about 5000 km, Mexico was very important for the American ruling class in its lust for exploiting its resources including human labour and other strategic interests of US imperialism. These events took place close to the time of 1968 Olympics.

Mexico was dramatically affected by revolutionary upheavals worldwide. Mexico's economy was actually growing quite fast, within the context of a general worldwide economic upswing. But this growth was very unequally spread, with a gaping social and economic polarization between the rich and poor. The President wanted to show to the world that Mexico was a 'modern' country, and his opportunity came in the 1968 Olympics, which were held in Mexico City.

The workers and youth had another idea. As in many parts of the world 1968 proved to be a year of revolution in Mexico also. This was dramatically confirmed on 27th August, when about 400,000 people converged on the centre of Mexico City chanting abuse against the president.

The movement started with the students but after severe police repression it began to spread to the workers. The movement initially began with two demonstrations, one in solidarity with the Cuban revolution and another by polytechnic students protesting against a police intervention in their schools. Both demonstrations suffered police repression. But the students would not be cowed. They organized to spread the movement and call a general strike of all students. Soon the demonstrations began to grow in size and number, from 30,000 at the beginning to half a million a month later.

The students consciously turned to the population at large, going to the neighbourhoods, the markets, bus stations, with leaflets. The workers responded magnificently. One example is when tanks were brought in to the main square of Mexico City to disperse a student demonstration. The President, Diaz Ordaz, in an attempt to show he had mass support, brought in thousands of government workers in a counter-demonstration. But those very same workers began shouting, "We have been transported here; we are the sheep of Diaz Ordaz".

Then a new rally was planned for October 2, just ten days before the Olympics were to open. The government was keen to put an end to the rising wave of revolt in the country, and present the country to the world as calm and under control.

At least 5,000 students and workers gathered in the Plaza de las Tres Culturas, calling for democratic reforms, such as autonomy for the country's universities, the freeing of political prisoners and social justice. But the security forces were waiting for them. At a certain point agents provocateurs opened fire, giving the army the 'excuse' to open start shooting into the vast crowd with machineguns. The estimates of those killed that day range from anything from 150 to 500. Hundreds were arrested, and many disappeared. To this day no one knows what happened to them.

The object of the massacre was clear. It was to destroy the leadership of the student movement and put an end to the movement that was spreading more and more, involving wider layers of the working class.

Earlier this year we had a hue and cry about the Olympics being held in Beijing, after the repression of the movement in Tibet. But back in 1968 there were no official complaints about the events in Mexico City, no US condemnation then! In fact, the truth about what had happened was not revealed for another three years!

This brutal massacre put an end to the movement ... for the time being. However, the effects of the movement were to be felt for years to come. It showed quite clearly that the old one-party rule of the PRI (Institutional Revolutionary Party) was in the process of decay. The 1968 movement was the first crack that was later to become a gaping chasm and eventually lead to the fall of the regime and prepare the ground for a new period, which we are still living in today.

The lessons of that tragic experience have come down to the new generations with the added experience of the rigged 2006 elections at the behest of US imperialism. The Marxist tendency in Mexico, working under the banner of El Militante, is emerging as a significant force of the revolutionary left in Mexico. Already it has been the subject of state repression. And this in itself is a proof of its growth and development. In the coming years El Militante, with a revolutionary programme and a Marxist internationalist strategy, can become the torch bearer of the first real socialist victory in central Latin America, and above all in the backyard of mighty US imperialism that is a "giant with feet of clay".

Czechoslovakia

At the end of the Second World War the imperialist powers made a deal with Stalinist Russia which divided Europe according to spheres of influence. On this basis it was agreed that Russia would have most of Eastern Europe. This was merely the recognition of the fact that Russia had now become a major world power and dominated that region militarily.

However, part of that deal also entailed betrayal of the revolution in the West. Thus potentially victorious movements in countries like Greece, Italy and France were defeated. In Eastern Europe the movement was also held back as Stalin imposed regimes that were modelled on the bureaucratic caricature of Socialism that Russia had become.

The arch reactionary British Prime Minister, Winston Churchill confirmed that this deal (with Stalin) had taken place at the Potsdam summit in October 1944 thus noted:

> The moment was apt for business, so I said, "Let us settle about our affairs in the Balkans. Your armies are in Romania and Bulgaria. We have interests, missions, and agents there. Don't let us get at cross-purposes in small ways. So far as Britain and Russia are concerned, how would it do for you to have 90 per cent predominance in Romania, for us to have 90 per cent of the say in Greece, and go 50-50

> about Yugoslavia?" While this was being translated I wrote out on a half sheet of paper: Romania: Russia 90 per cent, the others 10 per cent; Greece: Great Britain (in accord with USA) 90 per cent, Russia 10 per cent, Yugoslavia: 50-50 per cent, Hungary: 50-50 per cent, Bulgaria: Russia 75 per cent, the others 25 per cent.
>
> I pushed this across to Stalin, who had by then heard the translation. There was a slight pause. Then he took his blue pencil and made a large tick upon it, and passed it back to us. It was all settled in no more time than it takes to sit down. After this there was a long silence. The penciled paper lay in the centre of the table. At length I said, "might it not be thought rather cynical if it seemed we had disposed of these issues, so fateful to millions of people, in such an off-hand manner? Let us burn the paper". "No, you keep it" said Stalin.[12]

And according to Churchill, "Stalin adhered strictly and faithfully to our agreement of October and in all the long weeks of fighting the Communists in the streets of Athens not one word of reproach came from Pravda or Izvestia".[13] Thus was the Greek revolution betrayed!

As Ted Grant explained in Stalinism in the Postwar World, (June 1951):

> In Europe, the victory of Russia in the war and the upsurge of the masses following the defeat of German-Italian fascism also developed a tremendous revolutionary wave which threatened to sweep capitalism away over the entire continent. However, the victory of Russia in the war had complex and contradictory consequences. Temporarily, but nevertheless for an entire historical period, Stalinism had been enormously strengthened.[14]

The imperialists were forced to accept Russian hegemony of Eastern Europe and parts of Asia which they would never have agreed to concede even to reactionary Tsarism. The Russian Stalinist bureaucracy had achieved the domination of the region beyond the wildest dreams of Russia under the Tsars.

Comrade Ted Grant in his brilliant work *Russia: From Revolution to Counter revolution* gives an indepth analysis of this process.

> The process whereby capitalism was overthrown in Eastern Europe, and Stalinism extended, took place in a peculiar way, as explained by the author of the present work in documents published at that time. The vacuum in the state power in Eastern Europe, following the defeat

> of the Nazis and their quislings, was filled by the forces of the conquering Red Army. The weak bourgeoisie of these areas had been largely exterminated, absorbed as quislings by German imperialism or reduced to minor partners of the Nazis during the years of the war. They had been relatively weak in Eastern Europe even before the war, as the states of this region were largely semi-colonies of the great powers on the lines of the South American states. The pre-war regimes suffered from a chronic crisis due to the Balkanisation of the area and the incapacity of the ruling class to solve the problems of even the bourgeois democratic revolution. They were nearly all military police dictatorships of a weak character without any real roots among the masses.[15]

In spite of all this, Eastern Europe was to be shaken several times by mass movements challenging the rule of the bureaucracy, the most famous being Hungary 1956 where we had the making of the political revolution. That rising was drowned in blood when the Russian tanks went in.

However, the rising world tide of the 1968-9 revolution could not be curtailed or stopped even by the so-called Iron Curtain. The discontent amongst the masses that had accumulated against the bureaucratic Stalinist regimes in Eastern Europe was ignited once more by the events of 1968 in France and elsewhere. Among the East European regimes most affected was Czechoslovakia.

The movement became known as the 'Prague Spring'. Again it was the students who gave the initial spark to the movement.

The students, demonstrated in the winter of 1967-8 when the electricity failed and the lights went out in their hostels. They marched through the streets carrying posters bearing the short but clear slogan: "Give us light."

As Alan Woods, in his article 'Czechoslovakia (1968): Stalinism Rocked by Crisis', wrote at the time:

> The Secret Police brutally attacked the demonstration, wounding several students. It was a measure of the nervousness of the bureaucracy then that they strove to pacify the students by offering to pay the hospital bills of the injured demonstrators. This offer was met by the bold demand that those responsible for the outrage must be punished and the press must publish all the facts about the incident. The student leaders warned that if the papers did not tell the truth they would march to the factories and explain the facts to the workers. (...)

From the outset, Dubcek who coincidentally became the leader of this movement aimed to enlist the support primarily of the intellectuals and students, who have been the most vocal in his support. The Czech bureaucracy was clearly frightened that the ferment among the intelligentsia would spread to the workers. The lessons of the 'Crooked Circle' in Poland and the 'Petöfi Circle' in Hungary, whose agitation sparked off the violent mass movements in 1956, was not lost on Dubcek and the other bureaucrats. They were prepared to grant concessions temporarily, especially to the intelligentsia, in order to preserve their own privileged position. These reforms were far less sweeping than the reforms carried out by Gomulka in 1956. Why then did the Russian bureaucracy choose to intervene?

The first thing which alarmed Brezhnev and the leaders of the Russian bureaucracy was the rapid development of the mass movement in Czechoslovakia. For all the timidity of Dubcek's reforms (it now emerges that Dubcek himself was a 'compromise' candidate of the Central Committee, i.e. not even the most radical of the bureaucrats!) they undoubtedly acted as a catalyst to the profound feelings of discontent that were welling up in the working class.

The split in the bureaucracy precipitated an unparalleled outburst of discussion, protest meetings and demonstrations. In every factory, college and village a furious discussion raged. From all over the country resolutions poured in demanding the sacking of Novotny and the speeding up of reforms. For the first time, meetings of the CP themselves were the scene of noisy discussions, criticism and even the removal of candidates from the official lists. An attempted coup of Novotny followers merely acted as a whip to stir up the masses further. The movement was gathering impetus. The bureaucracy was forced to swim along with the current, to grant reform after reform. (...)

The movement in Czechoslovakia was nowhere as highly developed as the movement in Hungary or Poland in 1956. There were no workers' councils, nor were the workers armed, as in Hungary, where the Russians intervened. (...)

The tragedy of Czechoslovakia was that the Czech people found themselves leaderless, disarmed and unprepared. The Dubcek clique preferred to see the country occupied rather than arm the working class. For all his brave words, Dubcek was prepared to eat dirt, rather than risk sparking off the spontaneous mass movement of the working class. (...)

The Czech events, although far less advanced than the Polish and Hungarian events of 1956, had shaken to the core every one of the bureaucratic cliques in Eastern Europe and Russia.

In March, as a direct result of the ferment in Czechoslovakia, riots broke out in Poland, in which at one stage, a crowd of 10,000 people wrecked the Ministry of Culture, shouting "long live Czechoslovakia", and battling with the police. And whereas in 1956, the students and workers sang Polish nationalist songs, in 1968 they began their demonstration by singing the 'Internationale'. (...)

Even more significant were the disturbances in Yugoslavia. Inspired by the French events, and influenced by the crisis of the Yugoslav economy and the wide-spread suffering of the masses, students in Belgrade staged protest demonstrations against the wealth and privileges of the bureaucracy, demanding the equalization of salaries, an end to the power of the 'red bourgeoisie' and to the policies of breaking up the planned economy and handing back the state-owned property to private owners.

The students even took over a whole suburb and ran it for a time. The students' leaflets received an enthusiastic reception from the workers. Newspapers reported people standing in groups, studying and discussing the views expressed. Such was the sympathy of the whole population that violent repression was out of the question. The 'arbiter' Tito had to step forward and promise to "look into" the students' demands. (...)

The growing unrest, on the one hand, and the increasing nervousness of the bureaucracy on the other was clearly revealed at the recent World Youth Festival in Sofia, where the usual rigged Stalinist puppet-show of "Peace and Friendship" gave way to splits, disagreements and open violence, when the Bulgarian police beat up a number of delegates and cameramen. (...)

A week after the invasion [of Czechoslovakia], the effects were already apparent in the most repressive Stalinist regimes in Eastern Europe including East Germany.

Attempts by Ulbricht to get the East German workers to sign petitions in support of the action of the Warsaw Pact met with refusals to sign. Hundreds of people entered the Czech embassy and other buildings of Czech delegations in defiance of the government, which had surrounded these buildings with police.

There was even a demonstration of 4,000 workers at Eisenhüttenstadt protesting against the invasion.

In spite of all the ravings of the Ulbricht press, the jamming of Western broadcasts and the banning of Czechoslovak German language newspapers, the truth had seeped through to the East German working class. (...)

In Russia itself, for all the striking progress that had been made by the nationalized, planned economy, the figure for wastage of production had been put as high as 30–50%. Along this road, no further progress could be made. The needs of the planned economies themselves demanded an end to the rule of the parasites and the

> introduction of a democratic plan of production to meet the needs of the people themselves.
>
> Such a plan could have only succeeded on the basis of a Socialist Federation of Eastern Europe and Russia. The continuation of the old capitalist national divisions was the most powerful brake on the productive forces of Eastern Europe. It was a monstrous distortion of socialism that 'socialist' Rumania and 'socialist' Russia actually have territorial disputes. (...)
>
> Most criminal of all was the spectacle of Russian and Chinese divisions facing each other over a completely artificial line drawn up in the nineteenth century by the Russian Tsar and the Chinese Emperor!
>
> The survival of these senseless antiquated national divisions was not the result of 'nationalism' among the working classes of the East. They were never consulted about it. It was purely and simply the result of selfish greed and narrow nationalism of the bureaucratic cliques, who were not prepared to sacrifice an inch of 'their' territory, to share their privileges, power and income with the other bureaucrats. (...)
>
> As in 1953 and 1956, the capitalist press had had a field-day, exploiting the Russian invasion of Czechoslovakia as 'proof' of the barbarity of Communism, the impossibility of combining socialism and democracy, etc., etc.
>
> The resulting depths of cynicism to which the representatives of 'Western Democracy' could sink was typified by the crocodile tears of US president Johnson, who was waging a barbarous war against the people of Vietnam on behalf of World Imperialism. The words 'Freedom' and 'Democracy' on the lips of these gentlemen are made to smell rotten. (...)
>
> But now, in a manner which could hardly have been foreseen, the revolutionary movement is coming to a head in all the main areas of the globe simultaneously.
>
> The real balance of forces on a world scale is strikingly revealed in turn by the events in Vietnam, France and Czechoslovakia.[16]

The capitalist system in the West was becoming thoroughly rotten. From being a progressive system, which rapidly developed the productive forces of the world, it was turning into its opposite. And the tumultuous events in France and beyond were a confirmation of this.

But also in the East, Stalinism had entered into a phase of crisis, which threatened not only the parasitic Stalinist cliques of the East, but also the capitalist systems of the West. The events of 1968 in Czechoslovakia were an anticipation of what was to come. They anticipated the later crisis that was to bring all the East European regimes tumbling down in 1989. Unfortunately, due to the lack of a viable workers' alternative, the collapse of Stalinism ushered in the return of capitalism and this was to give a temporary respite to imperialism.

It used this collapse of Stalinism and capitalist restoration in Russia and Eastern Europe to aggressively launch a capitalist onslaught that has devastated the majority of humankind. Unprecedented poverty, misery and destitution have created hatred that will lead to much larger revolutionary upheavals in the period ahead. The overthrow of this rotten capitalism through a socialist revolution is the only alternative for human survival.

The USA, the Vietnam War and Radicalization

Such was the power of the 1968 movement that it affected the very bastion of imperialism, the United States of America. The movement brought together the Civil Rights movement, the anti-war movement and the student revolt, as well as a growing radical mood among the working class.

Such was the force of this mass revolt that the so-called "warrior president Lyndon B. Johnson" was forced to retreat. On 31 March, 1968 the president came under such pressure that he was forced to announce that he was abandoning his re-election campaign and that peace talks with the Vietnamese Liberation forces would soon begin. Literally within a few minutes students on campuses across the country were cheering.

The war in Vietnam, which completely transformed the situation in the USA, did not begin in a planned way. The USA was sucked into it almost by accident. It began with a covert operation, the sending of officers and 'advisers' to prop up an unpopular and corrupt government against its own people. This is the usual style of US imperialism! The regime of Ngo Dinh Diem was guilty of vicious repression in South Vietnam. Buddhist monks burned themselves alive in protest. Finally, Diem was assassinated by his own generals.

Three weeks later, the President of the USA suffered the

same fate. Kennedy was succeeded by his Vice President, Lyndon B. Johnson, who immediately announced that he was "not going to lose Vietnam". "Win the war!" was his clear instruction. But despite all its tremendous wealth and military firepower, the USA did not win the war. On the contrary, Vietnam was the first war America ever lost. Korea had been a draw. But in the steamy jungles and swamps of Vietnam, the Americans suffered a bitter defeat at the hands of a barefoot army.

In order to step up its military activities in Vietnam (as usual) an incident was required. This was (as usual) manufactured in the so-called Bay of Tonkin incident. It was alleged that a US warship, the *Maddox*, had been fired upon by North Vietnamese naval vessels in the Gulf of Tonkin. For years it was believed that the US navy had been the target of unprovoked 'Communist aggression'. That was completely untrue. Even at the time, the captain of the *Maddox* admitted that none of his crew had made "actual visual sightings" of North Vietnamese naval vessels, and not one sailor either on the *Maddox* or the *Turner Joy* had actually heard North Vietnamese gunfire. The opening of the Hanoi archives has proven conclusively that the North Vietnamese did not fire on the American ships, which were actually inside Vietnamese territorial waters at the time. Yet the American public was persuaded to back a foreign war on the basis of false information and not for the last time, as we know.

> The very next day Lyndon B. Johnson ordered the bombing of North Vietnamese naval bases and an oil depot. It was the start of a huge campaign of bombing that caused havoc in Vietnam, killing a large number of civilians and destroying its industry and infrastructure. On television, President Johnson declared: "Repeated acts of violence against the armed forces of the United States must be met not only with alert defense but with positive reply. That reply is being given as I speak to you tonight."[17]

There was not a word of truth in any of this. Johnson and co. had decided to send US troops to Vietnam and that was that. In the same way, George W. Bush and his friends decided long before 11 September to invade Iraq and lied through their teeth about the alleged weapons of mass destruction that were supposed to pose a deadly threat to American security to sell it to the public.

In the years that followed, high explosives, napalm and cluster bombs rained down on Vietnam. The U.S. Air Force dropped toxic chemicals, including the notorious Agent Orange on forests, allegedly to kill the vegetation and deny shelter to the Vietnamese guerrillas. A total of 18 million gallons of herbicide were dropped. Even today U.S. servicemen are dying from the effects of just handling these toxic agents, especially cancer. One shudders to think of the effects they had on the Vietnamese men, women and children on whom they were dropped. Tests have shown that the South Vietnamese have levels of dioxin three times higher than those in U.S. citizens. It will take many years to flush these toxins out of the fragile ecosystem. This was chemical warfare pursued with a vengeance!

In all, the US dropped more tones of explosives on Vietnam than were dropped by all sides in the Second World War. After bombing one village to rubble, one US officer was quoted as saying: "We had to destroy the town in order to save it." They are still "destroying towns in order to save them" today. Ask the inhabitants of Fallujah. And the tactic of dropping tones of poisonous chemicals still continues in Colombia, where herbicides are being used in the so-called war against drugs. The damage to people, vegetation and wildlife will be the same as in Vietnam. But nobody talks about that.

The name of this particular operation was *Rolling Thunder*. There must be somebody in the Pentagon, some frustrated poet, whose sole function is to think up picturesque names for such acts of barbarity. Lately we had *Operation Shock and Awe*. It is a pity such talented people were not around at the time of the fall of the Roman Empire, or Attila the Hun might have called his activities: *'Operation Sweetness and Light'*. No matter what the name was, it did not succeed. Once an entire people stands up and says "no!" to a foreign invader, no amount of troops, guns, bombs or chemical agents will make any difference, as George W. Bush will learn to his cost in Iraq. The Vietnamese continued to resist. More and more US troops had to be sent in and more and more body bags were being flown home. Alan Woods explains in his book *Marxism and the USA* :

> At first the U.S. authorities simply hid the facts of the growing escalation from the American public. They continued to lie and deceive with the active assistance of what is known in some quarters as the free press. But as Abe Lincoln pointed out: you can fool some of the people all the time, and all of the people some of the time, but you cannot fool all of the people all of the time. Slowly, by degrees, and not all at the same time, the people of the United States became aware of what the true situation was.
>
> The suffering of the Vietnamese population will never be fully known. Apart from the huge number killed and maimed, the war caused many other human casualties. The relentless bombing, shelling and defoliation drove tens of thousands of peasants from the countryside to the outskirts of the big cities where they lived in humiliating poverty. The traditional structures of Vietnamese village life were shattered. Young girls became prostitutes for the U.S. soldiers.
>
> A drug culture flourished, which later fed back into the cities of the U.S.A., with devastating results. In 1971 the Pentagon calculated that nearly 30 percent of the U.S. troops in Vietnam had taken heroin or opium, while smoking marijuana was commonplace. Attempts to stamp out the drug trade met with the opposition of the South Vietnamese puppet regime, which was heavily involved in it. That was an indication of the rottenness of the regime the U.S.A. was trying to prop up.
>
> By the end of 1967 the U.S. was spending $20 billion a year on the Vietnam War, which contributed massively to a balance of payments deficit of $7 billion. By the end of 1968, the number of U.S. troops in Vietnam was over 500,000. Towards the end of the war, the U.S. troops in Vietnam were completely demoralized. They understood the situation, that they were fighting an unwinnable war. The Vietnamese were fighting a just war of national liberation, while the U.S. army was a hated army of foreign occupation. In any army there is an element of killers and sadists, and in such a situation atrocities and brutality against civilians became routine. Eventually, these horrors became known at home, with the massacre at My Lai among the most infamous. The supposed moral justification for the war was blasted to pieces just as in Iraq today.
>
> In January 1968, President Johnson announced that the U.S.A. was winning the war. This was immediately blown apart by the Tet offensive. The Vietnamese mounted simultaneous attacks in more than a hundred cities. In Saigon a sapper unit even managed to penetrate the U.S. embassy compound. These events were shown all over America on the television screens to a shocked public. This cruelly

> exposed the fact that for all its military might, the U.S.A. had not succeeded. The war finished Johnson's political career. Richard Nixon, the Republican candidate, defeated L.B.J.'s Vice President Hubert Humphrey in the Presidential elections of November 1968.[18]

As we have already mentioned the anti-war movement intermingled with the movement for Civil Rights. In April 1968 Martin Luther King, Jr. was assassinated in Memphis. This provoked the anger of the Blacks in the United States as more than 100 cities erupted, with flames reaching within six blocks of the White House. Such was the power of the movement that it took 70,000 federal troops to restore order.

The Black Revolt of April 1968 was the culmination of an urban black rebellion that had been unfolding since the summer of 1964, in fact it reflected a process that had been brewing since the 1950s. Now it reached fever pitch and shook US society to its core. With this came a radicalization of the youth in particular who turned to radical and revolutionary politics.

This turn to revolutionary politics was embodied in one of the central figures of the time, Malcolm X, who was assassinated in 1965. In the last year of his life he began to move towards a class analysis of the Black question, drawing the conclusion that racism was an integral part of capitalism, that it was used to divide the workers and thus guarantee the profits of the capitalists.

The French events of 1968 were to accelerate this process. And the Tet offensive at the same time revealed that the giant did indeed have "feet of clay". Tangible evidence of this was the upsurge in student protests. In March 1968 saw the first University occupation at Harward University with the students winning most of their demands. Another occupation followed at Columbia in May, where one thousand students occupied the University. At San Francisco State University we saw a four-and-half month long strike. Again the University administration was forced to accept most demands.

This mood started infecting the working class, with wildcat strikes mushrooming. When this affected the auto industry the *Wall Street Journal* was forced to admit that, "the revolution of the sixties had finally arrived at one of the most vulnerable links of the American economic system—the point of mass production, the assembly line".

The upsurge in rank and file workers' protests had an impact on the official unions, where they were forced to take on a more radical stance, leading many strikes. In fact in the years 1969-70 they led far more strikes than at any time since 1946.

Such was the intensity of the conflict in American society that at one point the state forces opened fire on protesting students, killing four white students at Kent State university and two Black students at Jackson State university. There were strikes and protests at over 440 US campuses, with four million students taking part.

An opinion poll carried out in 1971 revealed that up to three million people were of the view that a revolution was necessary in the United States. Such was the impact of 1968 on the workers and youth of the most powerful capitalist country in the world.

Developments Elsewhere

The purpose of this book is to elaborate on the revolutionary events that unfolded in Pakistan in 1968, the year of revolution. It was part of an international tirade of revolutionary uprising in that period. May 1968 in France was clearly the most advanced revolutionary upsurge in the advanced capitalist countries. As we have observed, Italy was also affected as was Mexico. Even the mighty United States could not escape this process.

It is also true that the radical mood affected even what might seem to have been relatively stable countries. In Britain, for example, we witnessed a growing level of strikes, which culminated in the mass movement against the hated Industrial Relations Act in 1971. Such was the mood that there was talk of a possible general strike, the first that there would have been since 1926.

Even that much-loved (by the reformists) 'model' of class peace and class collaboration, Sweden was affected. Throughout 1969 strikes broke out in many places, and were more extensive and violent than at any previous time in the 25 years since 1945.

Germany also saw extreme radicalization of the students and growing militancy of the working class.

With some delay Spain, Portugal and Greece were affected. At the time of the 1968 wave of revolts these three countries were under the jackboot of military dictatorships. But in the early 1970s there were two mass movements brewing. In Portugal this combined with the liberation struggles in Mozambique and Angola, bringing down the hated dictatorship. At one point such was the situation in Portugal that the *British Times* even commented that the game was up. They felt that capitalism could not be saved. In Spain the decades-old Franco regime finally came tumbling down and in Greece the mass movement removed the hated Colonels' regime. In all three countries we witnessed pre-revolutionary situations where the workers could have taken power.

The Impact on the Former Colonial Countries

In the same period we had a parallel development in the former colonial countries where a whole series of countries saw social transformations that led to the setting up of regimes similar to Stalinist Russia and Maoist China. There was the example of the revolution in South Yemen in 1967, which Ted Grant commented on in his 1986 article 'The Colonial Revolution and Civil War in South Yemen' :

> The overthrow of British imperialism, which was forced to retreat from Aden and South Yemen because of the movement of the masses, marked the beginning of the revolution in South Yemen. However on the basis of bourgeois democracy, with the crisis which exists of world capitalism, a crisis above all in the colonial areas, it was clearly revealed that the bourgeois and petit-bourgeois democrats were incapable of taking action against landlordism and carrying the bourgeois democratic revolution to a conclusion.
>
> Thus the most revolutionary wing of the revolutionary forces was compelled to take power into its own hands. But in order to eliminate feudalism and landlordism they were compelled to go further and eliminate capitalism or rather those elements of capitalism that existed in South Yemen at that time.
>
> South Yemen declared itself a 'Marxist' state, i.e. in reality it was a military-police-bonapartist dictatorship, basing itself on a nationalised economy but with the support of the overwhelming

> majority, especially of the active population. The Yemeni revolutionaries had as their model the revolution in Cuba, in Russia and of course in China.[19]

We saw a similar development in Somalia in 1969, where the former Chief-of-Police, Siad Barre led and organized a coup which eventually finished up like South Yemen where these military officers discovered that they too were 'Marxist-Leninist' and modelled themselves on Soviet Russia. In the 1960s we saw Syria and Burma go down the same road. In 1974 there was the military coup in Ethiopia that brought to power the Derg which had been formed in June 1974 by military officers after a widespread mutiny in the armed forces. That regime also modelled itself on Stalinist Russia. The regimes that came to power in Angola and Mozambique after the defeat of Portuguese imperialism in 1974 were of a similar nature.

Ted Grant, writing in 1975 explained the process:

> The Ethiopian revolution, like that of Syria and Burma, seems to be developing on the lines of sections of the officer corps, leaning on the support of the workers and peasants, purging the country of feudalism and then with the incapacity and feebleness of the native bourgeois carrying the revolution through by expropriating the bourgeoisie which has shown itself incapable of leading the fight for the development of a modern economy. With the backwardness of the country, the limited understanding of the military caste leadership leads them to accept "socialism", i.e. the military-bureaucratic caste system on the model of Russia, China and Cuba, as the solution to the problems of economic expansion so imperatively necessary for the country. The economic might of Russia and China, which is abolishing backwardness with seven-league boots, acts as a mighty magnet. The narrow national limitedness of the rulers in Stalinist states far from repelling them acts as a mighty attraction. Not least of the attractions consists in the organisation of "socialism" and the privileges of the military and bureaucratic castes, which the intelligentsia and military middle layers would consider to be the natural order of society.
>
> Consequently, because the development of [the] productive forces is hampered by the elements of capitalism and big business which are subordinate to, and collaborators of, imperialism, they are swept away. In a twisted version of the permanent revolution this lower officer caste becomes—for a period—the unconscious agent of history, in carrying through the necessary tasks of the state-ification of the economy.

> All these processes are due to the delay of the proletarian revolution in the advanced countries. But they constitute the lappings at the edges and the undermining of the foundations of world capitalism. Not accidentally most of the bourgeois Bonapartist dictators and the rulers of most of the colonial countries which have gained their independence rule in the name of a mythical form of "socialism". This is because of the profound effects in the consciousness of myriads of the oppressed of the Russian and Chinese Revolutions. But this in turn for a whole epoch has reinforced the hold of the Russian bureaucracy over the Russian masses. At the same time it has strengthened the power of the reformist and Stalinist parties in the industrialised countries and deepened their nationalist limited outlook and de-generation.[20]

Since the collapse of Stalinist Russia, and its parallel in China with the adoption of the 'market', i.e. capitalism, all these processes have unravelled with most of these regimes drifting back towards capitalism, in some cases after internal conflict and upheaval such as the civil war in Yemen. But the return to capitalism has solved none of the problems. On the contrary, it has exacerbated them. A new wave of struggle is now being prepared, but this time the whole world is affected.

Venezuela and Latin America are at the heart of this process. And what we see is that just as world capitalism has entered one if its deepest ever crises in history, the concept of socialism is back on the agenda!

Conclusions

Almost a quarter of a century after the Second World War the youth and proletariat on a world scale entered the arena of history, to once again take their destiny into their own hands, feeling the experience of their own strength, of their revolutionary capacity and the valour of the labouring and exploited classes. This mighty movement registered in that epoch showed that revolution and socialist transformation was totally possible and practicable.

Although defeated, the events of 1968 shall not go in vain. As Trotsky said, "No struggle ever goes in vain". The imprint left on the realm of world history by the 1968-9 revolt cannot be removed. Describing that revolutionary epoch and the situation that developed in the following period and up till today, Alan Woods summed up in his article on the 40th anniversary of the French Revolution (1st May 2008):

> We have no time for those petty bourgeois ex-revolutionaries who talk about 1968 in sentimental and nostalgic terms as if it were ancient history of no practical relevance to the world we live in. Sooner or later the events of 1968 will reappear on an even higher level. Which country is the most likely candidate for this scenario? It could well be France, but it could also be Italy, Greece, Portugal, Spain or any one of a number of other countries, and not only in Europe. We look forward to this. We desire it and we are preparing for it. We are striving to prepare the vanguard so that the next time we will be successful. And on this glorious proletarian anniversary we say: The Revolution is dead. Long live the Revolution![21]

Revolutions are not everyday occurrences. It can take years, decades, for a new opportunity to arise. It is our duty to learn the vital lessons from those gigantic events, those historical moments of 1968-9. In truth the most important lesson drawn by Leon Trotsky exactly 70 years ago is once again the decisive and most crucial lessons from the 1968 revolutionary movement of 40 years ago. At the founding congress of the 4th International in 1938 Trotsky wrote: "The historical crisis of human mankind has been reduced today to the crisis of revolutionary leadership."

Trotsky was brutally assassinated just two years later in 1940 in his exile in Mexico by a Stalinist agent. The balance of forces changed tremendously after the Second World War. Western imperialism got a respite from the betrayals of the Social Democratic and Stalinist leaderships of the workers' traditional parties. The longest upswing of world capitalism in history from 1948 to 1973 was one of the factors that gave some credence to social democracy. This to some extent delayed the revolution in the West.

On the other hand in Russia, China and Eastern Europe the rise and spread of Stalinism, strengthened the authority of the 'Communist Parties' for a whole period. The planned economy introduced for the first time in history by the October 1917 Bolshevik revolution led by Lenin and Trotsky provided steady and in some cases dramatic growth for a whole historical period.

Even this Stalinist caricature of the October foundation of this economy gave tremendous growth rates and impetus to science, technology and production. This led to a rapid rise in the living standards in these Stalinist states.

In turn these states created a lot of illusions and also enormous ideological confusion amongst the toiling masses and left leaders especially in the colonial countries. Hence the developments again became impediments to the revolutionary upheavals of 1968-9 and derailed the potential socialist victories into tragic defeats.

However, since then the collapse of Stalinism on the one hand and the excruciating agony brought on to the human race by this crisis-ridden, bloodletting capitalist system has solved nothing. The vast majority of the human race has been forced into intolerable conditions. Life has become unbearable for the majority people on this planet. And with every passing day it worsens. This cannot go on forever and it cannot crush or remove the will and determination of humankind to struggle for the survival of its very existence.

Nothing is wasted in history; it all has a purpose. In the last few decades of reaction and onslaught of the ruling classes the credibility and authority of reformism and Stalinism within the labour movement has been severely diminished.

An epoch is opening up now where we see the predictions and perspectives of revolutionary Marxism being vindicated over and over again. Now we will see new movements and uprisings. Class struggle is back on the agenda. The revolutionary movement will erupt sooner rather than later. However, history does not repeat itself in exactly the same way; it repeats on a higher plane. Thus we will see a new 1968-9, more generalized, more global, and on a higher level and with greater zeal and vigour. And this time we must make sure that the errors of the past are not repeated, that we do not face once more a series of defeats.

Our task is to build the International Marxist Tendency and develop it as a leading force on this planet. We must make sure that this time round the voice of genuine Marxism is not a voice in the wilderness. In all countries we must strive to establish the Tendency as a recognized force within the labour movement. It must be organized and prepared to harness the energy of these massive upheavals of the youth and toilers. A successful socialist transformation, a socialist victory in such conditions will be the order of the day. The genuine communist future, through which the ultimate emancipation of the toiling masses will be achieved, will not be far away.

NOTES

1. Ted Grant, *The Unbroken Thread,* (Fortress), p. 414.
2. *Dual Power in France; A Militant Leaflet,* May 1968.
3. Quoted in *Revolutionary Rehearsals,* p. 12.
4. *London Times* 21.5.1968.
5. *Financial Times,* London 20.5.1968.
6. *Times,* London 23.5.1968.
7. *Times,* London 24.5.1968.
8. *Times,* London 21.5.1968.
9. Pp. 464-65.
10. www.marxist.com.
11. Alan Woods, *'The Revolutionary Dialectic of Republicanism—An Open Letter to Irish Republicans, (Part eight)',* October 2003.
12. W. Churchill, *Triumph and Tragedy,* Pp. 227-8.
13. Ibid, op. cit p. 229.
14. Ted Grant, *The Unbroken Thread,* (Fortress), p. 167.
15. Ted Grant, *Russia from Revolution to Counter Revolution,* Pp. 227-228.
16. Alan Woods, *Czechoslovakia (1968): Stalinism Rocked by Crisis,* September 1968.
17. Jeremy Isaacs and Taylor Downing, *Cold War,* p. 216.
18. Alan Woods, *Marxism and the USA.*
19. Ted Grant, *The Unbroken Thread,* (Fortress).
20. Ted Grant, *The Iberian Revolution—Marxism and the Historical Development of the international situation,* p. 17, 1975.
21. www.marxist.com, 01 May 2008.

Two

BLOODY PARTITION OF THE SUBCONTINENT

Birth Pangs of Pakistan

There is no real connection between these two unrests, labour and Congress opposition. But their very existence and coexistence, explains and fully justifies the attention, which Lord Irwin gave to the labour problems.

—*London Times*, 29 January 1928

Now a situation had arisen where we were becoming greater supporters of partition than Jinnah. I warned Jawaharlal that history would never forgive us if we agreed to partition. The verdict would be that India was divided not by the Muslim League but by Congress.

—Maulana Abul Kalam Azad (1888–1958)

As explained in the previous chapter, the end of the Second World War unleashed a revolutionary wave in its aftermath. Not only in the advanced capitalist countries, but also in countries like China, the red storms were raging across continents. They were threatening imperialism and the capitalist system on a world scale, with an unprecedented ferocity.

This was perhaps the biggest movement of the oppressed masses in human history. This was an enormous awakening of the colonial peoples of China, Africa, the Middle East, Indonesia and India. This was an inspiring movement in which countless millions of former colonial slaves rose against their masters, fighting for their national emancipation. The reasons why all Marxists supported the colonial revolution are obvious: it was a revolutionary movement, a blow against imperialism, it aroused the masses and advanced the class struggle.

If the intense struggle for independence in the Indian

subcontinent had run its course, it would not have stopped at overthrowing the direct rule of British imperialists and gaining national liberation; it would have advanced to socio-economic liberation by overthrowing capitalism and the feudal remnants of the British Raj. This would have put the existence of capitalism on a world scale in serious jeopardy. Hence, in connivance with their local political toadies, the Muslim and Hindu elitist leaders promoted, projected and indoctrinated by British imperialism, and subverted this movement on ethnic and religious lines. The Stalinist leaders of the CPI played no less horrendous a role in this disastrous outcome.

Ted Grant (1913–2006) in the foreword to the book *'Partition—Can it be Undone'* by the author in July 2001, wrote,

> The partition of the subcontinent into Pakistan and India was a crime carried out by British imperialism. Initially, British imperialism tried to maintain control of the whole of the subcontinent, but, during 1946–1947, a revolutionary situation erupted across the whole of the Indian subcontinent. British imperialism realised that it could no longer contain the situation. Its troops were mainly Indian, and they could not be relied on to do the dirty work for the imperialists.

The Partition of the Indian subcontinent led to the largest transmigration of mankind in modern history. It was also the bloodiest migration: at least one million innocent souls perished and about 16 million crossed borders. This was how the 200 years of direct British colonial rule ended in India. It ended with the same policy with which it had begun—divide and rule!

The first scientific, and perhaps the most correct, analysis of the colonization of India and perspectives of its development was written by Karl Marx even before the British formally took over India after the War of Independence of 1857.

Marx, in his writings of that period, explained the economic and social basis of British colonization and its impact on future developments in India. On 22 July 1853 he wrote:

> (...) if we knew nothing of the past history of Hindustan, would there not be the one great and incontestable fact, that even at this moment India is held in English thraldom by an Indian army maintained at the cost of India? England has to fulfil a double mission in India: one destructive, the other regenerating the annihilation of the old Asiatic

society, and laying the material foundations of Western society in Asia. Arabs, Turks, Tartars, Moguls, who had successively overrun India, soon became Hinduised, the barbarian conquerors from primitive cultures, by an eternal law of history, were conquered themselves by the superior civilisation of their subjects. The British were the first conquerors superior in culture, and therefore, inaccessible to Hindu civilisation. They destroyed it by breaking up the native communities, by uprooting the native industry, and levelling all that was great and elevated in the native society. The historical pages of the British rule in India report hardly anything beyond that destruction. The work of the regeneration hardly transpires through a heap of ruins. Nevertheless it has begun. The political unity of India, more consolidated then it ever was under the great Mughals, was the first condition of regeneration. That unity imposed by the British sword will now be strengthened and perpetuated by the electric telegraph. The day is not far distant when, by combination of railway and steam vessels, the distance between England and India measured by time will be shortened. The ruling classes of Great Britain have had till now but an accidental transitory and exceptional interest in the progress of India. The aristocracy wanted to conquer it, the moneyocracy wanted to plunder it, and the milliocracy to undersell it .... Nowhere more than in India, do we meet with such social destitution in the midst of natural plenty, for want of the means of exchange .... The profound hypocrisy and inherent barbarism of bourgeois civilisation lies unveiled before our eyes, turning from its home, where it assumes respectable forms, to the colonies where it goes naked .... Did they not in India, to borrow an experience of that great robber, Lord Clive himself, resort to atrocious extortion, and simple corruption could not keep pace with their rapacity?[1]

Resistance and Betrayals

Throughout the Raj, resistance continued in varying forms. Peasants participated in upsurges. Individual folklore heroes attacked the British forces and were termed bandits by most Western historians. Apart from the Afghan wars, no period was without some form of challenge to the rule of the Raj. Later on, in the 20th century, we witness the proletarian struggle of the soldiers' and sailors' revolts in the armed forces against direct imperialist domination.

The English educated Indian politicians set up the Congress. According to Collins and Lapierre:

> A dignified English civil servant founded Congress in 1885. Acting with the blessing of the Viceroy, Octavian Hume had sought to create an organisation which would canalise the protests of India's slowly growing educated classes into a moderate, responsible body prepared to engage in gentlemanly dialogue with India's English rulers.[2]

During the First World War, Congress fully collaborated with British imperialism.

In criminal silence, they acquiesced to the hangings of members of the Gadar Party, which represented the militant youth who had taken up arms against the British. In the 1915 and 1916 sessions, Congress paid its respects and gratitude to the British governors who were in attendance.

In 1939, in one of his last writings on India, Leon Trotsky (1879–1940), the leader of the Bolshevik Revolution (1917) in Russia along with Lenin wrote the following:

> The Indian bourgeoisie can never lead a revolutionary struggle. It is the slave of British capitalism and fully reliant on it. It has gone mad in its quest to protect its properties. It is terrified of the people. It wants to come to an agreement with British imperialism no matter at what price. It is singing lullabies of hopes of reforms to the masses. The leader and prophet of this bourgeoisie is Gandhi. He is an artificial leader and a false prophet.[3]

Gandhi was awarded the medal of Kaisar-e-Hind by Lord Harding, viceroy to India from 1910–1916. When the Mountbattens travelled to London for the wedding of Princess Elizabeth to their nephew Prince Philip in 1947, whom they had brought up since childhood, Gandhi manifested his affection for them with a touching gesture. Packed into their York MW 102, along with ivory carvings, Mughal miniatures, the jewels and silver plates offered to the royal couple by India's former ruling princes was a wedding gift to the girl who would one day wear Victoria's crown: a teacloth made from yarn that Gandhi had spun himself.

On 15th January 1948 Gandhi also stressed the ownership rights of the capitalists and landlords. He said:

> I will never be a participant in snatching away the properties from their owners and you should know that I will use all my influence and authority against the class war. If somebody wants to deprive

> you of your property you will find me standing shoulder to shoulder with you.[4]

Jinnah was no less anglicised. His habits, lifestyle, dress and attitude were much more British than those of the Muslims of the subcontinent he claimed to represent. He actually never contemplated a total break with the British. In April 1947, in his negotiations with Lord Mountbatten, Jinnah said:

> I do not care how little you give me so long as you give it to me completely. I do not wish to make any improper suggestion to you, but you must realise that the new Pakistan is almost certain to ask for dominion status with the British Empire.

Such was his passion for Partition that in August 1946 he vowed: "We shall have India divided or we shall have India destroyed". Here Jinnah had made a complete u-turn, however: at an 'oyster dinner', held in 1933 by Cambridge student Rahmat Ali at London's rather non-Islamic Waldorf Hotel, to propose a country called Pakistan, for Muslims, he laughed at the idea. He later described it to the Joint Select Committee of the British parliament as "only a student's scheme, chimerical and impractical".[5]

Christina Lamb, in her 1980s book, *Waiting for Allah*, wrote the following:

> In fact, were Jinnah alive today, he could be flogged under Pakistan's strict Islamic laws. A cold nationalist who disliked connecting religion and politics and who, right up to mid 1930s, claimed he was an Indian first and Muslim second, Jinnah saw in the Mullahs' slogans the route to safeguard both his own future and that of the Muslim entrepreneurs and landowning elite.

Jinnah's break with the Congress was not on a communal basis, but was the outcome of tactical differences. Separatism was still a decade away, though the path towards it was already being carefully prepared by the colonial state.

As London began to feel the pressure of agitation, it became clear that some form of self-rule was essential to forestall social upheavals and revolutionary outbreaks. In 1932, Sir Theodore Morrison, a former principal of the staunchly loyalist M.A.O (Mohammadan Anglo Oriental) College in Aligarh, wrote an influential essay in support of separatism. He developed a mystical theme which was to become the leitmotif of Muslim communalism:

> The Hindus and Muslims were two distinct nations, as different from each other as any two European nations; Muslim civilization could not survive under an 'alien' government especially a democratic government which tended toward standardization of citizens; the Muslims should rest assured that they were not alone in their concern for the preservation of their characteristic civilization.[6]

The principle of separate electorates for Muslims had already been accepted and was to play a major role in institutionalizing communal politics in India; but the demand for Pakistan, a separated Muslim state, was only to become meaningful in 1944-6, both for the leaders of the Muslim League and for the sections of the Muslim masses. Those who argue that the notion of Pakistan was contained in the 'fact' that the Muslims were a 'distinct community' are simply re-writing history. If the question is posed: 'When did the Muslims become a distinct nation?' it would be impossible to elicit a common answer from the communal historians.

Apart from the Shi'a–Sunni divide, there were numerous other currents which defined themselves as reformers or defenders of orthodoxy. They argued amongst themselves on questions of theology.

Some theologians were in the pay of the British and wrote sermons on command. Others backed the Congress and declared in favour of a 'composite nationalism'. Others still argued for a universal Islamic republic, and refused even to consider the notion of Islam in One Country. This was the view of Abul-Ala Moududi, who founded the Jamat-i-Islami in 1941 to oppose the secular nationalism of his declared rivals, the Deoband Group, and the aims of the Muslim League. Moududi accused Jinnah of being motivated "by the worldly socio-economic interests of the Muslims" rather than by religion. He insisted that:

> Not a single leader of the Muslim League, from Jinnah himself to the rank and file, has an Islamic mentality or Islamic habits of thought, or looks at political and social problems from the Islamic viewpoint

> ... their ignoble role is to safeguard the material interests of Indian Muslims by every possible manoeuvre or trickery.[7]

The decisive turning point for the national liberation struggle came with the advent of the Bolshevik revolution in October 1917 in Russia. A whole cross-section of activists and leaders in the national liberation struggle were inspired by the mighty events that were taking place in Russia.

Poets like Iqbal called Marx: "A prophet with a book [Capital] but no prophet-hood".

The impact on youth was tremendous. The formation of the Hindu Socialist Revolutionary Army (H.S.R.A.) was the main expression of this radicalization. The heroic deeds of Bhagat Singh, Sukhdev, Raj Guru and B.K. Dutt, although ultra Left, were actions of youth seething with revolt against the British tyranny. Unable to find a Marxist road to independence and revolution, they resorted to armed struggle.

Some of the militants of the H.S.R.A shot and killed an assistant superintendent of police, John Poyants Saunders, on 8 April 1929. Two young men were arrested for throwing bombs at the treasury benches of the central legislative assembly in Delhi. One of them was Bhagat Singh. Most of the youth arrested went on hunger strike in prison. Jatin Das, a young man, is believed to have died during an attempt to feed him forcibly after he had completed sixty-three days of fasting.

The trial of Bhagat Singh and those of the other accused men, gained enormous publicity throughout India, and a mass base started to form around this radical Left trend. The case was much discussed in society, and such was the sympathy for the accused that witnesses started turning hostile to the prosecution. Even a British policeman refused to identify Bhagat Singh as a person present at the time of the murder.

Bhagat Singh's trial lasted five months. Judgement was pronounced on 7 October 1930. The popularity of these radical youths and their assertion of left ideas in the movement for national independence sent shock waves through the bourgeois leaders in the movement.

A British visitor to India, C.F. Andrews, wrote in 1932:

> The scene in India at the present time is that of the Roman Empire nineteen hundred years ago. There was the same vast order outwardly maintained. But within this area of apparent calm a surging, heaving ferment had suddenly begun to appear like volcanic lava cracking through the surface of the soil. Men call it the national movement.

British rulers continuously imprisoned and released Congress leaders including Gandhi, prompting the media of colonial India to give extensive coverage of the sacrifice, courage and commitment of Gandhi and other bourgeois leaders. The British ruling class used Gandhi in a manipulative manner to quell the rising tide of the left and derail the class struggle.

Reaction from within Congress, however, was also intense. Subhas Chandra Bose, a leading figure of the Left wing in Congress, told Congress supporters that: "Between us and the British lies an ocean of blood and a mountain of corpses. Nothing on earth can induce us to accept this compromise which Gandhi has signed". Wherever Gandhi went, youth with red flags met him with angry questions, sometimes he was even manhandled. At the All India Congress meeting in Karachi, the main slogan chanted was "Gandhi's truce sent Bhagat Singh to the gallows!"

On the day of Gandhi's visit to Lord Irwin (19 March 1931), Bhagat Singh and his comrades, encouraged by their friends, sent a letter to the viceroy. In that letter, instead of asking for clemency, they asked the viceroy to treat them as prisoners of war and to have them shot rather than hanged. Four days later the four were hanged at Lahore central prison. Bhagat Singh's prison diary makes very interesting reading; in it he described the evolution of his ideology and thoughts while languishing in his death cell. He renounced individual violence, but condemned Gandhi's non-violence. He put forward the proposition that a socialist revolution in the Indian subcontinent was the logical conclusion of the liberation struggle. It should have been the responsibility of the Communist Party of India to unite, develop and take forward the Left currents that inevitably develop in every struggle for national liberation. If the Communist Party of India (CPI) had been based on Marxist methods and perspectives, the whole course of history would have been different and the tragedy of Partition averted.

The Communist Party

The Communist Party of India (CPI) was founded at the Kanpur communist conference of 26–28 December 1925. It was convened by Satyabhakata and the chairman of the reception committee was Hasrat Mohani. Comrade Singaravelu delivered the presidential address. The first nucleus was set up in Berlin in 1919, and an organization in the name of Indian communists was established in Tashkent UŜSR in December 1920. Manabendra Nath Roy, the main theoretician of the party who was in exile, played a leading role in affiliating the CPI to the Third International.

The Kanpur communist conference brought together various Left groups across India. The main leaders were Muzaffar Ahmed from Bengal, Shaukat Usmani from the United Provinces, S. A. Dange from Bombay, Abdul Majeed from Lahore and representatives from other regions of the subcontinent. Nearly three years earlier, on 27th April 1923, a circular from 'Inquilab' Office, Railway Road, Lahore, was sent to twenty-five prominent Leftist leaders, with the aim of forming a new political party. It was signed by comrades Ghulam Hussain and Shamsuddin Hassan. The rising tide of the workers' struggle and the interest in communist ideas that swept through the wider layers of society terrified the British imperialists.

Communists, right from the beginning, had to work under clandestine conditions, whereas the leaders and parties of the bourgeoisie worked more or less in connivance with the British rulers.

The regime instituted several cases against the CPI, two of which gained mass publicity. The first was the Kanpur Bolshevik conspiracy case, which took place in 1924. The main accused was Manabendra Nath Roy, who was convicted in absentia. Eight other leading members of the CEC (Central Executive Committee) of the CPI were arrested: Shaukat Usmani, M. Singaravelu Chettair, S.A. Dange, R.C.L. Sharma, Muzaffer Ahmed, Nalini Das Gupta, Maula Baksh and Professor Ghulam Hussain. The prosecution case lodged on behalf of the Crown made a mockery of British democratic values:

> The accused are charged under section 121A with conspiracy to establish a branch organisation of the communist international throughout British India with objective to deprive the King Emperor of the sovereignty of British India...

Eventually, only four of the accused were convicted: Muzaffer Ahmed, Shaukat Usmani, S.A. Dange and Nalini Gupta (Roy's emissary from Berlin); they were sentenced to four years of rigorous imprisonment.

A centre was set up in Tashkent to train and send cadres to India to spread communist ideas. Most of these communists, known as Muhajirun, were arrested as they filtered into India from the North West Frontier at the end of 1922. Except for one or two, the rest abandoned Communism. In spite of the setbacks, however, communist groups had sprung up in major cities throughout India: Madras, Bombay, Lahore, Karachi, Calcutta and parts of the United Provinces. In the first two decades of the 20th century, two major upsurges occurred in the mass movement against the British Raj. The first wave was in the period 1919–1922, and then a second more militant upsurge began in 1926–1927. These were the first major strike waves of the Indian proletariat, which was making its mark on history. When the Simon Commission landed in Bombay in February 1928, it was greeted by nationwide strikes. Unrest was growing among the industrial proletariat, and, from 1928 to 1929, 209 strikes took place compared with 129 in 1927. A mass general strike led by the textile workers was held in Bombay. This textile strike caused the shutdown of fifty mills and lasted from 26 April to 6 October, 1928.

In the Bardoli district of Bombay state, the peasants went on a campaign of non-payment of taxes. At the steel works of Tata Limited, staff dismissals and wage decreases led to a strike that lasted five months. The workers of the Eastern Railway Company at Liloolah were locked out for four months. From the North Western Railway (NWR) to the South Indian Railway (SIR), the railway workers went on strike in almost all sectors of the huge Indian railway network. An increase in the armed struggle also occurred, and in December a bomb explosion wrecked parts of the train in which Viceroy Irwin was travelling.

Not surprisingly, Gandhi, Nehru and the Congress condemned the attack.

Chronic unemployment and deteriorating conditions created enormous discontent and turmoil amongst peasants, workers, and the educated youth. In the northwest frontier the conflict became more violent. According to the Simon Commission report, between 1858 and 1922, British troops carried out seventy-two expeditions against rebellious tribesmen in this region.

In Gujarat, at the end of June, a movement for the non-payment of rent and revenue began. In Bengal, a student movement developed and semi-guerrilla insurgency increased. The Communist Party led these struggles. The British imperialists were terrified of this red threat. They used the Indian national bourgeois leaders to distract the movement and started a new wave of repression against the Communist Party. This culminated in the infamous 'Meerut Conspiracy Case' in 1929. This was similar to the Kanpur Bolshevik conspiracy and aimed to crush the CPI's leadership. Thirty-one leaders of the CPI were arrested on 20 March 1929, after the preparation of an elaborate dossier by the state's secret agencies against active communists. The trial of the Meerut conspiracy case began in June 1929. Not until 16 January 1933 did the trial court conduct its hearings and sentenced all but four of the accused to terms of imprisonment varying from three years to life. Phillip Spratt and Benjamin Frances Bradley, who had come from England to India to work for the CPI, were sentenced to transportation for ten years. The Chief Justice of the Allahabad High Court dismissed all the appeals, but the sentences were reduced and by the autumn of 1935 all the prisoners were released. During the trial, the accused had been able to evoke considerable national sympathy by exploiting anti-British feelings in the nationalist movement. The Indian bourgeoisie retaliated and formed a defence committee including Motilal Nehru as chairman and Jawaharlal Nehru as a member. The accused took advantage of the opportunity provided by the trial to propagate communist ideas. The Chief Justice observed:

> They took an inordinately long time in reading out well-prepared statements, which the court had to take down word for word. In most cases they had nothing more than an exposition, on an elaborate scale, of the doctrines of communism, its tenets and its programme.

After the Meerut trial began, attacks were launched against the Giridih Kamgar Union ... the textile union of Bombay. The government not only arrested the communists and the leading trade unionists but also appointed a Riots Enquiry Committee and a Strike Enquiry Committee, with the intention of removing all communists from leading positions in trade unions throughout India. The Whitley Royal Commission on Indian Labour was also appointed and arrived in India in October 1929. The 'Manchester Guardian' reported that the real aim behind this commission was to repress the communists. On 25 October 1929 it wrote:

> Experience of the past two years has shown that the industrial workers in the biggest centres are peculiarly malleable material in the hands of unscrupulous communist organisers naturally, and this is one of the circumstances which give such importance to the recently appointed commission on Indian labour.

Although the Giridih Kamgar union was forced to call off the textile strike, more strikes broke out in other parts of the country. The tinplate workers in Jamshedpur took strike action, while the strike of oil and petroleum workers in Calcutta and dock workers in Karachi threatened the supremacy of the Raj.

The question arises as to why the Communist Party could not take the lead in spite of the sacrifices and struggle of its workers. One of the explanations that most Stalinists tend to give is that repression was the main cause of the failure of the CPI to take charge of the situation. The Meerut Conspiracy Case is cited often as an example. It is true that repression does damage an organization and leads to serious setbacks. A Marxist organization has to be able to built solidarity and support out of repression, both nationally and internationally. Some of the CPI leaders of the time accepted this position. Soumy Endranath Tagore in his pamphlet *Historical Development* wrote,

> Nothing made so much propaganda in India for communism as did the Meerut conspiracy case. The entire attention of political India was

> focused on this case and hundreds of radical youth were drawn to the Communist Party because of it. There was also a good bit of propaganda in the international press. One can say with justice that the Meerut conspiracy case placed communism on a sure footing in India.

The Programme of *The Communist International*, which was adopted at the second congress and published in September 1920, had stated:

> Tendencies like Gandhi's in India, thoroughly imbued with religious conceptions, idealize the most backward and economically most reactionary forms of social life. They see the solution of the social problem not in proletarian socialism, but in a reversion to these backward forms, preaching passivity and repudiating the class struggle, and in the process of the development of the revolution they become transformed into an openly reactionary force. Gandhi's is more and more becoming an ideology directed against mass revolution. It must be strongly combated by communism.

The zigzags and right and left turns of the Stalinist Comintern resulted in the defeat of several revolutions, as well as some important revolutionaries, throughout the world.

After Roy's return from the China mission in 1927 he had fallen from Stalin's grace. He was eventually expelled from the Comintern in 1929.

In spite of mistakes, the CPI still maintained a considerable base, mainly because of its links with the heritage of '4 October'. In 1936, the railway strike paralyzed the British Empire in India. It had an important impact on the newly emerging proletariat in other sections of industry. In 1938, with the slogan of a 'Workers Socialist Republic', the CPI was able to mobilize 50,000 workers in Calcutta. It was able to lead a massive strike under the slogan 'Government of Workers and Poor Peasants'. Similarly, a new wave of class struggle had forced the CPI leadership to move further Left. In the 1938 Kissan Sabha [Peasants' Conference] of the CPI, more than 500,000 poor peasants had registered for attendance. In 1939, the resolution passed by this conference strongly criticized the Congress Ministries. The resolution demanded the full political freedom and independence that could be obtained only under the rule of the people.

The Communist Party was banned until 1937. In Maharashtra and the United Provinces, thousands of members of the CPI were put behind bars. In Bengal and Punjab, they were subjected to atrocities and torture. In Sholapur, four leaders of the Communist Party were hanged; these included one main trade union leader. In Malabar, the workers of the Communist Party were subjected to constant repression. In Madras, several workers were hanged.The changes and zigzags in the policies of the Moscow bureaucracy influenced the policies of the CPI leadership. The policy of "defence of the fatherland" severely dented the clear class perception of the revolutionary struggle among the activists of the CPI.

At the beginning of the Second World War the CPI launched an intensive anti-war campaign. It called it an imperialist war, and the CPI was in the forefront of anti-war and anti-British agitation. This was a golden chance for the CPI to present itself as a revolutionary alternative to the masses. At the start of the anti-war campaign, the CPI took the courageous step of organizing mass strikes against the war. The first ever anti-war workers' demonstration in the world took place in India on 22 October 1939 with a one-day protest general strike; 90,000 people participated. The main slogans of the demonstration were: 'Defeat This Treachery against the Human Race!', 'Down with the Imperialist War!', 'Long Live the Freedom of India!' etc. The British colonialists increased state repression and thousands of CPI workers were put into jail during this anti-war agitation. Congress was polarized, and a number of Leftist groups, including those around Subhas Chandra Bose, identified with the CPI. In the 1939 convention, Bose defeated Gandhi in the election for President of Congress, thus creating a strong possibility of forming a United Front with the Left wing of Congress. This would have led to a formidable force of the left which, with a correct Marxist programme and methods, could have led to a socialist conclusion of the national independence movement.

Degeneration of the Left Leadership

While the process of Left unity on the basis of the anti-war and anti-British policy of the CPI was forging ahead, changes in Moscow's policy struck a devastating blow.

The Stalinist compromise with British and American imperialism forced the CPI to change its attitude towards British imperialist rule. In 1942, Comrade Khushi Mohammad, a CPI leader, spoke at a mass rally in Azamgarh, in United Provinces (now Uttar Pradesh). He was at the height of a fiery, anti-imperialist speech when he was passed a note that had just been brought by a messenger from the CPI's high command containing strongly worded instructions from Stalin—the capitulation had begun. After he glanced at the note, he made a U-turn in his speech. He retreated from his staunch anti-imperialist position and said that as British democracy had formed an alliance with fatherland Russia, the main thrust of agitation and struggle had to be directed against the fascists (Germany and Japan) and not the democratic allied governments, including Britain.

The CPI paid a heavy price for this opportunistic turn. Apart from its attitude of appeasement towards the British, it started to develop a conciliatory attitude towards the national bourgeois leadership. In reality, large sections of the CPI were absorbed into Congress. At the same time, its reversal of previous policies led to a head-on clash with Bose and other Left-wing tendencies inside and outside Congress. The CPI cadres who were in Congress were moving to form a block with liberal socialists like Nehru and social democrats like Jayaparkash Narayan. Nehru, like Gandhi, was used as a tool of the British to control the workers' and the peasants' upsurge and to subvert the radicalisation of the youth.

In some instances, CPI even cooperated with the bourgeois nationalist leaders at the heart of the movement, instead of aiming to develop the movement on class lines to break the stranglehold of the bourgeois leaders. The preliminary draft thesis on the National and Colonial Question, drafted by Lenin, was presented to the Plenary Session on 28 July 1920 at the second Congress of the Communist International. It stated: "The Communist International must enter into a temporary alliances with bourgeois democracy in the colonial and backward countries, but should not merge with it, and should under all circumstances uphold the independence of the proletarian movement even if it is in its most embryonic form..."

The CPI cadres should have exposed the real class interests of Nehru and Gandhi to the toiling masses.

Their main aim should have been to recruit the socialist youth and militants who were in Congress into the CPI and create a mass movement of the workers and peasants to put an end to imperialist rule. That should have been the real revolutionary course of the struggle a class war! The change in the CPI's position on the war created disillusionment amongst the masses and confusion and apathy in the party ranks.

Gandhi launched the 'Quit India' movement on 8 August 1942. Like his previous manoeuvres, it was passive in character and did not threaten the British rule or the colonial structures. It aimed to water down the militancy of the struggle and at the same time consolidate and perpetuate the bourgeois leadership and ideology of the national liberation struggle. Stalin had abolished the rudimentary organization of the Third International to appease Churchill and Roosevelt, but he was still calling the shots in the CPI's policy and actions in India. The imprisoned CPI leaders started a secret correspondence with the British rulers from their jails. They were laying their "voluntary services" at the doorstep of the colonial rulers. They were offering to put up resistance against Congress activists and "fifth columnists" who were still active in the struggle against the Raj. Dange, the general secretary of CPI at the time, wrote a letter to the Viceroy, Lord Wavell, pledging the services of the Communist Party in the war effort. The CPI leadership not only isolated itself from the ever-rising tide of the national liberation movement, but also frustrated and disillusioned its own cadres and members.

In this period, while thousands were being hanged, lashed, tortured and imprisoned, leaders and activists of the CPI were being released from prisons. The ban on the party was lifted, and CPI publications started getting funds from the British Colonial government.

Ironically, the first congress of the CPI was held in this period of collaboration with the British in 1943. During this period the party was trying to stop strikes, restrain youth from going on demonstrations and soldiers from deserting. As a result of this betrayal, the mass reaction against the CPI was enormous. It became so severe that CPI offices were attacked. Ranadive, the CPI ideologue of the 1940s and 1950s, confessed: "The voice of the CPI was reaching deaf ears. They had never been so isolated from the masses."

The crucial test for the CPI came during the Second World War. At the outbreak of the war, the Indian communists opposed any support for Britain and France and argued that India's freedom should not be compromised by any deals with the occupying power. Their opposition to the war led to widespread arrests of party leaders on a national, provincial, and local level, but it also brought them closer to the Left wing of the Congress.

A minority of party leaders, among them K. Damodaran of Kerala, opposed the thesis developed by Moscow that the war had now been transformed into a 'People's War', and accordingly that the duty of communists everywhere was to support the Allied war effort. The CPI fell into line and became a virtual recruiting agent for the British authorities, but those communists who opposed the new line were not released till much later.

In August 1942, when Congress launched its 'Quit India' movement, the Viceroy responded by unleashing a new wave of repressive measures. Congress leaders and activists were now being locked in prison cells which had only recently been vacated by CPI inmates. Many decades later Damodaran revealed in an interview how damaging the consequences of the CPI's servile compliance with Stalin's dictate had been:

> There is a view developed by some of the apologists for the 'People's War' line which argues that the CPI gained a lot of support as a consequence of "swimming against the stream". I do not subscribe to this view. Of course the party took advantage of the legality granted to it by British imperialism to gain new members and increase its trade-union strength, but the point is that it was swimming against the stream of the mass movement and was to all intents and purposes considered an ally of British imperialism; it became respectable to be a communist. Many young communists joined the British army to go

> and 'defend the Soviet Union' in Italy and North Africa. Some of them rapidly shed their 'communism' and stayed in the army even after the war and not to do clandestine work. It is true that the membership of the party increased from about 4,500 in July 1942 to well over 15,500 in May 1943, at the time of the First Party Congress. However, most of these new members had no experience of any militant mass struggle or police repression, but only the peaceful campaign conducted by the party to 'grow more food', 'increase production', 'release national leaders', 'form a national government' and 'defend the Motherland' from a Japanese invasion which never came; strikes were denounced as sabotage. On the other hand, the growth of the Congress and its influence after the 'Quit India' struggle of August 1942 was phenomenal. Millions of men and women, especially the youth, were attracted and radicalized by the struggle, which was considered as a revolution against imperialism they branded the Congress Socialists, and Bose's followers and other radicals who braved arrests and police repression, as fifth columnists and saboteurs. In reality the CPI was isolated from the mainstream of the nationalist movement for the second time within a decade. In my view the party's policy virtually delivered the entire anti-imperialist movement to the Congress and the Indian bourgeoisie on a platter. At the time, if the CPI had adopted a correct position the possibility existed of winning over a sizable and influential section of the Congress to communism: "On my release from prison I experienced the wrath of the left-wing nationalists who used to chant 'Down with supporters of British imperialism' at our meetings. So swimming against the stream when the stream was flowing in the right direction resulted in drowning the possibility of genuine independence and a socialist transformation. We were outmanoeuvred and outflanked by the Indian bourgeoisie."[8]

CPI's position during the war was untenable on all counts. It created a sharp divide between party activists and the base of the nationalist movement.

The CPI thesis on the war brought it closer to the Muslim League.

It was the League's growth that was to provide an opportunity for the CPI to make another major strategic error. Instead of providing its supporters with a trenchant critical analysis of all brands of communal politics and offering an alternative, the CPI, in the words of its theorist Adikhari: "began to see that the so-called communal problem, especially the Hindu–Muslim problem, was really a problem of growing nationalities". It was during the 'People's War' years (1942–5) that the CPI, forced into the same political camp as the Muslim League, first discovered the intricacies of the national question. A resolution, 'Pakistan and National Unity', was passed by the Enlarged Plenum of the Central Committee in September 1942 amidst opportunist politics and theoretical confusion. It took as its starting-point Stalin's insufficient definition of a 'nation', went on to develop a completely false analogy between India and Tsarist Russia, and drew the conclusion that the Muslims constituted a national minority which should be granted the right of self-determination.[9]

The CPI leaders failed even to refer to the classical definition of a nation within the Marxist tradition. To have done so would merely have revealed the political distance they had travelled over the years. For Marx and Lenin alike, neither a common language nor a common culture constituted the basis of a bourgeois nation. The latter was a synonym for the modern state. Religion merely expressed the separation of an individual from the community as a whole, and could not constitute the basis for a community.

This was a time when the CPI should have swum against the stream of Muslim communalism; but their approach of 'national unity in the holy defence of our Motherland' against 'pitiless and powerful enemies' (the Japanese) made any application of Marxist politics impossible. The politics being effectively applied became ipso facto the only possible politics. It was only after the conclusion of the war that the CPI altered its position, this time on the urging of R. Palme Dutt, a leader of the British Communist Party. Dutt argued in 1946 that Pakistan was based on religion and not on nationality. The CPI obligingly changed its position and denounced Pakistan as a plot between British imperialism and "Muslim bourgeois-feudal vested interests". Many Muslim communists, however, were slow to catch up with this change in line, and found themselves in 1947 still members of the Muslim League, which they had been instructed to enter by the Stalinist leadership in order to help the 'progressive' elements against the landlords.

One of the oldest living 'communists' from Sindh and a former member of the CPI, Sobho Gianchandani explained the situation from this turn at the time. In a recent interview Comrade Sobho said,

> In 1943 Communist Party switched sides and started supporting the British. The Communist Parties all over the world had changed their stand on the war: from being viewed as an imperialist war, it had now become the people's war. A meeting was arranged to sell the new idea to the students. The Communist Party sent Muqeeb-ud-din Farooqi, Sajjad Zaheer and Mian Iftikhar to do the job.
>
> Addressing the students, Farooqi, the secretary of the Communist Party of Delhi, a gentleman from Delhi University, told the students not to feel betrayed and that the world was changing and, they [the Communist Party] with it. The Sindhi comrades, who had grown up in revolutionary times, were shocked at hearing that they were being asked to support the British.
>
> While the leadership of the Indian Communist Party abided by this reversal, they were unable to convince some of the students of the wisdom of their choice. I came to the conclusion that when thousands of students were prepared to go to jail, I couldn't back out, so I resolved to join them against the British.[10]

Defiance and Revolution

In the 1940s, a revolutionary blizzard swept across Asia and the world. In India, 1946 was the year of revolution. It began with a mass movement that forced the British rulers to release the leaders of INA (Indian National Army) who were imprisoned in Indian jails facing charges of treason. The massive popularity of INA at that time revealed that the masses had no sympathy for the non-violence and passivity of Congress. After the Second World War, there was enormous ferment and tumult in the British army. The British soldiers and young officers, exhausted from the war, led widespread revolts from Hong Kong to Egypt. At the same time, the mass upsurge was unstoppable and gained momentum day by day. In the countryside, the sleepy hamlets and small towns had been awakened by these winds of change and the end of imperialist rule was in sight.

On 1 March 1946 a soldier's revolt occurred in the military barracks at Jabalpur, and on 18 March the Gurkha Sepoys deployed at Dehradun revolted against the regime. The unrest among the Indian officers manifested itself in many incidents in the army and the air force.

One of the most spectacular episodes of the revolt against the British Raj was the uprising of the sailors of the British Indian Navy in 1946. On 18 February the sailors of the British Indian Navy battleship *HMS Talwaar*, posted at the Bombay harbour, went on strike in protest against the bad food and poor conditions.

Although at first it was a peaceful hunger strike, signs of an imminent and much bigger rebellion against the British rulers were evident. On 19 February, the sailors announced the strike to the naval personnel stationed in the fortress and to those in the naval barracks. They took over the naval trucks, boarded them, hoisted Red Flags and started patrolling the city of Bombay. They invited the masses of the city to join in the struggle they had started. As a result, anti-British imperialist sentiments started to spread like wildfire throughout the region.

On the evening of 19 February 1946 increasing numbers of naval personnel joined this revolt. The Union Jacks on most of the ships of the Royal Indian Navy in the Bombay harbour were torn down, and the rebel sailors hoisted Red Flags along with the flags of the political parties involved in the struggle for independence.

Within 48 hours, the British imperialists were faced with the largest ever revolt of their naval units. The message of this rebellion started to spread by word of mouth and then over the radio (the radio station had been taken over by the rebels) to military garrisons and barracks across India. Some of the sailors' leaders broadcast the message of the uprising, as well as revolutionary songs and poetry, round the clock. The revolt spread to 74 ships, 20 fleets and 22 units of the navy along the coast. These naval stations included Bombay, Calcutta, Karachi, Madras, Cochin and Vishakapatam. On 20 February only ten ships and two naval stations were not in complete revolt.

In the beginning, this revolt was considered to be spontaneous, but that is not completely true. On the evening of 19 February, a strike committee was formally set up. Signalman M.S. Khan and petty officer telegraph operator Madan Singh unanimously were elected president and vice president of the committee. Both of them were under the age of 25 years. One was a Muslim and the other a Sikh: this was a conscious act to reject the religious divide being fed into the liberation movement by the native bourgeois leaders and their British masters.

Apart from the other tasks on the strike committee agenda, it was also agreed to involve the political parties in this movement and to gain their support. The CPI lost the leadership of the independence movement because of its disastrous policy of supporting the British imperialists. At that time, the Indian bourgeoisie and their leaders were negotiating a settlement with the British. They were as hostile as the British to any revolutionary upsurge at this delicate juncture in the history of the subcontinent.

Gandhi outrightly condemned the uprising of the sailors, while the CPI leaders even lost the opportunity to link this naval revolt with the strikes taking place in the textile industry, on the railways, and in other industrial sectors throughout India. Likewise, leaders like Subhas Chandra Bose were unable to connect this movement with the revolts taking place in the British Indian army. Bose had gone too far in launching the Indian National Army to fight British forces under the auspices of the reactionary Japanese regime!

Congress and the Muslim League were afraid that revolutionary and class struggle ideas would penetrate into the movement they had done so much to tear apart along religious lines. In spite of this betrayal and the contemptuous attitude of the national bourgeois leaders, the revolutionary momentum of the uprising continued unabated, and the whole country was filled with the echoes of the slogan "long live the revolution"!

The passions and sentiments of these slogans resonated throughout the whole of Bombay. One of the poets of the era, Josh Malihabadi, wrote enthralling verses like:

> My task is my growth; my name is martyr. My slogan is revolution, revolution, revolution.

On 21 February, British shock troops opened fire on the sailors as they came out of their barracks in the Bombay fortress. This provocation changed a peaceful uprising into an armed rebellion. Armed clashes occurred between the British elite troops and the rebellious sailors throughout the day. On the first day, one death was reported in Bombay, but on the second day 14 sailors were martyred in Karachi. The industrial workers who had joined the revolt with the sailors were subjected to brutal attacks by the British forces.

On 22 and 23 February, 25 sailors and workers were martyred by the imperialist forces. According to some eyewitness accounts, on 21 February, it seemed that the oppressed masses of the whole subcontinent had risen up in a revolutionary movement against British rule. In these events, the revolutionary strike committee had shifted its command to the Narba fleet. The sailors now aimed the barrels of their guns at ships and targeted British Naval installations and command centres on the coast. Sirens were sounded from all ship decks. The sailors announced through loudspeakers that they would destroy the British military bases and installations to defend their comrades in the cities and in the harbour if the British dared to attack.

The British government in London was in shock. The British Labour Prime Minister, Clement Attlee, ordered the uprising to be crushed. The commander of the British Indian Navy, Admiral Godfrey, ordered the rebellious sailors to "surrender or perish". One of the stalwarts of the Indian National Congress, Sardar Vallabhbhai Patel, openly came out on the side of the British, denouncing the uprising and supported the 'imperialists' ultimatum. In this uprising, the national leadership of India, both Hindu and Muslim, became allies of the British imperialists. This exposed their real class character and their collaborationist role in the saga of transition from British to native rule after Independence.

Meanwhile, British fighter aircraft were carrying out sorties over the rebellious fleet. In such conditions, Sardar Patel made the following infamous statement:

> Only a small band of insolent, hot headed and insane youngsters are trying to get involved in politics through these acts, when they have nothing to do with politics.[11]

Isolated, desperate, and disillusioned by the treacherous role and attitude of the national leadership towards the uprising,

M.S. Khan proposed surrender to the strike committee. The 36-member committee, however, rejected this plea. Several tense hours passed. The mainstream national leadership intensified its efforts to isolate the naval uprising from the mass movement for independence that was surging across the subcontinent. Demoralization started to set in among the members of the strike committee.

Another session of the committee started in the early hours of 24 February on *HMS Talwaar*. By now it was evident that surrender was the only option. At 0600 hours on 24 February 1946 black flags were raised to announce surrender. In its last session the strike committee passed a resolution which became the last message of the revolutionary sailors to the toiling masses of the South Asian subcontinent. The resolution stated:

> Our uprising was an important historical event in the lives of our people. For the first time the blood of uniformed and non-uniformed workers flowed in one current for the same collective cause. We, the workers in uniform, shall never forget this. We also know that you, our proletarian brothers and sisters shall also never forget this. The coming generations, learning its lessons, shall accomplish what we have not been able to achieve. Long live the working masses. Long live the Revolution.[12]

After the Revolt

After the surrender most leaders and activists of this uprising were prosecuted, imprisoned and executed in spite of their surrender. On 15 March the rebellious sailors of the Royal Indian Navy who were still imprisoned started a hunger strike. The nationalist bourgeois leaders refused to raise any protest. The nationalist parties, masquerading as upholders of independence, also made no protest.

In the early 1980s there emerged in India a school of history that goes by the name of Subaltern Studies. Inspired by the writings of the Italian Marxist Antonio Gramsci, these historians denounced both the Cambridge and the nationalist schools since both assumed that nationalism was a product of elite action and had no place in it for the independent political actions of the subaltern classes (rural peasants or urban workers). The document's aim was to highlight the actions of the men and women from the subaltern classes, and their remarkable resilience against the British between November 1945 and February 1946.

The display of Hindu–Muslim unity, students' and workers' protests against the trial of prisoners of the Indian National Army (INA), and the heroic strike of the Royal Indian Navy (RIN) from 18 to 23 February, were marked by massive solidarity actions in Calcutta, Bombay and Karachi. Order in Bombay city could be restored only after the killing of 228 civilians, while 1,046 were injured in the aftermath of the mutiny. The RIN Mutiny shook the Raj to its very foundations, and it was probably no coincidence that the British Prime Minister, Clement Attlee, announced on 19 February 1946 the decision to send a Cabinet Mission to India. This event was the single most contributory factor in hastening the process of independence.

The mutiny was the culmination of the erosion of imperial authority, but curiously this incredible feat has been erased from history. After Independence, many of the RIN Muslim mutineers came to Pakistan in search of a new identity, but their hopes were shattered as they were not considered suitable for re-employment in the then Royal Pakistan Navy (RPN). The fate of their counterparts in India was no different. Nonetheless, in 1973, the government of India accorded official recognition to the ex-personnel of RIN who participated in the mutiny, and granted them freedom fighters' pension.

How surprising that the official history, both in India and Pakistan, has seldom commemorated the RIN Mutiny. No doubt the attitude of the Congress and Muslim League leadership had been lukewarm if not hostile. The treatment meted out to the mutineers by Congress and Muslim League leadership S.K. Patil and Chundrigar, presidents of Congress and Muslim League respectively displayed a rare unanimity in "offering the help of volunteers to assist the police". Patel argued that "discipline in the army cannot be tampered with, we will want an army even in free India". "Even Gandhi thought that the sailors had set 'a bad and unbecoming example for India. A combination of Hindus, Muslims and others for the purpose of violent action is unholy.' Jinnah told the RIN men: 'If they would adopt constitutional, lawful and peaceful methods and apprise him fully of what will satisfy them, he would assure that their just grievances are redressed'".[13]

Interestingly, Aruna Asaf Ali disagreed with Gandhi and said in a rejoinder, "it would be far easier to unite Hindus and the Muslims at the barricade than on the constitutional front". Sarkar supports this view and notes that "if the British had been forced to give up tentative plans for holding onto political power, the logically opposite scenario of radical united mass actions forcing an unqualified imperial retreat also did not materialise".

The documents, particularly those related to Captain Abdul Rashid Day (14 Punjab Regiment) disturbances and the RIN strike, vividly illustrate the 'restraining role' of the national leadership. Political parties had opposed the disturbances for the very good reason that they were about to assume power and had no wish to inherit rebellious and undisciplined armed forces. In this volume excerpts from the statements of the top leadership of both the Congress and Muslim League have been kept minimal, as they are easily accessible and highlighted in various other documents.

These documents, probably for the first time, provide a unique insight and rare glimpses into the labour and peasants' movements. The year 1946 witnessed remarkable and unprecedented labour unrest, and it also saw the beginning of several powerful movements. This volume contains 250 documents pertaining to labour and kissan affairs, extracted from various sources and some private papers. One is amazed to note the range of participation which extended from sweepers, miners and railway workers, to white-collar post office and bank employees, as well as the military establishments. Railway and postal workers all over India were on strike and a mob of 80,000 stormed ration centres in Allahabad. These strikes were ruthlessly suppressed at the time.

The documents illustrate the central role of the communists in the labour movements in 1946. However, documents relating to the peasant movements have a somewhat distinct time frame and character. Apart from some scattered items from Punjab, the United Provinces and Bihar, the bulk of the documents refer to the Tanjore, Ramnad and Malabar regions, the agitation of the Warli tribals in Bombay, and the beginnings of the Tebhaga movement by sharecroppers in Bengal demanding a two-third share of the crop, instead of one-half, from rich farmers.

At this point the author notes that "communist predominance in all these movements was even clearer than in the case of labour, and once again left-led agitations emerged as a potential, never fully-realised, and yet memorable and moving alternative to Stalinist leaders".

Nevertheless, "the nationalist leadership's choice of the path of compromise, and the eventual acceptance of Partition as a necessary price" was made at the cost of millions of displaced people and innumerable sacrifices.

This episode stands out, however, as one of the greatest chapters in the history of the struggle for independence from British rule. Although the uprising was defeated, the movement showed the British what lay ahead. As a direct result of this uprising, the British Prime Minister, Clement Attlee, announced that the British would leave India before June 1948. Such was the blow inflicted on the confidence of the British rulers that they were forced to beat a retreat. The British, in connivance with the native bourgeois leaders, hastened the process of Partition along ethnic and religious lines. After this episode they were determined not to leave the subcontinent united in any form whatsoever either as a confederation or with any political superstructure they may have envisaged before these revolutionary events. The British policy of divide and rule thus came into play.

The details of this glorious uprising remain unrecorded both in India and Pakistan, just as several similar events and great episodes have yet to see the light of day. Rising generations of youth and workers have the task of carrying out the message and aspirations of the sailors' strike committee of the February 1946 uprising.

The mass upsurge jolted the CPI leaders and the impact of the uprising was enormous. The leadership was under pressure to do something; there was enormous ferment within party ranks, full-timers, and the youth. The CPI called a general strike in Bombay, which paralyzed the city. When the armed personal carriers were sent to crush the protest the workers put up barricades to stop their advance, and street battles broke out throughout the city. In three days, more than 400 people were killed and hundreds were injured in clashes with the state forces.

On 19 March, a strike wave penetrated the police force throughout the major centres of the country. At Allahabad, the police went on a hunger strike. The Delhi police joined them on 22 March. On 3 April 10,000 police personnel in Bihar joined the strike movement. Soon the workers also joined this mass wave of strikes. On 2 May 1946, the workers of the North Western Railway went on strike, then, on 11th July, more than 100,000 postal workers started an all-India strike. Industrial workers across the subcontinent joined the movement with massive strike action. The whole of India was engulfed in these mass uprisings, revolts and strikes. The British were losing control over the armed forces. The first to come to the rescue of the imperialist Raj were the political leaders of all religions.

This revolutionary outburst spread alarm throughout the Congress leadership; the president of Congress between 1939 and 1946, Maulana Abul Kalam Azad, thought that it was not the appropriate time for direct action: "We must watch the course of events and carry on negotiations with the British Government".

Nehru said:

> (...) what has happened clearly demonstrated how anti-social elements in a vast city like Bombay exploited a situation. Our freedom is near at hand today. We have all the virtues for winning our freedom, but I confess we lack discipline, which is essential in a free country.[14]

In February 1946 outbreaks occurred in Calcutta and Madras. A serious uprising at Karachi was suppressed with considerable loss of life, and many casualties occurred among the revolutionary sailors and soldiers. In a telegram to Whitehall, London, Auchinleck said: "...if you don't grant them independence in three days they will take it by force". India's chief of staff, General Lord Ismay, who had been Winston

Churchill's chief of staff from 1940 to 1945 and a veteran of the subcontinent in the British Indian army, stated: "India was a ship on fire in mid-ocean with ammunition in her hold." The question he asked Lord Mountbatten was whether they could get the fire out before it reached the ammunition? Because of the revolutionary ferment throughout the subcontinent, it was obvious that the British imperialists would not be able to leave behind a united India. India had to be divided. Again, during the movement of 1946, Hindu and Muslim soldiers fought shoulder to shoulder. More than half of the armed forces personnel were Muslims. Rejecting sectarianism, Muslim soldiers, navy sailors and air force personnel fought alongside their Hindu brothers. Muslim and Hindu workers jointly set up barricades during the Bombay strike. In Calcutta and other cities, Hindus and Muslims launched a united movement and demonstrations for the release of the INA personnel of all faiths. The Red Flag was the symbol of the mass uprisings that had spread throughout the subcontinent. Although the leadership wavered, thousands of CPI workers and young full-timers were burning with the desire to march on the road of socialist revolution.

The condition and frustration of the CPI activists and young full-timers is portrayed in some of the literary writings of that period. The liberal novelist and literary critic Khushwant Singh, in his famous novel on Partition, *Train to Pakistan*, described the state of mind of CPI full-timer Iqbal Singh, who had been sent from an advanced urban locality to the hamlet of Manomarja near the new Indo–Pak border:

> Lying on a cot in the courtyard of the village Sikh Temple, gazing at the stars he thought: "Everyone, Hindu, Muslim, Sikh, Congressite, Leaguer, Akali or communist was deep in it. All that was needed was to divert the kill and grab instinct from communal channels and turn it against the propertied classes. That was the proletarian revolution, the easy way." To his anguish, the party bosses would not see it in this light.[15]

A workers' movement on a class basis and a proletarian revolution was the only way out of the communal frenzy unleashed by the Partition. The ingredients of a proletarian revolution were there, but they lacked leadership; when the custodians of the proletariat err in such times, generations have to suffer.

A revolutionary or a pre-revolutionary situation does not last forever. Mass movements and uprisings move in ebbs and flows. Once a movement ebbs, the reaction in society comes to the fore.

As the movement ebbed in the subcontinent and the revolution was betrayed, the impoverished masses suffered the consequences. With the exit of the CPI from the leadership of the national liberation movement, the political representatives of the Indian bourgeoisie took over.

If the truth be told, the Indian bourgeoisie never fought a freedom struggle. They actually negotiated and bargained the struggle of the masses with the British rulers. They wanted direct rule in their own hands. The British could not hold on to power. As the movement surged ahead, mass revolts and desertions occurred in the British armies.

Winston Churchill and his Conservative Party faced a humiliating defeat in the first post-war elections in Britain; anti-war sentiment had had a strong impact on the electorate. On 26 July 1945 the results of the British national elections were announced. Labour, under the leadership of Clement Attlee, won a sweeping victory, winning 388 seats in the British Parliament. The British government now had no choice but to quit India.

The Labour administration, in spite of its reformist posture, was as committed as the Tories to the continuation of capitalist rule in what would become the former colonies of the Empire.

Attlee's choice of Lord Mountbatten (a grandson of Queen Victoria) as India's last Viceroy made it clear that the Labour government would continue with the same policies as its Tory predecessors.

The British Empire and its political representatives had no fixed plan on how to leave India. Like all rulers, on the one hand, they were afraid of a revolution, and on the other, they wanted to avoid anarchy. Both outcomes would have hindered and disrupted the profit system and endangered the properties and assets of the ruling elites. They therefore tried to effect a peaceful transition. They sent several missions from Whitehall to develop a feasible plan that would ensure the continuation of the capitalist rule and imperialist plunder. One of these missions was the Cabinet Mission sent to India in 1946.

The Cabinet Mission Plan

The Cabinet Mission arrived in India in early May and on 16 May the 'Cabinet Mission Plan' was published: the central government would be responsible solely for defence, foreign affairs and communications. It divided the subcontinent into three zones: A, B and C. Section B would include Punjab, Sindh, NWFP (North Western Frontier Province) and British Baluchistan. A majority of Muslims would be in this area. In section C, which included Bengal and Assam, the Muslims would have a small majority. It was thought that this arrangement would give assurance to the Muslim minority and satisfy all the legitimate fears of the Muslim League. At first, Jinnah was opposed completely to the scheme; the Muslim League had gone so far in its demand for a separate independent state that it was difficult for it to retract its stance. Azad, president of Congress, was in favour of accepting the proposal. The Muslim League Council deliberated for three days before coming to a decision. On the final day, Jinnah seemed to favour acceptance of the plan. He told the council that the scheme was the best that they could hope for and, as such, he advised the Muslim League to accept it. The council voted unanimously in its favour. This in reality meant a retreat from Partition. The acceptance of the Cabinet Mission Plan, both by Congress and the Muslim League, was an important event in the history of the liberation movement of India.

On 26 April 1946 Azad issued a statement that proposed Nehru's name for the coveted post of Congress President and appealed to Congress that they should elect him unanimously.

Nehru was accepted unanimously. The Muslim League Council had accepted the Cabinet Mission Plan, as had the Congress working committee. However, it needed the approval of the All India Congress Committee (AICC). It was thought that this would be a formality as the AICC always had ratified the decisions of the working committee. Accordingly, a meeting of the AICC was called at Bombay on 7 July 1946. After an intense debate, a vote was taken, and a resolution of acceptance was passed with an overwhelming majority. On 10 July 1946 however, Nehru held a press conference in Bombay in which he made an astonishing statement. Some press representatives asked him whether the passing of the resolution meant the AICC Congress accepted the plan in total, including the composition of the interim Government. Jawaharlal Nehru in reply stated that Congress would enter the Constituent Assembly: "completely unfettered by agreements and free to meet all situations as they arise". In reply to another question, Nehru said emphatically that Congress had agreed only to participate in the Constituent Assembly and regarded itself free to change or modify the Cabinet Mission Plan as it thought best.

This change of heart on Nehru's part made it impossible to avoid Partition on a bourgeois basis forever. This sudden turn by Nehru exposed the narrow-mindedness of the Indian bourgeoisie and the secretive forces that were working behind the scenes, bent on partitioning the subcontinent. Obviously those forces were afraid that in an undivided India, the threat of class struggle and revolutionary upheavals against capitalism and imperialist domination would remain very much alive and vibrant. The extent to which Lady Edwina played a role in coaxing Nehru into this remains a secret of history. Now this love affair has been exposed in Alex von Tunzelman's book *Indian Summer*, published in 2007. Cate Blanchett plays Edwina Mountbatten in the film on this book to be released in 2009.

The Muslim League had only accepted the Cabinet Mission plan under duress. Naturally, Jinnah was not very happy about it. In his speech to the League Council, he had clearly stated that he recommended acceptance only because nothing better could be obtained. His political adversaries started to criticize him by saying that he had failed to deliver his promises. They accused him of having given up the idea of an independent Islamic state.

Nehru's statement had been a complete surprise and Jinnah

immediately demanded a complete review of the whole situation, asking Liaquat Ali Khan to call a meeting of the League Council to discuss this demand. Now that the Congress president had declared that Congress could change the scheme through its majority in the Constituent Assembly, this left the minorities at the mercy of the majority. Jinnah felt that Nehru's declaration meant that Congress had rejected the Cabinet Mission Plan and that, because of this, the Viceroy should call upon the Muslim League, which had accepted the plan, to form the government.

Jinnah was a man of towering vanity and he took Congress's action as a personal rebuke. The former apostle of Hindu–Muslim unity became the unyielding advocate of Pakistan.

Collins and Lapierre describe Jinnah in *Freedom at Midnight*:

> A more improbable leader of India's Muslim masses could hardly be imagined. The only thing Muslim about Mohammed Ali Jinnah was his parents' religion. He drank, ate pork, religiously shaved his beard each morning and just as religiously avoided the mosque each Friday. God and the Koran had no place in Jinnah's vision of the world; his political foe, Gandhi, knew more verses of the Muslim Holy Book than he did. Jinnah had been able to achieve the remarkable feat of securing the allegiance of the vast majority of India's Muslims without being able to articulate more than a few sentences in their traditional tongue, Urdu.[18]

Jinnah had only scorn for his Hindu rivals. He labelled Nehru a Peter Pan, a "literary figure" who "should have been an English professor, not a politician", "an arrogant Brahmin who covers his Hindu trickiness under a veneer of Western education". Gandhi, to Jinnah, was "a cunning fox", "a Hindu revivalist". Jinnah never forgot the sight of the Mahatma in his mansion, stretched out on one of his priceless Persian carpets with his mudpack on his belly.

On 27 July 1946 the Muslim League Council met in Bombay. Jinnah in his opening speech reiterated the demand for Pakistan as the only course open to the Muslim League. After three days' discussion, the Council passed the resolution rejecting the Cabinet Mission Plan. It decided to resort to direct action for the achievement of Pakistan.

Azad and several leading members of Congress were

perturbed by this new development. The Congress working committee met on 8 August 1946 and Azad pointed out that if they wanted to save the situation they must make it clear that the statement of Congress at the Bombay press conference was Nehru's personal opinion, and did not conform to the decisions of Congress. Nehru responded that it would be embarrassing to Congress, and to him personally, if the working committee passed a resolution maintaining that the statement of the Congress President did not represent the policy of Congress.

Commenting on these events, Azad, in his book *India Wins Freedom* dedicated to 'Jawaharlal Nehru, friend and comrade', attributed the tragedy as follows:

> This was one of the greatest tragedies of the Indian History and I have to say with the deepest regret that a large part of the responsibility for this development rests with Jawaharlal. His unfortunate statement that Congress would be free to modify the Cabinet Mission Plan reopened the whole question of political and communal settlement. Mr. Jinnah took full advantage of his [Nehru's] mistake and withdrew from the League's early acceptance of the Plan.[17]

Nehru, again according to Azad:

> Within a month of Mountbatten's arrival in India, Jawaharlal, the firm opponent of Partition had become, if not a supporter at least acquiescent to the idea. I have wondered how Jawaharlal was won over by Lord Mountbatten. He is a man of principle but he is also impulsive and amenable to personal influences. I think one factor responsible for the change was the personality of Lady [Edwina] Mountbatten. She is not only extremely intelligent but has a most attractive and friendly temperament.[18]

In his book Azad had this to say about Gandhi:

> But when I met Gandhi again, I had the greatest shock of my life to find that he had changed. He was still not openly in favour of Partition but he no longer spoke so vehemently against it. What surprised and shocked me even more was that he began to repeat the arguments which Sardar Patel had already used. For over two hours I pleaded with him, but could make no impression on him.[21]

In the same book he describes the role of Patel: "It would not perhaps be unfair to say that Vallabhbhai Patel was the founder of Indian Partition."

Azad continued:

> I was surprised when Patel said that, whether we liked it or not, there were two nations in India. He was now convinced that Muslims and Hindus could not be united into one nation. It was better to have one clean fight and then separate, than have bickering everyday. I was surprised that Patel was now an even greater supporter of the two-nation theory than Jinnah. Jinnah may have raised the flag of Partition, but now the real flag bearer was Patel.[22]

The AICC met on 14 June 1947. Congress, which had always "fought for the unity and independence" of India, was considering an official resolution for dividing the country.

Gandhi intervened in the debate, appealing to the members to support the Congress Working Committee by accepting the resolution moved by Pandit Pant. When the resolution was put to the vote, only 29 voted for Partition while 15 voted against.

Even Gandhi could not persuade more members to vote for the Partition of the country!

In the meeting of AICC, the members from Sindh vehemently opposed the resolution. They were given all kinds of assurances. In private discussions they were told that if they suffered any disability or indignity in Pakistan, India would retaliate on the Muslims in India. This implied that both in India and Pakistan, hostages would be held responsible for the security of the minority community in the other State. This was a barbarous idea and could only escalate tensions.

Slaughter of the Innocents (The Aftermath of Partition)

Acharya Kripalani, who was president of Congress at this time, realized the danger of these implications and understood that once such a feeling was allowed to grow, it could only lead to oppression and the murder of Hindus in Pakistan and Muslims in India. The rivers of blood, which flowed after Partition on both sides of the new frontier, had their origins in this concept of hostage and retaliation.

It was decided that the Indian Dominion would come into existence on the 15th of August 1947. The Muslim League decided that Pakistan should be constituted a day earlier on the 14th of August.

On the 14th of August Lord Mountbatten went to Karachi to inaugurate the Dominion of Pakistan. He returned the next day, and at midnight on 15 August 1947 the Indian Dominion was born. Once again, according to Azad: "If a united India had become free, there was little chance that the British could retain her position in the economic and industrial life of India".[25]

The two new states were born amidst slaughter and bloodshed. Thousands of years of religious, ethnic and communal harmony was shattered in a matter of days as families were uprooted from their ancestral towns and villages; whole trainloads of people were killed in the carnage. The dawn of 14th of August 1947 had turned red, not with revolution, but with the blood of millions of innocent oppressed people. Blood spilled by the reactionary madness of religious bigotry. The magnitude of the carnage stunned even those who had been the main advocates of Partition.

The most brutalized regions were Punjab and Bengal. The irony is that the first two papers of the Communist Party of India came out in Punjabi, *Kirti* (Worker) from Amritsar and in Bengali, *Langal* (Plough) from Calcutta. Yet the workers and peasants of Bengal and Punjab suffered the biggest massacre of Partition. The stiletto of Partition drenched in the poison of communal hatred had pierced two nationalities right through the heart.

Between August and September 1947, Punjab was a living hell. This was a cataclysm without precedent, unforeseen in magnitude, unordered in pattern, and unreasoned in its savagery.

Collins and Lapierre narrate the episode in *Freedom at Midnight* as follows:

> The gutters of Lahore were running red with blood. The beautiful Paris of the Orient was a vista of desolation and destruction ... In nearby Amritsar, broad sections of the city, its Muslim sections, were nothing but heaps of brick and debris, twisting curls of smoke drifting above them into the sky, vultures keeping their vigil on their shattered walls, the pungent aroma of decomposing corpses permeating the ruins. Everywhere the face of the Punjab was disfigured by similar scenes.[22]

Robert Trumbull, a veteran correspondent of the *New York Times* wrote in the issue of 12 September 1947:

> Death by shooting is more merciful than to be beaten to death with clubs and stones and left to die, their death agony intensified by heat and flies.
>
> Horror had no race, and the terrible anguish of those August days in the Punjab was meted out with almost biblical balance ... an eye for an eye, massacre for massacre, rape for rape, blind cruelty for blind cruelty.
>
> For tens of thousands the trains became rolling coffins. Like a ship's prow cutting through a heavy sea, the train rolled through the mass of scrambling humans choking the platforms, crushing to a pulp of blood and bone the hapless few inevitably pushed across its path. In a concert of tears and shrieks, the crowd would throw itself on the doors and windows of each wagon. There were periods of four and five days at a stretch during which not a single train reached Lahore or Amritsar without its complement of dead and wounded. Along the roads, the refugees plodded dumbly forward, eyes and throats raw with dust, feet bruised by stones or searing asphalt, tortured by hunger and thirst, enrobed in a stench of sweat, urine, and defecation.

These Hindus, Muslims and Sikhs were innocent illiterate peasants whose only life had been the fields they worked. Most of them did not know who a viceroy was, were indifferent to Congress Party and the Muslim League, and had never bothered with issues like Partition or boundary lines. They were unaware of the freedom in whose name they had been plunged into despair.

Their haggard faces turned to the blazing sky to beg Allah, Shiva, the Guru Nanak, for the monsoon that refused to come. The human debris left behind was gruesome. The forty-five miles of roadside from Lahore to Amritsar became a long, open graveyard.

As in every conflict since the dawn of history, the tragedies and atrocities of Partition were accompanied by an outpouring of sexual savagery and rape. The Sikh's tenth guru specifically instructed his followers against sexual intercourse with Muslim women in an attempt to prevent what happened in the Punjab. The Sikhs ignored the guru's admonishment and gave free rein to their fantasies, falling upon Muslim women everywhere; this resulted in the legend that Muslim women were capable of particular sexual prowess. During Partition the rulers of India and Pakistan were more concerned about the division of assets than the agonies of the Hindu, Muslim and the Sikh masses. In terms of the distribution of armies, assets and wealth, they exhibited meanness and greed.

Each dominion was extremely interested in owning the gaudiest symbols of the imperial power which had ruled them for so long.

Partition was a wound inflicted upon the living body of one of the oldest civilizations on earth. A civilization that was rich in art, architecture, music, literature and other forms of human culture ... its cultural diversity was its greatest beauty. The pain still remains and has left an indelible scar upon millions of people. Partition was one of the most counter-revolutionary events in recent history. More than half a century later, one question is asked throughout the subcontinent ... can Partition be undone? The famous Punjabi poet Ustad Daman summed up the agony of the people on both sides of the Frontier in the verses below.

Devastated through these Freedoms
Are you and so are we;
The redness of the eyes is telling
Wept you have, a lot
And weeping we have been too!

(Translated from Punjabi)

Barbaaad Ainah Azadian Toon
Hoey Tusee ve Ao
Hoey Ase vee Aaan
Akhiaan di laali pai dasdi Ae
Roaey Tusee vee Ao
Roaey Asee vee aan

NOTES

1. Azad, *India Wins Freedom,* (Orient Longman), p. 202.
2. Published in the *New York Daily Tribune* No. 3840 of 8th August 1853.
3. Collins and Lapierre, *Freedom at Midnight*, p. 58.
4. Trotsky writings 1939, p. 169.
5. *Times of India,* 16 January 1948.

6. Lal Khan, *Partition: can it be undone?* p. 26, Indian edition published by Aakar Books, 2007.
7. Sir John Cumming (ed.), *Political India*, Oxford, 1932.
8. P. Hardy, *The Muslims of British India*, Cambridge, 1972.
9. Lal Khan, *Partition: can it be undone?* p. 34, Indian edition published by Aakar Books, 2007.
10. K. Damodaran, 'Memoirs of Indian Communism', *New Left Review* No. 93, London, 1975.
11. *Pakistan and National Unity*, Bombay, 1944.
12. *Newsline* (Karachi), October 2008, p. 82.
13. Mazdoor Morcha, Faridabad, July 1978.
14. Ibid. p.12.
15. Lal Khan, *Partition: can it be undone?* p. 57, Indian edition published by Aakar Books, 2007.
16. Azad, *India wins Freedom*, (Orient Longman) p. 61.
17. Khushwant Singh, *Train to Pakistan*, p. 50.
18. Collins and Lapierre, *Freedom at Midnight*, p. 127.
19. Azad, *India Wins Freedom*, (Orient Longman), p. 170.
20. Ibid. p. 198.
21. Ibid. p. 203.
22. Ibid. p. 201.
23. Pp. 224, 209.
24. Collins and Lapierre, *Freedom at Midnight*, pp. 359, 360.

Three

A FAILED START—THE FAILURE OF BOURGEOIS DEMOCRACY

Military Rule and the Gathering Storm

I don't know about businessmen elsewhere, but ours are damn rascals. He will not hesitate to suck people's blood if he gets half a chance. I wonder how long we would be able to protect him and the private sector against the people. One day people will take their revenge on him.

—Field Marshal M. Ayub Khan[1]

According to the official medium of Pakistan's State ideology is based on a dream conceived by the philosopher poet Allama Sir Mohammad Iqbal. But even the creator of Pakistan's mythological ideology had reservations about how his dream would be realized. He had died about a decade before Pakistan's inception in 1938. A year before his death he wrote a letter to Jinnah about his fears of his dream turning into a nightmare for the oppressed Muslims of the Indian subcontinent. In his letter written on 28 May 1937 Iqbal astutely drew attention to the political problems confronting the Muslim League:

> I have no doubt that you fully realize the gravity of the situation as far as Muslim India is concerned. The League will have to finally decide whether it will remain a body representing the upper classes of Indian Muslims or the Muslim masses, who have so far, with good reason, taken no interest in it. Personally, I believe that a political organization which gives no promise of improving the lot of the ordinary Muslim cannot attract our masses. Under the new constitution the higher posts go to the sons of upper classes; the smaller ones go to the friends or relatives of Ministers. Our political institutions have never thought of improving the lot of Muslims generally. The problem of bread is becoming more and more acute.[2]

The first planning commission of Pakistan was set up in 1948. Out of 15 members there were 11 from the US and imperialist institutions. It was self evident what course of political and economic development this new confessional State would embark upon.

Most of the Muslim entrepreneurs who had a tough competition and were subdued and dominated by Tatas, Birlas and other major nominally 'Hindu' conglomerates had a false perception that by getting a separate 'independent' state and market they would be able to amass huge profits. Hence the Habibs, Valikas, Adamjees, Saigols, Isphahanis and many other nominally Muslim business houses had showered Jinnah and the Muslim League with large sums of money for a greater share of the market and facilities in the new Muslim Republic.

After the disastrous summer of 1947, the leaders of Pakistan tried to take control. They had envisaged building a new modern capitalist state. The newly emerged bourgeoisie in Pakistan had an enormous opportunity to show its calibre and capabilities: they had the state, a massive market and a country rich in natural resources, together with a huge reservoir of human manpower.

Crisis of Identity

Jinnah wanted to create Pakistan as a modern industrialized secular capitalist state. He believed in sound law and sound procedures. He was, according to one intimate: "a parliamentarian in the mode of Gladstone..." At the inauguration of Pakistan, Jinnah was a frail, sick man who already, in the words of his physician, had been living for three years on "willpower, whisky and cigarettes". When he became Pakistan's first governor general, Jinnah said to his new ADC, Syed Ahsan, "Do you know I never expected to see Pakistan in my lifetime".[3] He died in mysterious circumstances on 11 September 1948. On its inception, Pakistan went into an internal crisis, which intensified after Jinnah's death. Disagreements within the feudal hierarchy and the semi-capitalist elite created political chaos. Pakistan's first Prime Minister, Liaquat Ali Khan, was assassinated by Akbar Khan at

Company Bagh Rawalpindi, in 1951. Most domestic and foreign policy decisions of the 1950s reflect these conflicts. Pakistan was founded as a theocratic state, and the newly emerging ruling elite tried to impose this artificial ideology on a multinational, multilingual and multiethnic society in order to perpetuate its rule. Jinnah's promised secularism was fading fast. The educational curriculum was modified to fit in with the state's official theology. The history syllabus was distorted to reflect the official line. Urdu was imposed as the national language, although the state bureaucracy, commerce, trade and the elite continued to use English. The first two commanders-in-chief were British: although Jinnah had refused to accept Lord Mountbatten as a joint governor general of Pakistan and India, the army was receptive to a British commander as head of the armed forces to ensure the continuity of colonial structures. The first commander-in-chief of the Pakistan Army was General Messervy, who was later replaced by Major General Douglas Gracey. The land revenue system, military chain of command, civil administration, legal code and judicial system continued as created by the British. In fact they still remain intact to a large extent in all countries of the subcontinent. Even 'left-hand drive' on roads and railways is still in practice. The ruling elite tilted its foreign policy towards the United States of America and became its stooge at a very early stage. The United States and the Central Intelligence Agency became involved in the affairs of the Pakistan army early on.

The main reason behind this chaos and anarchy and the shattered dream of the nascent Pakistani bourgeois class was the historical belatedness of this class itself. Its advent in history came when imperialism had attained a crushing domination of the world market. During the Second World War, when most of the world was in the throes of devastation and destruction, the US mainland remained untouched by the ravages of war. But during the war period the emergency war regime and laws were in full force in the USA. This enabled the US ruling classes to extract and exploit maximum labour from the American proletariat. It resulted in an enormous boost to US industry, accumulating enormous surplus in the process. They now had the luxury to invest larger sums of this surplus in research and technological innovation, thus further increasing productivity and profits; hence an even greater accumulation of capital by the US bourgeoisie. Consequently, in the post-war scenario, their technological superiority, financial domination and military hegemony gave them a greater control of the world capitalist economy and the international market. Institutions like the World Bank, the Bretton Woods Treaty, which later became the IMF (International Monetary Fund) and the GATT (General Agreement on Tariffs and Trade), now WTO (World Trade Organization), were used for the implementation of US financial and economic domination. In the political and diplomatic sphere they used the United Nations, its subsidiaries, NATO (North Atlantic Treaty Organization), CENTO (Central Treaty Organization), SEATO (South East Asia Treaty Organization) and other treaties and alliances, to assert their diplomatic, political and military hegemony.

Meanwhile, European imperialists, financially weakened and exhausted by the war, had lost their capacity to continue with direct colonial rule. The revolutionary movements of the European proletariat, and the reactions of the soldiers of the returning armies, exhausted and sickened by the Second World War, further aggravated this process. Hence European imperialism had to withdraw from direct colonial rule; the growth and spread of national liberation movements further accelerated this imperialist retreat. But in the colonial revolutions the only Third World countries that could get a temporary respite from the stranglehold of this new structure of capitalist imperialism were those proletarian Bonapartist states that arose through their own peculiar methods and forms of revolutionary movements. These were mainly through guerrilla armies led by petty bourgeois intelligentsia or the military coups led by radical officers who were disgusted by the glaring and rapacious imperialist exploitation ravaging their societies. They had no option except to overthrow capitalism and feudalism to escape from the exploitation and plunder of imperialism.

Apart from these exceptions, most other neo colonial

countries were trapped in capitalist/landlord regimes dominated by corrupt and reactionary rulers incapable of developing these societies and laying the social, economic and political foundations of modern industrialized capitalist states. In the period of post-colonialism the so-called independence of these countries was paralytic and debilitated in its character; their ruling classes had a comprador character and were subservient to imperialist hegemony. On the other hand, due to the intrinsic and organic weakness of these colonial ruling elites, their economic base was in constant dearth and at the mercy of the technology and finance capital of Western imperialism. Owing to this historical backwardness and economic, technological, and financial dependence on the advanced capitalist countries, these subservient and subdued nascent ruling classes were forced to submit to the new post-war world order that was designed and structured to enhance and facilitate the blatant plunder of imperialism.

The bloody partition of 1947 ensured that the imperialist exploitation and the rule of capital continued in the phase of neo colonialism where the world market domination subjugated these societies under the yoke of imperialism. The Pakistani nascent capitalist class soon realized this but was impotent to break this cordon. Their weakness forced them to rely on imperialism on the one hand and the landed aristocracy, including religious mystagogues (pirs) owning vast tracts of rural lands, mainly introduced in the subcontinent by the British Raj to perpetuate its rule, on the other. These 'Nawabs', feudal landlords and religious mystagogues had already switched over to the Muslim League for reasons not dissimilar to the nascent Muslim bourgeoisie cashing in on support for a separate Muslim entity. Politics began at the top and was marked by a distinctly feudal approach to problems. Individual landlords could make or break parties by utilizing the 'parcelled-out sovereignty' they enjoyed over their lands and their tenants.

Jinnah favoured the creation of a bourgeois-democratic state, but the theocratic inconsistencies of the advocates of the 'two-nation' theory now made themselves felt in the practice of fashioning the new republic.

Kashmir

But within a year war broke out in Kashmir which was a dispute deliberately left behind by British imperialists. Their motive was to continue the divide-and-rule policy even after they retreated from direct colonial rule in the South Asian subcontinent; they aimed to maintain a greater imperialist control by sowing the seeds of instability and antagonism between India and Pakistan. After the Hindu Maharaja of Muslim-dominated Kashmir signed accession with India, the Pakistani rulers wanted to take Kashmir by force. A secret plan was agreed upon in which Pathan tribesmen were used to start the offensive.

The Pathan tribesmen crossed the Jhelum River into Kashmir on the night of 23-24 October, 1947. The plan was to capture Srinagar by 26 October in time for the Eid celebrations. However, instead of marching straight to Srinagar, they indulged themselves in arson and plunder in Muzaffarabad and nearby towns, getting only as far as Baramulla (though they did manage to cut off the power supply to the Kashmiri capital). This gave the Indian army crucial time to amass troops and force the raiders into retreat. Hence the history of the subcontinent took a strange twist: more than two-thirds of Kashmir was taken by India and the other one-third, of mostly rugged terrain, came under Pakistani control.

Indian troops, replacing National Conference supporters in the defence of Kashmir, succeeded in halting the tribal advance before Srinagar was captured. They also launched a counter-offensive, recapturing Baramulla. Once India had sent her forces into Jammu and Kashmir, Pakistan's Governor General M.A. Jinnah wanted to send his country's regular troops in as well. But such a move was blocked by the Pakistan Army's acting Commander-in-Chief, General Sir Douglas Gracey, who feared that it would spark off a war between the two new states (the two armies were still under the same supreme command). Jinnah still attempted to send help to the pro-Pakistan 'Azad Kashmir' forces, for example, encouraging Pakistan regulars 'on leave' to make their way to the state. In May 1948, Gracey reversed his earlier decision, and Pakistan 'officially' sent its troops into Jammu and Kashmir.

A series of offensives and counter-offensives ended with Pakistan controlling Gilgit (which had 'acceded' to that country on 3 November 1947), Baltistan, part of the Vale, most of Poonch, and the Mirpur area of Jammu. Indian forces controlled Ladakh, most of the Kashmir and Jammu provinces, and a small part of Poonch. By the end of 1948 the war, which had so far been confined to Jammu and Kashmir, threatened to spread to India 'proper' and Pakistan. Such an escalation was avoided by the declaration of a ceasefire, partly the result of the intervention of the United Nations which took effect on 1 January 1949. The ceasefire line was defined in an agreement between Indian and Pakistani military representatives on 27 July 1949 and remained unchanged until the 1965 Indo–Pakistan War.

Jinnah

The only 'political party' Jinnah could rely on was the civil service of Pakistan, born out of the Indian civil service and conceived by the British imperial administration. Jinnah clearly viewed Pakistan as a constitutional social democracy. His first address to the Constituent Assembly in Karachi, on 11 August 1947, explicitly dissociated itself from interpretations which stressed the confessional character of the new state:

> You are free; you are free to go to your temples, you are free to go to your mosques or to any other place of worship in this State of Pakistan. You may belong to any religion or caste or creed that has nothing to do with the business of the State ... We are starting with this fundamental principle that we are all citizens and equal citizens of one State. Now I think we should keep that in front of us as our ideal and you will find that in the course of time Hindus would cease to be Hindus and Muslims would cease to be Muslims, not in the religious sense, because that is the personal faith of each individual, but in the political sense as citizens of the State.[4]

This speech has been strongly criticized by religious divines, confessional sects and Right-wing political parties because of its opposition to the creation of an 'Islamic state'. The criticisms are not without logic. If Pakistan was the culmination of the struggle for a 'Muslim nation', then clearly secularism was a somewhat inappropriate ideology for it. If its aspirations could be implemented in Pakistan, then surely they could equally have been put into practice in a united India.

Jinnah's addiction to constitutionalism merely brought to the fore the confused character of the campaign which had preceded the formation of the new state. Soon after Partition, Jinnah seriously considered the possibility of declaring the Muslim League a secular party and changing its name to the Pakistan National League. His intention, however, was prematurely revealed by the *Pakistan Times*, and the effect of Jinnah's death in 1948 and Liaquat Ali Khan's assassination in 1951 left the civil service in total command.

The economic situation was not much better. The agrarian character of the new state was highlighted by the fact that agriculture accounted for 60 per cent of total output and 70 per cent of total employment. The comparable figures for industry were 6 per cent for output and 10 per cent for employment. Service sector made up the remainder. Large-scale production was non-existent: 41 per cent of all industrial enterprises were devoted to the processing of agriculture raw material and were in seasonal operation.

The country was seen as a producer of raw materials tied to Britain by a whole network of economic and political links.

The 1954 Election

It was in the countryside that the situation was at its worst: in Pakistan as a whole, 6000 landlords owned more land than 3.5 million peasant households. The landlords were the largest single group on the Muslim League National Council.

An attempt was made to create a cohesive ruling class, a stable ruling party, and a permanent constitution; but all these attempts failed, and the decades that followed exacerbated the 'crisis of identity' that had consistently confounded the ideologists of the new state.

Pakistan's refusal to devalue the rupee during the Korean War had resulted in a temporary boom, but with the end of the war there was a sharp drop in the prices of agricultural raw materials. This was coupled in 1952-3 with a massive food shortage and a famine, during which the Muslim League proved incompetent to deal with either the black market in food or the economic crisis.

It was mainly Mohajir (the refugee Urdu-speaking population from India that came after Partition mostly from Central and Northern India) and Punjabi civil servants, moulded by the Raj, who determined political developments in the country. The Muslim League was a creature of the state bureaucracy. Its isolation was revealed in stark fashion following the provincial elections of 1954. The elections were preceded by a fresh outbreak of mass struggles on the thorny issue of language. On 21 February 1952 a large student demonstration was 'dispersed' by the police in time-honoured fashion: they fired on the protestors, killing twenty-six and wounding 400 others.

As the date for the elections approached, the bureaucracy was in a state of panic; it postponed them for a fortnight in order to silence the Left. Twelve hundred communists and trade-unionists were arrested within the space of forty-eight hours. When the voting was finally allowed from 8 March till 12 March 1954, the Bengalis showed how isolated the Muslim League was from the mainstream of political consciousness in the province: out of 309 seats, the League won only ten.

The Communist Party won four of the ten seats it contested, and interestingly enough it was communists of Hindu origin who were elected rather than their Muslim comrades—a revealing footnote to illustrate the outrageous character of the 1947 division!

The Central government dissolved the newly elected Assembly only two months after the elections and proclaimed Governor's rule under Section 92A of the Constitution. The Communist Party was banned and employers were instructed to dismiss communist workers or face the wrath of the administration. While repression was used to demobilize the left, the Right wing of the United Front was offered a number of inducements.

In West Pakistan, as it continued to suffer defeats in successive by-elections, it became clear that if free elections were permitted the Muslim League would lose three provinces.

Shaking hands with Uncle Sam

The bureaucracy was petrified. The scheme of 'One Unit' was conceived.

For a start, it split the Muslim League. The Governor-General, Ghulam Mohammed, was a foul mouthed bureaucrat closely in league with the Dulles brothers in the United States. The country's Prime Minister, Mohammad Ali Bogra, was himself a favoured protégé of John Foster Dulles, US secretary of state. Together with the commander-in-chief of the army, General Ayub Khan, Bogra was dispatched by Ghulam Mohammed to the United States to negotiate a long-term military and economic aid pact and obtain authority to run the country. On their return to Karachi they went straight to the Governor-General's residence, where the decision was taken to dissolve the Constituent Assembly and proclaim a 'state of emergency', the first of many to be inflicted on the country. The One Unit plan was forced through by the Central government, and provincial assemblies were ordered to vote in its favour.

On 14 October 1955 the new 'province' of West Pakistan came into existence. On 23 March 1956, Pakistan became an Islamic Republic.

Pakistan's first Prime Minister, Liaquat Ali Khan had rejected an invitation to visit Moscow and, instead, boarded a plane for Washington. His successors formally cemented the alliance. Ghulam Mohammed and Iskander Mirza, the two bureaucrats who effectively ran the country as heads of state in the 1950s, needed the alliance with the United States to shore up their position at home. American aid had already started in 1951.

John Foster Dulles acclaimed Pakistan as "a bulwark of freedom in Asia". Any idea that the aid came without any attached strings was brutally dispelled by an official US document which laid down the guidelines:

> Technical Assistance is not something to be done, as a Government enterprise, for its own sake or for the sake of others. The US Government is not a charitable institution, nor is it an appropriate outlet for the charitable spirit of the American people. That spirit finds its proper instrumentality in the numerous private philanthropic and

> religious institutions which have done so much good work abroad. Technical Assistance is only one of a number of instruments available to the US to carry out its foreign policy and to promote its national interests abroad ... these tools of foreign policy include economic aid, military assistance, security treaties, overseas information programmes, participation in the UN and other international organizations, the exchange of persons programmes, tariff and trade policies, surplus agricultural commodities disposal policies and the traditional processes of diplomatic representation.[5]

The refusal of India or Afghanistan to become part of the Western alliance gave Pakistan a certain geopolitical importance. The army and bureaucracy agreed to make the country an American base.

The very circumstances of its birth had rendered Pakistan into a security state from day one. And from then onwards all of its policies, including that of its economy, were being dictated and shaped by the state's security concerns.

In the immediate bloody aftermath of Independence, India was seen by the ruling classes of Pakistan as the bully on the block who was perceived to be hell-bent on wolfing down its smaller neighbour. This partly real and partly imagined threat had sent the ruling elite in Pakistan, soon after Independence, scurrying desperately in pursuit of defence parity with the larger, more powerful and more developed India, although its own internal organic weakness, plus its fear of its own toiling masses, also created this psychology of heavily arming the state.

> Pakistan would be willing if necessary to be a satellite of the US if she remained secure from India. But we can never accept a relationship which would expose us to being a satellite of India.[6]

Although it was on 3 January 1966 that Ayub Khan uttered this demeaning, servile statement to the American ambassador, it was precisely this blinding fear of Indian hegemony which had driven Pakistan into the lap of the US from the very beginning.

Over the years Pakistan has poured, overtly, at least 25% of its total federal budgets on defence needs, over and above what was spent covertly; the real figure would be astronomical. Still, it lost all the wars that were fought, losing in the process half of Kashmir in 1948, half of Pakistan itself in 1971, and Siachen in the early 1980s. The real story of Kargil is yet to be told.

A recent study by the New Delhi-based strategic Foresight Group, that included former Pakistani Foreign Secretary Niaz A. Naik, has estimated that the ISI alone comprised 10,000 professional staff, and its wages and operations, including the 'Jihadi operations', cost around Rs 26 billion. Subversion costs by Pakistan and India are said to have exceeded their defence budgets.

On gaining independence in 1947 the country inherited a 95,000-strong army and immediately planned to raise its strength to 150,000. To fund this plan Mohammad Ali Jinnah, Liaqat Ali Khan, and Nazimuddun, in their respective tenures, sought $2 billion of immediate assistance from the US, but the latter kept refusing to oblige.

Pakistan's first budget, announced on 28 February 1948 allocated a staggering 85 per cent of its total resources to defence; this priority continued during the first ten years of independence, except in 1953-4.

Ayub's first budget (1958-9) allocated twice as much as the defence budget (which was being taken care of by that time mostly by the US military assistance) to development, helped by US economic assistance.

In 1952, Pakistan was hit by a food shortage. The government approached the United States for assistance, and negotiations led to an agreement for the importation of one million tones of wheat under a $15-million commercial loan provided by the Export-Import Bank of the United States (USEXIM).

On 19 May 1954 Pakistan and the United States signed the 'Mutual Defence Agreement' and on 8 September 1954, Pakistan joined SEATO (South East Asia Treaty Organization): "The sky is the limit," said Ayub Khan.

But SEATO neither enhanced US aid to Pakistan nor guaranteed help from the US in the case of Pakistan being attacked. Nor did the infamous Badabair basing facility that was given to the US in 1959 bring Pakistan any additional security: instead the Russians warned that they would wipe Pakistan from the face of the earth if any further U-2s took off from the base after one was shot down in 1962 by the Russians.

On 11 July 1950 Pakistan joined the World Bank and a team of World Bank officials visited Pakistan the following year, offering $60 million for projects in irrigation, rehabilitation of railways, extension of telecommunication and hydro projects. Pakistan contracted the first loan of its history—a $27 million loan from the World Bank—for the Pakistan Railways on 22 February 1952.

In May 1967, when aid from America had ceased, Ayub's government approached the World Bank for the first debt relief of Pakistan's history, but no consortium meeting was held for two years. General Yahya Khan was therefore compelled on 25 March 1969 to impose a unilateral moratorium on repayment of debt.

US military and economic aid produces a shift in the domestic relationship of political and social forces in favour of reactionary and conservative parties and institutions. The United States is strongly conscious of this; it admits that "from a political viewpoint US military aid has strengthened Pakistan's armed services, the greatest single stabilizing force in the country, and has encouraged Pakistan to participate in collective defence agreements".[7]

The climax was reached when Pakistan justified the Anglo–French-Israeli invasion of Egypt in October 1956. The overthrow of the pro-British monarch Farouk and the rise to power of Nasser in Egypt marked a turning point for Middle-East politics. Arab nationalism was on the ascent! On 26 July 1956 Nasser reacted to the refusal of the West to finance the building of the Aswan Dam by nationalizing the Suez Canal. The imperialists could, he stated, "choke in their rage". Nasser's defiance of the British evoked a responsive chord in other former colonies.

The Communist Party in West Pakistan

In early 1957 Bhashani visited West Pakistan, where he conferred with Left-wing leaders and decided to convene an All-Pakistan conference of progressive organizations. This was held in Dacca on 25 and 26 July 1957, and resulted in the creation of the National Awami Party. The social composition of the party varied from province to province, but overall it was a 'United Front' of the communist and non-communist left throughout the country. Its stated aims were a combination of radical nationalism and social democracy. Its programme and contents were basically different variants of Stalinism.

Partition had resulted in a severe dislocation of the Left. The effects of this were especially felt in West Pakistan, where the communist movement had never acquired a mass following.

A limited peasant agitation was organized by the Left, and areas like Lyallpur (now Faisalabad), Montgomery (now Sahiwal), Multan, Khanewal and several other districts saw a number of peasant strikes and peasant-landlord clashes. The Punjab premier and Unionist leader, Sir Sikandar Hyat, used a combination of repression and concessions to end the agitation.

The Communist Party of Pakistan (CPP) was set up by decision of the CPI in 1948, and the latter obligingly sent a number of Muslim communists to lead the new organization.

The first general secretary of the CPP was Sajjad Zaheer, a resident of the United Provinces and scion of a landed family, who held a commanding position as a critic in the realm of Urdu literature. His organizing abilities, however, did not match his literary skills.

> The membership of the CPP in West Pakistan was less than two hundred. With committed cadres a party could have been developed and an influential trade-union network established.[8]

However, the skills and talents which existed were not put to their proper use, and the CPP leadership was constantly engaged in a search for short-cuts. The curse of Stalinist two-stage development was always an impediment to its growth and development.

In 1951 the Rawalpindi Conspiracy Case exploded on an unsuspecting country. The mastermind of this attempted putsch was Major-General Akbar Khan, chief of staff of the Pakistan army and widely regarded as an audacious and relatively progressive officer. The officers who supported him were a mixed bag of radical nationalists, outright chauvinists and religious freaks. The infant CPP became embroiled in the plan when Sajjad Zaheer met General Akbar at a cocktail party. The general broached the subject of the intended coup, and requested help in drafting manifestos and hit-lists. The CPP leadership approved of the enterprise and participated in various meetings with army officers. It was decided that the plan be shelved for a period, but one of the military conspirators, fearing that the truth might come out, turned informer and unveiled the whole affair. The plotters were arrested. General Ayub, commander-in-chief of the armed forces, was shocked to learn that he was to be shot. The amateurishness of the plot ensured that those involved received light sentences. Sajjad Zaheer returned to India after his release. The CPP virtually dissolved itself after being banned, and many of its cadres joined the Azad Pakistan Party. This debacle was to leave a lasting impact on the demoralized remnants of the party, which was never again to emerge as a national, independent force. Its politics was instead to be submerged in successive multi-class formations of one variety or another.

1958

In the spring 1958 budget, military spending was increased while price controls were abolished. The cost of living in the towns registered a phenomenal rise: an average of 8.2 per cent.

The result was increasing agitation in town and countryside. Strikes became commonplace and were crushed by private armies in the pay of the employers or by state repression.

In Lahore, capital of West Pakistan, hundreds of thousands of peasants marched through the streets to demand that: (a) eviction of tenants be outlawed; (b) landlordism be abolished; and (c), all uncultivated land be given to landless tenants.

> On 8 May 1958, in one of numerous episodes, the police attacked peasants in the village of Lundo in the heart of the province of Sind. They attacked the Haris (poor peasants), seized their harvest, ransacked their homes, raped the women and arrested seventy peasants. The local landlords provided valuable aid by burning hari dwellings.[9]

On 20 June 1958 workers attempted to occupy a strike-bound factory in Lyallpur in protest against the imprisonment of a union leader. The police opened fire, killing six workers and seriously injuring another twenty-one.

The country's first ever general election was scheduled to be held in March 1959. The bureaucracy was extremely worried, and with good reason. There was every likelihood that the Left would make gains on a provincial and national level. There was also a real possibility that the mere holding of a general election could trigger off a mass upsurge which might overflow electoral channels.

Under Military Rule

The bureaucracy, in ten years, had failed to build a stable bourgeois political party. On 7 October 1958, eleven years after Pakistan was created, its political structures lay in shambles and the army took political power through a coup d'etat.

The new regime was an undisguised dictatorship of the bureaucratic military elite. General Ayub's own reflections on the post-colonial state: "Democracy cannot work in a hot climate, to have democracy we must have a cold climate as in Britain",[10] were treated seriously by State Department policy-makers and their satraps elsewhere in the world.

The two dominant institutions, the army and the bureaucracy, were the direct descendants of the colonial state, and the importance of these institutions in maintaining colonial rule cannot be overestimated.

It was the politically backward rural hinterlands of the Punjab and the North-West Frontier which were to be the catchment area for the new style army.

The simple reality is that even before completing the first decade of its existence the state of Pakistan had proved that it could not develop into a modern industrialized and developed capitalist country. The quest of the 'lefts' who were ignoring the tragedy of Partition, that the nascent ruling class of the 'new' country would create a democratic set up, equality of nationalities, genuine election, sovereignty and other democratic tasks, was a utopian dream at best and a conscious betrayal of revolutionary Marxism at worst. The traditional Muslim bourgeoisie could in reality only hope against hope.

The political conflagration, the crisis of the state and the subservience to imperialist hegemony was basically the reflection of the economic failure of capitalism in a newly independent colonial country now trapped in an epoch of the resurgence of rapacious imperialism.

But above all it was carved out, and two of its nationalities were pierced, by the stiletto of partition. It was not just a geographical bifurcation but a historical, economic and cultural separation, the wounds of which needed healing through a high level of socio-economic development and growth which the new Pakistani ruling class could not even begin to deliver. The squabbling, ruling, political elites created such an anarchic situation that imperialism and the vested interests of Pakistani capital had no option other than direct military rule to safeguard the crisis-ridden Pakistani capitalism. This in itself exposed the real reactionary character of the Pakistani ruling class, even when it had just begun its rule of the new state.

The use of religion to create such a state was a retrogressive act in itself. But the promulgation of Martial Law further exposed the historical, ideological and economic bankruptcy of the ruling classes and their state. But, as subsequent events would prove, military rule with all its repression and might could not develop a stable and functioning Pakistani capitalism. Paradoxically, it sharpened the contradictions so much that after a decade it ignited a social revolution which suspended the state in mid-air, and the overthrow of capitalism through a socialist revolution was the order of the day.

Nasser

The new regime established as a result of the military coup of 27 October 1958 was an undisguised dictatorship of the bureaucratic military elite. It lasted for a decade and was marked by two distinct phases: the first period (1958–62) was dominated by the army, then the years that followed (1962–9) saw the bureaucracy re-asserting its dominant role in the country's politics.

The situation in the Middle East and Asia had become very fragile, especially for the declining force of British imperialism. This was especially due to the 1956 Suez crisis, during which Britain, Israel and France had been defeated by an awakened

Egypt and Nasserism was on the rise. For many army officers, especially in the Arab and so-called Muslim world, Gamal Abdel Nasser was a beacon of hope, an icon to follow.

Hence a military coup, even by the very pro-Western Field Marshal Ayub Khan, raised a lot of eyebrows, especially in the corridors of the White Hall in London. Some of the immediate diplomatic correspondence after the coup expresses apprehension. In a telegram, published in the recently declassified British papers published by Oxford, these fears are very much evident:

> Outward Telegram from Commonwealth Relations Office
> TO: Karachi
> (Sent: 20.12 hours 28 October 1958)
>
> No. 2300 TOP SECRET
> Addressed Karachi No. 2300, repeated Ottawa No. 1694 and Delhi No. 2050.
> My telegram W. No. 927
> PAKISTAN
>
> Brief for Prime Minister's talk with Mr. Diefenbaker follows lines of paragraph 2 of my telegram under reference, but continues as follows:
>
> New regime has, however, many difficulties to surmount. Future is uncertain and there are grounds for anxiety. Although a strong personality and a man of vigorous action, General Ayub is not of high intellectual stature. This raises question whether there is not some more capable and designing mind or minds in Pakistan Army providing impetus behind scenes. It is to be feared that if General Ayub were in turn replaced, his successor is likely to be less favourably disposed towards Commonwealth and West. The danger is that he might be neutralist or, worse, a Nasserite. Sad as it is to see democracy extinguished, even temporarily, in a fellow Member of the Commonwealth, and uncertain as future of General Ayub's regime may be, it would seem nevertheless in our interests to give them every possible encouragement.[11]

The fears of British Imperialism were not unfounded, mainly because of their experiences in Iraq, Syria and of course Egypt. The entire leading melange of twenty officers who constituted the effective leadership of the 'Free Officers' were university graduates, most having studied at Cairo University. They were imbued with the main urban influences of the time: Islamic revivalism as preached by the Muslim Brotherhood and socialism as advocated by the Egyptian Left. While Anwar Al Sadat had been an activist of the Muslim Brotherhood, Gamal Abdel Nasser, Khalid Mohieddine and Gamal Salem were all associated with the Left. During his period as a cadet, and later as an officer, Nasser for his part had read Voltaire, Garibaldi, Ataturk, Napoleon, Clausewitz and, according to some, even Marx. They were successful in overthrowing the monarchy of the corrupt king Farouq and tried to carry out radical reforms, especially in the agrarian sector, that dented the authority of the rural oppressor and had a nationalist, anti-imperialist, programme.

McArthur

Paradoxically, with autocratic and rural backgrounds, the Pakistani generals were a different breed. Their vision of the world was some what jaundiced.

But the Americans had a different game plan and motives: they wanted to repeat the experiment of the Far East in Pakistan. In South Korea, Hong Kong, Formosa (now Taiwan), Japan, Singapore and other states and state-lets in South East Asia, they had laid the foundations of relatively sound capitalist economic bases under the jackboot of military dictatorships.

With military brute force US General Douglas McArthur, the Commander of the US military's Eastern Command, carried out extensive land reforms and other steps to develop a base for modern industrial capitalist states. These experiments were successful mainly because most of these states, like Taiwan and South Korea, were bifurcated lands from main countries: China, Korean peninsula and Malaya. Japan also had a certain development and industrial base in these regions, even before the war. Hence US imperialism invested under General McArthur's despotic rule, and created a subservient bourgeoisie that was entangled in a thousand straps to ensure that US hegemony over these states remained intact, even after the departure of General McArthur and his forces.

This was to curb the raging tide of red revolution in China and other countries of the region and required substantial capitalist development; America had to put in some of the surplus it had accumulated, mainly from the labour of the US proletariat during the war years. This investment was necessary to maintain the political, military, diplomatic and strategic hegemony of US Imperialism in the post-war period of the Cold War. The Stalinists in China who headed the regime after the 1949 revolution also facilitated this process through their narrow, nationalist approach. The despotic regime of General McArthur also removed some of the remaining feudal impediments to this process, such as the monarchy in Japan, etc. This was to create modern nation states.

Ayub Khan

In Pakistan it was not to be. Even today some of the bourgeois politicians are fond of raising this option of the 'miracle' of the Asian tigers although after the 1990s' crash they are not much of an example to boast about. In Pakistan this process was initiated through Robert McNamara, who had been the World Bank President and US Secretary of Defence in the 1960s. He was the main instructor of Field Marshal Ayub Khan in formulating and executing these policies, by means of the jackboots of the Pakistani Generals. The blueprint of the plan for the Green Revolution and the land reforms was drawn up in Washington. The motive of US policy in Pakistan was the same as those in East and South East Asia: to curb and quell any revolutionary wave in the region. But in Pakistan this had the opposite effect; instead of preventing, this pattern of capitalist development actually provoked revolution. One of the most significant outcomes of Partition was a geopolitical situation of the period, where revolutionary waves were charging all around the subcontinent and had started to dominate the Independence struggle in spite of the Hindu/Muslim bourgeois political leadership.

In his autobiography, *Friends not masters* Ayub devotes a whole chapter on the first military coup in Pakistan. In this chapter, he tried to interpret this coup as a revolution and not a coup. But also his apprehensions on the ramifications are very evident. He wrote:

> Another worry I had was how, if the Army once got drawn into political life and this seemed inevitable how it could withdraw itself from the situation. The outside world was going to interpret the action of the Army in terms of the coup d'etat which frequently occurred in certain other countries. This would have had a damaging effect on the image and reputation of Pakistan. A well organized, trained and disciplined army would find it distasteful to be turned into an instrument for securing political power. But as conditions were, the army alone could act as a coercive force and restore normalcy... Revolutions take long and painstaking preparations, detailed planning, clandestine meetings and countrywide movement of troops. In our case, there was very little preparation. It was handled as a military operation. What happened was that a brigade was moved, actually two brigades.[12]

The weakness of the Pakistani bourgeoisie has vastly enhanced the role of the army as the arbiter of political power. The civilians are heavily dependent on the army for their rulership. Hence it is not an accident that all the bourgeois politicians, in spite of this endless rhetoric against military rule, always end up allocating greater sums of money for the military during their sham democratic stints than the funds overtly allocated under direct military rule. They are very much aware that, in the final analysis, the institution that protects their exploitative class and system against revolutionary uprisings is the institution of the armed forces of Pakistan.

British influence was gradually displaced after Independence by that of the United States, a reflection of changing political realities on a world scale. In February 1954, USMAAG (United States Military Assistance Advisory Group) was set up in the army GHQ in Rawalpindi; as Pakistan's domestic and external policies had by then become largely subservient to US interests, few politicians were bothered by the fact that there was now a direct link between the army chiefs and the Pentagon. There can be little doubt that the relevant authorities in the United States were fully aware in the late 1950s that the Pakistani army was planning a coup d'etat: some years later Ayub's brother, Sardar Bahadur, was to allege that the CIA had been fully involved in the military takeover.

After October 1958, the military chiefs and their civil-service collaborators argued that the coup had been essential in order to save Pakistan from the politicians. It is perfectly true that Pakistani politics was notoriously unstable and the country's parliamentary institutions were in a shambles.

These, however, were not the real reasons for the army action. The Pakistani state was not a viable entity; its ruling class was weak. The possibilities of radical advance and mass explosion were built into the very structure of the new state. So the army, with guidance from abroad, decided to circumvent the whole process of obtaining mass consent, substituting itself for a homogeneous ruling class and a strong ruling political party alike. It was aided and abetted by the civil service.

The first phase of the Ayub dictatorship saw the regime attempting a 'cleaning-up' operation: politicians were prosecuted and barred from political activity for several years, trade unions and peasant organizations were banned, and students were warned against initiating or participating in any form of political activity. The progressive chain of newspapers owned by the veteran Leftist Mian Iftikhar-ud-Din was taken over by the state, on the grounds that Mian was a 'foreign agent'. This was a severe blow against the Left, at a stroke depriving it of its voice and providing the new regime with newspapers under its direct control. At the same time, the military attempted to modernize the country, setting up commissions to prepare recommendations on land reform, education, marriage and family law, pay and services, and a number of other subjects. With the exception of the Family Laws Ordinance (which placed serious restrictions on polygamy and allowed women to sue for divorce), none of the other commissions resulted in any serious reforms.

Domestic and Economic Policy

But this reform could only be realized and exercised by women from the middle and upper classes. Working-class women and destitute sections of society did not have the financial resources or the social acumen to benefit from this reform and these comprised the vast majority of women in Pakistan.

The Pay and Services Commission report did propose a drastic overhauling of the country's civil service, which would have challenged the traditional elitism inherited from the Raj, but this report was conveniently shelved.

The Land Reforms Commission proved to be the biggest disappointment. The reforms proposed and subsequently implemented were designed to preserve the status quo (after making a few cosmetic adjustments). In sharp contrast to the Nasserite reforms in Egypt or the Cardenas agrarian measures in Mexico, the land reforms in Pakistan were actually welcomed by the country's main landlords. Though the ownership ceiling was placed at 500 acres of irrigated and 1,000 acres of unirrigated lands, orchards and cattle-farms were exempted, as were landlords who had gifted some of their land to their heirs or dependants. A leading Sindhi landlord, Mir Ghulam Ali Talpur, declared that the reforms were exceedingly generous "because of the big heart of the President". In reality, the reforms evaded the central issue in the countryside: the separation of ownership and cultivation. The only equality embodied in the reforms was equality between landlords. Even though limited areas of excess land made available through the reforms were offered to tenants, the latter did not possess the money to make an offer. Since the departure of the Hindu moneylenders, the peasants had had no access to ready cash; landlords had taken over the functions of the moneylenders, and the government did not set up rural credit institutions to aid poor peasants.

At the time of the land reforms, 6,000 landlords owned 7.5 million acres of land in estates of 500 acres and over; 2.2 million peasant families owned an average of less than 5 acres per family; 2.5 million peasants owned no land and worked as share-croppers or seasonal workers. This situation was not qualitatively altered by the reforms. As the *Pakistan Times* pointed out, a few months before it was seized by the army: "even a conservative body like the Muslim League Land Reform Committee recommended an upper limit of 150 acres of irrigated land."[13]

The total land surrendered by the landlords was only 6 per cent of the total area under cultivation, and it was also the worst land. General Ayub strongly condemned absentee landlords. As a result, many landlords evicted weak tenants and put their retainers or heirs in charge of direct cultivation. The dispossessed tenants joined the growing army of landless labourers.

Thus the new regime failed to alter the basic structure of class relations that prevailed in the countryside, although it did begin to inject government subsidies to raise agricultural output. Capitalist farming was encouraged and the area under cultivation grew. But small farmers were virtually ignored. The main beneficiaries of the 'green revolution' were the big landlords. They were the major recipients of subsidies and loans, and were not required to pay income-tax. Hardly any money was made available to build village schools or rural hospitals and dispensaries; to improve sanitation facilities; or to carry out welfare measures. The rural poor, who comprised the overwhelming majority of the population, received few benefits from the 'green revolution'.

Dramatic economic developments, however, were to take place in the cities. The military made Pakistan a haven for capital investment by removing cumbersome restrictions, particularly by suppressing trade unions. Pakistan had not possessed a capitalist class in 1947. The North Western areas of the subcontinent had not been particularly hospitable to the industrial entrepreneur. It was Bohra and Ismaili Khoja traders from Bombay who were destined to become the agency of Pakistan's limited industrialization. Together with their Chinioti counterparts from the Punjab, the traders became the clients of a powerful civil service. It was the latter, acting on behalf of the new Pakistani state that put into effect a series of measures designed to aid capital formation. Government aid involved supplying cheap machinery, raw materials and interest free loans, while turning a blind eye to large-scale tax evasion.

Immediately after Partition an industries' conference was convened in September 1947 in Karachi to consider the country's future industrial development. On 2 April 1948 the government issued a statement of its industrial policy, setting out the priorities which were prescribed as basic for subsequent industrial development.[14]

The weakness of the indigenous entrepreneurial class, in

addition to the lack of industry, caused the government to play an active role in the promotion and fostering of a class of industrial entrepreneurs. In this respect, Mohammed Ali Jinnah, speaking as the governor-general of Pakistan, set the goals quite clearly in a speech to the Karachi Chamber of Commerce shortly after the industrial policy was issued in April 1948:

> Government will seek to create conditions in which industry and trade may develop and prosper ... I would like to call to your particular attention the keen desire of the Government of Pakistan to associate individual initiative and private enterprise at every stage of industrialization ... I can no more visualize a Pakistan without traders than I can without cultivators and civil servants. I have no doubt that in Pakistan traders and merchants will always be welcome and that they, in building up their own fortune (...)[15]

The government took a variety of measures to promote industrial development and to foster the growth of an industrialist class. In March 1949 the Karachi Stock Exchange was established to provide a broad-based capital market. In September 1949 the Pakistan Industrial Finance Corporation was established for financing private sector industries. Various fiscal incentives were used by the government to encourage private investment in industry.

The New Industrialists

As a more concrete measure, the Pakistan Industrial Development Corporation Act of 1950 (which was implemented in January 1952) provided for the establishment of a corporation that was to take initiative in the field of industry.

It would also, in certain cases, assist private capital in its projects: it was intended that when the projects were completed and successfully in operation, the Pakistan Industrial Development Corporation (PIDC) would transfer the share capital to private investors.

The government suspended the open general licence for imports in November 1952, stemming the import of consumer goods, allowing only 'essential' goods and machinery to be imported. All these factors together created conditions for profitable industrial investment in Pakistan.

There followed what has been termed a period of 'austerity and development' during which there was large scale investment in industry. Because of the large differential between the foreign exchange cost and the extremely high domestic prices of imported goods, traders who had import licences made extraordinary windfall profits which then provided them the capital to invest in industry. They were sufficiently assured of a protected domestic market free of any uncertainties over future government policy.

> Throughout the 1950s, new industrialists earned extremely high profits, investing mainly in consumer-goods industries where the entire initial investment could sometimes be recovered within a year. Even during the early 1960s, the profit rate was about 25 to 35 percent of the paid-up capital and net value. During this period and into the 1960s, the government, favouring private ownership, awarded large subsidies and tax concessions to private industry.
>
> Profits were subject to various exemptions from taxes: these were in the form of 'tax holidays' for certain types of industries in specified geographical areas of the country, accelerated depreciation allowances, various exemptions on reinvested income from both corporation and personal income taxes, etc. During the 1950s the government invested in a few industries which private enterprise found unattractive on account of technological complexity, high initial outlay and overhead costs or doubtful profitability. But the government embarked on that programme with the declared purpose of selling such industries to private enterprise when it was ready to take these over.[16]

By 1958 the momentum of the initial period of growth seemed to be at an end. Stagnation in agricultural production resulted in inadequate food supplies, which meant rising prices and the risk of inflation. The strategy of import substitution through domestic production of consumer goods had come close to the end of its potential.

Ayub Khan's martial law government imposed greater controls to counteract the deteriorating economic and political situation that had preceded their coming to power. Such initial measures caused a short period of uncertainty among investors, but the government soon made it clear that its basic aim was to promote private enterprise. This promotion was to be based primarily on the growth of new industry, which was to be export oriented and was to be financed through large amounts of foreign aid; it soon began to implement policies designed to secure those ends.

Ayub Khan pointed out that the needs of economic development were such that new countries could not progress under the "strains and stresses of the western democratic systems. Their development, if you study their history carefully, took place under almost a totalitarian system (...)"[17]

During the 1960s, in keeping with government policy of decontrolling the private sector, the emphasis was more on assistance to private industry, through finance corporations in the form of loans. The Pakistan Industrial Finance Corporation (PIFCO) had already been created for this purpose as early as 1948. The Pakistan Industrial Credit and Investment Corporation (PICIC) was established in 1957, with World Bank assistance, to provide foreign exchange facilities to the larger private enterprises which had been outside PIFCO's realm of activity. In the 1960s, PIFCO was transformed into the Industrial Development Bank of Pakistan (IDBP), which serviced medium-scale industry while PICIC operated in the field of large-scale industry.

In those sectors where private enterprise was still reluctant to invest, despite being offered optimal terms of assistance, the government undertook direct investment in new projects. This was mainly in the capital-goods industry, for creating employment in the industrially underdeveloped areas of Pakistan.

Interests of Capitalism come Before the Interests of the People

PIDC preferred to 'disinvest' by selling its projects to the private sector on very favourable terms. In the absence of any formal procedures for selecting those who were to benefit from the corporation's resources, transfers were made on the basis of political patronage. Thus, handovers were made to those leading industrialists who had cultivated the top bureaucracy.

This relationship between business and bureaucracy resulted in increasing the concentration of wealth in the hands of leading industrial houses of the country, and was in keeping with the government's general policy of rapid industrialization at the expense of social distribution of benefits. The rationale behind such a policy was that, in the overall interest of capital accumulation, it was essential to develop industrial entrepreneurship. It was argued that only high-income groups of investors should be promoted for this purpose, because of their "high marginal propensity to save".

The average growth of large-scale manufacturing industry, which had been 16 per cent per annum during the 1950s, continued to be about 15 per cent during the early 1960s. The share of GNP originating in the industrial sector increased from 8.4 per cent during 1954/55–1959/60 to 10.9 per cent during 1959/60–1968/69.

By 1959 twenty-four industrial houses owned 45.9 per cent of the total assets in Pakistan. By 1968 twenty-two families (one of them being Ayub Khan's family) controlled 66 per cent of the country's total industrial capital, 70 per cent of insurance and 80 per cent of banking.[18]

Government resources continued to flow in favour of leading industrial houses through public finance corporations, because the former had by then strengthened their monopolistic position, both on the boards of the corporations and in the market in general.

Despite the government's professed goal articulated in the Third Plan Period (1965-70) to accord special priority to the promotion of capital-goods industries, and its stated desire to provide the required financing, private entrepreneurs continued to invest in only those industries which guaranteed a high rate of return.

In the period 1965–68, 83 per cent of PICIC loans were sanctioned to the textile (including jute and other fibres) industry, and only 6.6 per cent went to engineering, metal and electrical industries—the sectors in which the government had stated it wished to invest at that stage.[19]

This was due to the concern of Ayub Khan's government that Karachi was receiving too much importance, also resulting in the concentration of a large industrial workforce in that city. In 1954, over 25 per cent of the workers engaged in large-scale manufacturing were employed in Karachi.

Karachi accounted for 40 per cent of industrial employment in 1959-60, 45 per cent in 1964-65 and 30 per cent in 1969-70, numbers which assumed greater significance because they constituted the largest single concentration of the organized workforce:

> The government's policy to disperse industry and thus reduce the importance of the few centres where industries were initially concentrated, particularly Karachi, is of obvious importance for a study of the organization of industrial workers since it entails a concomitant regional dispersal of new entrants into the industrial workforce.
>
> However, it appears that in the long term the dispersal of industrial growth resulted in a much wider impact of the industrial workforce on national politics, notably in the great revolution of 1968-69 that brought down the Ayub regime.[20]

Corruption and Oppression

The state had decided to create and strengthen private capitalism in Pakistan, ensuring that the new bourgeoisie would be tied to the coat tails of the bureaucracy. There thus developed a close and mutually profitable relationship between bureaucrats and businessmen; after the 1958 coup the army top brass also entered this relationship, and corruption increased manifold. While the army and bureaucracy exercised political power, the capitalists exercised economic power. Profits increased, but real wages in manufacturing industry declined drastically, as the working class grew in size in the industrial centres of Karachi, Lyallpur, Lahore, Rawalpindi and other cities.

Although the period under Ayub Khan seems to be relatively quiet compared to the chequered history of Pakistan, it was far from establishing any real stability in society: it was a brutal, repressive regime which committed several atrocities, especially against the Left-wing. The notoriety of the Mughal Shahi Fort at Lahore, used as a torture centre by the Ayub dictatorship, is well established in modern times.

The most infamous incident to gain publicity was the incarceration and gruesome murder in 1964 of Hasan Nasir, a leader of the Communist Party of Pakistan, by the military rulers. Several other political and trade union activists were also tortured and brutalized in the dungeons of this sinister fort.

But torture was far more widespread: the police were unleashed in every nook and cranny of the country to execute its brutalities, especially against the political opponents and dissidents of Ayub's dictatorship. Bribery and corruption was rampant in the bureaucracy, and among the police it was so notorious that it became a social norm. The system of 'basic democracies' was also introduced by this dictatorship to 'depoliticize' society while pretending to take democracy to the grass roots. Ever since, every subsequent military dictator in Pakistan has followed this same course to perpetuate its own rule. In the first presidential elections on 2 January 1965 the modus operandi was also these 'basic democracies'. Incidentally, even these tightly-controlled and easy-to-rig Presidential elections became a headache for Ayub Khan. The foxy feudal politicians who had been discarded by the Ayub dictatorship played a cunning trick on him. They put up Miss Fatima Jinnah, the old frail sister of Muhammad Ali Jinnah, as the opposition's joint candidate against Ayub Khan. She had been very prominent with Jinnah during his public appearances and was his companion for a long time after his wife had left him.

Let's Have a War

Although Ayub Khan 'comfortably' won the presidential election, the blatant rigging was too exposed to the masses to be covered up by the propaganda churned out by the State machinery and the official media.

The discontent seething under the surface began to come to the fore; the calm of the corridors of power began to shatter; the unease was palpable amongst the strategists of the regime. They were so baffled by this 'unexpected' stirring in society that they embarked upon another more dangerous misadventure in order to divert the attention of the masses, who were beginning to question the credibility and existence of the regime. They decided to make an incursion into Kashmir and provoke a conflict with India. Some even had the audacity to imagine that they would capture Kashmir to give the regime a solid foundation. In the words of Clausewitz, it was "the continuation of politics by other, violent means".

They intended to divert the domestic conflict on to the foreign front. Some were so naive that they imagined the war zone would be restricted to the disputed border within Kashmir. It turned out to be a full-fledged war between India and Pakistan that spread to the so-called International Borders. The war of September 1965 was a seventeen-day affair, and, as in every war, the first casualty was truth.

It is difficult to imagine who really won the war. After the ceasefire, brokered for a change by the Soviet diplomacy, both India and Pakistan claimed victory. In reality Pakistan being a weaker state had suffered greater ramifications of this destruction, both on the economy and in the stability of the state itself. The crisis above had already enhanced tensions amongst the ruling elite, and the war itself led to an even greater discord amongst the different factions of the regime. The most significant was the aggravation of the conflict between Ayub Khan and his blue-eyed-boy, the most able of his lieutenants, Zulfiqar Ali Bhutto.

This parting of ways became evident even during the parlays between Ayub Khan's cabinet team and the Indian delegation led by Prime Minister Lal Bahadur Shastri at Tashkent, where the negotiations were taking place under the supervision of the Soviet Prime Minister Alexei Kosygin, and Foreign Minister Andrei Gromyko. Bhutto later called the Tashkent Accord an outright sell-out of Pakistan's sovereignty by Ayub Khan. This break-up with Bhutto was to prove fatal for Ayub Khan; it was one of the main factors that had led to his demise.

Revolution

It is said that revolutions emerge from the wombs of wars. The national and social chauvinism pent up by the war hysteria, and the patriotism inculcated in the minds of the masses, was shortlived. The burden of war devastation, as in every capitalist society, was borne by the working classes and the impoverished masses. Social and political opposition and resistance started to emerge, in the beginning, amongst the unemployed graduates and students. They started burning their professional degrees as a result of their extreme frustration at the unemployment and social distress which they faced, even in a rather rapidly growing economy.

In many ways the September 1965 war became a significant factor in triggering the 1968-9 revolution. The war inevitably took its toll on the economy and further aggravated the burgeoning gap between economic growth and social development. The strong economic growth and industrial and infrastructural development under Ayub Khan's regime, and its incapability to develop society simultaneously, once again proved the historical inability of the neo colonial bourgeoisie to complete the tasks of the National Democratic Revolution.

The Pakistani bourgeoisie could not have imagined better conditions: infrastructural and financial support of the state along with such favourable trade conditions and tariff barriers. The list of state facilitation is a very long one. Yet they failed to carry through the agrarian revolution and abolish feudalism, create a genuine nation state and resolve the national question through an equitable integration, or give a secular character to the state and establish a genuine parliamentary democracy through adult franchise. The whole pattern of industrial and social development, in this 'decade of reforms', was of a strikingly uneven and combined nature; they had failed to create national sovereignty and break out of the imperialist stranglehold. All the government had done was to expose its own weakness and corruption. Their inability to become a progressive class was evident in their necessity to form alliances with the remnants of feudalism and religious obscurantism, and their dependence on imperialism. Such a ruling class was fated to be doomed by history. The 1968-9 revolution almost did it.

One of the positive aspects of the industrial development under Ayub Khan was the arrival of a fresh and virgin proletariat on to the arena of history. The relative absence of major trade unions and established trade unionism was also an important factor. Such established trade unions were routinely accompanied by corruption and conciliatory opportunism, always an impediment to the revolutionary development of the proletariat. The trade unions that the revolution threw up were of a totally different character, although they acquired the same classical trade union role when the revolution was derailed, the tide ebbed, and normalcy was restored.

These workers, mainly from villages and suburban areas, were sucked in by rapid industrialization, the crises in rural farming, and the slow and sporadic mechanization of the agriculture sector. However, industry and advanced technology gave them new insight and brought out the innovative skills of their untarnished minds. They had not yet suffered betrayal by their trade union and political leaders; the complexities of compromise had not convulsed their thoughts. Their consciousness was rising at lightening speed, and when they realized that the only way forward for them was a collective struggle for collective gains, they plunged into the erupting volcano of the revolution.

This virgin proletariat was the product of relatively rapid development. Karl Marx said in his epic work on the 1857 Indian War of Independence: "By laying every mile of the Railway track and telegraph the British Imperialism was digging its own grave". The same observation could equally be applied to the industrial development under the Ayub Khan regime. These contradictions of the lag of the social development with economic growth exploded into 'The 1968-9 Revolution'.

It is a historical fact that Pakistan's highest and the fastest growth was during the rule of Ayub Khan, when more industrialization took place than during any other regime. In the year of the revolution the growth rate of the economy was 9.1 per cent, the highest Pakistan has ever experienced. These high growth rates and the industrialization process were not due to the wonders of military rule: there were a number of totally different factors involved. Mainly it coincided with the boom in the West and the spin-off effects of the upswing of World Capitalism, which gave the Pakistani rulers room to manoeuvre. At that time they could adopt Keynesianism and state intervention in the economy was quite significant.

Pakistan's growth was to become a reference point for US economists 'advising' other neo-colonial regimes, a 'model' for the rest of the Third World and a shining example of free enterprise.

Yet there was nothing free about this enterprise. It was state subsidies and protection which enabled capitalism to establish itself. Where this was insufficient the state established factories (through bodies such as the Pakistan Industrial Development Corporation) and subsequently offered them to private capitalists at 'reasonable prices'. This process was labelled as 'Harvard's Development Advisory Service'. Papanek affectionately referred to Pakistan's fledgling bourgeoisie as "robber barons", and defended the growing exploitation which accompanied their progress. In what might seem an unconscious parody of Lewis Caroll, Papanek acknowledged the rising inequalities in his Wonderland, but wrote: "Inequalities in income contribute to the growth of economy which makes possible a real improvement for the lower income groups".[21] The social explosions which ended Ayub's rule were to prove Professor Papanek wrong.

The Harvard advisors gravely underestimated the damage being done to Pakistani agriculture in the same period that funds were pouring into industry. Moreover, two-thirds of capital investment in West Pakistan came from outside the country, as a stable military regime induced foreign investors to help the growth of indigenous capital.

The policies of the military regime led to an incredible concentration of wealth in the country. When the country's economists began to assemble in 1964 to discuss a third five-year plan, they were gripped by the realization that Papanek's plaudits could not conceal the stagnation of real income so far as the bulk of the population was concerned. Dr. Mahbubul Haq, chief economist of the Planning Commission, revealed a set of figures which startled the country. He stated that 66 per cent of the country's industrial capital was in the hands of twenty-two families, Dawood, Adamjee, Saigols, Valika, Bhimjee, Dinshaw, Fancy, Marker, Isphani and Habib being the most prominent. At the same time, the draft outlines of the third plan showed that the real condition of the economy did not give much reason for optimism. Growth of the national income and economic expansion had gone side-by-side with deterioration in the living standards of the mass of the population, whose food consumption had actually declined over the preceding five years.

In the towns, the army and the bureaucracy had helped to create a monstrous millionaire elite on the basis of intensive and large scale exploitation, while in the countryside they had similarly concentrated on promoting the interests of landlords and capitalist farmers at the expense of peasants and landless labourers.

Any attempt by the people to challenge this state of affairs was met by repression. In the urban areas, all trade-union activity was kept firmly under control. There were a number of reasons for the slow growth of trade unionism: acceptance by many workers on the shop-floor, who had only recently entered the factories of a tenant-landlord, was one factor. Also significant were official co-optation and repression. The bureaucrats of company unions were encouraged by the state, while local bureaucrats aided factory-owners in victimising those who tried to organize representative unions. During the Ayub years, all strikes were outlawed and many union leaders were put on the regime's payroll. But there is an important objective reason for the weakness of trade-unionism in Pakistan. The existence of a very large pool of unemployed labour does not facilitate strong unions. In the countryside, meanwhile, the combined powers of the bureaucracy and the landlords ensured the passivity of the tenants.

On the development front, the regime's much vaunted 'tube-well revolution' benefited only the rural rich. Instead of being geared to planned investment in rural infrastructure, social welfare, and producer technologies, the Pakistan economy was geared to the consumption habits of the urban upper class, which lay behind the country's topsy-turvy imports policy.

Capitalism in Pakistan was not an independent, developing system, but a very dependent client of the major capitalist powers, unable to finance its investment plans without massive foreign aid.

Industrial growth had two major consequences for Pakistan: it highlighted the differences between East and West, and it led to a rapid increase in the size of the working class in the cities.

The Pakistani ruling class was so busy congratulating itself that it was blind to the political developments which would soon threaten the entire fabric of the State.

At least in Asia the 1968-9 uprising in Pakistan was unprecedented for almost two decades. And in the world scenario it came close to a social revolution, the success of which could have had scintillating effects far beyond South Asia.

NOTES

1. Ayub Khan, *Diaries of Ayub Khan 1966-72*, Wednesday 16th October 1968, (Oxford), p. 273.
2. *Letters of Iqbal to Jinnah*, (Lahore 1942).
3. Collins and Lapierre, *Freedom at Midnight*, p. 285.
4. *Dawn*, Karachi 12 August 1947.
5. *Technical Assistance: Final Report of Committee on Foreign Relations*, Washington, 12 March 1957.
6. Zafar Shaheed, *The Labour Movement in Pakistan*, (Oxford), 2007, p. 25.
7. *Technical Assistance: Final Report of Committee on Foreign Relations*, Washington, 12 March 1957.
8. Tariq Ali, *Can Pakistan Survive?* p. 56.
9. *Pakistan Times*, 16 May 1958.
10. Tariq Ali, *Can Pakistan Survive?* p. 63.
11. The British Papers 1958-69, (Oxford), p. 49.
12. Ayub Khan, *Friends not Masters*, p. 71.
13. *Pakistan Times*, Lahore, 26 January 1959.
14. The Industrial Policy of 1948 is reprinted in Arnold 1955, as Appendix III pp. 283-8.
15. Zafar Shaheed, *The Labour Movement in Pakistan*, (Oxford) 2007, p. 18.
16. Zafar Shaheed, *The Labour Movement in Pakistan*, (Oxford), 2007, p. 20.
17. Ibid, p. 25.
18. *Business Recorder* 25 April 1968.
19. IBRD 1970: Vol. III, p. 63.
20. Zafar Shaheed, *The Labour Movement in Pakistan*, (Oxford), 2007, p. 24.
21. Gustav F. Papanek, *Pakistan's Development*, (Harvard), 1967.

Four

THE MASS REVOLT

When Socialist Victory was on the Agenda

The most indubitable feature of a revolution is the direct interference of the masses in historical events. In ordinary times the state, be it monarchical or democratic, elevates itself above the nation, and history is made by specialists in that line of business—kings, ministers, bureaucrats, parliamentarians, journalists. But at those crucial moments when the old order becomes no longer endurable to the masses, they break over the barriers excluding them from the political arena, sweep aside their traditional representatives, and create by their own interference the initial groundwork for a new regime. Whether this is good or bad we leave to the judgment of moralists. We ourselves will take the facts as they are given by the objective course of development. The history of a revolution is for us first of all a history of the forcible entrance of the masses into the realm of rulership over their own destiny.

—Leon Trotsky (1879–1940)

First Stirrings of the Revolution

On Thursday, 7 November 1968 it was the fifty-first anniversary of the great October Revolution of 1917. On that day there were hardly any celebrations or commemoratory meetings organized amongst the masses in the cities and towns of Pakistan. The practice had become that the Stalinist leaders of various 'communist', 'socialist' and 'progressive' parties along with the government ministers and high officials, 'respectable' citizenry, were invited to the embassies and consulates of the USSR for the celebrations. The Stalinist bureaucracy had confined the 'Bolshevik Revolution' within the high walls of their diplomatic compounds. It was converted into a Russian National day rather than a symbol of the solidarity of proletariat internationalism.

This in itself was a sharp reminder of the killing of the

internationalist essence of Bolshevism that the 1917 revolution led by Lenin and Trotsky had so forcefully elaborated and practised. The formation of the USSR as a union aimed at uniting workers of all countries had inspired revolutionary uprisings of the workers and youth across the planet.

Yet not far away from the Soviet Embassy in Islamabad the first stirrings of a revolution were taking place. This mighty mass upheaval that erupted in the aftermath of the events of 6 and 7 November could have become for Pakistan, what the 1917 revolution was for Russia. The revolutionary storm that engulfed Pakistan for the next 138 days began a few kilometres from Rawalpindi/Islamabad in front of the Government Polytechnic College, where the students of Gordon College and Polytechnic College had their first clash with the state forces that triggered this revolutionary upsurge. Such was the ferocity of this blizzard of mass revolt that it shook the corridors of power not just in Islamabad and Dacca but also as far as London and Washington.

The first incidents that triggered this uprising and the events in its aftermath are well documented in the diplomatic messages sent to Whitehall in London by the British High Commission in Rawalpindi. Their narration even in the hypocritical diplomatic language exposes the fear the imperialists had of the revolutionary wave that swept across Pakistan from the autumn of 1968 to the spring of 1969.Their experiences during the period of the Raj and their vested interests in the preservation of Pakistani capitalism in order to continue their plunder was the main reason behind their worries. This is evident in the dispatches that have been recently declassified and published. In any case the British had a greater understanding and insight of this region than any other imperialist power, including the United States. The draft dispatch on "disturbances in West Pakistan" was sent by a diplomat with the name of Pickard from the British High Commission in Rawalpindi on 16 November 1968. We quote it in detail, not to test the patience of the reader but to show the deep interest and apprehensions of British imperialism faced with these events, and this interest was not without reason, most probably to begin preparations to combat what was about to come.

This dispatch was sent to Michael Stewart MP at Whitehall, SW1, London:

Sir,

I have the honour to report that demonstrations by students, joined later by others, occurred in Rawalpindi from 7 to 10 November. The death of a student as a result of police firing led to a wave of sympathetic demonstrations, often violent in character, in many places in West Pakistan. On 10 November President Ayub, addressing in a large public meeting in Peshawar, was reportedly fired at by a student. On 13 November Mr. Z.A. Bhutto, Mr. Wali Khan and certain other opposition politicians were arrested under Section 32 of Defence of Pakistan Rules.

There is a good deal of combustible material lying around in West Pakistan. Student demonstrations were held in Karachi in October and again in early November to draw attention to local educational grievances. They took an ugly turn and places of higher education, were closed. There has also been trouble in the University at Hyderabad. There were disorders involving tear gassing and police lathi charges in some of the Frontier towns visited by Mr. Bhutto during his tour of the region in late October and early November. Students in particular were thus in a mood to take to the streets should an excuse present itself.

The occasion came in Rawalpindi on 7 November. A party of students from the Gordon College (the oldest institution of higher education in the town and affiliated to the University of the Punjab) recently had an outing to Landi Kotal (beyond the Khyber Pass near the Afghan border). As is customary they there bought smuggled goods unobtainable elsewhere in Pakistan but these were later impounded by the Customs authorities. Aggrieved at this 'discriminatory' treatment the students organized a strike in Gordon College on 7 November and marched in procession that morning to the office of the Deputy Commissioner to seek redress. The D.C. however was unsympathetic and at about noon they repaired to the Intercontinental Hotel at which Mr. Bhutto, then on his way by road from Peshawar, was scheduled to spend the next two nights. Mr. Bhutto has a considerable following among students in the West Wing and the Gordon College party planned to give him a welcome and incidentally seek his help over what they considered to be a grievance against the authorities. At this stage they were exuberant but harmless.

Meanwhile a separate welcome party was despatched to meet Mr. Bhutto on the Grand Trunk Road at the north western limit of the town and here they were joined by students from neighbouring Polytechnic. The gathering, which was quiet to begin with, would not disperse when ordered to do so by the police. The latter then charged with lathis and later opened fire, killing one Polytechnic student. From this point the situation rapidly deteriorated.

When the news of the firing reached Rawalpindi students, later joined by other elements, they resorted to violence in the Cantonment and Saddar area. Public service vehicles were stoned and set on fire, traffic lights smashed and government cars stoned and destroyed. Plate glass windows in the Inter-Continental hotel and the Government-sponsored Pakistan Bookshop were broken.

After a lull during the night of 7-8 November and the following morning (apart from some minor demonstrations, well shepherded by the police, in Islamabad) there was a recrudescence of disturbances in Rawalpindi from about 1230 hours on 8 November. This centred mainly on the area near Gordon College in Saddar and in the neighbouring Satellite Town. There was further damage to property, the targets for the most part being either Government-owned or in some way identifiable with the administration. Troops were called in and a dusk-to-dawn curfew imposed on the affected areas of the town. The victim of the previous day's firing was buried at his home in Pindi Gheb, some 70 miles from the capital, so that Rawalpindi was spared the further tension which would have been the inevitable result of a local funeral.

The following morning (Saturday, 9 November) a large crowd gathered in the troubled Murree Road area when Mr. Bhutto was due to leave by train for Lahore. Two persons were killed as a result of firing by the security forces. After this however the disturbances gradually subsided in Rawalpindi. The following day the curfew was partially relaxed and troops returned to barracks. The curfew was lifted altogether on Monday 11 November.

Official casualty figure (over and above the three persons killed in police firing) for Rawalpindi since 7 November is five injured and in hospital. Judging by eyewitness accounts these are almost certainly an understatement. In addition one Assistant Superintendent of Police was seriously injured and nine constables were hurt. Vehicles of some diplomatic missions were damaged (notably the Turkish ambassador's and the Iranian Minister-Counsellor cars). Among these a High Commission bus and land-rover, caught in a riot area, were damaged by stones and one of our local drivers was manhandled. Otherwise there was no damage to British lives or property, nor were there any reports of mobs showing xenophobic tendencies.

Meanwhile demonstrations in sympathy for the Rawalpindi student killed on 7 November took place at a number of places in West Pakistan. These were fairly harmless on 8 November but on the following day reports were coming in that a considerable number of towns in the Punjab, Sind and the old Frontier Province were experiencing disturbances with varying degrees of violence. In Karachi where purely local issues were already the cause of student unrest the Rawalpindi incident exacerbated the situation. Public property has been damaged there and schools and colleges and the University are all closed. In Lahore rioting began on 8 November and continued on 9 November especially in the railway station area, where crowds gathered to meet Mr. Bhutto on his arrival from Rawalpindi. Educational institutions in Lahore are also closed. Similar disturbances took place on either on both days in Peshawar, Nowshera, Mardan, Charsadda, Abbottabad, Dera Ismail Khan, Lyallpur, Sialkot, Kohat, Sukkur, Sargodha, Gujranwala, Bahawalpur and other places in West Pakistan.

There were further disturbances on 10 November in towns of the Northern Punjab and Frontier region. Among others, Mardan, Charsadda, Campbellpur and Nowshera were scenes of violence with crowds shouting anti-Ayub slogans and stoning vehicles and trains. Police firing at Nowhsera resulted in one death. At Charsadda a mob ransacked the office of a sugar mill (a reflection of public feeling which blames the Government for the current sugar shortage).

I turn now to a consideration of Mr. Z.A. Bhutto in the events so far described and who, with Mr. Wali Khan (President, National Awami Party, Pro-Moscow group) and certain other opposition politicians, was arrested on 13 November under section 32 of the Defence of Pakistan Rules. It is not too much to say that Mr. Bhutto's political standing has been transformed during the last few weeks, particularly as a result of tours of the Frontier which began on 28 October. This is partly the Government's own fault. In a speech at Hyderabad on 21 September Bhutto made a personal attack on the President which appears to have needled the regime. A somewhat ponderous and unedifying attack was launched on Bhutto first by Governor Musa and then a number of the party faithful, the statements being dutifully recorded in the Press Trust newspapers. To an impartial observer Bhutto seemed to come off the better in the public wrangle that developed during October. Bhutto then set off for his Frontier tour, receiving a tremendous welcome wherever he went from crowds who defied Section 144 of the Criminal code (which, when imposed, makes illegal the gathering in a public place of more than five people and forbids the carrying of any kind of offensive weapon) and the threat of lathi charges, tear gas or bloodshed.

What are the reasons for this success? In my despatch of 10 July on the internal politics of Pakistan I set out reasons for the reputation and political following that Mr. Bhutto then enjoyed. These advantages were enhanced by the success he had achieved and the publicity he had received in his October exchanges with the regime. He came to Peshawar, it was said, "as a man with a halo". (As far away as

Khanewal, 30 miles ENE of Multan, a group of teachers told me last week "Bhutto is our hero". The current political mood of the Frontier region is such that any person of note who is prepared to denounce the regime in public is assured of a following. In short, it was a situation which might have been hand-tailored for Bhutto: the latter, with his shrewd political sense and instinctive sense of catching the mood of his audience, exploited it to the full. He played on the emotions of the crowds in Peshawar, Kohat, Dera Ismail Khan and Charsadda by simply denouncing the regime and few of his hearers paused to subject his outpourings to anything approaching a cool analysis.

Having become in the public estimation the champion of the neglected Frontier region, Bhutto moved on to Rawalpindi and the Punjab where his student supporters and other representatives of "the defenceless masses" had taken to the streets and were being "victimized by the brutal forces" of the Government.

The arrest of Mr. Bhutto opens a new chapter. It is clear that Mr. Bhutto's progress worried the Government. Mr. Bhutto himself I believe, welcomes the martyrdom of political imprisonment; he has seen what this can do in the case of Sheikh Mujibur Rahman, who as a result of imprisonment and the much publicised Agartala trial has become something approaching a public hero in East Bengal. Cooler heads in the Governments are probably aware of this. But the regime saw fit to launch such a propaganda campaign against Bhutto, accusing him of every political crime in the calendar from near-treason down, that they lost all room for manoeuvre. The Government publicly laid the blame for the disturbances at Bhutto's door. Bhutto responded by refusing to appeal to the students for calm, saying "they are fighting and I am with them". In the circumstances the Government had little option but to arrest him, though the results of this course on the political life of the country are unpredictable.

East Pakistan has long-standing grievances sharpened by the Agartala conspiracy Trial, against the Centre, but the Government, believing itself secure in its power-base in the West, has learned to live with the problem of uneasy relations with the East. But now the Government is faced by disorders which are directed, not against a specific act of policy such as its action in signing the Tashkent Agreement, but against its policies overall and, indeed, its very existence; this is something which, on this scale, has not happened since the regime assumed power in 1958. The Government of course disposes of considerable forces, the civil service, the Basic Democrats, the police and finally the army wherewith it can contain the situation. But a second eruption (now, with Bhutto's arrest, a more likely possibility) would weaken its position and the Government must therefore move decisively to prevent a recurrence.

The authorities are faced with a difficult task of reconciliation and of building bridges between the rulers and the ruled; the arrest of Mr. Bhutto may well prejudice this. Even without this added complication it is a role for which the regime is ill-equipped since the Pakistan Muslim League is singularly lacking in the grass roots contacts which ought to have warned the Government in good time of the growing discontent which led to the disturbances and which are now essential if there is to be an effective reconciliation between the regime and its aggrieved opponents in the Province. I am told that the President left officials of the Pakistan Muslim League in no doubts of his displeasure at the time of the Rawalpindi disturbances.

I am sending copies of this despatch to the High Commissioner in New Delhi and to Her Majesty's Ambassador in Kabul.

I have the honour to be,

Sir,

Your obedient Servant,

Pickard.[2]

Again on 18 November the military advisor to the British High Commissioner in Pakistan sent a sensitive dispatch to the Ministry of Defence in London. This pertained to the people challenging the armed forces of Pakistan and that also in the historically sensitive region of the North West Frontier (Pushtoonkhwa). This region had a special historical nostalgia for the British Raj in India as the Imperialists faced a fierce resistance and could never fully occupy and control this territory. It is rather brief so we also quote this in full.

18 November 1968,
Ministry of Defence (DI 2)
Main Building, Whitehall,
London, SW1

DISTURBANCES IN PAKISTAN

Reference: My MA/81 dated 14 November 1968.

As a follow-up to my recent letter, we have had recent reports of serious incidents concerning the Services.

During the riots in Abbottabad the house rented by the Pakistan Military Academy and occupied by a Major who was decorated for gallantry in 1965, was ransacked. The house was wrecked and all personal belongings were looted or smashed. The house belongs to President Ayub.

In Peshawar a Medical Corps Colonel, his driver and orderly, were beaten up and stripped of much of their uniform. An Army Order now forbids Services in uniform to go into the old city of Peshawar. Peshawar has long been one of the historic and important military centres.

In Rawalpindi Air Marshal Nur Khan, the Commander in-Chief of the Air Force had his staff car stoned, and was saved from being manhandled by Police.

In Rawalpindi Begum Wasi-ud-Din, wife of Major General Wasi-ud-din Master General of Ordnance was roughly handled when collecting her two children from the local school. She was in the General's staff car, with the stars covered.

The Services were called out in aid of the Civil Power in Rawalpindi and Peshawar.

These incidents have been reported to the diplomatic staff.

(J.D.W. Millar)
Brigadier
Military Adviser

Copy to: Major General J.M. McNeil[3]

The Masses Arise

There were several dispatches sent from the British High Commission and British Consulates in both East and West Pakistan to Whitehall in London. Similarly the answers to these dispatches with further instructions were sent back from London. However, there are three diplomatic dispatches that show the anguish of the British imperialists and the grave threat they felt from the 1968-9 revolution in Pakistan. The first of these three was sent by Roy Fox, the Deputy High Commissioner in Dacca, as early as 20 November 1968:

> For us, I think, the lesson is clear. If East Pakistan is to be saved from communism there is little time in which to work and all our effort is needed to make the world and our own people realise this.[4]

Apart from the diplomatic garb it is obvious that Roy Fox was very clearly contemplating the overthrow of capitalism through a Socialist Revolution. The second message that exposes a British diplomatic service terrified by the revolutionary movement was sent from the High Commission in Rawalpindi on 29 January 1969. In this message the diplomats give a stark warning to London:

> In any case, many young army officers are likely to be attracted by Bhutto's 'doctrines' and personality; a Young Turk movement, joining hands with his civilian followers to seize control of the Army and put Bhutto in power, may not be beyond the bounds of possibility (...)[5]

In spite of the diplomatic camouflage the message is more than clear. Bhutto's 'doctrine' in those days was very clearly inscribed in the founding documents of the Pakistan People's Party. It called for the overthrow of capitalism/landlordism through revolutionary socialism. Young military officers beginning to support such a doctrine had sent shivers down the spines of the ruling classes in Pakistan and of their imperialist masters. At that time in his speeches Bhutto was advocating revolutionary socialism. His speeches were fired up with a revolutionary message stirring up the masses wherever he went.

The third vital diplomatic dispatch that was sent by Mr. C.A. Pickard from the British High Commission in Rawalpindi on 19 February 1969, states the following:

> There is a danger to British economic and commercial interests. Moreover a revolutionary situation will develop ... This cannot fail to be related to the developments in West Bengal and will lead to increasing dangers toward peace.[6]

Here Mr. Pickard is clearly visualizing the immediate spread of the revolution to West Bengal in India. This means that he was expressing the fear of a socialist revolution throughout the South Asian subcontinent. And when he refers to the "increasing dangers to world peace", he in fact means that world capitalism's stability and existence was in danger. And that was true had the revolution been victorious.

An alarming rate of inflation in the expensive aftermath of the 1965 Indo–Pakistan war exacerbated the existing poverty of the vast majority of the population.

Since people were unable to fight for their rights through normal political channels, and because government machinery was corrupt, they adopted extra-parliamentary methods which met with dramatic success. Workers joined students and unemployed elements in all the major cities of West and East Pakistan in a protest movement that rapidly created a revolutionary situation.

Traditional labour leaders who operated within the parameters of the government's labour policies and institutional framework, and who had already been discredited in the 1963 industrial action in Karachi, were definitely left behind. On the other hand, through shared political organizational work in several strike action committees which sprang up during the struggle, young radicals who until then had been largely limited to student politics an important element of opposition to the government during a period of severe restrictions on labour and political activity now joined and interacted with workers for a common cause. This interaction between militants who originated from student cadres and workers' organizations had already been apparent in the 1963 movement. The overt political character of the 1968-9 movement made this form of united action all the more effective and qualitatively different in terms of creating organizational links between such intellectuals and workers. In some cases this interaction led to the forming of new labour organizations with goals more politically and socially revolutionary than those of modest wage settlements.

Comparable coalitions between workers and students have been formed in other countries. For example, in Egypt during 1945–47, an alliance between workers and students led a mass movement which was directed both against imperialist rule and internal repression.

Spark of the Students' Rebellion

As in many other revolutions of the 20th century, students played the role of the initial spark that inflamed the 1968-9 revolution in Pakistan. The main Left student organization was the NSF. The National Students Federation (NSF) was actually formed as a result of the movement of 1953. It was banned after some time.

There were also other Left wing organizations of students in the 1950s' like the High School Students Federation and the Girls Students Congress which was later changed to the Girls Students Organization. Its main activists were Zahida Taqi, Hamza Baji, Rahat Shakoor, Zarina Saliha, Malika Hussain and others. After the 1958 Martial Law of Ayub Khan the NSF was banned again due to its increasing popularity amongst the students and its Left wing character. In 1959 US President Eisenhower visited Pakistan. He was to have his last meeting in Karachi and from there he was scheduled to fly back home. The NSF planned a big demonstration to protest Eisenhower's visit and decided to stop his caravan towards the airport. All the planning was finalized in a clandestine manner but somehow it leaked out to the government. Mairaj Muhammad Khan along with many other student leaders was arrested one night before the planned date. That demonstration couldn't be held due to the arrests of leadership.

Another important demonstration was in January 1961 against the killing of Patrice Lumumba, the Left leaning Prime Minister of Congo, which was also led by the NSF. The bourgeois press and the Islamic obscurantist party, the Jamat-i-Islami, criticized this agitation and asked the leaders whether they had forgotten the Muslims who were being mercilessly killed in ethnic violence in Jabalpur, India at that time.

After two days the NSF led a rally in support of poor Muslims being slaughtered in Jabalpur, India. These demonstrations were very militant and spread to most of the colleges of Karachi. This also led to a strike in Karachi University. The State reacted and arrested all the leading student leaders. Fifteen of the main leaders were tried under Military Law. Five were released while others, including Khan, were banned from entering the city for nine months. Habib Jalib's verse on this oppression of these students became very popular:

> Jin Naujwanon ne apna lahoo hawa mein uchhaal diya
> Sitamgaron ne unhein shehar se nikal diya
> (The Youth that spilled its blood in the air;
> The tyrants have expelled them from the city)

The expulsion of these leaders from the city gave them the opportunity to spread their message to other cities. They visited almost all of the other big cities during this period and raised revolutionary fervour in the hearts of students.

In the General Strike of Karachi 1963 the NSF played an active role and supported the workers of the Railways, KESC (Karachi Electric Supply Corp.), Shipyards, SITE industrial area and Landhi industrial zone.

An important incident took place on 12 September 1962 when Ayub Khan's Convention Muslim League held a public meeting at the Polo Ground Karachi. A big stage was set up and all the ministers and leading figures of the Convention League were due to address the gathering.

NSF activists went on to the stage and tried to intervene in the proceedings. They threw the reactionary sycophant of Ayub Khan Ch. Khaleeq uz Zaman from the stage and a clash took place. Z.A. Bhutto, the General Secretary of Ayub Khan's Convention League at the time, was also on the stage and he also had a scuffle with the NSF students. Later many students were arrested and sentenced to jail. However, they were able to get a lot of their demands accepted in which the Bachelor's degree was reduced to two years from three, fees were reduced in all educational institutions and several other demands were accepted.

In the 1964 presidential elections the NSF had supported Fatima Jinnah against Ayub Khan. The 1965 convention of the NSF in the Gul-e-Ranaa club in Karachi was a historic one. In that convention the NSF split into pro-Moscow and pro-Peking factions, NSF-Mairaj and NSF- Kazmi.

NSF then played a major role in the student agitation in 1968-9 and supported the PPP. In the 1970 elections it withdrew its support for the PPP and opposed Bhutto's reformist turn in the politics of the party after it came to power and its induction into the state establishment.

During the revolution of 1968-9 the Punjab University Lahore was the hub of student politics, where along with other student organizations the National Students Organization, NSO, was active against the Islamic fundamentalists. In those days the fundamentalists were weak and the Left had a complete hold over the University.

However, in the elections of the student unions the joint candidate of all the Left-wing organizations lost to a fundamentalist by 162 votes. It was more due to the internal split within the Left rather than any major Islamic following. In fact, in spite of the 'victory' the fundamentalist Jamiat was not able to regain control of the campus.

In an interview Imtiaz Alam, a student of Punjab University at that time, told the author of this work:

> It was a marvellous period. Every student was reading Marx, Lenin, Mao, Tolstoy or other progressive literature as well as literary classics. Everywhere there were debates between students. Every other day there were demonstrations against Ayub Khan and on various student demands. Frequent agitations became the norm. Those days were full of energy and romance. Every body had a romance with revolution ...
>
> I still remember my last day at University. We had a farewell party at night in an open ground where 60 to 70 students had gathered. We gave revolutionary speeches and were very emotional. At the end we sang the International and tore apart our degrees and promised that from here on we will not go to our homes rather we will go to the factories and the fields to work for revolution. It is the call of revolution that from here we must set out for revolutionary work.[7]

The student movement against Ayub spread out into the fields and factories:

> After the protests in university, the campuses were closed down for indefinite periods and the hostels were forcibly vacated. From there when students went to their homes, they started struggle in their particular areas and conveyed the message of revolution there to the peasants and workers.[8]

The militant students, youth and workers were therefore searching for an alternative type of organization. Through their participation in the 1968-9 movement, they interacted with other militant labour leaders, especially those associated with radical political groupings, as well as militant shop-floor workers and student leaders who had become active in the labour field.

1967 Railways Strike—A Prelude to the Revolution

During the decade of the 1960s, under Ayub Khan's regime, it clearly became difficult for workers to receive just and expeditious awards in an industrial relations' system which had become increasingly dominated by state adjudication procedures. Those labour leaders who were frustrated with lengthy court processes opted for other, more direct methods of dispute settlement, often in response to the mounting pressure from the rank-and-file trade union members who wanted faster results. Those labour leaders who did not change their modus operandi according to changing conditions and rapidly radicalizing consciousness were discredited amongst workers, and lost their following to a considerable extent. The parameters of the existing social order which had been delimited with respect to workers through comprehensive labour laws and government-controlled procedures were challenged by forces working outside and against the legal boundaries. In these conditions one of the main strikes that became the precursor to the 1968-9 revolution was the magnificent Railway Strike of January 1967.

This Railways strike lasted for 13 days. There were two Right-wing unions in the Railways at that time, the Railways Mazdoor Union (CBA) in the workshops led by M.A. Rahim, while the Railways United Union (CBA) on the open lines was led by Umar Din. The only Left-wing union was the Railways Workers Union which was led by Mirza Ibrahim.

The protest started with the demand that special Rashan (food) Depots should be established for Railway workers to facilitate them in their work. This demand was rejected by the government. After that, independent committees started to form among the Railway workers. The appeal for strike action spread by word of mouth among the workers. Some leaflets were published. When the strike started not a single rail wagon moved from its place. Old longstanding trade union activists said they had not seen such a strike in the history of Indo–Pak trade unionism. The yellow unions were obviously not participating but the pro-Chinese trade union of Mirza Ibrahim also was not in a position to lead this due to the close Ayub–Mao friendship and support of the Chinese bureaucracy for the regime in Pakistan. Hence, the strike went out of control of the leadership. The regime had no clue of how to end this paralyzing and forceful strike. The Minister for Labour, Ahmed Saeed Kirmani, contacted Mirza Ibrahim to get a deal between the workers and government. Mirza tried his best to end this strike but was not able to do so. The government finally arrested Mirza Ibrahim and started an orgy of severe repression against the railway workers. In Hyderabad the workers lay down on the railway tracks to stop the traitors from moving the trains.

But the trains moved on and due to this militancy two workers were killed while many others were injured. Finally the government had to accept most of the demands, and the strike ended.

A fresh young leadership of the workers emerged after this strike and all the official and 'non-official' structures of the unions were bypassed. The weakness lay in the fact that the strike failed to link up with the workers of other sectors. In spite of this, the working class realized its immense power and the ability to weaken the Ayub regime and shake the whole system.

One of the main problems for the Ayub government was that of finding a way of creating a democratic legitimacy for itself which meant converting the government conquered by military power into a civilian government. This they did by introducing the system of 'Basic Democracy'. This scheme was introduced in 1959 under which 80,000 BD members were directly elected, 40,000 each from East and West Pakistan. Ayub thought he could get 80,000 members elected of his own choice and if he had such people he could control the politics of the whole country. US imperialism gave a lot of money for this system. Ayub got a vote of confidence through these newly elected BD members. The question asked by these members was "Do you have confidence in President (Field Marshal) Mohammad Ayub Khan, 'Hilal-e-Pakistan', and 'Hilal-e-Jurat' (gallantry awards)? The BD members replied "yes". After this Ayub Khan took an oath as the first elected President of Pakistan in 1960. A new constitution was prepared. It was designed in such a way that all powers were in the hands of the President. A parliament was also elected through these BD members.

But all these gimmicks manufactured by the dictatorship were shattered as the mass revolt erupted. Bhutto was already in the forefront of the opposition against Ayub. He grabbed the historic opportunity. Stanley Wolpert describes Bhutto's intervention after the 7 November 1968 incident when Abdul Hameed was killed by police firing on a demonstration as described earlier in the diplomatic mail quoted at the beginning of this chapter.

Unleashing of the Stormy Events

> Z.A. Bhutto by then had rolled on to Rawalpindi, where Mustafa Khar and Mumtaz Bhutto were waiting for him at the Intercontinental Hotel. Thousands of students, many from neighbouring Gordon College, had just been chased from the Intercontinental lawn by the police. Pindi was the site of the army's general headquarters (GHQ), so crowds of raucous students were not welcomed there, especially on the anniversary of the Russian Revolution.
>
> 'When I arrived at the Hotel Intercontinental I found the whole Mall area thick with teargas smoke,' Zulfi later recalled 'About one-and a-half hours after my arrival ... I received a telephone call from the Polytechnic institute informing me that the police had opened fire there resulting in the death of a student, Abdul Hamid. I was told that the students were insisting on taking the body ... to the President's House and that they wanted me to lead the procession.'[9]

After his tumultuous reception in Rawalpindi, Bhutto proceeded on an eventful journey to Lahore by train. He was accompanied by student leaders of Rawalpindi. Thousands had thronged on the Railway stations along the route to Lahore to get a glimpse of him.

Stanley Wolpert again describes Bhutto's first arrival in the historic city of Lahore after being deposed by the Ayub regime:

> He had come back to Lahore, more than two years after his eloquent silence and tear-filled eyes spoke to a hundred thousand or more young men who gathered at the railway station hanging from precarious perches like bats in midday, filling every platform, tightly locked together on every step just to catch a glimpse of this Shaheed.[10]

On 13 and 14 November all the Left-wing leaders of the country were arrested including Z.A. Bhutto and Wali Khan. These acts of the regime further inflamed the revolutionary inferno. On this there was a protest by lawyers on 15 November. On 19 November there were demonstrations by Lahore, Karachi and High Court Bars of several other cities and towns across the country.

A general strike had closed down Pindi for a day in late November 1968, and the police continued to clash with students and workers, while the army watched warily from its barracks. Little more than a week later another general strike paralyzed Dacca on 7 December. This time police fire drew young Bengali blood, and radical Maulana Bhashani, whose National Awami Party was ideologically modelled on Maoist doctrine, issued a call for the complete shutdown of East Pakistan in mid-December. Mujib's Awami League endorsed Bhashani's call, and soon all the small shops and businesses of East Bengal closed their doors.

Ayub saw that his days in power were numbered. He could speak nowhere in public without getting shot at or causing a riot. Nor had his once-robust health returned. Still, he thought the army, might not be powerful enough to beat India, but that its strength was more than sufficient to quell street disturbances and political opposition. He was far from reality, as it might have been able to fight with India but to curb a ferocious revolutionary upsurge was beyond the capacity of the army. Paradoxically had the armed force, at that stage been used to crush the revolt, the army itself would have crumbled to pieces.

On 28 November the PPP and NAP organized joint processions and demonstrations. On 8 December Ayub Khan visited Dacca where students protested against him. Two students got killed in police shootings. On 10 December 1968 there was a countrywide strike of journalists on the call of the Federal Union of Journalists. On 13 December there was a general strike in East Pakistan.

Ayub Khan wrote in his diaries at that time:

> Today, reports indicate that there have been widespread disturbances by students and hooligans in several towns. They indulged in looting and arson. Muslim League and family planning offices were made a special target. The curious thing is that young school children of 10-12 years of age have also taken to violence.[11]

Ayub Khan was now feeling the heat of the mass inferno rising from below:

> Cars and other vehicles were stoned and in places shops looted. A convoy of East Pakistan Rifles was brick batted. The East Pakistan Rifles opened fire in self-defence. Some people were wounded (...)
>
> (...) Bhashani and his followers declared a total hartal (General Strike) for two days. Meanwhile, Section 144 was imposed in Dacca and Narayanganj area. However, he decided to defy Section 144 after

> mid-day prayers. When police entreaties failed to dissuade him, coloured water was sprinkled on him and his crowd, whereupon they beat a hasty retreat and dispersed.[12]

On 20 January 1969 a Communist student leader Asad was killed in police firing at Dacca and his death intensified the student militancy in the country. On 21 January the first demonstration by doctors was held in Lahore and they put forward their demands. On 24 January a general strike was observed in Lahore. A 24-hour curfew was imposed on the city and the army was deployed to control the people. However, elsewhere, students and thousands of people took to the streets in defiance of the curfew.

In a police shooting, Matiur, a student of Class 9 of the Nabakumar Institute in East Pakistan was killed in East Pakistan. Outraged students and people burned the offices of two government newspapers because of their anti-people role. They were *The Morning News* and *Dainik Pakistan* published in Dacca. They also ransacked the office of the daily *Paigam* owned by the Governor of East Pakistan, Munim Khan.

On 25 January there was a big demonstration in Karachi. There was a lot of rioting and many buses were set on fire. A curfew was imposed in Karachi. On 26 January three civilians were killed in Dacca and Narayangunj while breaking the curfew; after that demonstrators attacked BD members. The office of the Karachi Development Authority was attacked and set on fire. Along with Karachi, curfew timings were increased in Gujranwala, Lahore, Dacca and other cities.

According to the telegraphic narration of the stormy events of those days in Dr. Mubashar Hasan's book, *The Crises of Pakistan and Their Solution*:

> On 14 February 1969 workers of Railways, WAPDA (Water & Power Development Authority) and rickshaw taxi union went on strike and held a demonstration in Lahore. West Pakistan Federation of Trade Unions presented their financial demands in which increase in wages and other facilities for workers were demanded. On 17 February PIDC (Pakistan Industrial Development Corporation) workers went on strike in Multan. On 19 February 30 trade unions held a joint demonstration in Lahore. On 20 February all the overseers in government jobs held a demonstration and presented their demands.

On 21 February all the clerical staff of West Pakistan secretariat went on strike and held a demonstration. On 23 February Road Transport workers held a demonstration, hospital workers and PWD employees also joined in. On 24 February Road Transport workers held another demonstration, also the school teachers of Bahawalpur held a demonstration same day.

On 3 March Workers of Basco factory in Gujarat went on strike for 13 days. On 4 March post men went on strike which continued for 13 days. On the same day two thousand workers of Telephone & Telegraph announced to go on a total strike. On 5 March ten thousand workers of Karachi Port Trust went on strike which continued for 5 days. On 6 March Railway workers of Lahore went on strike and held a demonstration. A person thought about as the supporter of Ayub was beaten to death.

On 7 March workers of National Bank went on strike while Railway workers held a demonstration. West Pakistan Federation of Trade Unions took out a big rally in Lahore. On 8 March teachers held a demonstration in Karachi, which was supported by another big demonstration of workers. On 9 March a demonstration was held by Central Hydro Electric Union of WAPDA in which they put forward their demands. One of the demands was of fixing basic pay at Rs. 150. For the first time a declaration about nationalization of basic industries was issued. Eastern Federal Union (insurance company) workers also announced a strike on the same day. On 11 March workers of WAPDA held a demonstration and a rally in Lahore. Telecommunication workers started a strike on 11 March which continued for 8 days. 5000 School teachers of Karachi held a demonstration which was joined by 14000 postal clerks and postmen. On 12 March telephone operators went on strike. On 13 March telecommunication workers held a demonstration and after that engineering staff went on strike along with the workers. On 14 March long distance operators also joined the strike. On 15 March staff of National and Grindlays Bank went on strike. On 17 March 20 thousand primary school teachers of Lahore held a one mile long demonstration in which teachers from 12 districts of Punjab participated. On 18 March 2.5 million workers went on country wide strike on the call of Joint Labour Committee. On 19 March 6,000 workers of Karachi Port trust went on strike without any notice. On 21 March workers of India flour mills and Karachi steam roller mills took control of the mills and formed a committee of workers for administration. On the same day 20,000 workers of Accounts Department went on strike. On 21 March Grade 4 workers of hospitals went on strike. In all this period 24 incidents of gherao (siege tactics), took place in East Pakistan in which workers took control of large factories and many government and semi government buildings and got their demands accepted. On 25 March Joint Labour Council celebrated the week of workers' demands.

In this movement a total of 239 people were killed, 196 in East Pakistan and 43 in West Pakistan. According to details police firing killed 41 in West Pakistan and 88 in East Pakistan. Most of them were students. In East Pakistan they included Asad, Matiur, Anwar, Rostom, Dr. Shamsuzzoha and Sergeant Zahurul Huq.[13]

Ayub Khan wrote his confession of defeat in his diaries on Sunday 9 March 1969:

> (...) law and order situation in the province, which is very bad indeed. In fact, it does not seem to exist. The civil administration is rendered ineffective. Apart from the mischief makers, gangs of communists and terrorists on the prompting of Bhashani are raiding police stations, the houses and properties of Muslim Leaguers, and asking the chairmen and members of Basic Democrats to resign.
>
> (...) In consequence, most of the civil officers have left their posts and so have the local rent collectors, and their records have been burnt.
>
> Labour trouble is rampant in many places, constant demonstrations, etc., have affected production. Investment is drying up. The stock exchange has slumped and money is being taken out of the country. The coming days are going to be hard for Pakistan.[14]

On 20 March Ayub Khan conceded how the movement had paralyzed the functioning of the state and society.

> The civilian labour force in Karachi dockyards had struck and stopped work. No loading or unloading of ships was being done. In one case a ship went back empty as it could not be loaded with cotton. Bhashani has been in Karachi and elsewhere spreading disaffection. Expectations are that the situation is likely to deteriorate.[15]

None of the heads of the three top services—Army General Yahya Khan, Navy Admiral S.M. Ahsan, Air Marshal Nur Khan—was willing to order troops to fire on civilians, advising instead a negotiated settlement.

Ayub announced on 21 February 1969 that he would not be a candidate in the scheduled 1970 presidential election. This bolstered the revolution even more.

Ayub's announcement marked the passing of the Movement into a new momentous phase. This announcement coincided with the first protest action by lower ranking government servants. A short strike by the clerks of the government of the West Pakistan Secretariat at Lahore soon spread through the ranks of Class III and IV government servants. Within days it involved the staff and low-paid employees of government hospitals, the Public Works Department and the Posts and Telegraph Department, as well as more autonomous government bodies, like the Road Transport Corporation, the National Bank of Pakistan and the Water and Power Development Authority. During this period, organized labour became much more active and militant. The leaders of the major unions and federations in West Pakistan joined together to form the Joint Labour Council (JLC). The JLC organized the first week of March as the workers' 'demands week', and called for a nationwide general strike on 17 March 1969, which was a brilliant success as the whole country came to a standstill. On this day, the electrical workers cut off electricity to the President's House, Islamabad Civil Secretariat, government offices and the GHQ of the Pakistan Army in Rawalpindi for two hours. According to Bashir Bakhtiar, president of the West Pakistan Federation of Trade Unions (WPFTU), "It was our signal to Ayub Khan: If you don't go, we will keep this up."[16]

March was a month of massive labour unrest throughout Pakistan, as factory workers resorted to gherao (siege tactics), jalao (burning), and takeovers of factory premises. These conditions, together with the strikes by government employees, brought both the ponderous government bureaucracy and much of the urban economy to a virtual halt. The entry of the workers into the arena of revolution, their discovery of the efficacy of political methods to win higher wages, and their wider demands for the right to strike, the nationalization of industry and an end to capitalism in Pakistan, ushered in the most ideologically advanced phase of the Movement. Inevitably, this meant a growing ideological polarization in Pakistan. The Movement, increasingly represented by Bhutto and Bhashani, continued to insist on the immediate ousting of Ayub, but it also began to emphasize more revolutionary themes. Maulana Bhashani, whom "Feldman aptly characterized as 'that inexplicable Savonarola',"[17] was particularly vocal during this period in his call for a revolution. As he told factory workers in Karachi, "it is time to talk less and sharpen [our] weapons".[18]

The Peasant Revolt

Bhashani was a typical peasant leader and believed in guerrilla struggle. He was a staunch follower of Mao. Pakistan was still an agriculture-based country in 1968-9 in spite of rapid industrialization under Ayub Khan in the preceding decade. The majority of the population lived in the countryside. The revolutionary message from the cities and towns was resonating throughout the rural heartlands louder and louder. It was having a deep impact on the minds, psyche and nerves of the peasant masses.

Soon a gigantic peasant struggle had erupted and joined the revolution raging in the cities and towns. Peasants in both East and West Pakistan came out to challenge the authority of feudal lords in their villages. The popular slogan of the movement was "He that tills the land, shall reap the harvest".

Mass peasant movements took place in Chambar in Sindh, Hasht Nagar in Pushtoonkhwa and a number of districts in East Bengal. In Chambar the peasants subdued the arrogant wrath of the feudal lords through their unity and went as far as challenging the right of property and establishing peasant courts. This also linked up with the workers of Hyderabad when a joint demonstration was held with nearly 700 peasants from Chambar and 800 workers from Zeal Pak Cement Factory under the leadership of its president Ustad Murtaza. Workers from the Municipal Authority, Road Transport and other sectors also joined in.

This struggle ended with the feudals of the area publicly asking for forgiveness from the poor peasants and accepting the demands that peasants should divide the harvest in peasant courts, no wageless work (Begaar), no ejections of poor haris (tenants) from their lands. The peasants raised the slogans Hari Haqdar, Jageerdar Dastbardar (The tenants have rights; Landlords should abdicate).

The Mazdoor Kissan Party (MKP) was a Left-wing party founded on Maoist lines. According to Wikipedia, it soon started to work together with several factions in Pakistan including the Major Ishaque Mohammad group in Punjab and Leftist groups in East Pakistan. In 1970 the Ishaque group merged with the MKP. The party's main focus was on the peasantry, inspired by the struggles of the Chinese, Vietnamese and African people. It achieved immediate success in Pushtoonkhwa, where spontaneous clashes between peasants and landlords were already taking place due to Ayub Khan's land reforms and the imposition of farm machinery. The MKP provided the organization and leadership needed by the peasant rebellion and in turn the movement gained a tremendous following in the late 1960s and early 1970s. The movement was not only facing the private armies of the landlords but also attempts by the state to crush it by force. The fight continued through three governments of those tumultous years. Soon even the landlords belonging to the different parties banded together in the Ittehad Party in order to crush the peasant rebellion.The provincial governments stood firmly behind the landlords in this repression and breaking up of the peasant movement.

One of the greatest clashes between the peasantry and the state took place in July 1971 at Mandani in Pushtoonkhwa. In a day-long pitched battle an army of 1,500 heavily armed policemen were routed with casualties of about 20 peasants and party cadres. Another struggle took place at the end of the NAP-JUI government period. Around 8,000 militia and Rangers were deployed in the Malakand Agency in order to stop the MKP. During this time the party's vice-president Maulvi Mohammad Sadiq was assassinated.

The MKP ignored the parliamentary form of struggle and did not participate in the general elections in 1970. Also the question of nationality in Pakistan was not addressed properly by the MKP, and it also failed to organize in Sindh and Baluchistan. Still, the MKP had strong support among the peasantry of the Peshawar and Mardan districts, the Malakand Agency and the former states of Swat and Dir. It also built support in parts of Hazara and Punjab.

The first national congress of the party was held in May 1973 at Shergarh in the Mardan District. Armed security guards were placed around the area, and a strike of bus owners was organized in order to prevent people from attending. This failed, however, as 5,000 delegates, helped by disobeying drivers and MKP militants, attended the congress. In the congress Ishaque Mohammad was elected as president of the party.

As in 1970, the MKP did not participate in the general elections of 1977, although it had good prospects of winning more than a dozen parliamentary seats. Instead it held the slogan of 'Intikhab Naheen, Inqilab' (Revolution, not elections) and organized mass rallies following a relaxation of political restrictions. Around 50,000 participated in Peshawar and 30,000 in Shergarh.

Another important peasant struggle was held at the Chishtian Sugar mill which they occupied in 1972 and it continued to be under workers' control for two years. There were almost 1,200 workers in the mill. The occupation was mostly supported by the peasants of adjoining areas who used to sell their harvest to the mill.

Former MKP leader Imtiaz Alam narrated to the author of this work:

> In those days the Chishitan sugar mill was like a commune for workers and peasants. Everything was free for the workers and a lot of political work was done from there. There were nearly 25 full timers who went on visits to other areas and built unions in other industries. We had formed a federation of Sugar mill workers at national level and its centre was Chishtian. The Bhutto government had to deploy rangers in order to break this occupation. But actually it had collapsed internally because it was not feasible financially to run the factory. In the end we were actually living by the support of peasants of the area and funds collected through the Trade Union Federation.[19]

He also said that they had "organised women peasants in the countryside. Women came out to work mostly in the cotton picking season and harvesting of the wheat crop. They were given in compensation 1/16th of the whole crop for picking. A peasant women's conference was also organized in Chishtian in 1974 in which nearly 10,000 women participated. We had an expense of only 48 rupees for this conference and that was mainly on the loud speaker and setting of the stage. All the women had travelled on their own expenses and brought cooked food with them."

Apart from Pushtoonkhwa this movement had spread to many villages in Punjab and land occupations had started in Khanewal, Rajanpur, D.G. Khan, Vehari, Burewala and other areas.

The movements started mainly against ejections, wageless labour (Begaar) and distribution of harvest (Batai). They were able to get a greater share for the peasants after this movement.

There is a long history of peasant struggles in Pakistan. This created a tradition of Kissan (peasant) conferences that gave a certain organizational base to the peasant movement. The first Kissan Conference was organized in March 1948 and held in Tehsil Toba Tek Singh of District Lyallpur (now Faisalabad). In this conference, the Punjab Kissan Committee was re-organized and founded, attracting peasants from rural and urban areas all across the province.

In the wake of the outbursts of the revolutionary wave Kissan conferences were held in different parts of the Punjab in 1970 in Toba Tek Singh, and in 1971 at Khanewal. The Toba Tek Singh conference of 22-23 March 1970 was the most successful in the history of Pakistan. Around 0.5 million peasants from all over the country participated in that conference, according to veterans of the Pakistan Kissan Committee. The most prominent people who spoke on that conference were Maulana Abdul Hameed Bhashani, Faiz Ahmed Faiz, Ahmad Rahi and Mairaj Muhammad Khan.

People had begun to whirl around it like a tornado. The landlords of Punjab and Sindh were shivering in their shoes. The capitalists who were subservient to American and Western capital felt as if the blood in their veins was drying up. The mullahs were boiling with anger because a few mortal human beings were trying to change what the mullahs preached was the will of God. The bureaucracy was always a worshipper of the past, its ideals and views unchanged since the time of the East India Company.

Peasant organizations within the NWFP (Pushtoonkhwa) were also very active in holding meetings and processions throughout the province. Many conferences were held throughout the 1960s and 1970s, from which demands for the rights of peasants were projected through mass agitations, processions, and sometimes armed struggle.

In April 1967, in village Shah Abad, district Peshawar, a Kissan Jirga was held in which a joint resolution regarding the occupation of land by the Khans and their unjustified eviction of peasants was passed.

The Sindh Hari Committee also left no stone unturned in terms of their massive support to the peasants' struggle. On 21-22 June 1970, a historic Sakrand Hari Conference in village Sakrand, district Nawab Shah was organized by the Sindh Hari Committee. This conference was headed by Sheikh Abdul Majeed Sindhi; significantly, peasants from across the district and province traveled to attend this conference, many barefooted, for many kilometres.

Sheikh Abdul Majeed in his presidential speech said:

> This conference is a representative forum of all the peasants of the province, this is the conference of workers and peasants of the province. Our struggle is against the brutal policies and control of the Landlords. It is the peasant who has claim over the lands of Sindh not the Landlords, they must ensure their dominance and claim over their lands.[20]

The revolution had put an end to the vacillations and reluctance of the middle classes. Lawyers, doctors, engineers, artistes, scientists, intellectuals, poets, journalists and people from all sections of society that are used by the ruling classes in 'normal' times to perpetuate their rule, had come decisively onto the side of the proletariat. They jumped on to the rising tide of revolutionary ferment. One of the most important organized struggles at that time was that of the journalists.

Struggle of Left Journalists

The Pakistan Federal Union of Journalists (PFUJ) was formed on 2 August 1950 after a newspaper workers' convention was held in April 1950 in Karachi. In this convention newspaper workers from the Delhi Union of Journalists also participated. The leading figures at that time were Minhaj Barna and I.H. Rasheed.

The PFUJ's past history is marked by memorable milestones

such as the 49-day long strike in 1949 in the daily *Sindh Observer*, Karachi, led by the Sindh Union of Journalists which later played a leading role in the formation of the PFUJ in 1950, the strike at the *Times of Karachi* in 1954, the daily *Anjam* Karachi in 1966, daily *Kohistan* Lahore in 1969, the hunger strike led by the PPL (Progressive Papers Limited) workers union and innumerable other struggles.

In 1959 due to the demands of the PFUJ the first wage board was formed which declared a first wage award in 1960. It was decided that wage award would be announced after every five years but a second wage award could only be announced in 1969, a direct result of the pressure generated by the revolutionary upsurge of the masses from below.

With the advent of Ayub Khan's Martial Law regime the press in Pakistan suffered the greatest setback. The regime introduced the blackest law 'The Press and Publications (Amendment) Ordinance, 1963'. It started its invasion of the Fourth Estate by taking over the independent newspapers, *The Pakistan Times*, *Imroze* and weekly *Lail-o-Nahar* belonging to the Progressive Papers Ltd. and owned by the well-known Left leader, Mian Iftekharuddin, under a Martial Law Ordinance. Not content with these actions the regime went further and brought into existence what came to be known as the 'National Press Trust' (NPT) by taking over at least fourteen established national dailies and weeklies. It was obvious that the NPT was established with the aim of coercing the press and setting loyalist and conformist unions to be followed by others. It was in this period also that the news agency, the Associated Press of Pakistan (APP) was taken over by the Ayub government. The aim for the public consumption was to "improve the financial and administrative affairs of the agency". But the real purpose was to control the dissemination of news.

The PFUJ opposed and criticized all these dictatorial measures. It called for a joint action against the Press Ordinance, formed a joint committee with the APNS (All Pakistan Newspapers Society) and CPNE (Council of Pakistan Newspapers Editors) and observed a countrywide protest strike on 9 September 1963. However, the APNS and CPNE (the two are the same commodity except the name and the label) disassociated from the Joint Action Committee and accepted the government's proposal to frame a so-called 'Code of ethics'. For more than three decades these two organizations have belonged to the owners of the media in Pakistan. These billionaires ruthlessly suppress and exploit the journalists and other workers of the media industry. While the government assured that it will observe a "moratorium" on the use of the Press Ordinance, very soon violated its assurance and banned the daily *Ittefaq*, the opposition paper published from Dacca, under the Ordinance.

By the mid-1960s *Ittefaq* had emerged as the virtual voice of the people of East Bengal. Tofazzal Hossain's post-editorial column 'Rajnaitik Mancha' (political platform) earned great popularity in East Pakistan. Consequently, the government of Ayub Khan censored the publication of the paper from 17 June to 11 July 1966 and then again from 17 July 1966 to 9 February 1969. Tofazzal Hossain, the editor of the paper, was detained several times. This triggered a nationwide strike of journalists. Ittefaq was revived on 10 February 1969.

Minhaj Barna writes in his article on the history of the PFUJ:

> 1968 was a significant year in the history of PFUJ in regard to its struggle for freedom of the press. The entire period of 1968 and beginning of 1969 (Ultimately ending in a new Martial Law of General Yahya Khan) was marked by a great upsurge of the people against the autocratic rule of General Ayub. Desperate and frustrated, the Ayub regime resorted to more and more repressive measures. The noose around the press was further tightened. After banning the daily "Ittefaq" in 1966, the government closed down the weekly "Purbani" Dacca and weekly "Chattaan", Lahore. It detained journalists without trial, withdrew allotment of official advertisements to "Nawa-i-Waqt, Lahore, "Ibrat", Hyderabad and "Pakistan Observer", "Azad" and "Sangbad" published from Dacca. Besides, it resorted to the obnoxious system of "press advice", which was made a regular practice and its scope was enlarged even to day to day functioning of newsmen and newspapers.
>
> The Federal Executive Council (FEC) of the PFUJ in its meeting held in Karachi from December 15 to 17, 1968, reviewed the situation and adopted a detailed resolution, observing: In recent months the functioning of the national press as a constructive and democratic

> instrument of public opinion has become almost impossible. The situation has deteriorated to such an extent that people have lost faith in the printed world and the position of the journalists as watchdogs of society has been compromised. The FEC believes that this constituted the greatest peril the national press has ever faced and, therefore, affirms that restoration of press freedom has become ever more imperative than ever before. It maintained that the present situation was the accumulated result of a series of repressive measures adopted over the last decade to stifle the press.
>
> The FEC however noted with satisfaction that the working journalists throughout the country in keeping with their traditions of struggle for press freedom had shown that they had risen to the occasion. During the last two months they had shown that they would never be cowed down. The various meetings, demonstrations, rallies and processions organized during this period and the successful countrywide strike on December 10 had again demonstrated their determination to resist the onslaught on press and carry their struggle for the press freedom through to the end. In this regard the FEC appreciated the cooperation of press workers, calligraphists, proof readers, and hawkers who had joined hands with the journalists in these demonstrations, and expressed the hope that this unity of the newspaper employees would grow further (...)

Minhaj Barna continues:

> (...) This period was also marked by physical attacks and violence by the minions of law and order on the one hand, and political opponents of the regime on the other. The targets were reporters, press photographers/and even newspaper offices all over Pakistan, particularly at Dacca, Karachi, Lahore and, Rawalpindi. In Dacca, the offices of "Morning News" and "Dainik Pakistan" were burnt down as a result of mob fury. Both papers were the property of the government controlled National Press Trust (NPT). The offices of the daily "Unity" and daily "Insaf" of Chittagong, and the daily "Kohistan" of Lahore and Rawalpindi were attacked.[21]

With the advent of General Yahya's Martial Law perhaps a vicious and sinister smear campaign was launched against the PFUJ under the direct patronage of the regime's Information Minister, General Sher Ali. Pampered by the military government some of the reactionary political leaders and vested proprietary interests organized a concerted attack against the leading and active members of the PFUJ. They were assisted in their designs by a couple of dailies and one particular weekly from Lahore. They started clamouring for what they called a "sweeping purge of all communists and anti-Islam elements" from the newspaper industry, radio, television and other institutions. These were the same people who had welcomed the takeover of the *Pakistan Times* and *Imroze* by the Ayub regime. One of the prominent leaders like Nawabzada Nasarullah Khan of Majlis-e-Ahrar orientation went so far as to claim that "most of the journalists in newspapers, particularly in the NPT papers, are 'reds', and, therefore, should be thrown out to safeguard Islam and ideology of Pakistan".[22] The weekly, *Zindagi* wrote a series of articles against the PFUJ and its leadership and appealed to the Martial Law authorities to dismiss them from jobs. It is interesting to note that these detractors of PFUJ (some of them were paid for their service) were never tired of giving lip service to democratic values and freedom of the press. Another powerful strike of the PFUJ started on 15 April 1970 which lasted for 10 days both in East and West Pakistan.

The 1970 ten-day countrywide strike may be remembered for a number of significant reasons. The main reason of course was the intransigence and refusal by the proprietors' body (the All Pakistan Newspapers Society) to accept and implement the award announced by the Second Wage Board for 35 per cent interim relief after a decade-long wage freeze. At that time the Wage Board and its award was legally meant for the journalists alone and did not cover other employees of newspapers and news agencies and yet the APNS was not prepared to accept and implement it. It was because of the APNS's refusal to implement the Second Wage Board Award even after losing their petitions in the High Court that the PFUJ had to take strike action.

In desperation the fourteen newspaper editors and proprietors issued a joint statement a few days before the strike began alleging that the strike was inspired by "Communists and Maulana Bhashani". They asked General Yahya's Military Government to intervene and take action against the PFUJ and its leaders under Martial Law Regulations.

Another significant aspect of the 1970 strike was that for the first time it provided a joint platform of action for the entire newspaper workers community-journalists, calligraphists and press workers. As the first and second Wage Board were for journalists alone, PFUJ repeatedly asked the government to either form a separate Wage Board for other workers of the newspaper industry or include them in the board meant for journalists. The PFUJ's argument was that a newspaper was produced not only by journalists, but by the collective labour and effort of all the employees of a newspaper establishment who worked under the same roof, were paid by the same employer, and equally affected by vagaries of socio-economic conditions including the price hike. It was for this reason that the PFUJ's four-point strike charter included the demand for payment of the interim relief to the non-journalists employees also. It was because of the united struggle of the newspaper industry workers that the strike was successful and the employers were made to pay the interim relief not only to the journalists but to the non-journalists employees as well.

After this strike of 1970 about 250 journalists including office-bearers and active members of the PFUJ and its affiliated unions belonging to different newspapers and news agencies in West Pakistan were dismissed from their services by the managements in collusion with the authorities led by the then Information Minister, General Sher Ali. The journalists thus dismissed belonged to such leading newspapers as the *Pakistan Times*, *Imroze*, *Morning News*, *Jang*, *Nawa-i-Waqt*, and *Mashriq*.

The office of the *Ittefaq* was burnt down by the Pakistan army on 25 March 1971, and consequently from that day the publication of the paper ceased. However, the *Ittefaq* was revived from 21 May 1971 under the surveillance of the Pakistani government.

Serajuddin, a renowned journalist in Dacca was abducted on 10 December 1971 and later killed by religious zealots. He was President of the East Pakistan Union of Journalists (EPUJ) in 1964-65 and Vice-President of the Pakistan Federal Union of Journalists (PFUJ) in 1970-71.

Even during the ferocious Zia dictatorship the journalists were in the forefront of the struggle. They were one of the first sections of the resistance who were publicly flogged and lashed by the military regime for demanding the right of free expression.

On the other side of the ideological spectrum, industrial and business circles moved to support the conservative religious parties, the Nizam-i-Islam and the Jamat-i-Islami, as Ayub's position weakened. These parties began to insist that Ayub ought to stay for an interim period to ensure a smooth transition to the political leaders of the country a position that was also urged by S.M. Zafar, Ayub's Minister for Law and Parliamentary Affairs. On 2 March 1969, Mian Tufail Muhammad, Acting Amir of the Jamat-i-Islami, announced that his party "opposed the exit of Ayub at this stage, as it would sabotage the desires of the people expressed through the Round Table Conference (RTC)".[23]

The response of the Regime during the fourth phase centred on the Round Table Conference, which met on 26 February and

RETURNS IN MILITARY CANTONMENT AREAS
NA ELECTION, 1970 (Percentage of votes cast through postal ballots)

Cantonments	Muslim League	PPP	JI	Other Islamic	Ind	Others
Wah	3.2	67.2	16.7	5.2	1.9	5.8
Jhelum	21.2	61.2	7.1	5.6	1.4	3.6
PAF Bases Area	11.6	37.8	11.9	13.1	25.5	-
Sargodha Cantt.	8.0	58.3	8.8	8.1	16.9	-
Shorkot Road	-	67.6	-	22.8	9.6	-
Lahore Garrison	29.2	58.2	-	-	0.7	11.9
Lahore Cantt.	25.7	64.7	-	-	0.7	8.0
Sialkot Lines	7.2	72.3	8.4	8.8	3.1	0.2
Sialkot Cantt.	20.8	55.7	8.0	14.6	0.7	0.2
Gujranwala	23.4	67.4	7.5	1.7	-	-
Multan	-	55.9	-	44.1	-	-

(Philip E. Jones, *PPP Rise to Power,* Oxford, 2003, p. 324)

again from 10 March to 13 March. On the final day of the RTC, President Ayub accepted the two demands on which the opposition leaders had been able to agree—direct adult suffrage and a parliamentary system—and directed that a constitutional amendment to this effect be drafted. These concessions, however, failed to halt the Movement. The masses refused to accept the stage of bourgeois democracy, the revolution had propelled the working classes towards a socialist transformation. The bourgeois opposition who wanted to derail the revolution on 'democratic' lines was cast aside by the movement.

Ferment in the Army

There is little information, for obvious reasons, about the repercussions of the 1968-9 movement within the armed forces. However, in the abdication of Ayub Khan on 25 March 1969, dissent within the armed forces was an important factor. The reformist and compromising policies of General Yahya Khan's regime also reflect pressures from within the armed forces. One of the factors of waging a war and whipping up Pakistani chauvinist frenzy, mainly in West Pakistan, from where the bulk of the armed forces came was not just to distract the revolution in society but was also intended to dissipate the dissent within the army. After all the army in the last analysis is a reflection of the society from which it is derived. But the situation was so explosive that they had to actually go to war and even to lose half of the country to preserve and safeguard the rule of Capital. We have quoted from some works of army generals that give vague accounts of tremors within the armed forces, later on in this book. A more subtle proof of which side the garrison was on, was reflected in just a few results of postal ballots collected from some of the Military Cantonments in the 1970 elections. The wave of revolutionary socialism that was linked to the PPP had also engulfed the consciousness of the workers in uniform, the soldiers and lower ranks of the armed forces. Philip E. Jones was somehow able to dig out some of these results which he has produced in his work *PPP Rise to Power*.

This would tend to support reports that the officer corps, as a group, did not vote for any one political party. The GHQ was concerned about security and political implications that might result if the whole army vote was made public. Possibly, also, the GHQ wanted to shield the troops from the ideologically Left tendencies engendered in the volatile election campaign.

The known results are important because they support claims that the PPP enjoyed strong support among the ranks of the Pakistan Army, a fact that greatly strengthened Bhutto's leverage in the manoeuvring in the negotiations after the election with the Yahya's military regime and Sheikh Mujibur Rehman. But above all these results reflected the revolutionary ferment within the armed forces of Pakistan.

During the upsurge there were several incidents of army officers refusing to fire at the charging crowds and processions of the workers and the students in the cities. There were several occasions when the army and police deployed to crush the protests actually sided with the protesting masses. Several middle-ranking army officers were court martialled for their support of the revolutionary demonstrations and strikes. Such was the revolutionary fervour that heavily armed troops had to retreat when the workers demonstrations defied their authority with their will and determination unleashed by the revolution.

One of the incidents in Karachi graphically illustrates the situation. A retired army officer who was a major at the time of the 1968-9 revolution on condition of anonymity narrated the following to the author in 1996:

> In February 1969 I was in Karachi. I was deputed to disperse a huge workers demonstration on the Karachi's most famous avenue, the Bandar Road (now M.A. Jinnah Road). There were at least 50,000 workers from different unions and factories of Karachi in that demonstration. It was being led by left wing labour and student leaders. Near the Empress market a tank squadron comprising of perhaps 16 tanks was lined up blocking the avenue. The tanks were giving aggressive signals by the movement of their gun barrels. I was with few army officers clad in war outfit standing in front of those columns of tanks. One of the officers approached the leaders asked them to retreat and disperse the demonstration in an aggressive militaristic tone. The workers refused point blank. The workers kept on marching with the thunder of the slogans of a socialist Revolution now resonating even louder.

> The Army officer again approached the leaders. The threat in the tone had some what softened. On the blank refusal again he drew a line with a white chalk on the black tarmac a few feet ahead of the demonstration and warned that anyone crossing that line would be immediately shot. The rage of the workers was now intense. The demonstration with red flags with yellow hammer and sickle signs and banners with slogans like 'Struggle till socialist victory', moved on. When the demonstration crossed the line, the officer drew a second line, then the third, the fourth and the fifth line. The demonstration had crossed all the 'dead lines'. The columns of the armoured cars and tanks had now started to roll back, we had to retreat. Myself and my officer colleagues felt so feeble. We could not fire upon our own people who were struggling to end their grievances and sufferings. There were shouts of jubilation and thunderous applause by the crowd. A sense of victory was almost palpable among the workers involved intensely in this historical display of the strength and courage of a proletarian unity. The menacingly huge vehicles of the Pakistan Army's armoured corps had failed to terrify the workers and disperse the procession.[25]

From such incidents it becomes so clear that in the fervour of a revolution, such is the enraged spirit and bravery of the working classes that they psychologically almost conquer the fear of death. Here the state had been defeated in one of the most significant battles of the class war fought by the Pakistani proletariat during the 1968-9 revolution.

Several soldiers now have reminiscences of the discussions with high-pitched revolutionary zeal that went on in the military barracks throughout the nights after 'light off'. They were seething with vengeance against the brutalities and insults inflicted upon them by their commanding officers and the generals. There was an overwhelming support for socialism expressed by the soldiers on these private but rampant discussions.

The movement of the students and the youth had electrified the whole society. The workers were taking over factories and brought the country to a halt through their magnificent 'wheel jam' strikes. The agrarian workers and the poor peasants had seized the lands of the feudal aristocracy and were burning their luxurious palaces and mansions built with the blood and sweat of the toilers of the soil. This movement in the countryside was a huge reservoir of support and source of courage for the proletariat in revolutionary struggle. The involvement of the soldiers and lower ranks of the armed forces would have made the decisive strike to defeat the system of drudgery and exploitation of the toiling masses of Pakistan.

Had a revolutionary party been there to mobilize and organize that support of the army ranks then the outcome of the 1968-9 upheaval would have been a victory for revolutionary socialism. This would have changed the course of history.

NOTES

1. Trotsky, *History of Russian Revolution*, (Pathfinder), p. 17.
2. The British Papers, (Oxford), pp. 734–739.
3. The British Papers, (Oxford), p. 743.
4. Roy Fox, 20th of November 1968.
5. The British Papers,(Oxford), p. 775.
6. The British Papers, (Oxford), p. 795.
7. Interview with the author, September 2008, Lahore.
8. Ibid.
9. Stanley Wolpert, *Zulfi Bhutto of Pakistan*, p. 126.
10. Ibid, p. 127.
11. Ayub Khan, *Ayub Khan Diaries*,Thursday, 28 November 1968, (Oxford), p. 287.
12. Ibid, Sunday, 8 December 1968, p. 289.
13. Dr. Mubashar Hasan, *The Crises of Pakistan and Their Solution*, pp. 49–55
14. Ayub Khan, *Ayub Khan Diaries*, Sunday, 9 March 1969, (Oxford), p. 305.
15. Ibid, Thursday, 20 March 1969, p. 308.
16. Bashir Bakhtiar, interview with Philip E. Jones at the Labour Hall, Nisbet Road, Lahore, 31 October 1973, published in *PPP Rise to Power*, p. 166.
17. Feldman, *Crisis to Crisis*, p. 261.
18. *The Pakistan Times*, 19 March 1969.
19. Interview with author, September 2008.
20. Sakrand Conference, Weekly *Lail-o-Nehar*, Karachi, 19 July 1970.
21. Minhaj Barna, *A Movement called PFUJ*, www.pfuj.info
22. Ibid.
23. *Dawn*, 03 March 1969.
24. Philip E. Jones, *PPP Rise to Power*, (Oxford), 2003, p. 324.
25. Interview with the author, June 1996, Rawalpindi.

Five

WITNESSES TO REVOLUTION

Veterans of the 1968-9 Upheaval

Men make their own history, but they do not make it just as they please; they do not make it under circumstances chosen by themselves, but under given circumstances directly encountered and inherited from the past. The tradition of all the generations of dead weighs like a nightmare on the brain of living. And just when they seem involved in revolutionizing themselves and things, in creating something that has never before existed, it is precisely in such periods of revolutionary crisis that they anxiously conjure up the spirits of the past to their service and borrow names, battles cries and costumes from them in order to act out the new scene of world history.

—Karl Marx (1815–1883)[1]

Millions of workers, peasants and students had actively participated in these gigantic events of the 1968-9 revolution. A whole generation had entered the arena of history to change their destiny in Pakistan. They had fought to the finish, and played their utmost role in the revolution. Many of the leading activists have passed away in the last forty years. Some of the veterans who are still around have a strong nostalgia and pride of participating in those stormy events. We were able to meet up with a few of them. Some of these comrades are long-standing friends of the author.

A series of interviews and discussion with some of these prominent leaders and activists of the movement revealed details of the revolution perhaps hitherto never printed in any work on this movement.

USMAN BALOCH (Karachi)

One of the most militant figures and workers' leaders of the 1968-9 revolution in Pakistan was Usman Baloch, who acquired legendary character during the course of the revolution. A labour leader in the shanty towns of Karachi, he became a legend when the revolutionary events exploded on the arena of history. Still a lot of heroic stories are related to this man, some of which he denies. In an interview with the author he narrated the memories of those heady days with a spirited nostalgia.

At the start of the decade of the 1960s he was a young man whose father was working in Gregs Salt Company in Karachi and was a union leader there. He lived in the shanty town of Lyari, which was home to thousands of workers, most of them belonging to informal sectors. His father and his colleagues often discussed matters of the unions and their disputes with employers which were keenly heard by this young man.

This was a time when there were no legal rights for workers and the employers had all the powers to exploit the labourers. If someone resisted this oppression he was called a traitor of the fatherland and a sympathizer of India. Like most other workers and youth of that area Usman was also inspired by the revolutionary ideas of socialism and had a keen interest in Marxist literature. He had read Lenin's *State and Revolution* and *What is to be Done?* at an early age. The subsequent events in his life proved to him the real character of the State as described by Lenin.

The event that inspired him along with many others was the general strike of workers in Karachi in 1963. This strike continued for many days and workers from most industries participated. It had a deep impact on the consciousness of the workers. An important lesson of this strike was the real character of trade union leaders who betrayed the workers in their struggle.

Workers were determined to fight for their rights but their leaders capitulated to the brutal civil administration. Usman told us that the "leaders of the movement came in a police van and appealed to workers to end the strike". Later on the all-powerful Deputy Commissioner of Karachi S.K. Mahmood authoritatively dismissed all agreements between workers and the management and said that his orders shall prevail. This capitulation of the leaders to the State authority shattered the confidence of the workers in them. Also this strike could not link to the common people outside the industrial area and was not able to gather sympathy of the masses. After the strike not only was the State against the working class but the public opinion also turned against them.

Another important incident narrated by Baloch was Ayub Khan's visit to Karachi Shipyard in 1967 to inaugurate a new Naval Warship. A grand ceremony was arranged to welcome the president and an exquisite dinner was to be served to the presidential delegation. Before the inauguration the workers of Karachi Shipyard put forward their demands for better wages and labour conditions. At that time Ayub was in his full grandeur and decorum as Field Marshal. He got furious by this behaviour of workers and simply rejected their demands. This invited the rage of shipyard workers who overturned all the dinner tables and the porcelain crockery was thrown into the sea. They also raised slogans against Ayub.

Usman Baloch's other important venture was forming the labour union in KANUPP (Karachi Atomic Nuclear Power Plant). In those days it was being built with the support of the Soviet Union and it was being considered an important strategic venture of the State. Any activity like trade unionism was strictly prohibited. At the same time the workers employed there for construction purposes were treated like slaves and given meagre salaries with no social security and other benefits. Construction workers were coming those days to Karachi from across West Pakistan including workers from Balochistan and those who had been working on the Mangla Dam project. Most of the traditional trade union leaders were afraid of these rowdy construction workers from the informal construction sector.

But Usman Baloch took the task to organize them and lead them towards the struggle for their rights. He told us that in the beginning it was a bit difficult to win the trust of these workers as an outsider, but with close association with them and meeting them daily in their free time, Usman not only gained their trust but also developed a warm personal affiliation with them.

In the period of a few months an informal union was formed with Usman Baloch as the president. When they went to the Labour Department for its registration they were disallowed on the pretext that no such activity can be allowed at a 'sensitive' site like this nuclear power plant.

However, workers had their own agenda and one evening they took over the plant and closed all the gates of KANUPP, with workers taking guard. The foreign nationals of the management were locked in their premises. This siege of the nuclear site lasted for a few hours and after that workers withdrew the control voluntarily. This was a clear warning to the State.

They had planned this only to show their power to retaliate. After this siege all the demands of 2,500 workers at the nuclear power plant, including the registration of their union, were accepted and their wages were given on time through the intervention of the Labour department. After the Martial Law of Yahya Khan, the Army took over strategic installations, but KANUPP was captured by this regime one month before the coup.

Usman Baloch was arrested on 10 October 1969 with 62 other workers, while he was organizing the construction workers working at KANUPP. At the time of arrest he was bargaining with the management for giving more rights to the workers. He was sentenced to one year of prison. His popularity was the envy of many other trade union leaders, and to express their hatred other leaders called him a 'communist'.

Usman Baloch also had close connections with the construction workers of Lee Market, workers of Rasheed Textile mills and Valika Textile mills. He was not one of the mainstream trade union leaders of the time but with his close ties with workers and their families and because he used to live with them, he was one of the most popular labour leaders of his time. He was inspired by Lenin and used to publish leaflets and handbills among the workers on their current issues. Funds for these leaflets were collected from the workers, usually 50 paisa or 1 rupee from each worker when the average wage of an ordinary worker was Rs. 50. A special team of workers was deputed to collect funds.

Workers at that time were coming from various nationalities and far-away regions. Workers of various industries were not united on any one platform. There were various Trade Union Federations but they were almost indifferent to the problems of the daily life of ordinary workers.

Usman took the initiative in bringing the multicultural workers closer. Class unity was being developed among workers of different nationalities at the moment of marriage, death and other social occasions. He convinced the workers that it is important for them to attend the funeral or marriage of a worker whether he belongs to his nationality, caste, creed or not.

Another important step was the practice of saying goodbye to a worker who was going on leave. Usually workers from far-off Northern areas went on leave for two to three months after many years of hard labour. When they came back factory management didn't recognize their past service and they had to start anew. They had to plead hard to get their job back as there was no concept of leave and they had to start again at a lower wage scale. Their leave was also no respite for them. They had to work in their hometowns, mostly in remote villages to earn a living for those few months when they were supposed to be on leave. Their meagre savings were not enough.

The new custom of saying goodbye to one of their companions who was going on leave was introduced by Usman Baloch. It proved to be economically beneficial for the workers. One of their companions would give an empty sack to the worker who was going on leave to a far-off place from the industrial city of Karachi. Other workers came with things he would need for his stay in his home including sugar, tea, flour, cooking oil and other necessary items and fill his sack to the full. Also they would go to the Railway Station to see him off.

When these workers went to their hometowns they were proud that they had not come back empty-handed. They could also spend their leave a bit more comfortably. When any worker came back his factory management was forced to recognize him due to the pressures of his fellow comrades. When the manager would refuse to recognize him, the fellow workers would tell the manager that they have given him flour, sugar and other things from their own pockets and he was one of their colleagues. In this way he could get his job back. This was one of the several unique ways of developing a close cultural bondage amongst the workers.

Another such effort of cultural bondage was practised in the Zaibtan Textile mills, where Usman was the workers' leader. He raised funds from the workers and opened a canteen and a small hotel from the collected money. This canteen was run by workers themselves and with their collections became the centre of social and political gatherings. Workers from other nearby factories also came there to pass their free time and have discussions, play games and enjoy cultural activities. This small canteen grew bigger with the passage of time as more and more workers joined in. One could see dozens of workers sitting there at any time of the day, discussing their problems, sharing their joys and sorrows.

Important meetings also started taking place here when the movement started to pick up. The management tried various methods to shut it down but the workers' resistance defeated their plans.

An important struggle of this movement was when workers took control of the Valika Textile mills in Karachi in February 1971. Usman Baloch was instrumental in the takeover of the Valika Textile Mills.

He narrated the whole incident to the author. He said that in the beginning there were no intentions of going to that extent but it was the momentum of the movement and the rising gigantic spirit and proletarian determination that took the ordinary workers to take such courageous steps.

Saleem was one of the active trade unionists inside the Mills and was involved in various labour-related disputes with management along with Usman Baloch. On 14 February 1971 the management wanted the arrest of Saleem to punish him severely for his activities. Usman feared that if Saleem got arrested he would be severely tortured and that would send a negative message to the workers of the mills. He also thought that an all-out strike would be premature.

There was heavy police presence inside and outside the mills on that day. They were keeping a close watch on the movement of Saleem and workers around him. One option for Baloch was either to somehow get Saleem out of the factory area and take him into hiding. If that was not possible he would ask the workers not to change the shift and the same shift would carry on. This would make it harder for the police to arrest him, as they wanted to arrest him during the shift change.

When the time of shift change came the management and police started to argue with Saleem and tried to provoke him. On seeing the heavy presence of police, workers were enraged and seeing the intentions of management they raised the alarm and closed all the doors of the factory and evicted the police from the premises.

After the occupation the first thing the workers did was to protect the chemicals, wool and cotton inside the factory so that nobody could damage it or put the chemicals on fire.

An urgent meeting was called of all the workers and it was decided that no personnel from management or police would be allowed to enter the premises and workers would run the factory themselves.

An administrative committee was elected in a short time and workers took control of the entire mill. All the supervisory staff was expelled and collective decision-making was initiated on various aspects of running the mill. Though this control lasted just a few days, it revealed the abilities of the workers to run the industry and was a precedent for workers in other factories.

In a factory meeting it was decided that old redundant machinery would not be sold but would be repaired and used again. Various decisions about the handling of accounts and wages were made, though they could not be fully implemented.

There was no theft from the factory during the whole episode. However, some policemen, as they entered the factory, looted some sweaters and socks. Workers collectively protected the entire factory and its materials as their own belongings.

After a few days there was a heavy crackdown of police and army and the management took back the control from the workers. Leading workers were severely tortured and others had to face dire consequences.

In 1972 workers took over many industries in Karachi. An important takeover was that of Dawood Mills in Karachi, which was led by Aziz-ul-Hasan and Riaz Ahmed. The government arrested these two leaders and they were presented handcuffed in court. The takeover lasted for 10 days.

Another important incident of the 1968-9 movement was when Usman Baloch slapped US Secretary of Defence Robert McNamara. McNamara had a meeting at the Orient Hotel in Hyderabad and was addressing a press conference when Baloch went there along with a popular labour leader of Hyderabad Ihsan Azeem.

The US Secretary of Defence was there with all the pomp and grandeur of the imperialist might. All the Pakistan government officials were behaving in a slavish manner. Usman narrated the episode.

He said that in the questions session he asked McNamara about the workers' struggles in the United States and about the martyrs of Chicago. The Secretary of Defence told him that the US government protected the right of workers and stood by their legal struggles. Usman argued that in the Bank of America, which also had its branch in Pakistan, unions were not allowed. Saying this he went closer and closer to McNamara.

McNamara was furious by this argument and said that, "We are not here to be engaged by every sucker." Baloch answered this insult by slapping McNamara on his face and said, "Down with US Imperialism". This created panic in the whole meeting and it was dispersed. Usman was again arrested.

An important incident in the labour movement of Pakistan is the incident of Feroz Sultan Mills, which took place on 6 June 1972 when the PPP was in power. While narrating this incident Baloch's eyes were red with anger and grief and he was breathing heavily.

The Union of Feroz Sultan was led by Kaniz Fatima, who was always envious of the popularity of Usman Baloch. Kaniz

Fatima was another labour leader of the Karachi shipyard workers. In an interview with the author she said that the workers were protesting for their wages. When she contacted the management, they told her that they could be given wages in two days and there is no serious problem. Then she condemned Usman Baloch for his 'adventurous' role in that struggle.

According to Usman Baloch workers of Feroz Sultan were in protest against non-payment of their wages, and the bonus that the management had refused to pay. The management was furious over the workers' attitude for the last many years and wanted to crush them.

They called the police and asked them to take strict action against the workers. When the police inspector confronted the protesting workers he opened fire from his pistol. This killed three workers on the spot.

The police and management took hold of two dead bodies but the workers were able to retrieve the body of Shoaib Khan. The enraged workers took the body towards Pathan colony, which was the locality of thousands of ordinary workers.

Usman Baloch came with a big rally of workers from the Zaibtan Textile mills and joined the workers of Feroz Sultan Textile Mills. There was a meeting of Trade Union Federations planned on the same day in which the demands of the workers were to be chalked out. The police attacked the venue and the Trade Union leaders went underground.

In this situation Usman Baloch was left on his own to lead the workers. When the body of the slain worker reached Pathan Colony there was a seething anger and resentment amongst thousands of workers who had gathered in anguish and protest. Usman Baloch asked them to take the body towards the governor's house. Workers marched behind the coffin. Led by Baloch they were in a violent mood and anything that came in their way was smashed. Any worker in Karachi who heard this news rushed to express their solidarity and support. The numbers grew more and more.

When this tide of rebellious workers started to move they faced heavy contingents of police pointing their guns towards them. As they tried to leave the Pathan colony, the police opened fire. Three more workers were killed. The police announced that whoever tried to get out of the area would be killed.

The militant mood of the rally was ready to face anything while police had orders to stop them at any cost. They tried to terrify the rally. On this Usman went to the graveyard in Pathan Colony and asked the workers to dig 20 more graves.

He said that it was just to boost the morale of the workers. We gave the message that we shall die rather than give in. The picture of 20 open graves was published in the daily *Mashriq* the next day.

Then came the PPP government and ministers and officials. They said they wanted to negotiate and end all this matter in a calm way. Many workers had been arrested by that time. Usman said that he was confused whether to go for negotiations or not. Workers were asking him not to go, that they would arrest him and torture him severely. They might even kill him.

He went on, but for him it was the start of a new government of the PPP and any of his actions at this time could give them the excuse of turning away from the pro-workers' programme.

Negotiations took place between Usman Baloch and PPP minister for Labour affairs Sattar Gabol, who was elected from Lyari, the hometown of Usman Baloch.

Gabol knew very little about the problems of labour. During the negotiations whenever Usman raised a new issue, he asked to go to the toilet. He asked Gabol if he was having some serious kidney problem. At a certain moment when he went to the toilet, a waiter came to serve tea. He told Usman in Balochi, as in front of other government officials he couldn't speak openly, that a pimp of the bosses was sitting in another room who was advising Gabol in these negotiations. That man was actually a famous Maoist leader of that era.

Usman asked the minister that the PPP should fulfil its promise of socialism or they would continue their struggle. He demanded electricity, roads, water, sewerage and other facilities for the residents of the Pathan colony and all the other workers' shanty towns. Gabol assured him that all demands would be met and the protest was ended. But the reformists couldn't fulfil any promises and it was a manoeuvre to dissipate the struggle.

This incident had a deep impact on the workers of Landhi, the SITE area and also on the workers of Hyderabad, Multan, Lahore and other places. The next day all trade union leaders accused Usman for his adventurism and opportunism. PPP leaders called him a communist, while Stalinists called him a stooge of the PPP.

A meeting was called by leaders of the official PNFTU (Pakistan National Federation of Trade Unions) in which Usman was accused of working against the cause of workers. PNFTU was actually against Bhutto before that meeting. But after that incident a meeting took place in Karachi between all the labour leaders and Bhutto in which they settled down on an agreement and decided to cooperate with each other.

They told Bhutto, "We are with you but you should talk to Usman". Bhutto then threatened Usman and asked him to calm down or face dire consequences.

That was the end of a long relationship between Usman Baloch and Bhutto.

When Bhutto resigned from Ayub's cabinet he wanted to become a mass leader. He usually took tips from those who already had roots in the working class and were popular amongst the masses. He also had close relations with the workers of the Pathan colony, Frontier colony and workers of the SITE area. Bhutto always used to get tips from Usman for getting support of the workers of Karachi.

Usman told Bhutto to go to Lyari and have lunch at a small workers' cafeteria, and after having lunch go to a nearby Paan (betel leaf) and cigarette stall of Azeem Bhai and ask for Paan. When you take out your wallet and Azeem Bhai tells you, *Are Bhutto Saab tu apna bhai hai, tere se paisa nahin le ga,* (Mr. Bhutto you are like my brother, I will not take money from you) then it would mean you have succeeded in winning the workers' support. If he accepts payment from you it means you failed to get it.

The next day Bhutto went to Lyari's dusty streets in his car. He had lunch with workers in that shabby cafeteria and then went to Azeem Bhai's kiosk. Bhutto had a very interesting chat with him and talked warmly with him. When he tried to pay for Paan and cigarettes, Azeem Bhai told him, "Forget it, you are my brother". This was the first time Bhutto got his footing in Lyari, which to this day is a stronghold of the PPP.

Workers often went to see movies at weekends in groups of 20 to 30. Usman advised Bhutto to come at the main gate of Capri cinema when the show ended and pretend that he was just passing by. Usman told him that he would come to him with his friends and that he would have a large gathering there.

The next evening Bhutto just came at the time of the end of the show at the front gate of Capri Cinema where a popular English film was being screened. Usman as a routine had 30 or so worker friends with him who had come to watch the movie. When he saw Bhutto, he loudly asked his friends, "Oh look, Bhutto is here, let's meet him". They all went towards him and all the crowd that had come to watch the movie gathered around Bhutto.

Usman Baloch to this day believes that socialism is the only way out of this misery of capitalism.

DR. MUBASHAR HASAN (Lahore)

Dr. Mubashar Hasan, an engineer by profession, was one of the founders of the Pakistan People's Party. The founding convention of the PPP was held at the lawns of his residence on the main boulevard, Gulberg, Lahore. Hardly any of the participants of the convention had imagined what the historical significance of this founding of a new party would be. This party was to become the largest ever political tradition of the masses in the history of Pakistan in such a short span of time. In the 41 years since then, not much has changed of Dr. Mubashar Hasan's house. The furniture, the structure and even the Volkswagen Beetle of those times are still very much there in their original posture. There is hardly any other house of the period along the Gulberg's main boulevard that has not been brought down and replaced by high-rise commercial plazas and the prices of land have shot up to astronomical levels, yet it is a feat in itself that Dr. Mubashar has been able to retain this house in its original form and shape. In a wide-ranging discussion with the author on the events of four decades ago at his house,

Dr. Mubashar gave his first-hand experiences of the 1968-9 revolution.

The gleam in his eyes was portraying the enthusiasm and nostalgia of those revolutionary memories. He explained that the founding documents and resolutions of the PPP founding convention had been worked on for more than a year. The railway strike of Jan-Feb 1967 had given a new impetus and hope to the revolutionary Left and most of the activists who felt suffocated and blocked by the Stalinist leaders were looking for an alternative revolutionary way out. These underlying currents led to the formation of the PPP and its socialist founding programme.

Dr. Mubashar gave details of how the founding document was formulated. It was mainly compiled from three papers written by Zulfiqar Ali Bhutto, Jalaluddin Akbar Rahim and Dr. Mubashar Hasan himself. Bhutto wrote mainly on the need of building a new party and the socio-economic and political crisis in Pakistan. Rahim wrote on the necessity of socialism and transformation of society. Mubashar wrote the detailed economic policies concerning health, education and infrastructure envisaged from a socialist perspective. According to Dr. Mubashar in all the sessions of the convention there were no religious rituals allowed, which used to be and still is the usual practice in Pakistani politics.

He also asserted that Zulfiqar Ali Bhutto, who was elected as the founding chairman of PPP, was more against the capitalists than the feudal landlords. This was of significance because the traditional Left supported the nascent bourgeoisie while Bhutto and the PPP came clearly against capitalism and called for a socialist alternative to the bourgeois regime and system.

However, it was clear from Dr. Mubashar's discussion that although most of the participants in the 1967 founding convention had little or no in-depth understanding of scientific socialism and Marxist philosophy and economy, still there was enormous enthusiasm for socialism in that historical convention. The convention was held under the rule of the hostile Ayub dictatorship and many hurdles were created by the administration such as denying any proper hall or meeting place where such political events were traditionally held. Hence the only choice was Dr. Mubashar's house. The convention was held in a semi-clandestine manner. The main reason was that the regime was so obtuse that it didn't imagine the impact of this new party on the events that erupted in the next few months. Ayub Khan himself undermined the importance of this convention at the time. In his diary he wrote:

> From official press reports it is said that Mr. Bhutto has held a two-day convention in Lahore to launch his so-called People's Party. Reports further said that it was a tame and childish affair. His major attempt is to misuse the student community, a dangerous game. But we are watching his activities. He will be dealt with in no uncertain fashion if he crosses the limit.[2]

Dr. Mubashar raised another important point in the discussion, i.e. that even after the abdication of Ayub Khan from power the movement did not wither away as is generally presumed. The movement had a decisive impact on the elections of 1970, which were held mainly to divert the movement on to the electoral plane from the revolutionary path it was treading upon. In the months preceding the elections, the PPP was rapidly expanding. In Lahore, which had a much smaller population than today, 450 branches of the party grew within weeks of the outbreak of the revolution. Certainly these were not the branches of a Bolshevik party as the rapidity of the expansion and the intense activities of the revolutionary upsurge did not allow much time for the education, organizational development and ideological preparations of the cadres and the party. It was more of a loose formation. It lacked ideological homogeneity, structures and democratic centralist methods of a Leninist organization. They were neither well-defined nor practised nor was the leadership prepared for nor expected such a rapid change in the situation. The enthusiasm for socialism was enormous but it lacked the in-depth understanding of the ideology and the strategy of the revolution that could achieve this goal.

Dr. Mubashar's view was that the branches of the PPP in Lahore were actually a form of soviets that had taken up a number of tasks to run society. They chalked out the different centres of crime, gambling dens, etc. in their respective localities and formed committees to keep the social order. This was actually a situation of dual power, where the State had a superficial presence, but in reality these People's Party branches were having control from below. According to Dr. Mubashar at least in Lahore it was so where he was the main leader of the party. These committees also drew up lists of different thugs and criminal gangsters and used the mass collectives to stop their crime and violence. The mullahs had very little or no social influence in the committees at the time. These committees were having even a greater control and command in the workers' quarters and the shantytowns of Lahore. The growth of these committees on the one hand defied the repression of police and the State forces while they maintained order and supplies of essential services and needs to the masses. These same committees later on became the main electoral machines that not only made the PPP victorious but also ensured the most non-controversial electoral result ever in Pakistan. This election led to the defeats of the politicians who were considered invincible and even surprised many workers and middle class candidates of the PPP who won in those elections. Bhutto had public meetings with hundreds of thousands of people who came from far-off places just to listen to his speeches that were becoming increasingly revolutionary in content.

Dr. Mubashar Hasan was himself a candidate from the North East Lahore National Assembly constituency, where 92 per cent of the electorate was the proletariat, mainly the railway workers and their families.

The PPP branches ensured a massive victory for Dr. Mubashar, who secured a huge 87,000 votes. The Jamat-i-Islami was second with 15,000 votes while the Stalinists could manage only 4,000 votes from perhaps Pakistan's most dense proletarian constituency. Dr. Mubashar got the highest votes in the country and he was the stalwart of a Party that was calling for a socialist revolution as the only solution to the problems confronted by the workers and peasants of the Islamic Republic of Pakistan.

ZAKIR HUSSAIN (Malakand)

In Pukhtoonkhwa still officially named as NWFP (North West Frontier Province) from the times of British colonialism, the wave of the 1968-9 revolution was as severe as anywhere else. Comrade Zakir Hussain was a schoolgoing boy when the revolution broke out in 1968. He was deeply affected and radicalized by mass upheaval at a tender age. In the next few years he became the leader of the students and youth wing of the Communist Party of Pakistan in Pukhtoonkhwa. In his discussions with the author, he explained how the students in Peshawar, Mardan and other main cities and towns of Pukhtoonkhwa took part in those events.

The initial spark came from the students in the universities, colleges and schools as had happened elsewhere in the country. But soon the freshly emerging proletariat had struck. There were strikes and occupations in several industries. The main factories where the workers were in the forefront of the movement were sugar mills in Mardan, Bannu Mills, Colony Textile mills in Nowshera, Charsadda paper and sugar mills, silk processing factories in Swat, several industries in Peshawar, Malakand and other industrial units in the province. In early 1972 there was a police strike that was so complete that it shocked the state. An important organ of the state in such a sensitive province had dared to revolt against the law. The lawyers of various district bar associations, doctors, engineers and several other sections of the society were in revolt.

The peasants' movement in Pukhtoonkhwa (late 1960s until early 1970s) was a natural outcome of the historical events in the process of a class upsurge. The movement was necessarily a part of the 1968-9 revolution. The factors behind this movement were development in content of the society, dictating an entirely new form of social relations with capitalist modes being introduced into the old system. This was breaking the intransigent cells of feudalism. There were widespread brutalities of the landowners on the peasantry and a widespread explosion of class contradictions. The movement though could not empower the peasants and it too fell prey to the counter-revolutionary manoeuvres, yet it brought about some fundamental changes in the very structure of the society. It was successful in breaking control of the feudals to exclude other segments of society to own land. It also succeeded in abolishing Begaar (forced labour without any wage). It proved a success in eliminating the ancient curse of bonded labour. The primitive forms of social subjugation of the peasantry were dismantled and it brought some relief from drudgery to the lives of the poor peasants.

In the subcontinent British colonialists, during their colonial occupation, operated through an installed feudal hierarchy. The shift of imperialism from colonialism to neo-colonialism yielded a new breed of bourgeoisie—the comprador bourgeoisie, which was reactionary in its character as a requisite of the assignments, allocated by their imperialist masters to them.

Areas of Pukhtoonkhwa that were under feudal productive relations experienced a lengthy wave of feudal cruelties. In the event of surplus production and historical developments, business currents brought about a change in the state of affairs and a change occurred in the psyche of the working peasantry. Just like the revolutionary upsurge in all other classes of Pakistan, the peasantry of Pukhtoonkhwa also struggled. Had it been channelled on a scientific basis, the revolutionary zeal of the peasantry could indeed have been led into the channels of a revolutionary change. The subjective factor was missing. The movement did succeed in creating new, smaller ownership of land. But this eventually only created a column of new landowners (kulaks) rather than a revolutionary change in the foundations of the agrarian society.

The movement included peasantry from rural areas of Pukhtoonkhwa. The connection with the urban industrial labour class and even middle classes was confined to a few rural areas. The class structure in rural Pukhtoonkhwa consisted of four main classes (i) landowners (ii) peasants (iii) agricultural labourers and (iv) lease-holders of land. The leaders of the movement had narrowed its base only in the peasants as its objectives remained confined to the interests of the peasantry and the programme was exclusive of the demands of other oppressed rural and urban classes.

Eventually these clashes of interests deepened the schism within the movement and none of the allied classes including the rural working classes (mainly agricultural workers), could be integrated in the mainstream movement. The diversity of interests among these naturally allied classes increased and there was hardly any unity. This isolation of the peasantry resulted in a very limited geographical expansion of the movement. The movement could expand to Charsadda, Malakand, and some portion of Swat and Rustam area of Mardan. The limited geographical range of the movement and a limited class inclusion caused another indictment to it; the reactionary forces dubbed it as a feud between local tribes. In Hasht Nagar (Charsadda), for example, it was called a fight between Ahmadzai and Mohmand tribes, in Malakand between Yousafzai and Roghani tribes and in Mardan between Yousafzai and Mohmand tribes. Hence the movement could not integrate itself with other revolutionary upsurges raging in the country.

The peasants' movement of Pukhtoonkhwa, although not triumphant, brought about a series of positive changes. It was one of the landmarks in the revolutionary process of 1968-9 and an inspiration for the future revolutionary movements of the working classes of the region.

In spite of all the drawbacks, the conflicts were fierce and bloody clashes took place between the peasant movement and landlords. In Malakand district a landlord Mukaram Khan and the peasant leader Mullah Mohammad Sadiq were killed in a clash. In Hasht Nagar a big landlord Vava Khan was defeated, his landed estates were besieged by the peasants and he was forced to retreat. Similarly in Dir and Swat owners of hundreds of acres of the land, known as 'Khans' had their landed estates taken over by the peasant movement.

MUNNOO BHAI (Rawalpindi)

Munnoo Bhai, a noted columnist and a famous playwright, was the Secretary General of Rawalpindi press club in 1968-9. He has been writing columns in mainstream newspapers on a daily basis for 55 years. He had organized many protest activities against the regime. He wrote his famous play Jaloos (Procession) inspired by a sit-in by the girl students of Rawalpindi in front of the entrance of the Rawalpindi cantonment. They wanted to cross Nala Lai bridge and go inside the military cantonment area but the police stopped them. They did a sit-in on the road for six hours when at last Nusrat Bhutto, wife of Z.A. Bhutto, came there and led the girls into the cantonment area.

While Munnoo Bhai was organizing a public meeting of the PFUJ in Liaqat Bagh, the information minister General Sher Ali approached him and tried to bribe him by giving 10,000 rupees. He returned this money with thanks. On this he was transferred to Multan.

While recollecting memories of the 1968-9 revolution he was enthused and told the author that there were hundreds of thousands of people on Mall Road in Lahore every other day, men wearing red turbans and women wearing red dupattas (shawls). Nobody here had seen so many red turbans and flags before that.

He recalled his memory of a public meeting in Ichra Lahore in which Jamat-i-Islami head Maulana Modoudi held bread in his one hand and the Holy Koran in his other and asked the people, "Do you want Roti (bread) or Koran?" The people replied, "We have the Koran in our homes, but we don't have bread".

After Bhutto's assassination, Munno Bhai met Nusrat Bhutto for an interview for the daily *Musawat*. She told him that when she met Bhutto the last time in his death cell in Rawalpindi Bhutto had asked her, "Why is the party not doing anything for me? I have done so much for the masses and the party." On this Nusrat replied, "Zulfiqar, you haven't left a Bolshevik Party outside so how do you expect that they will do anything for you?"

In another interesting anecdote Munnoo Bhai told the author that he was travelling by car on GT Road from Lahore to Jhelum with Zulfiqar Ali Bhutto during the election campaign in the summer of 1970. Mustafa Khar (later Governor of Punjab) was driving and Hanif Ramay (later Chief Minister of Punjab) was sitting on the back seat with Munnoo Bhai. When they reached the town of Gujarat there was a procession of shirtless workers from the local factories that stopped Bhutto's motorcade and asked him to give a speech. Some were lying down on the hot tarmac and blocked further movement. Bhutto was reluctant as they were already late for the public meeting in Jhelum. Sensing the delicate situation Khar persuaded Bhutto to come out and say a few words. Bhutto gave a fiery revolutionary speech and thrilled the procession. When he came back into the car and the motorcade sped off towards Jhelum, the chest naked workers were shouting slogans of "Socialism! Socialism!" and were beating their wrists on the bonnet of the car. When they passed them, after a few minutes Bhutto turned back from the front seat and addressing Ramay and Munnoo Bhai said, "We may not mean it but they really mean it!"

MAIRAJ MUHAMMAD KHAN (Karachi)

One of the main leaders of the movement of the 1960s, especially amongst students was Mairaj Muhammad Khan.

He was a symbolic figure of struggle for the youth in the Ayub era. He told the author in a recent discussion that he was a small drop in that storm, but a drop that loved dancing on thorns!

In this discussion he narrated some important events of his life. He is an old man now having serious problems with his lungs and cannot talk much and participate in activities. When he came in his sitting room for the discussion he was breathing heavily and had a severe cough. His sitting room is decorated with his large pictures addressing public gatherings of hundreds of thousands in several big cities of Pakistan.

At the end of discussion he told us that when he came for the interview he was thinking to finish it within 15 minutes. But when he started recollecting his memories on the momentous events of the revolution of 1968-9 he got so charged that he went on speaking for five hours.

He was a young boy studying in High School when he came to Karachi from a small city of Quetta. He loved to play football but also had some oratory skills. In his college there was a debating competition in which students from all the colleges of Karachi were participating. With his eloquent style and powerful language he won that competition.

Some activists of the Communist Party were sitting in the audience, who asked him to join the Party. After that his discussions with the communists began and thus started his thrilling journey on the road to revolutionary politics.

Mairaj Muhammad Khan turned NSF into a militant students' political organization that campaigned for the rights of students. In the elections of students' unions in 1957 NSF won in 90 per cent of the colleges and universities in Karachi. Its stronghold was Dow Medical College and DJ Science colleges.

Other main student leaders in Karachi were Hussain Naqi, Fatehyab Ali Khan, Khurram Mirza, Nafees Siddiqui, Ali Mukhtar Rizvi, Amir Haider Kazmi, Syed Saeed Hassan, Agha Jaffer,Wahid Bashir, Nawaz Butt, Johar Hassan and Ali Yawar.

Mairaj Mohammad Khan remained president of NSF until 1967 and was later replaced by Rasheed Hassan Khan (student of Dow Medical College Karachi) in a council session held in Lahore in 1970.

Mairaj then went into mainstream politics and by the instructions of the party leadership joined PPP after it had become a mass political force and Bhutto had emerged as a mass leader.

In the 1970 election campaign Mairaj was nominated by Bhutto as his candidate from Lalu Khait Karachi. He was very popular among the ordinary people of that area. During the Ayub regime he was often chased by the police and used to take sanctuary in this area. He told the author that when he was chased by police he ran into the streets of Lalu Khait and suddenly would enter any home whose door was open. To the people inside that home he introduced himself and would say, "I am Mairaj Muhammad Khan and police is chasing me". They gave him enormous respect and showed him the back door to run away. When police came to that house, those men and women were maltreated and tortured for harbouring Mairaj. But they never told them where he had gone.

He was tipped to win elections with a big margin from that area. But the Communist Party leader met him while he was in prison and asked him to return Bhutto's ticket and announce a boycott of the elections. Mairaj said that he was really surprised at this decision. However, he told them that though he didn't agree with them he would abide by the party discipline. Bhutto then nominated an ordinary man for this seat that lost to the Jamat-i-Islami candidate by a small margin of 5,000 votes.

Mairaj Muhammad Khan was made a minister without portfolio in Bhutto's first cabinet but both NSF and Mairaj fell out with the Bhutto government in 1973 when Bhutto started to compromise on his so-called Socialist agenda and the regime resorted to repressive measures.

In later years due to his differences with Bhutto, Mairaj left the PPP. He formed Qaumi Mohaz-e-Azadi and his own faction of NSF. And a once flamboyant student leader like Mairaj fell into political isolation, never to regain his political credibility and popularity.

On recollecting the memories of the incident in which two NSF students were killed by the police on 7 November 1968 and that sparked off the 1968-9 movement, Mairaj Muhammad Khan was very emotional.

He said that actually they were planning to take special measures to intensify the resistance movement in Punjab. However, even Mairaj had not expected that this police killing of students would unleash a revolution of such gigantic proportions.

PERVAIZ MALIK (Campbellpur, now Attock)

Comrade Pervaiz Malik was a young student and activist of NSF during the 1968-9 revolution in Campbellpur, now Attock. In an interview with the author he recollects his memories of that revolutionary period.

In 1968 when Ayub decided to celebrate his 'Decade of Development', NSF decided to condemn it and announced it as 'Decade of Decadence' and decided to organize a 'week of demands'.

After the incident of 7 November, there was a mass eruption of revolt. There was not a single city, town or village where the masses had not poured on to the streets to condemn the Ayub regime and yearned for a change of the system. The masses were not only protesting but were challenging the existing relations of production. They were not paying their rents of the houses and shops and passengers were not paying bus and railway fares.

A students' action committee was formed at Rawalpindi Division, which was organizing students of the whole division. When the leader of this action committee, Sheikh Abdul Rasheed from the Government Degree College union, was arrested, a shutter down and wheel jam strike was observed in the whole division. The BBC presented a report on it saying that after the strike the whole area was paralyzed.

The NSF was formed in Campbellpur during the same period and an organizing committee was set up. A district body was elected later in the District convention. Before the departure of Ayub Khan all the political prisoners booked under DPR (Defence of Pakistan Rules) were released. Four central leaders of NSF from Karachi were released from Campbellpur prison. They got a huge welcome and were brought to a public meeting in a huge rally. These leaders addressed the public gathering in which thousands of people had participated.

Pervaiz Malik remembered the names of three of them, Shehryar Mirza, Munir Uzair Saud and Kanwar Qutub ud din. The fourth was a student leader from Baloch Students Organization (BSO). They thanked the people and students for this huge reception in that area which was totally unexpected for them.

Three of these student leaders went back while Shehryar Mirza stayed on in Campbellpur until the departure of Ayub Khan. During his stay he went to various public gatherings and meetings in Rawalpindi Division and gave revolutionary speeches. They also took advantage of the presence of Shehryar Mirza and made NSF very active in their area. This was the only organization which had an office in the city that was also shared by the PPP.

They also met the leaders of Democratic Action Committee (DAC) at the residence of Mahmood Hassan Minto. In this meeting Nawabzada Nasrullah, Maulvi Fareed Ahmed, Ch. Muhammad Ali and other such leaders of the Right wing were present. When Maulvi Fareed Ahmed tried to introduce Mirza to other people as a mass leader Mirza obstructed him and said, "What I am today is because of my organisation and ideas and in organisations personalities are not important". Mirza presented the demands of students to them and then walked out from there. On his way back Mirza told Pervaiz Malik and others, "These reactionary beasts are trying to secure the State and the system, we should not have any links with them. Their interests are antagonistic from those of workers. If there had been a revolutionary organisation today in the country then this revolutionary situation could have brought a socialist revolution in Pakistan".

After the abdication of Ayub Khan the power was handed over to Yahya Khan. The movement did pause but then continued again.

An important incident took place in Nowshehra College in Pushtoonkhwa. The police entered the College and opened fire on protesting students, which resulted in the death of Zahir Naqvi, an activist of NSF who was a resident of Campbellpur city. Perhaps this incident took place in October 1969. This killing caused a mass uprising in the city and huge rallies and demonstrations took place. The police used tear gas to disperse people but the masses kept on moving and at the end the police had to run away.

On the Chehlum (40th day after death) of Zaheer Naqvi a big public meeting was held in which hundreds of students from Nowshehra College participated. The police again cordoned the meeting. Some guest students were arrested. All the participants of the meeting marched to the police station, which forced the administration to release the arrested students.

MANZOOR RAZI (Karachi)

According to the veteran Manzoor Razi the railway workers' leader, Mirza Ibrahim (1905–1999) pioneered the trade union movement in Pakistan. When Mirza Ibrahim passed away on 11 August 1999, at the age of 94, he had spent almost a quarter of his life behind bars, besides having lived the horrors of the notorious torture cell at the Lahore Fort.

In 1924, Mirza Ibrahim moved to Rawalpindi and found employment as a brick kiln worker. Briefly, he also worked as a gardener at a British household. Finally, in 1926, he was employed at the railway workshops at Jhelum. It was this job at the railways that became his lifetime identity. His metamorphosis, however, occurred when he was posted to Lahore in 1930. Lahore was an important political and cultural centre even during the colonial era. Here he came in contact with the trade union movement and Left-wing activists.

At that time there were two unions in Railways. One was North Western Railways (NWR) whose president was a Britisher, J.B. Mills, a Railway Guard, while the General Secretary of that union was M.A. Khan.

The other union, United Union, which was a pocket union led by Chaudhary Muhammad Din Mirza joined NWR and was elected its president in workshops.

He later joined the Communist Party of India, became active in the trade union movement and was consequently elected as vice president of the Railways Federation. At the time, the federation's president was V.V. Giri, who was later to become the President of India. Jyoti Basu, the long-time communist chief minister of West Bengal, was also active at that time in trade union activities under Ibrahim's leadership.

The year 1946 was a revolutionary year in India. At the end of World War II, the government wanted to fire railway workers in their hundreds of thousands on the plea that with the end of the war their services were not required any more. On 1 May railway workers went on strike under the leadership of Mirza Ibrahim, who in those days was the president of the North-Western Railway Workers' Union.

On 1 May 1946 after a huge public meeting from 7 a.m. to 11 a.m. the wheel was jammed and the trains ceased to move. On 27 June 1946 the call for a strike was issued at 12 o'clock midnight. Many associated unions of the Federation detached themselves from the strike but Mirza intervened and formed a Strike Committee. As many as 96,000 workers voted in favour of the strike. Mirza Ibrahim was offered Rs. 10 million and a job as Assistant Works Manager in the Workshop if he dissociated himself from the strike. But he refused.

The government had to bow before the striking workers. The strike action not merely helped save their jobs, they won a twenty-rupees rise in their salaries.

Due to this activity Mirza Ibrahim lost his job five months before the partition in 1947. He was doing a job of water man at the time.

After the Partition of India in 1947, he became active in establishing the Pakistan Trade Union Federation (PTUF). The PTUF was affiliated with the Communist Party of Pakistan (CPP), and stalwarts like the famous poet Faiz Ahmed Faiz and C.R. Aslam were advised by the CPP to help the PTUF in organizing industrial workers. However, it was Mirza Ibrahim whom the PTUF elected as its president. Although Faiz's presence in PTUF ranks was symbolic, he was elected as vice president of the Federation. In 1951, he was implicated in the Rawalpindi Conspiracy Case and was tortured in the notorious Lahore Fort.

Manzoor Razi, a veteran of the struggle of the 1960s, described the Railway strike of 1967 at Karachi Railway Station to the author.

The Karachi railways installations had become a hub of revolutionary resilience of the workers. Red flags and revolutionary banners were hoisted on the top of the Railway station, workshops, locomotives and main gates of the railway premises. Marx and Lenin were studied and discussed in the study circles of the striking workers. The state had failed to intervene. There was a complete wheel jam and a revolutionary spirit was felt all around.

Manzoor Razi was a loyal lieutenant of Mirza Ibrahim and he spoke forty years later how the two-stage theory was responsible for the decline of such great militant workers' leaders in the electoral process of 1970s.

Mirza Ibrahim contested the elections in 1970, but this time his legendary role did not attract the voters amid the Bhutto bandwagon. The railway activists lobbied with the Pakistan People's Party (PPP) to nominate him as PPP candidate and it would have materialised, but Mirza did not want to contest elections from the PPP platform. Mainly because he professed the ideology of two stages and the PPP was at least verbally calling for a socialist revolution.

PROF. MOHD. YAHYA (Dera Ismail Khan)

The 1968-9 revolution reverberated in some of the most primitive regions of the country. In an interview with the author one of the veterans of this movement, Prof. Yahya from Dera Ismail Khan, narrated the events that unfolded around 1968-9 to the author.

In the D.I. Khan Region NSF and a local organization 'Dehqan Qalam' (peasant's pen) was campaigning for the awareness of class struggle amongst the masses. Before Bhutto came here Comrade Shaista Baloch, Hameed Khakwani and Comrade Haqnawaz Gandapur had participated in the founding convention of PPP at Lahore, in 1967.

Before Bhutto the left tradition of D.I. Khan goes back to Madan Mohan Malaviya, a comrade of Bhagat Singh. When he was being arrested he killed many and then himself in protest against Gandhi's non-violence to kill the revolutionary currents in the National Liberation struggle. Another comrade was Sarfraz, who was apparently in Congress but was a great admirer of the Bolshevik Revolution.

Many hurdles were created for sabotaging Bhutto's visit to D.I. Khan. Leaders of the Convention Muslim League brought twelve buses of hoodlums to disperse the crowd. A big banner was hoisted on which was written, 'Coward Bhutto Go back!' However, more than a dozen founding workers of the PPP were working day and night for his reception. They had erected welcoming gates from the stems of banana trees and were hoisting party flags, writing basic PPP slogans on the walls of the city.

When hooligans started tearing the banners of the PPP these few workers fought with them in the main bazzar. This was a fight between two classes—one group was representing the feudals, while the other represented peasants and workers. At last at the instructions of Haqnawaz Gandapur people lay down in front of the twelve buses to stop them from disrupting the meeting. Workers were fighting with sticks but in the end the whole bazaar was shut down.

On 31 October 1968 Bhutto was to address a mass gathering in Haqnawaz Park (then Jalal Park). Muhammad Nawaz Advocate had invited him to address the Bar while a workers' convention was arranged on 1 November.

The hooligans brought to disrupt the convention were forced to flee as the workers and peasants in a rising tide of revolutionary fervour came out with a vengeance against these intruders of the ruling classes. The masses were in a rage and at the moment when Revenue Minister Sarwar Khan of Patiala passed through D.I. Khan he was forced by the masses to salute the flag of the PPP. However, one tactic of the opponents was successful; Jalal Park, where the public meeting was taking place, was littered with water and garbage.

Deputy Commissioner of the area Sajjad Hussain was instructed to make all efforts to sabotage this political meeting, whereas on the other side the masses were desperately waiting to hear a leader proclaiming socialist change. Thousands of people gathered on a circular road anxious to see how the battle would end. When Bhutto saw that it was not possible to hold a public meeting at the declared venue, he took the procession towards the main bazaar. Bhutto climbed over a shop into the Shahani Manzil, the property of Shahani family of Bhakkar. Their gatekeepers tried to stop him but failed. The pictures of this speech are still on record. Bhutto along with his delegation and Shaista Baloch were in the Balcony of Shahani Manzil, which has now become a market. Haqnawaz was holding his gun below like a guerrilla warrior.

Bhutto spoke for only 70 seconds after which the police attacked the rally to disrupt it. Yet these 70 seconds brought about a big change in D.I. Khan. In his short speech he said:

> "Do you get flour here, do you get cooking oil?", and the masses replied "No!" He said, "Today sugar is dearer. The poor can't live a proper life. The PPP will give you all necessities of life. The PPP will give you bread, clothing and shelter through socialism".[3]

After that the police started to attack the crowd. Eyewitnesses reported that it was a barbaric baton charge that tried to disperse the meeting. For the first time in this city tear gas was fired and the violence spread all over the city. The masses were still present there in thousands, and after that the police started firing on the crowd. Many people were injured. Prof. Yahya himself had walked many miles to attend this historic meeting.

Bhutto went even to small towns and villages to arouse mass support. He visited Kulachi, Tank, Galoti and other places near D.I. Khan.

Ayub Khan had once said, "A spark started from a small city and the fire spread across the whole country". By this he meant the battle of D.I. Khan between the Convention Muslim League and the PPP. Before that a student was killed in Rawalpindi. The whole country was resounding with the slogan "Asia is red".

Haqnawaz Gandapur was a zealous revolutionary and an inspiration for the movement. He was the founding member of the PPP and had attended the Hala convention at Makhdoom Talib ul Maula's place in Sindh. Haqnawaz was a socialist at heart and from the early stages of his life he had struggled against the feudal tribal chiefs.

When feudals started to enter the PPP he was angry with Bhutto and restored his own peasant party and went on to Mount Suleman, a hilltop at 12,000 ft, along with nearly two dozen people. They held study circles there and cooked their own food in big utensils. These utensils are still present there in which food is cooked every day in the memory of Gandapur and people get free meals from there. However, Gandapur returned to the PPP in 1969.

Gandapur took out a rally every Friday with socialist slogans written on banners. They used to block the main crossing in D.I. Khan and hold public meetings. The participants of the rally were mostly poor peasants of the area. The main speakers used to be Farouq Shaista, Safdar Bukhari, Zardad and Gandapur himself.

After Bhutto's visit, the PPP started to get a large following in the area. The die-hard workers went from house to house to discuss with people. They were being invited by people every day. The movement was growing and D.I. Khan was resounding with the slogans of socialism. Many feudals also joined the PPP to save their skin.

Haqnawaz was the provincial and central leader of the Party. He kept an onion and a piece of bread with him for food and went from one village to another to raise revolutionary ideas in the hearts of people. He gave lectures against capitalism and feudal tyranny and people kept on joining the PPP in large numbers. His lectures were always attended by a large audience.

He was arrested for burning a fundamentalist bastion, which was being used to train fanatics that often attacked PPP workers and youth, but after a 14-day hunger strike, the government had to release him along with his comrades. He became a popular leader and all the feudal lords of the area feared him. They thought Haqnawaz would destroy them. On the night of 25 August 1970 he was coming back after attending a socialist study circle at the village Budh when some people killed him. The regime claimed that he was struck by lightning on that stormy night.

This was a great shock for the poor people of the area and the entire city remained closed for three days. Even the shops of eatables and medicines remained closed. At his funeral thousands of people came to attend the last rituals of a martyr of the revolution. Bhutto came the day after his funeral and went to his grave. Some people tried to spread rumours that he was killed by lightning but the original story, which his son Tufail Gandapur told Prof. Yahya, was that he was killed by the goons of local feudals.

On the second death anniversary of Haqnawaz Gandapur, Bhutto built the Gomal University in the backward region of D.I. Khan.

The Park where Bhutto couldn't hold a public meeting during his first visit was named Haqnawaz Gandapur Park. This became the place of revolutionary public meetings.

Sohna Khan Baloch had a tea stall in the main bazaar of D.I. Khan at that time. If any mullah came there to have tea he would pass comments on him and then praise socialism. He made the environment of his tea stall always political and also linked their personal problems with the system of exploitation.

For example, if the rent of his place was increased, he would say it is because the owner of his shop is a Mullah and would add that Bhutto will nationalize his small hotel. Kalu Khan Maniari was in the same condition. He was a progressive person and had a shop. He propagated socialist ideas amongst people at a grass roots level. His subject was always the latest statement of Bhutto in the newspapers. His son Buland Iqbal later joined the NSF and was very active.

Those days Miraj Muhammad Khan was at the peak of his popularity. An NSF office was established in Phatia Bazaar near the post office. This office was established by a person named Qamar Iqbal who had a romance with the slogans of "Asia is red". *Musawat* (Equality) and the socialist magazine *Nusrat* (Victory) could be found in this office. Comrades like Sheen Aadil, Yunas Thaeem, Daood Khan, Buland Iqbal, Tasleem Feroz, Salah ud din Gandapur and many other trade unionists used to come to this place.

These people always took out a rally on May Day with red flags and at a main crossing of the city held a public meeting saluting the martyrs of Chicago. They demanded better wages and living conditions for workers. Many of them were arrested later on for their agitation activities and were sentenced to seven years.

The events in the D.I. Khan region show that the idea of a socialist change had inspired the masses in the most primitive areas of Pakistan.

SHAHID MAHMOOD NADEEM (Lahore)

Shahid Nadeem is a playwright, a theatre and television director producer, a Left-wing intellectual and a political activist in his own right. He is one of the stalwarts reviving progressive theatre in Pakistan. His anti-establishment plays exhibiting class struggle on the television since the late 1980s have been extremely popular amongst the masses. He was recently sacked as Deputy Managing Director of PTV, the national state television network, by a Right-wing boss installed by the Zardari regime. In the contribution to this work he narrated his experiences, which are quoted below.

I graduated from Government College in 1967 and joined Punjab University for my Masters in Applied Psychology. GC was housed in a magnificent Gothic building and was famous for its educational records, sports, debates and discipline. GC students were not supposed to indulge in politics or get involved in agitation or street protest. I was among the students who cheered General Ayub Khan when he visited GC to inaugurate its Centenary celebrations.

The Punjab University New Campus was another world. It was a social and cultural island as well. It was open, liberal and somehow the monitoring agencies appeared less overbearing. The much larger presence of girl students was both a distraction and source of inspiration. The lawns around the cafeteria and the path along the canal were ideally suited for romantic rendezvous. Students came from varied social classes, ranging from the urban elite to village students from remote parts of the country, from dare-devil car-driving spoilt brats of top industrialists or feudal families to burqa-clad timid but hard-working females. There was space and demand for Marxists study circles and tablighi preaching circles. Alcohol was easily available, poetry was rampant and heated ideological debates were well attended. The students were passionate, committed, eager to express themselves and hoped for a better tomorrow. It was a melting pot of ideas and cultures.

I found the atmosphere very inspiring and mind-opening. I started becoming politically and socially aware and got interested in taking part in the process of change. Some of us set up a discussion group 'Nae log' (The New People) where we read stories, poems, essays and had serious political discussions. I read my first short story at this forum. It was at the 'Nae Log' meetings that we got introduced to some Left-wing teachers and some socialist intellectuals who frequently visited the campus. They were an important influence on some of the uninitiated students like me who were ready for radicalization but needed a catalyst. Prominent among them were Aziz-ul-Haq, Aziz-ud-Din, Khalid Mahmood and Anis Alam.

That was the time when we realised that the Punjab University was without a students' union. The Union had been banned by General Ayub Khan's government some years ago and had been replaced by indirectly elected societies. This was a miniature version of the basic democracy system introduced by the General at the national level. Some of my friends and I felt cheated and insulted for being deprived of freely electing a representative to an empowered students' body. The existing political wings of political parties had meekly accepted the banning of the union and there was no platform from where a campaign for the restoration of the union could be launched.

Punjab University was being ruled by an autocratic Vice-Chancellor, Hameed Ahmad Khan, who was a mirror image of Ayub Khan. He was a very powerful VC and believed in very strict old-fashioned policy of discipline through fear and tight control. Teachers and students dreaded his wrath. The Students Affairs department had become the intelligence and punishment arm of the management and kept a close watch on the students' activities. No one dared to talk about the union. I initiated dialogue with some self-proclaimed revolutionaries. They were not interested and found revival of the union meaningless. I did not give up and talked to apparently non-political non-serious friends. I found a couple of volunteers there.

We set up a clandestine Students Union Revival Committee and started distributing pamphlets and sticking hand-made posters. The most dramatic incident was at the exhibition at the Psychology Department. The VC had come to inaugurate the exhibition. When he went back he had a bundle of 'Revive the Union' handbills in his pocket, which I had inserted when he was keenly examining the psychological instruments at my stall. When the VC emptied his pocket at home, he hit the roof. The Head of the Applied Psychology Department was summoned and taken to task. He was told, "You have only seven boys in your department and you can't even control them". Like most psychologists, the Applied Psychology Head, Dr. Ghulam Jilani, was a nutcase himself. He almost had a nervous breakdown.

The union revival movement was now getting off the ground. We were able to organize small demonstrations in the campus, raise slogans and have emotional speeches challenging the dictator ruling the University and the dictator ruling the country. Students from different departments were slowly joining the protests. Even some left-wing activists had also seen the light.

In the meantime elections for the societies were announced. Like the BD elections in the country, the societies were elections were indirect. Department representatives were to elect office-bearers of the societies who then would have elected an ad-hoc Committee. We had long discussions whether we should contest the societies elections or boycott them. Contesting would legitimise the process, boycotting could isolate the pro-union elements. I was for contesting on the grounds that if we succeeded in capturing a majority, we could expose the sham process and announce our support for the union. I was confident that our candidates would win. Finally, my position was endorsed. We contested elections on a pro-union platform and won most of the seats. Soon after the elections, we announced our support for the restoration of the union. A majority of the society presidents announced their support for my candidature as Convenor of the ad-hoc Committee. But before the elections could be held, momentous events took place in the country.

It was October 1968. The Fortress Stadium was the venue for week-long celebrations of the achievements of the Ayub dictatorship. Every day there were parades, exhibitions, and demonstrations paying tribute to the great dictator. Like many other institutions, Punjab University was instructed to provide a certain number of students to fill the stadium. Every day a number of departments were asked to send the students to the stadium. We had secretly prepared a song, not praising but condemning the dictator and what we called 'The Decade of Sadness'. We were seated in the Brigadiers Enclosure along with senior army officers and bureaucrats. When the parade started and the announcer began praising the great saviour, we began singing the song that was an adaptation of a famous film song. The opening verse was, 'We have suffered the Ten Years of Sadness. We have lost, not one, my friend'. The red faces of the army officers and bureaucrats were a sight worth seeing. They were shocked, embarrassed, and angry. They could have eaten us alive. But we were young students, boys and girls and every one was watching. Dr. Jilani received another hammering and had more fits of nervousness. He confessed to one of my class-fellows, "I have nightmares, I see him in my dreams". We were reading about dreams in our clinical psychology class and had a great time in analyzing the Head's dreams.

Our little protest movement for the restoration of the union was now taking on the form of a campaign for restoration of democracy. These were exciting and radical times all over the world. National liberation movements were gaining momentum. The anti-Vietnam war movement had caught the fancy of young peace campaigners. Radical students in the US, UK, France and Germany had shaken capitalist society. The dream of a world revolution seemed possible. We regularly followed the events in Europe and the clashes between students and the police. Another source of strength was the students' agitation in East Pakistan that was gaining strength. We regarded East Pakistani students as politically more mature and organized and admired their struggle.

Another force that was gaining ground was Zulfiqar Ali Bhutto, the young charismatic populist leader from Sindh. After leaving Ayub Khan's cabinet and forming his Pakistan People's Party, Z.A. Bhutto had adopted a quasi-socialist stance and had boldly challenged Ayub Khan's all-pervasive rule. Many among us admired Bhutto: he was young, charismatic, bold and left-leaning. I was one such youngster. The first article I ever published was about Bhutto, titled 'The Desert Flower'. When Bhutto arrived in Lahore by train after resigning from Ayub's cabinet, I was at the Lahore Railway Station to witness the historic and hysterical reception.

Then came November. The death of Rawalpindi Polytechnic

student, Abdul Hameed, provoked protests, first in Rawalpindi, then in Lahore and Karachi. As if the youth of Pakistan was waiting for an incident like that. Ten years of dictatorship, controlled democracy, persecution of political workers, widening of the gap between the rich and the poor, alienation of the smaller provinces and denial of freedoms for the youth had made the students ready for a remarkable political movement. We at the new campus were already warmed up because of the union revival and anti-decade of development activities. The Rawalpindi killing was the turning point. We decided to call for a march from New Campus to the Old Campus in the city, a distance of more than six kilometres, and were surprised by the response. A couple of hundred boys and girls, all charged up, waving flags and placards, willing to walk all the way to the Old Campus. The march was joined by students from FC College and some other colleges on the way. It took us over four hours to reach the Old Campus in the heart of the city. The march was well-organised and peaceful. This was the first New to Old Campus march which was followed by many during the movement.

We were now connected to the students from city colleges like MAO College, Islamia College, Dyal Singh College. We would start from the New Campus and march on the Canal Bank Road, turning on Upper Mall and reaching the Charing Cross or Regal Square. There we would be joined by students from other colleges. The area between Charing Cross and Regal would be taken over by the students. The smooth flow of traffic and orderly march by the protesters became the students' responsibility. I myself acted as traffic warden a few times. Controlling the flow of the traffic, making cars stop or go with a gesture of my hands was a strange and uplifting experience. I still remember that feeling of power standing on the box and telling the cars, scooters when to stop and when to move.

We were also establishing contacts with student leadership in Rawalpindi, Peshawar, Karachi and Quetta. Rawalpindi students, who were in the forefront in the beginning, were losing steam. They were not ideologically motivated or politically mature. But Karachi and Peshawar students were seasoned and organized and had political support. The East Pakistani student leadership was in a different league. They were fired by the nationalist and political ideals and had massive public appeal. We were inspired by them, overawed in fact. But there was a strong sense of solidarity with them. Whenever there was a severe police crackdown on East Pakistani students, they were arrested or killed, we would organize solidarity rallies and loudly expressed our support for them.

In West Pakistan Bhutto was becoming a national hero, leading the movement from the front. His Islamic Socialism slogan had become quite popular, especially among the youth. It provided a reasonable and safe compromise and did not force a choice between Islam and Socialism. Bhutto adopted a populist style that was a mixture of revolutionary rhetoric and 'desi' (local) bravado, and the masses loved it. He displayed a loud disdain for the rulers, made fun of them, mimicked them, insulted them, abused them and the crowds would go wild.

Bhutto's visit to Lahore gave a big boost to the movement. It was still a students' dominated movement but now pro-PPP students were playing a prominent part in it. Student leaders from established colleges were more prominent in making speeches, issuing statements, holding press conferences and holding talks with the authorities. But when it came to showing street muscle, confronting the police, playing hide and seek with the plain-clothes policemen, breaking the shop window glasses, the PPP youth were unbeatable. Their ability to withstand police beatings and tear gas was astonishing. It was only a matter of time before student supporters of other political parties also got interested in a movement they had called bourgeois. Now you could see party flags and political banners along with the non-party banners for an end to dictatorship and students' demands. The regular student leaders who had initiated the movement felt that political youth were hijacking "their" movement and giving it a party political colour. Initially students' demos and party demos were separate and had distinctly different characters. Soon this distinction began to disappear or appear irrelevant. One uniting factor was the indiscriminate police brutalities and arrests perpetrated on both types of protesters.

I had been elected General Secretary of the Inter-Collegiate Body which comprised of elected student bodies of the city and hence could claim to be the authentic democratic voice of Lahore students. The ICB formulated students' and minimum political demands and gave calls to students to wage struggle on that agenda. For a while ICB maintained its identity and clout but the movement was growing very rapidly. More sections of society were joining. More political parties were getting involved. NAP (Bhashani) and NAP (Wali Khan), Socialist Party, Mazdoor Kissan Party and Awami League had all come out. The National Students Federation and Nationalist Students Organization were actively participating. Trade union and other workers organizations had joined the movement. It was now looking unrealistic or even foolish to insist on a "students only" movement.

By now police were looking for me and I was learning to dodge them. I would suddenly appear in a big demo, make my speech and then under the cover of a group, disappear in the narrow streets of Lahore. It was fun but there was always fear of arrest and what happens afterwards. But I could not stop. The momentum of the movement, the expectations of others, the excitement of challenging a dictator was irresistible. Finally the arrest came. It was February 1969. I had gone into hiding knowing that I was wanted. But the administration had gone berserk by then. They raided my house in the middle of night in commando style. They entered my room through windows and back doors and turned the room upside down. They took my father into custody and on their way out beat up the son of our neighbours who had come out to see what was going on. When I learned that my father had been taken to the police station, I obviously had no choice but to turn myself in. I was received at the Civil Lines Police Station by an anxious DSP, Asghar Khan alias Halaku Khan. He asked me to sit on a stool and turned the table lamp on my face. "Who are your associates?" he asked pacing up and down moving his stick menacingly. I was bewildered of course. "Who are associated?" he fired the next question. I almost laughed at the grimness and contrived menace with which he uttered these lines. "He must have seen too many suspense thrillers" I thought. But Halaku was well-prepared.

At the end he had given the formula for a Molotov Cocktail bomb, which had been quite popular among the student radicals in France and Germany. "This book belongs to you!". He kept pacing and grilling me in a dramatic style but failed to get a confession out of me that I was Trotskyite revolutionary who was planning to bomb installations and had a secret network of comrades. Finally, he let me go to my solitary cell. I spent a couple of nights in the cell, which was totally empty. No bed, no blanket in the freezing February night. Even the windows and the door had iron bars only. There wasn't even a piece of paper except a piece of newspaper that had been used to wrap something. I spent most of the night in the attached toilet, which was warmer in spite of the unbearable stench. Imprisonment was a watershed for me, another bridge crossed, another fear overcome. We were released on bail on High Court orders after a few days but I was a changed person. The PPP 'jialas' (activists) who looked at the softy students leaders who were afraid of being beaten up by the police or arrested or throwing stones at the police and the shops, were now willing to give me a chance. I came up to their expectations when I joined them in invading the Punjab Secretariat of the Government. The GC-educated debater was now acting like a firebrand radical.

The change was not just in appearance and radical postures, there was a more meaningful change taking place, an ideological change. I had moved to the left in terms of my world view, my political beliefs. I had seen the glimpses of the proletarian power, the strength of the masses. By the end of February the workers had started pouring into the city, taking over the control of the Mall and the main city locations. Squares and roads where we, the students, had ruled, were now under control. The workers were followed by the peasants and farmers in early March. It was not happening in Lahore only. All over Pakistan, people had arisen. Massive demonstrations were taking place everywhere, in towns big and small. Clashes with the police were taking place as a matter of routine. Thousands were arrested, including most opposition political leaders who had risen from the Elective Bodies Disqualification Order (EBDO) graves (dug by Ayub Khan). Ayub Khan tried round-table talks with the opposition but it was too late. The flood waves of the peoples movement were unstoppable. In end March General Ayub Khan resigned but true to his military mindset, abdicated in favour of General Yahya Khan.

I, like many student leaders, had by now become convinced that change of the general was no solution; what we needed was a change of system, a democratic, just system, a socialist system. Soon the people became disillusioned with the Yahya regime and protests started. I was now a member of the left-wing NSF and Young People's Front, a small leftist group formed by Dr Aziz-ul-Haq. Bhutto and Bengali left-wing leader Bhashani were leading the challenge against the right-dominated Yahya regime. Jamat-i-Islami, encouraged by Yahya's Information Minister Sher Ali, decided that the leftists were their main adversaries and military rulers were their allies. In East Pakistan, Awami League and NAP were riding the popular wave while the Jamat was collaborating with the military government to check their march.

However, at least one of our key demands was met. The Punjab University Union was restored and the elections called. But very soon it became apparent that the Yahya regime wanted to hoist Islami Jamiat-i-Talba (the student wing of Jamat-i-Islami) on the University. When we protested at the rigged, manipulated elections, we were arrested again. This time we were tried by a summary military court. We challenged the court and bravely faced the trial. This time I spent a couple of months in prison. We were now a part of the left-wing popular movement for a democratic change. The time I spent in prison gave me a rare chance to meet political activists, hardened criminals and the poor hapless prisoners. It was like an internship after my University degree in political activism. Some of my prison mates became characters in my plays and the prison governance system gave me invaluable insight into the political and social system in the country. When I was released, I was even more determined to work for the revolutionary cause. I almost went straight to the legendary Toba Tek Singh conference of peasants and workers, a convention of red-capped workers, passionate students, fiery trade unionists, and socialist intellectuals, all committed to the cause of a revolutionary change.

October 1968–March 1969 was a historic period. It was the first Pakistani people's movement against a dictator, it was the first and last movement started and initially led by the students. The movement was essentially popular and left-wing and the right-wing forces remained inactive or active only in name during the movement. This movement radicalised a whole generation of students who later played an important part in shaping the future of Pakistani politics. Some of them are still in leadership roles in mainstream political parties. Others made valuable contributions in cultural, academic and literary fields. As artists, writers, poets, journalists, thinkers, political activists, trade unionists, they still carry the spirit of 1968 with them. The revolution we dreamed of never came. In fact there were major setbacks to the cause of world revolution. But 1968 changed our lives, it was indeed a revolution for me and many of my comrades and in our own ways, we are still carrying the flag.

JAM SAQI (Hyderabad)

Comrade Jam Saqi is one of the most renowned veteran leaders of the Left in the Indian subcontinent. He was the Secretary General of the Communist Party of Pakistan (CPP) at the end of the 1980s and early 1990s. He was incarcerated by almost every regime, especially the military dictatorships. He spent eight long years in prison during the despotic rule of General Zia-ul-Haq. Now a member of the IMT (International Marxist Tendency), he has been a household name in Sindh's Leftist politics. He is an eyewitness and an active participant in the movement of 1968-9, which shook the roots of Ayub Khan's regime and the capitalist system in Pakistan. Comrade Jam Saqi was an active student leader then. He shared his experiences of the movement with the author.

On 4 March 1967 a movement of the workers, peasants, students and other oppressed sections of society started in Sindh. Jam Saqi was one of the main organizers and leaders of that movement. The demands were for the overthrow of the dictatorship and radical social and economic changes in society.

Comrade Jam Saqi recalls that he was a student leader in the days when the movement broke out. They visited different colleges and universities mobilizing students and youth for the movement. He says that students and workers went on strike even if they were called for it in a simple press release in newspapers.

When the movement broke out, he was Secretary of the Communist Party of Pakistan's Provincial Committee for Sindh. The central leadership of CPP made a Talba-Mazdoor-Kissan-Rabta Committee (Students-Workers-Peasants-Coordinating Committee) to support each other's work and coordinate the struggles of different groups. The Sindh Hari (landless peasants) Committee founded by Hyder Bux Jatoi was giving them support.

Bhutto was already in politics, but he was not popular until the movement had surged. The movement gave him popularity because he came with the slogan of socialism. In return, the revolutionary fervour of the masses radicalized Bhutto more and more to the Left.

Jam recalls that the movement gave such an impetus to the masses that policemen and army men dared not degrade even a poor and helpless person in those days as was their routine before.

Jam Saqi said that the trade union of the workers of Pakistan Railways was one of the biggest and influential ones. In fact, the strike of Railways' workers in 1967 was one of the events that he still remembers in detail. It was a famous strike.

Another influential trade union was that of WAPDA (Water and Power Development Authority) workers. These two trade unions along with some others shook the roots of capitalist system and the state.

He remembers an event that when workers of Pakistan Railways were on strike, the authorities tried to defeat the strike by forcefully running the trains. The workers at Rohri Station laid themselves on the railway track to block the railway traffic. Such was the ferment and courage in those times.

Sections of WAPDA and Railways workers were in support of the then CPP, but their trade unions didn't follow the discipline of the party. Only one trade union federation belonged to the CPP, and it was APTO (All Pakistan Trade Union Organization).

On 14 February 1969 the alliance of Pakistan's Right and

Left wing political parties DAC (Democratic Action Committee) called a strike. The Communist Party also decided that it would participate in the strike, and would struggle for participation of the working class in this strike. Two leaders of the CPP, Shamim Wasti (a famous trade union leader) and Dr. Aizaz Nazeer were sent to attend the meeting of DAC. There, they didn't put the suggestion of the participation of industrial workers in strike. Thus, trade unions of workers called for strike on a different date. Had there been participation of industrial workers it would have become another successful general strike and the CPP could have gained wide support and become a force in those moments of mass upheaval.

Comrade Jam Saqi revealed in his discussion that during the movement when he was a student leader state agencies tried to corrupt him by offering bribes of different sorts. He was offered a scholarship in Dhaka University or Peshawar University. On his refusal he was offered the post of Deputy Commissioner if he only appeared in civil service exams. But he rejected all such bribes to corruption.

Comrade Jam Saqi said that in the days of the movement, the reactionary forces and religious fundamentalists were in retreat. Seeing the rage of the masses in revolutionary ferment, the mullahs and their political parties like Jamat-i-Islami never dared to confront the Left.

The reactionary religious party, the Jamait-i-Islami, had arranged a demonstration in Hyderabad in 1967. It had to march from 'Talak Incline' to the 'Gari Khata' area of the city. Comrade Jam Saqi along with a few more comrades came to know that they had plans to burn pictures of Gamal Abdel Nasser, the President of Egypt who had crushed the Islamic fundamentalists to stop their neo-fascist attacks on the Egyptian left. Comrade Jam Saqi with his comrades entered the demonstration and marched along with it. In the middle, they warned the Amir (head) of Jamat-i-Islami that if they burnt pictures of Nasser, they would not let them do it, and if necessary they would fight to stop it.

Hearing this, Jamat-i-Islami declined to burn pictures of Nasser. Jam said that although there was a whole procession behind them, the Mullahs did not dare to do such an act, in spite of the fact that he was with only ten comrades. It was because they knew that these student comrades were popular with the masses and if they would oppose them, people could interfere and come in support of the comrades.

Comrade Jam Saqi now thinks that the main weaknesses of the leadership of the Communist Party of Pakistan and the Left in 1968-9 was its ideological position of the two stage theory. Due to this they failed to understand the socialist character of the movement. Hence, the movement was taken over by Zulfiqar Ali Bhutto. The CPP and its leaders thought the movement was a mere reaction against Ayub Khan's regime, and was not a threat to the system. Though they actively participated in the movement, they failed to give a clear programme in accordance to its character, which was socialist in nature. This was a sheer blunder of the CPP leadership in Pakistan.

Bhutto tried to win several communists into the PPP, including Jam Saqi at that time. Bhutto had again offered Jam Saqi and Sobho Gyan Chandani party tickets in elections but they declined his offer.

Comrade Jam Saqi concluded on this note:

"The CPP couldn't understand the importance of the movement. Had they understood the theory of permanent revolution and prepared revolutionary cadres and youth, the CPP would have built a mass support rapidly and led the revolution and achieve a socialist victory in Pakistan. It was because of the Stalinist doctrine that they failed at this crucial juncture in Pakistan's history."

KHAWAR NAEEM HASHMI (Lahore)

Khawar Naeem Hashmi is a famous film journalist and bureau chief of Geo Television in Lahore. He played a leading role in the struggle against the Zia dictatorship. He was flogged publicly in Lahore by the military junta on 13 May 1978. His only crime was to demand freedom of expression.

He was a 10th class student in 1968 at the N.D. Islamia high school near Ichra Mor in Lahore. Later on he went to Islamia

College Civil lines. During the movement nearly 20 teachers and 50 students were expelled from the Civil Lines College for being socialist and against the Ayub Khan dictatorship. Famous among those teachers were Eric Siprian, Manzoor Hussain and Amin Mughal. These teachers founded their own Shah Hussain College at Lawrence Road. Soon it became the centre of political and ideological discussions and protests in Lahore.

While recollecting the memories of 1968-9, Khawar said that young college and school students were extremely energetic in those days. Membership forms of the People's Party were available for 25 paisa in those days. He told the author that although he was not adult enough to caste his vote he still became a formal member of the People's Party. He zealously participated in protests and strikes along with his schoolmates.

Khawar's father, Naeem Hashmi, was a renowned progressive actor of the 1950s, 1960s and 1970s. His acting career had started in Bombay before Partition, then from the 1950s most of his films were made in studios in Lahore.

Being a film critic and historian himself, Khawar also revealed the sharp changes in the cultural environment due to the advent of revolutionary conditions.

Poets, film, TV and radio artistes, painters, dancers and musicians, all of them were impressed by the revolutionary upsurge of that time and came out with the best of their talents with creations that became masterpieces of film and arts.

In 1968 more than a hundred feature films were released, 64 of them were Urdu films, which is the record number of Urdu films in a single year in the history of Pakistani films.

Prominent writer Riaz Shahid's *Zarqa*, released in 1969, became the first ever diamond jubilee film in Pakistan when it crossed 101 weeks in Karachi. This is still the record holder in popularity among all historical films on Palestinian resistance made in Pakistan.

This film was about Palestinian people who were suffering and struggling against Israeli occupation of their homeland. Lyrics of the film were written by famous revolutionary poet Habib Jalib. A famous song by legendary Mehdi Hasan, *Raqs zanjeer pehen kar bhi kiya jata hai* (One has also to dance wearing chains and fetters), broke all records of popularity.

Regional films were also at their peak with a large number of films being made in Pushto, Sindhi, Bengali and Punjabi. The artistes from East Pakistan were actually dominating the film industry in Lahore and were very popular in the whole country.

Not only in films but also in other forms of art this mass revolutionary movement infused a strong inspiration.

Sadequain produced some of his best paintings in those days when he executed giant murals at the Mangla Dam in 1967 and in the Punjab University Library in 1968. He had joined the Progressive Writers and Artists Movement in the 1940s.

Bashir Mirza was also portraying his emotions stirred by the upheavals in society with pen and ink. In the 1965 'War Series' he drew a number of 'Screams' directly on to the canvas pouring out his inner turmoil and the devastations of war. Though packing his work with explosive power he also exhibited considerable control over his medium, earning media coverage and raising public interest in fine arts. Another highlight of his artistic career was 'Portfolio of Pakistan' produced in 1967. Basically portraits of people of Pakistan from various provinces, these were sketched in pen and ink in a single tone.

Shakir Ali, one of the most remarkable painters in the history of this country inspired cubism at that time amongst the artistes of Lahore.

KANIZ FATIMA (Karachi)

In an interview in Karachi Kaniz Fatima narrated her story.

She came from a family of renowned trade unionists and Communists. Her father was a veteran member of the Communist Party of India (CPI) who was deputed to work in the Indian National Congress. He served 14 years of imprisonment for his anti-State activities. Her elder brother was also a member of the Communist Party.

Due to her political background she joined the National Awami Party NAP at an early age. Her first public activity was her supportive role in the 1963 movement of workers of Karachi.

The strike that started in the Security Printing Press in Karachi in 1963 continued for many days. Due to their compromising role the old leadership was exposed and discredited in this strike and the new leadership had emerged. Kaniz Fatima went there to express solidarity with the families of workers who were on strike for the last three months.

She gathered all the women and children of the area and brought them to Regal Chowk (Square) in Karachi to raise Jholi Fund (money collection tradition by spreading the long shirt to collect donations). Workers' wives and sisters were sitting there in veils carrying their little children. This raised not only enough funds but also sympathies with the people outside the working class area. On the third day when they were collecting funds, the demands of the workers were accepted.

Due to her interest in the trade unions Bhashani on his visit to Karachi asked her to work in his party's trade union bureau. Then she went to the Rasheed Textile Mills and other industries and started gate meetings. She also went to labour colonies and organized study circles. She was arrested many times during the Ayub regime and expelled from the city. During her disputes with industrialists life attempts were made on her many times.

In 1966, she led a large rally of women workers for the rights of labourers working in various industries.

Then the all-powerful Deputy Commissioner of Karachi called her in his office and said that he had all the powers and could destroy her. She replied by throwing a paperweight on his face and said, "I have all the powers". The next day she was expelled from the city and sent to Thatta, where again she organized the workers.

Her main strength was the union of the Karachi Shipyard workers that had a militant character. She also organized the municipal workers of Karachi in KMC (Karachi Municipal Corporation).

She went to East Pakistan, to attend Santosh Conference in which all the Left parties gathered to chalk out a new strategy. She was not allowed to leave the premises of Dacca airport by the government officials but the masses who had come there to receive her broke the doors of the airport and took her to attend the conference.

She came back to Karachi in 1967 and was involved in labour activities. Yahya Khan again expelled her from the city in 1969. She was elected president of the Shipyard Union in her absence and when she came back 7,500 workers welcomed her at the Karachi Shipyard. Her role in the 1968-9 movement was not as significant as her stature in the Trade Union movement.

Though she was a leading figure among the workers and had a background of resistance against Ayub, due to the Maoist degeneration of the NAP she was not able to play a leading role. She was vice-president of NAP with Bhashani as President, and they had a pacifist stand against Ayub Khan's regime due to his deep friendship with the Chinese Stalinists.

In this interview with the author, she said that she herself persuaded Bhashani to go to China and broker a deal between Ayub and the Chinese government. "At first Maulana was not ready. He was in Karachi and was very ill. I was taking care of him and along with that persuading him to go to China. At last he agreed and I called Islamabad and told the officials that Maulana is ready. We were very excited".[4]

After this meeting with Mao, Bhashani abandoned the agitation against Ayub, and went back into his rather modest boathouse dwelling from which he never came out again. The bourgeois nationalist Mujib ur Rehman and his Awami League got hold of the movement in East Bengal on a platter.

A veteran trade unionist from PIA G.M. Anjum told the author that all the unions were going on strikes against Ayub except the unions led by Maoist parties. An example is the union of PIA led by Tufail Abbas.

Fatima also cited an incident about the Kissan conference in Toba Tek Singh. She said, "I was sitting along Maulana Bhashani and Mirza Ibrahim on a cart wheel while going to Toba Tek Singh. A group of young boys came to us holding flags of the PPP and raised slogans, 'Bhutto, Bhashani Bhai Bhai', (Bhutto and Bhashani are brothers). This made Maulana very angry. He snatched the flags from those boys and threw them away and said, 'Bhashani cannot become a brother of a feudal and a landlord, I will become brothers of peasants and workers'."[5] This incident shows the zigzags between opportunism and adventurism.

In the 1970 election she contested elections from the platform of NAP and came third while the candidate of Jamat-i-Islami won in that constituency in Karachi.

After losing the elections, Bhashani asked her if guerrilla war is possible in Karachi. I replied, 'no, it's not possible here, maybe in Balochistan and some areas of NWFP'. Bhashani replied that then revolution is not possible here.[6]

ILYAS KHAN (Multan)

Ilyas Khan, a revolutionary Marxist from Multan, explains the events of Multan in those revolutionary days.

Multan was also the hub of many revolutionary struggles and protests. In the historic conference of Toba Tek Singh many caravans from adjoining rural areas of Multan participated with hundreds of peasants travelling under the leadership of people like Taj Longah, Rabnawaz Chawan, Nur Muhammad Chohan, Parvez Aftab, Malik Altaf Ali Khokhar and Mahmood Nawaz Khan Babar.

In Multan workers took control of many factories, which included Allah Wasaya Textile mills and Gul Ahmed textile mills. These takeovers were led by Khan Muhammad Nisar, Aziz Niazi, Parvez Aftab and others.

Sheikh Rashid has written in his book *Jehde Musalsil* (Permanent Struggle) that he convened a meeting of the workers and peasants of Punjab and decided to take over all factories and lands in the province. Bhutto was in Dacca at that time and when he returned he was angry with Rashid on this act and rejected takeovers. In Faislabad Mukhtar Rana and his sister were leading factory occupations.

A party conference by Bhutto was convened in Hala, a city in Sindh, which is an unforgettable event in the history of Pakistan. A debate about the upcoming elections took place in that conference. Some Left-leaning leaders were demanding revolution, a destiny of the party instead of elections (Inqilaab ya Intikhab). They raised the slogan 'Barchi ya Parchi' (ballot or spear). However, due to the stronghold of Right-wing leaders it was decided to go for elections.

The capitulation of some of the PPP Left leaders to Bhutto's personality also led to this policy of degeneration.

KARAMAT ALI (Karachi)

Karamat Ali is a veteran trade unionist, a muralist, pioneer of the Indo–Pakistan people's initiative for peace and an active participant of the 1968-9 revolutionary movement. He was one of the first proclaimed Trotskyists in Pakistan. In an interview with the author he narrated his reminiscences of those heady days. He is the founding director of PILER (Pakistan Institute of Labour Education and Research).

> The 1968-9 movement against the decade old dictatorship of General Ayub Khan was perhaps the greatest mass mobilization in the history of Pakistan. It was unique in that it was initiated by the students and later energized and sustained, for almost six long months, by an unprecedented participation of labour.
>
> Given the nature of its movers, the social and political content of the movement had a clear stamp of the working classes from the very beginning. Its demands and slogans were unambiguous expressions of the aspirations of the workers, peasants and the lower middle classes—for a life of dignity, social justice and equality, and freedom for all. These were often stated in very direct demands for establishing a socialist order in the country.
>
> The movement began in the first week of October 1968 when the NSF (National Students Federation) decided to observe a Demands Week in Karachi. The NSF in those days was the most significant Left-oriented students organization. Even though it had split into two factions known as Mairaj group and Kazmi group, in 1966, this split was in fact a manifestation of the deep fissures that had occurred in the Left movement consequent to the Sino–Soviet rivalry in the communist movement across the globe. However this particular split materialized soon after the Tashkent Declaration was signed between Indian and Pakistani leadership in the aftermath of their war of September 1965. Since the deal was brokered by the Soviet leadership the supporters of Maoist Peking had to oppose it. In the event Mairaj group happened to be pro-Peking and the other one pro-Moscow in orientation.
>
> Meanwhile Ayub Khan's foreign minister Z.A. Bhutto had openly opposed the Tashkent Accord and was thrown out by his erstwhile mentor. Bhutto defiantly went public against the accord and the Ayub government and eventually formed his own political party—PPP, with

the help of radical student leaders like Mairaj Mohammad Khan and some trade union activists as well as some radical professionals among others. Bhutto put out a radical programme of economic reforms couched in socialist rhetoric coupled with extremely jingoistic anti-Indianism, and managed to attract large number of especially pro-Peking student and labour activists.

Despite these divisions the Left remained the largest influence over the labour and student organizations in Pakistan. In this backdrop the NSF gave out the call for a Demands Week, in response to the so-called Decade of Development celebrations of the Ayub Government.

A graduate student and a member of the NSF Mairaj group (by now known as Rasheed Group) I was at the time studying at the Jinnah College Nazimabad in Karachi, where the NSF had won the student union elections that year. Our college had some of the finest cadres of the NSF. There was Ziaullah, the president of the student union, Mumtaz Mehkri the great agitator of those times and of course Baseer Naveed to name a few.

On the first day of the demands week, we came to know of a seminar, to eulogize Ayub Khan for his achievements in the field of education, was being held at the auditorium of the Board of Secondary and Intermediate Education just opposite our college. The students marched into the building and disrupted the seminar. A procession then left for Burns Road where a large complex of colleges was situated and was traditionally a site of student protests. On the way large numbers of school and college students joined in and by the time it reached D.J.College the numbers had swelled to thousands. This was beyond all expectations of the organizers and set the tone for the days and months to come. The next six days saw protest rallies emerging from every nook and corner of the city. Schools and colleges remained shut. The Demands Week caused a big stir all around among all sections of the society in and beyond Karachi across the length and breadth of West Pakistan. There was hardly any direct contact among student between the two wings of Pakistan at that stage. After the Demands Week contacts were established with students and labour groups across the country. Thus the basis was created for a country wide movement culminating in the resignation of Ayub Khan and the imposition of a new Martial law by General Yahya Khan on 25 March 1969.

This great mobilization did not happen in isolation. It was indeed part of a process that began with student and labour protests, mainly in Karachi, since the early 1960s. The more important among these were the student protests against communal riots in Jabalpur, India, the movement against 3-year Degree course proposal (1961) when a group of 12 most prominent student leaders were expelled from

Karachi and subsequently from every other city they went to, till they landed at Multan and were able to mobilize students of Emerson College in their support. A fiery speech by the late Ali Mukhtar Rizvi so deeply motivated the audience that it decided to go on an indefinite strike, which eventually forced the Multan administration to allow the Karachi leaders to stay in Multan for as long as they wished to. I happened to be a first-year student at the college and came to know about the student movement through that interaction and forged linkages with the leadership which was picked up upon my shift to Karachi in 1963. I joined the NSF in 1964.

Similarly there were regular upsurges of labour during these years. The collapse of the state-sponsored, anti-communist trade union confederation APCOL, in 1962, paved the way for the formation of various independent unions as well as the emergence of numerous progressive labour leaders with close linkages with the shop-floor as well the student community. Thus the individual unit based mobilization of workers in 1962 led to the great struggle of Textile workers in March 1963. The strike by Railway workers in 1967 was an important milestone leading to the great upheavals of 1968-9. When the workers took over control of numerous large-scale Textile mills and other factories and forced the employers and the state to accept their long-standing demands.

Since the banning of the Communist Party in 1954, the left groups had to work mainly underground or within mainstream political parties. This coupled with continuing state oppression imposed severe constraints on them. However it must be recognized that they still managed to organize and radicalize both the labour and the student movement in the country. As observed earlier it soon managed to divide and fragment itself with concomitant negative impacts on the movements. However their greatest weakness lay in their incapacity to provide intellectual leadership.

The pro-Moscow and the pro-Peking factions both were almost blindly and slavishly following the ideological and strategic formulations devised by the Soviet and the Chinese leaderships respectively. In fact their perspectives were shaped more by the foreign policy imperatives of the two adversarial 'Socialist' states, than by an informed analysis of the society and the state.

They were completely sectarian in dealing with each other at all levels. There was no room for debate and discussion at inter or intra party level. While the Maoists were content with memorizing and holding the Red Book close to their chests, the Revisionists were religiously parroting the tracts coming out of the CPSU's publishing house. Both of them actively prevented their cadres from even touching a book published in the perceived rival's press!

> Similarly their relationship with Pakistan Government and the State were determined by its current relationship with Moscow or Peking respectively. In the late 1960s the Ayub government had become increasingly alienated from its patrons in the West specially the US and was per force leaning towards China and to lesser extent the Soviet Union. The leadership in the Left groups was quick to find shades of anti-imperialism in the government which should therefore not be opposed. Its brazenly capitalist, repressive and anti-people character not-withstanding!

Thus the 1968 student and later the labour movement began without the blessings of the Left leadership, even though it was being led by their own cadres. So, for example, the NSF launched the Demands Week at the behest of its former president Mairaj Mohammad Khan, as his party the PPP was keen on such agitation, while the top leadership of the Maoist party namely Tufail Abbas and others were yet undecided even openly sceptical about its advisability and success. On the other hand most of the Maoists found a natural affinity with Bhutto in his opposition to Tashkent accord as it had been brokered by the Soviets. Conversely the pro-Moscow groups developed a soft corner for the Ayub regime for signing the accord in Tashkent!

Thus when the 1968 movement erupted both the leaderships were taken by surprise. One very important leader of the pro-Moscow faction, Mr. Anis Hashmi summoned me to his house one October evening and gave me a long lecture that we people were being foolish in opposing the Ayub regime, as due to his closeness to the socialist camp the American CIA was determined to hound him out of power! I asked him if there was no substance in popular grievances against the regime? His answer was, 'Imperialism must be opposed above everything else'!

The Left leadership was evidently unable to grasp the pulse of the masses and their true aspirations. They therefore failed to take the initiative and benefit from this great opportunity to advance the cause of the teeming millions. This situation allowed Zulfiqar Ali Bhutto to monopolize the gains to the extent of West Pakistan. He expanded his organizational base as well as his mass support. He then very effectively converted and consolidated these gains in the form of his party's outstanding performance in the 1970 elections.

The initiators of the movement, on the other hand, failed miserably at all levels.

When General Yahya Khan imposed another martial law on 25 March 1969, there was no protest at all, as though the sole objective was to get rid of Ayub Khan!

> In the post-March 1969 period there were attempts at expanding the outreach of the NSF. A membership drive in Karachi alone enlisted over 10,000 members. However the Party leadership refused to allow an election through secret ballot to elect its leadership and insisted that the party must nominate leadership of all front organizations including students and labour!
>
> When the general elections were scheduled to be held in December 1970, the pro-Peking group came up with a ridiculous slogan-'Parchi Naheen Barchhi' (Spear, not Ballot) and announced a boycott of those contesting the election! Even Mairaj Mohammad Khan did not contest. Such ideological bankruptcy resulted in the loss of a big opportunity of sending close to 50 socialists/workers to the Parliament.
>
> To sum up, despite the avoidable failures on the part of Left leadership, the movement itself was a great emancipatory experience for thousands upon thousands of student and labour activists as well as for ordinary people who participated in it or witnessed it from close quarters.

The 1968-9 Revolution was a watershed in the history of not just Pakistan but the whole subcontinent. Never had the revolutionary torrents lashed throughout a country with such ferocity in the post-Partition period in South Asia. There was a classical situation of dual power for several months in Pakistan. Power had flowed down from the state and the grasp of the ruling class. In the streets, factories, towns, villages the masses had an intense feeling of that power. In spite of the fact that the revolution could not attain a socialist victory and overthrow of the rotten system, it changed the mass psychology in society. All methods of bourgeoisie rule, their ethics, morals, deceptions, mullahs, intellectuals, the media and structures were virtually smashed by the eruption of this mass revolt. It will go down in the annals of history as the greatest event of the hitherto history of the toiling masses of Pakistan. It set an example for the future generation that their ancestors had endeavoured to challenge the existing system and through this revolution they had brought the State and the ruling class to their knees. It was done here but will be repeated on a much higher plane, and this time it will not remain unfinished.

NOTES

1. Marx, *The Eighteenth Brumaire of Louis Bonaparte*, Foreign Languages Press, Peking 1978, pp. 9-10.
2. Ayub Khan, *Ayub Khan Diaries 1966-1972*, Saturday, 2 December 1967, (Oxford), p. 181.
3. Interview with the author, June 2008.
4. Interview with the author, July 2008.
5. Ibid.
6. Ibid.

Six

WAR, REPRESSION AND REFORMS

Lessons of a Derailed Revolution

A mere reform of the capitalist system is no longer a viable solution. The capitalist structure was rejected by the mass upsurge of 1969. The reformed system which is being demanded by the public and the politicians with minimum wages for all workers, participation of workers in profits, social responsibility of the capitalists, etc, may be in operation in Sweden or Yugoslavia but cannot be built in Pakistan through an evolutionary process.
—Dr. Mehboob ul Haq[1](1934–1998)

Field Marshal Mohammad Ayub Khan, the strongest ruler ever in the history of Pakistan, was forced to abdicate power on 25th of March 1969.

In his parting speech he had said:

> This is the last time I am addressing you as President of Pakistan ... The administrative institutions are being paralysed. The mobs are resorting to gheraos (siege) at will and get their demands accepted under duress. The persons who had come forward to serve the country have been intimidated into following these mobs.
>
> (...) It is my desire that the political power should continue to be transferred in a constitutional manner. In the conditions prevailing in the country, it is not possible to convene the National Assembly. Some members may not even dare to attend the Assembly session.
>
> (...) It hurts me deeply to say that the situation now is no longer under the control of the Government. All Government institutions have become victims of coercion, fear and intimidation. Every problem of the country is being decided in the streets.[2]

The Regime of Yahya Khan

His last speech resonates of the rising pressure of the revolution raging from below upon the state and the ruling elite. The main reason why he was urged to abdicate by US Imperialism, army red tape and the ruling classes was that they thought it would take the steam out the revolutionary situation which had engulfed society. Although the opposition bourgeois politicians and parties had named the 'Individual Ayub Khan' as the target of the movement, his abdication did not have the intended effect of dissipating the revolutionary movement of the workers, youth and the oppressed masses. The political leaders of almost all the political parties immediately went into negotiations and compromise with the new Military regime headed by General Yahya Khan. They were talking about parliamentary democracy, constitution, federative units formation in West Pakistan, equal rights of nationalities and other demands and tasks of the national democratic revolution. But the masses out in the streets, in spite of concession and reforms, were sensing victory and wanted it complete and total. They wanted to fight to the finish. The momentum and dynamics of the movement that had 'suddenly' burst into society were so intense that alarm bells were ringing in the echelons of power from Islamabad to London to Washington. The ruling classes and the state's elite were so terrified and shattered by its impact that they looked as if they had suffered a major defeat in war. Their fear knew no bounds, and when the movement showed little signs of subsiding after the fall of Ayub they immediately embarked upon reforms. At least on paper the labour policy of 1969 is supposed to be the most radical in the country's history and that too under the military dictatorship of General Yahya Khan.

As explained earlier the high growth rate of the economy under 'the Decade of reforms' of the Ayub regime did nothing to raise general living standards as had happened during the industrial revolutions in the advanced countries at the dawn of Capitalism. However, the economic burden of the growth had begun to bite the masses and workers who were absorbed in this Keynesian-based economic growth and development.

The imposition of Martial Law in 1969 was in response to a profound political and social crisis rooted in deep economic and social problems that were threatening the capitalist system itself. None of the established political leaders opposed its imposition. In fact they welcomed it at a time when the political situation had rapidly moved beyond their control with the masses, though leaderless, making a shattering impact on Pakistani politics. In view of the turbulent situation Yahya Khan made some conciliatory remarks concerning 'the need for social equality', harking back to speeches made on similar occasions in the past by his predecessors:

> In our circumstances, there is no alternative to planned socialist (our emphasis) economic development. But planned development cannot be isolated from the demands of social justice. The wide gap which separates the different sections of society must be narrowed, and the imbalance which led to social strife and discontent must be removed ... the objective of planned economic development should be the general raising of the standard of living all over the country and not the building up of a privileged class to the detriment and disadvantage of others.[3]

The turbulent period preceding the imposition of Martial Law had brought to the surface an unprecedented degree of militancy in the labour movement which the government needed to contain. As deputy chief Marshall Law administrator and overlord of the ministries of education, labour, health and social welfare, the first task that Air Marshal Nur Khan set himself under these circumstances was to win the confidence of the leadership of the labour movement.

To this end Nur Khan made some statements with reference to the socio-economic conditions under which the workers had never received fair treatment. A tripartite labour conference was called in Karachi to which labour leaders were invited to meet employers, government functionaries and advisors to formulate a new, more 'realistic' labour policy.

> This form of discussion served the important purpose of providing a forum where labour leaders could come together with those in power to express their grievances, give vent to their frustration and to achieve a sense of importance and equality with employers and government representatives.[4]

This was a new experience for many of them and something that was unthinkable during the Ayub period. This move by Nur Khan in reconstituting the tripartite labour conference and inviting numerous representatives of labour had an important psychological impact on the traditional trade union and labour leaders.

Many people involved in the movement against Ayub seriously expected that with his fall a new era would be introduced. As a result, the 'non political' labour leaders had high expectations about the government's intentions. The attitude of the employers on the other hand was openly criticized by the government to appease the workers in action. "Action", said Aristotle, "is the main principle of drama". In Pakistan it was the revolutionary drama being played on the stage of history. The wording of the threatened bourgeois state spoke volumes of its fear of the revolution.

> This by and large first generation of industrialists have failed to realise the contributions which a contented and well-motivated worker can make to productivity and profitability. They have looked upon trade unions as instruments of extortion rather than as institutions through which mutual give-and-take can lead to a peaceful resolution of conflict and possibly higher productivity.[5]

In the interest of 'harmonious labour relations' the government proposed the concept of a sole 'collective bargaining agent', purportedly to resolve the problem of rivalry and multiplicity of trade unions in the same establishment and to eliminate unrepresentative 'pocket' unions. Elections to determine which union would be elevated to the status of the 'collective bargaining agent' were to be held under the joint auspices of the government's labour department and the management of the establishment concerned. It is easy to see that once established as the collective bargaining agent, the leadership of a union would be in an advantageous position to perpetuate itself since rival groups and organizations would be deprived of the opportunity to operate legitimately until the next election, by which time such a rival organization would rarely survive the period of relative isolation from mainstream activity. However, it would appear that the practical implications of this legislation were not readily grasped by the labour leaders at the time.

There were two competing unions in Adamjee Cotton

Textile Mills, the second largest textile mill in Karachi. An election was held, as prescribed in the IRO, to choose between the two unions. The polls were conducted by the Sindh labour directorate on the mill premises. The union that had been the incumbent bargaining agent won the election to become the sole collective bargaining agent for another two years. The rival union criticized the labour directorate and the mill management for favouring the establishment union, alleging that the following means were used to prejudice its case:

The rival union was not allowed to operate inside the mill premises to canvass support.

The established union was afforded all facilities, and its workers were provided free food and drink.

The police prevented workers of the rival union from sitting in their union office outside the factory gate and removed their banners and badges from workers' shirts.

The mill management did not allow newsmen inside the mill premises to cover the polling process.

Thus, it was relatively easy for the management and the government to have a union of their choosing 'elected' as the collective bargaining agent with relative impunity for long periods of time. The goal of preventing illegal strikes and lockouts, which had always been foremost in the government's policy, was retained. The procedure leading up to a strike or lockout which could be considered legal was made extremely complicated and lengthy, and it provided for government mediation at a variety of possible stages.

If by some remote chance a legal strike or lockout could possibly materialize, the government added a further clause for restricting such industrial action if in its view the strike or lockout was causing hardship to the community, or was prejudicial to the national interest. It could then be prohibited by order of the government.

> A strike or lockout becomes illegal if it is continued against the orders of the federal government, the National Industrial Relations Commissions, a provincial government, a labour court or a tribunal.[6]

Zafar Shaheed makes a comment on this reformist manoeuvre of the new regime of Yahya Khan:

> In retrospect, some of the bold and 'liberal' declarations of the labour policy of 1969 sponsored by Nur Khan which misled certain people into believing that it was 'the most enlightened piece of labour legislation on the statute books' may be seen as a calculated move to create a structure of industrial relations that appeared to favour the interests of the workers even while its effect was quite the opposite. Also, it appealed to certain opportunist elements in the labour leadership now made vulnerable by grass-roots militancy.[7]

"The movement which workers had taken into their own hands was clearly not amenable to control through legal procedures and formalities. The industrial situation in this period was such that the President of the All Pakistan Textile Mills (owners) Association (APTMA) had occasion to complain to the government that the textile industry had been gheraoed (besieged) by labour since 1969.[8] In fact, there was a ban on political activities imposed at the beginning of Yahya Khan's government and this extended a fortiori to industrial activities. "A series of wide ranging retrenchments started in Karachi in 1969, coinciding with the imposition of Martial Law. In Karachi alone, 45,000 workers were retrenched during Yahya's regime".[9] The military court abounded with labour leaders and workers along with students and political activists. The practical labour policy of the government "seemed allied more with short-term objectives, aimed principally at minimising work stoppages and maintaining urban tranquillity".

This state of affairs indicated no fundamental change in government policy. Indeed, the 'caretaker' government of Yahya Khan was neither capable nor willing to undertake the fundamental changes in the economic system that were necessary prerequisites for nurturing the sort of amicable industrial relations which its labour policy purportedly sought. In any case, the government was too preoccupied with political campaigns for elections, which lasted from January to December 1970, and then with the political turmoil which led to war with India and the emergence of Bangladesh.

The PPP and Jamat-i-Islami

The imposition of Martial Law on 25 March 1969 provided Pakistan with only a short respite from the seismic forces set loose by the 1968-9 revolution. Indeed, there are many indications that the growth of religious obscurantism was related to efforts by industrial and big business circles to regain the leverage they had lost in the November Movement, to prepare for the elections and to derail the revolutionary mood of the masses.

In the major urban areas, the Jamat-i-Islami, abundantly financed by Saudi Arabia and indigenous industrial sources, became the cutting edge of the post-Movement reaction.

> As early as august 1969 re-emerging tensions between the JI and the PPP erupted into violence in down-country towns and in September there were serious JI-PPP clashes in Lahore, Lyallpur and Karachi.[10]

The Jamat-i-Islami began to talk about making Pakistan 'another Indonesia'. Part of the Left-Right polemic concerned the then US Ambassador to Pakistan, Joseph Farland. It was widely believed that he had been the US envoy to Indonesia during the Suharto coup against the Soekarno regime and the bloody massacre of the PKI. (In September 1965 in a coup against Soekarno, who was giving anti-imperialist statements, the CIA had used the Sarakat-a-Islam and other Islamic fundamentalist parties [some of them were sister organizations of JI in Pakistan] as an auxiliary force along with the Indonesian Army that carried out a genocide of the communists and their families. According to some estimate 1.5 million communists were slaughtered in the bloody counter revolution at the behest of US Imperialism.)

> Farland became the focus of the galloping anti-Americanism in Pakistan and the special bogey of the left.[11] On a number of trips around the country he was met by demonstrations. One of these occurred on 5 March 1970. "At the Nishtar Medical College, Multan, where the Ambassador Farland was surrounded by students shouting pro-Palestine, pro-Viet Cong, pro-China and anti-U.S. imperialism slogans."[12]

In Lahore wall posters announced the formation of a shadowy organization called the Musalman Sarfroshan ki Tanzim ('Organization of Muslim Fighters'), which warned all poets, writers and other intellectuals to behave or "we will break their pens, smother their tongues and smash their heads..."

The PPP and NAP-B leaders also identified a JI-backed organization of street fighters and claimed that the JI was using Nazi terror tactics to protect 'the interests of their masters', i.e., American imperialists, feudalists and monopoly capitalists.[13]

The anti-PPP campaign of the JI took a serious turn on 28 November 1969, when Bhutto was attacked by an infuriated, brick-throwing crowd of mullahs and youths at Sadiqabad in Rahim Yar Khan District. After this incident, PPP leaders began to make their own security arrangements. These evolved into the People's Guards, headed by Left-wing Major-General (retd.)Akbar Khan.[14]

The dismissal of Left activist teachers from Islamia College in May 1969 became a celebrated Left-Right issue. Islamia College was an institution run by the Anjuman-i-Himayat-i-Islam, a body now under the control of conservative business circles in Lahore.

In the union elections in the Pakistan International Airlines Corporation (PIAC) in early January 1970 the new JI-backed PIAC Employees Union was rigged to win and replace the Airway Employees union headed by Tufail Abbas, a colleague of Mairaj Muhammad Khan in the NSF.

The JI victory in the PIAC union elections was the most notable success in a broader JI effort to penetrate the labour movement in Pakistan with well-financed and well-organized parallel unions.

The People's Party had greater success in penetrating the labour sphere because it concentrated less on established unions and more on the newly industrialized sectors and older industries and occupations that had not been unionized.

Industrial labour had been deeply politicized during the November 1968 Movement. Its growing militancy was evident in the wave of factory takeovers during the last days of Ayub Regime. Tensions remained in industrial areas after the imposition of Martial Law as the 'retrenchments' occasioned by the post-Movement economic recession enabled managements to dismiss the most militant workers. This is what happened at Packages Ltd., a large factory employing some 2,500 workers in the industrial suburb of Kot Lakhpat, Lahore.

In the strike of 1 November 1969 a whole series of issues was at stake: retrenchment, victimization of union office holders, long-term use of 'temporary' labour, the work-charge system, and no implementation of minimum wage scales, etc. On 4 November the strikes were attacked by goons and on 7 November, the new Industrial Relations Ordinance was announced, which, while it permitted workers to strike, also legalized 'lockouts' by factory owners.

The Packages strike touched off strikes and lockouts in all of the other major factories at Kot Lakhpat and within three weeks industrial actions had spread across the Ravi river to BECO at Shahdara, up to the new chemical complex at Kala Shah Kaku, to the industrial cities of Lyallpur, Multan and eventually to the major industrial areas of Karachi, Landhi-Korangi and SITE. This massive strike wave involved not only industrial workers, but began to affect lower level government servants. Strikes in the latter sectors went unreported, but it is known that even the Military Accounts Service went out on a job action during this period. One of the most interesting aspects of the November-December 1969 strikes was the interaction between the industrial and nearby rural areas. Most of the workers in places like Kala Shah Kaku, Kot Lakhpat, and at the DaoodHercules Fertilizer Factory between Lahore and Sheikhupura, were essentially rural folk who regarded their industrial employment as a profitable interlude in an otherwise largely rural and agrarian existence. Many hoped to save enough to return to their villages and buy a plot of land, though few realized that they were likely never to return permanently to their ancestral villages.

It was certainly significant that when the strikes and lockouts around Lahore led to police and goon violence, and when the Nur Khan administration finally decided to crack down, thousands of rural folks from villages surrounding Lahore, Sheikhupura and Gujranwala came out to join the striking workers and battle with the police.

In the atmosphere of the times it was inevitable that the strike situation would become highly politicized. The Jamat-i-Islami backed the industrialists, one of its publications characterizing the strikes as a 'conspiracy' of the Left to prevent the holding of the general elections.

On 17 November 1969, Mian Tufail Muhammad, Amir of the West Pakistani branch of the Jamat-i-Islami, issued a statement which said: "The tools of the upholders of alien systems of life have so intensified the sense of hunger in the simple-minded working class, that under present conditions, even if all the factories were handed over to the workers, it will not satiate their hunger, nor give them satisfaction."

Bhutto visited the Packages Workers' strike camp and made a rousing speech in which he also denounced the lockout provision of the new Industrial Relations Ordinance.[15]

The PPP party journal *Nusrat* (victory) became the most important Urdu media source on the strike situation, while PPP Left cadres helped organize several industrial actions. Yet, behind the PPP display of militancy and support, there was a growing difference of opinion between the central cell and the Punjab party cell over the extent to which the People's Party ought to become involved in student and industrial politics. The Punjab cell had already organized student, worker, cultural and women's wings and argued that these ought to be developed into strong parallel organizations that would ensure solid blocs of PPP support in these social arenas.

> The left socialists maintained that the past weakness of the labour movement was primarily the result of its refusal to become involved in political actions.[16]

They looked forward to organizing a trade union federation that would be allied with the PPP and that would combine political and economic action. Indeed, some of them would later help to organize the Muttahida Mazdur Majlis-i-Amal, but by then they had broken with the PPP.

The central cell, however, did not want to lose broader student and labour support by identifying the party too closely with the radical Left segments of each grouping.

On the question of factory takeovers by workers, as happened at the Allah Wasaya Textile Mills in Multan under the leadership of left PPP figures (Mahmud Babar and Ishvak

Ahmad) and the Multan Mazdur Majli-i-Amal, the PPP Chairman opposed this kind of 'left adventurism'. On 25 November 1971, he assured a disquieted Multan Bar Association that the PPP was against violent means to achieve its political ends and that it believed in peaceful, constitutional methods.

In the cities, where PPP organizations were stronger, the rapid rise of prices after the elections and a wave of worker retrenchments in the large and medium industrial sectors created more palpable tensions. Buoyed by the PPP election victory in the 1970 elections, the party Left wing and its workers' committees demanded the immediate transfer of power to a Kisan-Mazdur Raj ('Peasant-Worker Rule'). Increasing incidents of factory takeovers, strikes (hartals), and blockades (gheraos) occurred in all of the major industrial cities, but it was in Lyallpur that the most serious outbreak occurred. There, on 25 March 1971 after the arrest of Mukhtar Rana, PPP MNA and Lyallpur party Chairman, worker-led mobs went on a city-wide rampage and brought it to a standstill through a city-wide successful general strike. People's Guards fought pitched battles with the police, destroying the Jhang bazaar Police station. "By nightfall the city was put under a curfew and the army called in to maintain civil order."[17]

It is interesting that not a single trade unionist from Punjab gained entry into either the national or the Punjab Assembly. All such ticket applicants (e.g. Ziauddin Butt) had been screened out by the Central Parliamentary Review board. Thus, even before the elections, the central cell had determined the relative strength in the assemblies of the various groups in the PPP coalition.

The PPP Left-wing had more success in making its influence felt in the industrial sector. There, high prices, worker retrenchments and the victimization of unionists fed a burgeoning crisis in worker–management tensions. Under Mukhtar Rana, MNA, a radical social critic and proponent of a Kisan-Mazdur Raj, pro-PPP unions began to occupy industrial units in Lyallpur, Multan and Sargodha. Rana, who claimed to be acting according to a party directive issued by Bhutto to seize control of industrial units which victimize workers, had the active support of Sheikh Rashid and the Punjab party organization. These efforts, which culminated in the Lyallpur riots of 25 March, were directed not only at the industrialists, but also at the establishment unions. Many of the pro-PPP workers' groupings to emerge during this and earlier periods were 'parallel unions' that aimed to replace older and less politicized trade unions, but their wrath was also directed to the persons from the elite and the Right-wing entering the PPP through the backdoors.

The strength of the PPP-backed thrust is evident in the reactions of the established unions, as well as in the violence of the elite response. The WPFTU (West Pakistan Federation of Trade Unions) had backed the JUI in the 1970 elections, only to see its own constituency vote overwhelmingly for the PPP. By the time the Punjab Assembly elections were held two weeks later, the WPFTU had come out in favour of the PPP. The established unions showed considerable nervousness about 'parallelism' at the All-Pakistan Labour Conference held at Lahore on 26 and 27 December 1970. It was at this point that Bashir Bakhtiar, President both of the WPFTU and the Pakistan Labour party, began to make pro-PPP speeches. Finally, on 22 March 1971 as worker actions moved toward a climax, the Pakistan Labour Party (PLP) dissolved itself into the PPP. This was seen largely as a measure of self-preservation, but there is also little doubt that the PLP's entry into the PPP was smoothed by the central cell's desire to offset the rapid growth of PPP leftwing influence among the industrial working class.

War

The occupation of factories by the workers, the seizure of land by the poor peasants, the awakening of women and the valour of the students and youth created a revolutionary situation in both East and West Pakistan. The delay in the revolution diverted the movement along national lines in East Bengal. War euphoria was whipped up, which led to a ferocious civil war and the separation of Bangladesh in 1971. The Pakistani Army suffered a humiliating defeat at the hands of the Bengali masses. During the civil war, hundreds of thousand of people were brutally killed and women raped by the Pakistan army.

The outright reactionary character of the onslaught of the Pakistan army against the Bengali masses was further compounded by the flagrant intervention of the Islamic fundamentalists as an auxiliary force of the Pakistan army in carrying out this grotesque genocide, even more brutally. The two main organizations were the subsidiaries of the main Islamic fundamentalist party, the Jamat-i-Islami. They were named 'Al-Badar' and 'Al-Shams'.[18] Comprising mainly lumpen elements, they were armed and heavily funded by the Pakistani state and in reality sponsored and bred by the CIA. Their atrocities far outnumbered those perpetuated by the Pakistan army, as it was under some military discipline and at least had to abide by some standards while carrying out the massacre of the Bengali civilians. At the same time, with the logistical and military support of the Pakistani Army, Al-Badar and Al-Shams targeted the communist and socialist students, trade unionists and activists in their orgy of mass murder and exterminations. They used this civil war to strike a savage reactionary blow at the revolutionary forces in the movement in East Bengal. This was one of the reasons that the nationalists came to dominate this movement and the socialist Left that had pioneered this revolt was sidelined. The deep involvement of the Jamat-i-Islami in this 'Operation Blitz' of the Pakistan army in East Bengal is exposed in a book by General Qureshi, who was a battalion commander in Dinajpur Saidpur districts of East Pakistan during the military operation. He narrates how the Amir (head) of the Jamat-i-Islami even went to the level of visiting combat troop formations in districts to expedite the role of these Islamic vigilante outfits, whose structures and methods had a close resemblance with the 'Black hundreds' in Russia and the 'Shock troopers' in Nazi Germany. General Qureshi writes:

> Maulana Tufail Muhammad of the Jamaat-e-Islami visited us after the military action. He was, I think, the only leader of national stature from West Pakistan who took the trouble of travelling to the remote corners of East Pakistan to make a personal assessment of the prevailing conditions. It was good to know that, besides men in uniform, there were others equally concerned about the future of this ideologically and geographically unique country. The Maulana was particularly concerned about the performance of the Razakars,

> (volunteers) locally recruited and belonging to his party, and was happy to learn that their conduct was commendable. He jokingly remarked that his party cadres had always come to the rescue of the Army in tough situations, but my state of mind at the time was not receptive to this light-hearted observation; I thought it limited the scope of co-operation between Jamat and the Army. In fact, neither was the Army acting to preserve itself, nor the mujahids to perpetuate army rule; they were co-operating in the national interest, not doing each other any favours. Let it be said, to the credit of Jamat-i-Islami and these motivated Bengali Muslims, that they stuck it out with us till the end. They were prepared to go all the way to their graves in the name of Islam and Pakistan; unfortunately we decided to raise the white flag.[19]

Again General Qureshi explains that how far the army went to amalgamate these fanatic fundamentalist gangs in the army operations:

> The GOC (General Officer Commanding) discussed the effectiveness of the newly-raised East Pakistan Civil Armed Forces (EPCAF) and Mujahid units, and we exchanged views on the question of mixing these outfits with the regulars, at the grass-roots level, leaving command to the army. It was felt that this would provide the necessary numbers to show the flag, in strength, in the entire area of responsibility, and also ease the problems of provision of rations, ammunition, and other administrative back-up support.[20]

In the aftermath of the Pakistan Army's surrender of December 1971, a new conflict began in Bangladesh. In the areas liberated from the Pakistani Army in East Bengal during the national liberation struggle, a form of soviets developed. The invading Indian army, in connivance with the reactionary bourgeois nationalist forces of East Bengal, tried to crush them. It is significant that during this time the seventh fleet of the American Navy was anchored in the Bay of Bengal with marines on board. American imperialists feared that the Indian Army might fail to crush the soviets that were rousing society in the new order, and that were mainly controlled by the Mukti Bahini and the JSD (Jatyo Samajtantrik Dal), the Left wing of the national liberation movement.

The fraternal spirit between senior army officers of the belligerent countries inspired by common service in the old India still remained a quarter of a century after India and

Pakistan had fought three wars. One day after India and Pakistan had faced each other on the battlefront at the end of the Bangladesh war, a group of officers of the Pakistan Armoured Corps sought an Indian unit to which they could surrender. They finally located an Indian cavalry officer in the bar of a newly conquered club: before accepting their surrender, he insisted on standing them a round of drinks.

> With the advance guard of Indian army, the first Indian General into the city, Major General Gandharu Nagra said, 'Casualties are severe. Very messy.' I asked him if he had already met General Niazi. 'Oh yes', he said, 'he was very happy to see me. We knew each other at college.'[21]

When the Pakistanis brought in their unit to lay down arms, Indians and Pakistanis fresh from the battle in the rice paddies of Bengal organized a round of hockey and football matches. From the office of Prime Minister of India Indira Gandhi came a sharp message to the Indian Commander: he was engaged, he was reminded, "In war, not cricket". Had the social revolution gone ahead in East Bengal, it would have been almost impossible to prevent it from spreading to West Bengal, where the Left was already strong and society already radicalized. In the post-war crisis-ridden subcontinent, a red Bengal with its traditions of uprisings and rebellions would have led to a revolution throughout the whole region. This would have threatened not only the rule of capital in the subcontinent, but its impacts would have had devastating repercussions for American and Western imperialism far and wide. The advent of the Seventh Fleet to the Bay of Bengal was not accidental.

In West Pakistan, the defeated, humiliated and shattered Pakistan army was in no state to resist a new mass uprising. The armed forces had lost the mass support and were exhausted and bewildered.

General Gul Hasan in his memoirs graphically illustrates the mass revolt in East Bengal. The movement had defeated an army and clearly the oppressed had overthrown the system. He describes the situation in Bengal even before the Indian army had moved in:

> Prior to the take-over by General Tikka Khan, our troops had been confined to cantonments. Their movement was limited, owing to the insults and abuse heaped upon them, and at times they were subjected to attacks by the Awami League followers. To make matters worse, their ration of fresh supplies was discontinued by Bengali contractors, and their electricity and water supplies were cut off. This was a totally dismal picture. It was natural that when Army action was ordered, the troops could not possibly forget the indignities they were subjected to by the Awami League minions.
>
> (...) On the way back from China, I stayed in East Pakistan for a couple of days, mostly touring and meeting with various commanders engaged in quelling the rebels. They were confident, but bewildered by the mass murders of West Pakistan officers serving with the Civil Armed Forces and the East Bengal Regiments, by their own men. From my talks with them I gathered and this was confirmed later by General Tikka Khan who was good enough to ask me for dinner the day before I returned to the West that nothing was moving. Trains, buses, steamers, etc., were all damaged or lying idle because the crews had either gone across the border or were in hiding, afraid of the Army or terrified of reprisals by the rebels if seen to be co-operating with the Government, the authority of which Tikka Khan was busy establishing. It was not an encouraging picture that I brought back with me.
>
> At Khulna HQ I listened to a wireless intercept of the rebels. At one end, the speaker was a Major Jalil, a good officer who had served with me in 1 Armoured Division. He had deserted the service to lead the rebels. I was most upset, the more so because I never thought for a moment that he would be one to abscond. East Pakistan was doomed and we were wasting our time by making futile attempts to appease them; that juncture had long passed.[22]

After failing to diffuse the revolutionary upheaval the ruling elites of the subcontinent had taken the extreme step of waging an all-out war to derail the revolution. The defeat of the Pakistani army in the war had sent tremors through the armed forces; there were open rebellions in several garrisons. There had been scattered reports of soldiers banishing, seizing and even lynching the officers of the top brass. However, as the most formidable pillar of the state was trembling and shaking to its foundations, the international and the Pakistani media, dominated by the interests of capitalism, maintained a strict censorship. This was more so on the question of the revolts within the ranks of the defeated army against the officer caste, the ruling classes, and the system itself. In any case we again quote perhaps the most relevant source on the subject, the first and the last Commander-in-Chief of the Pakistan Army after the emergence of Bangladesh, Lieutenant General Gul Hasan Khan. After sacking him Zulfiqar Ali Bhutto tried to change the chain of Command of the Pakistan Armed Forces, although it was more of a symbolic gesture and the changes were pretty cosmetic. The post of C-in-C was changed to COAS (Chief of the Army Staff). A JCSC (Joint Chief of Staff Committee) was set up to devolve the commander of the army. In his memoirs General Gul Hasan has this to say in the chapter 'Tremors in the army'. He wrote:

> 19 December will remain vivid in my memory as long as my faculties are not dimmed by the passage of time. The day itself was a bright one in Rawalpindi, but perhaps the weather did not feel inclined to share the tribulation which was entirely of our own making. The urge to drive to work to GHQ was not as compelling as it had been in better times. I was terribly depressed and demoralized by what we had done to ourselves. In the office there would be numerous inevitable cease-fire violations to be attended to.
>
> (...) Having initiated incorrect reports during the fighting, the Indians would be attacking desperately to regain lost ground to substantiate their previous false claims. Also, there would be a multitude of demands from our formations still occupying their battle locations. During the short drive, my thoughts reached out to the fate of our Prisoners of War: I was most distressed. With all this racing through my mind I noticed some people viewing the cars converging on to GHQ with undisguised contempt. I felt sorry for myself.
>
> (...) On entering my office, my staff officer informed me that the COS would be addressing all the officers of the Rawalpindi garrison later in the day. I did not know the purpose behind the talk but of one aspect I had no doubt: it would not be the easiest of tasks General Hamid had ever undertaken.
>
> (...) I received him at his arrival, escorted him to the lectern and sat in an empty chair in the front row. I cannot recall one word of what General Hamid said. I was emotionally too upset to pay attention, and in any case he was continuously interrupted by a near-rebellious audience. Once or twice, the COS left the stage and went out to collect himself, and then resumed his talk. I have never seen such a performance by a disciplined body of men, but I did not blame them; they too were charged with perturbation. The one incessant demand of the audience that I vaguely recall was that all officers'

> messes should be declared dry.
>
> (...) In my disturbed state, I could not figure out how that would help resolve our present dilemma, or any future ones that we were likely to inflict upon ourselves. In the afternoon I was told that Colonel Alim Afridi wished to speak me. The call was through soon, and he told me that the troops in Gujranwala were intensely agitated over the loss of East Pakistan and their demand was that I fly over to pacify them. I replied that I could not leave GHQ and that he should come over to see me, though I was not sure what good that would do. In the meanwhile Afridi did all the talking and I gained the impression that the troops in Gujranwala were on the verge of mutiny. Afridi also mentioned that the troops wished that General Yahya Khan should quit.

Exit Yahya Khan, Enter Bhutto

> (...) Major General M I Karim, an East Pakistani officer, commanding 6 Armoured Division confirmed that the troops were shocked over the loss of East Pakistan and there was visible unrest amongst them.
>
> (...) I enumerated the happenings of the afternoon to the President. At the end, he assured me that he would quit as soon as it was possible for him to hand over to an 'elected representative of the people'.
>
> (...) 19 December 1971 was indeed a day that I will never forget it was the worst I had ever experienced in all my long service. The discipline in the Army was on the verge of snapping and the repugnant odour of anarchy was in the air. The climate was all the more awesome because there would have been no authority to arrest the rot, should it have set in.
>
> All these alarmingly ominous happenings, putting the very existence of the Army in jeopardy, and hence whatever remained of Pakistan. But who was in a position to undertake the task of pacifying the Army?[23]

This was a situation when yet again, after several occasions since 7 November 1968, a socialist revolution could have been insurrected and the exploitative rule of capitalism and the yoke of imperialism could have been overthrown once and for ever. Trotsky had written in the founding documents of the Fourth International, the Transitional Programme that,

> The historical crisis of human mankind has been reduced today to the crisis of revolutionary leadership.[24]

The People's Party was not a Bolshevik party and Bhutto was no Lenin. The absence of a revolutionary party had let this revolutionary opportunity slip through the fingers of the Pakistani proletariat and the oppressed masses. Although many brilliant works have been done on the 1971 India–Pakistan war, the movement in East Pakistan, and the emergence of Bangladesh, there are very few books which give a class perspective of this saga of 1971 in East Bengal. Unfortunately, to dwell upon this subject a whole separate work is needed. Hence, due to the topic of this work, we must restrict our analysis to the momentous events that took place in those convulsive days in what still remains of Pakistan.

During the military operation and the defeat glaring in its face the Yahya dictatorship had inducted an artificial interim government into the fold of its regime. Nur ul Amin from East Bengal was made the Prime Minister and Zulfiqar Ali Bhutto was the supposedly deputy Prime Minister and Foreign Minister of this set-up.

Bhutto flew to New York on 8 December 1971, hoping to recoup on the diplomatic front some of the ground Pakistan had lost in Bangladesh. "We will not rest," he assured his cheering countrymen who had come to Karachi's airport to see him off, not if it took "a thousand years" to clear "Indian aggression from the sacred soil of Pakistan." He rested a bit at the Pierre, however, before going to the Waldorf Towers for breakfast with Henry Kissinger in the US Ambassador to UN George Bush's suite on 11 December.

Kissinger recalled. "Elegant, eloquent, subtle, Bhutto was at last a representative who would be able to compete with the Indian leaders for public attention. The legacy of distrust engendered by his flamboyant demeanour and occasionally cynical conduct haunted Bhutto within our government," wrote Z.A. Bhutto's American counterpart.[25] Kissinger advised Bhutto that

> "Pakistan would not be saved by mock-tough rhetoric. 'It is not that we do not want to help you; it is that we want to preserve you. It is all very well to proclaim principles but finally we have to assure your survival.' ... The next forty-eight hours would be decisive. We should not waste them in posturing for the history books. Bhutto was composed and understanding. He knew the facts as well as I; he was

> a man without illusions, prepared to do what was necessary, however painful, to save what was left of his country.[26]

'Tiger' Niazi surrendered on 16 December, signing a formal instrument in Dacca's race course the next afternoon and giving up the entire army, 93,000 of Pakistan's soldiers, and officers. It was the most ignominious defeat in the nation's history, one that even Bhutto's rhetoric was unable to conceal from millions in West Pakistan, who had hoped and prayed and desperately tried to believe every brave lie he told them.

From New York Bhutto flew to Key Biscayne, Florida on 17 December to meet with President Nixon and Kissinger on Bebe Rebozo's yacht, where he was assured of ample US military and monetary support. He boarded Pan Am flight 106 on the evening of 18 December for the long voyage home to the much-diminished nation he was now to lead, stepping down in Rome shortly the next day. Air Marshal Rahim Khan had ordered a Pakistan International Airlines Boeing to be sent specially for Bhutto from Karachi. The flight to Islamabad allowed Zulfiqar Ali Bhutto to stopover in Teheran to confer with the Shah before finishing the last lap of his sadly triumphal trip home.

> The cry of "Death to Yahya Khan" alternated with "Long life to Bhutto!" Yahya had wished to hang on, but when his chief of staff, Lieutenant Gereal Hamid Khan, briefed most of the junior officers at the National Defence College in Pindi on the morning of 20 December on the recent events in the East, he was met with angry questions and epithets, "The younger officers were shouting 'Bastards', 'Drunkards!', 'Disgraceful!' and " 'Shame' ... Lieutenant-General Hamid Khan's composure and that of generals of the front row had completely collapsed ... Yahya Khan had played his last card. The game was up.[27]

Zulfiqar Ali Bhutto landed at Rawalpindi soon after the well-staged drama in the NDC (National Defence College) had convinced Yahya that he had lost more than a war. Mustafa Khar, Bhutto's trusted lieutenant, was waiting in his blue Mercedes inside the airport gate and drove with Bhutto directly to the well-guarded President's House. The building surrounded by high barbed-wire walls with spiked steel gates would soon become Bhutto's residence. Yahya was nervously waiting inside with broken Generals, Peerzada and shaken

Hamid, sipping whiskey without any soda.

Bhutto had been driven to Pindi's Punjab House after having been 'sworn in' as the new president of Pakistan and chief martial law administrator, the two jobs he took over from Yahya on 20 December 1971. Yahya was left to pack up and vacate the President's House as soon as he could. Lieutenant General Gul Hasan had been called to Punjab House, and thought, in fact, that he was going to meet Yahya there as he ascended the narrow stairs, flanked by two six-foot-six Presidential House guards.

Bhutto asked Gul Hasan to take over Yahya's job of army commander-in-chief, for that was one position he knew he could not fill. As current chief of the general staff, Gul Hasan knew all the general officers personally, having trained many of them, including the obsequious 'dark horse,' Major General Zia-ul-Haq (1924–88). Gul Hasan asked for time to "think about it," still surprised to find himself with a new president.

After the defeat just sustained by Pakistan's army, the job of commander-in-chief must have sounded more like a crown of thorns than a high honour.

Let's go back to our bachelor C-in-C and see what he has to say on this episode. General Gul Hasan writes in his memoirs:

> At 1200 hours my Staff Officer told me that the President wished to see me urgently. In my mind I quickly went over the drill of how I should broach yesterday's events with him, and got into my car. Just then Javed Nasir came up and instructed the driver to take me to the Punjab House; I asked Javed Nasir what on earth the President was doing in the Punjab House. He replied that the Military secretary had called a minute ago and given him the message. This was an added enigma. The President was normally at the President's House or at his Secretariat. The Punjab House was where the Governor stayed when visiting Rawalpindi.
>
> (...) On reaching the Punjab House, I found the gates closed. When the guard saw my car, he opened them, but the driver had some considerable difficulty driving through crowds of people gathered outside the compound wall.
>
> Somehow I managed to get to the top of the steps, where I was met by the Military Secretary who showed me into one of the rooms. Inside, I was astonished to see Bhutto.
>
> Bhutto left his chair and embraced me and shed some tears, which

appeared genuine enough, though I was to learn later that he was equally adept at shedding the crocodile variety. He got down to business. He wished that I should take over the Army, informing me that General Yahya Khan and Hamid had been sacked. I was stunned by this disclosure and asked him how he fitted into the scheme of things. He replied that he had taken over the offices of President and Chief Martial Law Administrator from Yahya Khan.

I told him that I was just not interested in taking over the Army. Once the disengagement of troops had been accomplished on the border, I wished to retire: I had had enough.

'I do not accept that,' said Bhutto. 'You are a friend of mine and you have got to help me to get the Army on its feet.'

'I regret, but my mind is made up,' I replied. 'I am certain you will find plenty of others, senior to me, who will be more than willing to assist you.'

The conversation continued in the same vein for quite a while. He was very insistent, so I told him I wished for a few days to think over the matter.

'No, no there is no time. I am addressing the nation today and your appointment is the cornerstone of my speech.'

'I do not know how my appointment should become the cornerstone of your speech because I am sure there are more pressing matters the nation is anxious to learn about.'

'I will not take "no" for an answer,' he said.

'Well, then give me a couple of days to make up my mind, one way or the other.'

He again gave me a long sermon, stressing urgency, confidence in me, friendship, brotherhood, and so on. I knew I could not get out of it. I was now in a quandary.

'I must have time to think over it,' I insisted. 'I hope thirty minutes will not derange your plan.'

He took me into an adjoining room, where I sat down. As he was leaving, I asked him if it would be possible to have a cup of tea sent to me. This came presently.

After some forty minutes I entered the room where Bhutto was and told him that I would accept the job, but only if certain conditions were met: First, that I would serve in the same rank that I held then lieutenant-general despite the fact that the C-in-C was always a four star general.

Secondly, he should arrange to effect a disengagement of troops on the border. This was a prelude to the return of our Prisoners of War; the sooner they returned the better. He said this question was uppermost in his mind, and he was already working on these lines.

Finally, I told him that if I took over the Army, I wanted no

> interference from anyone, himself or any of his ministers included. At this he smiled and assured me that was the reason why he had selected me for the job.
>
> Bhutto having agreed to the conditions I had imposed for taking over the appointment of C-in-C of the Army, I had no option but to accept. I left Bhutto and returned to GHQ.
>
> I was not elated by my appointment. I felt no joy. I just felt worn out. It did not come as something which I had been yearning for. I was fully conscious that the job would be no bed of roses, especially in view of what the Army had endured in East Pakistan and more so because of the momentous and eventful 19 December. I was far from being thrilled: actually, I was the most unwilling occupant of that office.[28]

These were exceptionally historic moments which graphically demonstrate beyond all doubt that all the reformism, centrism, and revolutionary/socialist rhetoric of populist leaders ends up compromising a revolutionary opportunity with the bourgeoisie state and system.

All had been planned, arranged and organized in Washington, New York, Key Biscayne, and Florida before Bhutto returned to Pakistan.

The army had to be re-established with its credibility and its sacrosanctity in society restored, even though it was a difficult task for the ruling classes at that delicate juncture in Pakistan's chequered history. It was Herculean task which only the leader of the masses Z.A. Bhutto could have accomplished, and the populist medicine used for this miracle to have taken place was a mixture of rhetoric of the emancipation of the exploited oppressed along with Pakistani National Chauvinist overtones and acts of radical reforms. What else was expected of the PPP and its leader? The creation of a Bolshevik party to carry through a revolutionary transformation of society; a long patient persistent struggle and the building of Marxist cadres, like tempering steel in the white hot furnace of events and struggles were necessary. But that was not to be in Pakistan. It's not just that Bhutto had to pacify the army get it back on its feet again, he also had to deal with the revolutionary ferment seething in the bowels of society: the masses were still yearning for a change. After sorting out the problems within the state Bhutto immediately turned to the masses.

On the same freezing night of 20 December 1971 he spoke on the radio and television.

> My dear countrymen, my dear friends, my dear students, labourers, peasants ... 'Those who fought for Pakistan' I have come in at a very late hour, at a decisive moment in the history of Pakistan.
>
> We are facing the worst crisis in our country's life, a deadly crisis. We have to pick up the pieces, very small pieces, but we will make a new Pakistan, a prosperous and progressive Pakistan, a Pakistan free of exploitation, 'a Pakistan envisaged by the Quaid-e-Azam'. With your co-operation ... I am taller than the Himalayas.[29]

'Socialist Revolution' was missing in the first speech of Quaid-e-Awam as soon as he sat in the saddle of State power.

He went on to restore the stature of the army:

> I want to tell our gallant armed forces that have fought in East Pakistan that our hearts are with you," he said. "We will not rest till we have redeemed your honour ... These are not empty words.
>
> (...) We will stand by you, we are with you. If you go down, we all will go down together. Remember my words ... we are doing everything in our power.[30]

Although Bhutto had aroused expectations amongst the majority of the workers, the advanced layers, especially in Karachi, were not pacified with reforms. He went on a spree of radical reforms calculated to diffuse any new upsurge, but he was destined ultimately to failure in the crisis-ridden capitalist system

A substantial section of Left-wing radicals involved in the labour movement entered into alliance with the PPP from the outset, and were subsequently instrumental in acquiring working class votes for the party in the 1970 elections.

The workers expected electoral promises to be fulfilled and when the new government appeared on the scene, they insisted that their demands be met. A government publication for mass consumption and publicity described the industrial situation at the time the PPP came to office:

> Strikes, factory sit-ins and lockouts were rife, crippling the entire industrial complex and bringing production almost to a stop ... As soon as Mr Bhutto's Pakistan People's Party, pledged to Islamic

> Socialism, the end of exploitation of man by man and a betterment in the lot of the workers and peasants, assumed office, the dam containing over a decade of pent up workers' emotions burst.[31]

The government issued directives to employers demanding reinstatement of all workers who had been victimized during the preceding militancy and also spoke of a new 'comprehensive labour policy' with substantial benefits for the workers. As the federal labour minister put it, the party could not ignore the fact that the workers had rendered great sacrifices for the success of the PPP. However, on the other hand the government deplored the 'law and order situation' arising from labour unrest and warned labourers that enemy agents were also within their ranks. The employers' organizations were threatening to close down all industrial establishments unless industrial anarchy was curbed. The intent of the government and the role of the new labour policy were made clear by a statement it issued in conjunction with the announcement of this new labour policy. The government expressed confidence that with this announcement, "all intolerable activities such as gherao (besiege) will now come to an end"; otherwise, the government warned that the power of the street would be met by the power of the state.

The announcement of the new labour policy in February 1972 was a direct response to the heightened state of labour militancy and also reflected the fact that the government felt compelled at least to appear to service its debts to the workers' electoral support in some manner. This is somewhat ironic since the effects of the labour policy, far from bringing concessions, further tightened government controls over industrial relations, the reality of which became manifest through later practice.

The 1972 labour policy did not have its intended effect of calming the workers; they were compelled to resort to other means at their disposal.

Confrontation

Most of these more militant leaders had come into prominence during the 1968-9 upheavals and had been dismissed by their employers in the continuing cut-backs under Martial Law. They plunged into industrial action that the new government had to confront during its first six months in office. The primary goal of this phase of industrial action was the reinstatement of sacked colleagues and an end to the lockouts that had continued despite government directives to the contrary. "The widespread workers resurgence was such that the new government started arresting workers within forty days of assuming power."[32]

> The strong stand that the government resolved to take at the time of the announcement of its labour policy was given added impetus by the increasing pressure of industrialists who threatened en bloc closure of their industrial establishments if 'the lawlessness was not checked'.[33]
>
> In retaliation to the united stand of the employers, six major trade union federations joined to form the Sindh Workers' Convention. Between them, they represented over 75 per cent of the total organized labour force of Sindh province and the vast majority of the organized workers of Karachi.[34]

Their aim was to launch movements against 'anti-labour actions', the banning of strikes, etc. This convening of major labour federations was in part a response to an earlier coalition of workers in the industrial areas of Karachi. At the grass roots level, workers of plant unions in the same industrial areas had joined to form the Karachi Mazdoor Action Committee, with two representatives from each of the unions in SITE. In other major industrial area of Karachi, the Landhi/Korangi Labour Organizing Committee (LKLOC) had achieved a similar unification of forces early in 1970. To the extent that these grassroots organizations of workers were instrumental in making the movement more responsive to the demands and interests of workers, the labour federations and white-collar 'outsider' labour leaders who wished to maintain their position in the labour movement had to quickly align themselves with the fighting stance of activists who were becoming increasingly important in the movement. Indeed, one particular labour federation which was conspicuous by its absence from the Sindh Workers' Convention had already lost much of its support among workers and continued to do so because of its refusal or inability to pursue a militant policy.

A major confrontation between workers and the authorities

first took place in SITE, the larger of the two industrial areas of Karachi. At least three workers were killed on 7 June 1972 when police opened fire on workers who had gheraoed (besieged) Feroz Sultan, a textile mill when on payday they did not receive their wages.

> On the following day, when the funeral procession of one dead worker whose body had been retrieved by the workers was being taken out of the workers' colony at Banaras Chowk, police and paramilitary forces again opened fire. Police sources reported ten deaths, including a woman and a child.[35]

All the industrial units of SITE and Landhi went on strike, which continued for twelve days.

After the firing incident, militant shop-floor labour leaders had entrenched themselves in the workers' colonies in SITE in company with a few militant white-collar outsiders and other radicals who were basically representatives of one particular labour federation.

> The government made it clear that it wanted to negotiate with representatives of this group of leaders since they were evidently in control of the situation in the industrial areas.[36]

Regional committees were formed to organize meetings in their respective areas; two general meetings of workers were to be held daily to keep them informed of the latest developments.

> The conflict in Landhi started over wage demands in a government run machine tool factory. The protest spread to neighbouring textile mills and finally paramilitary forces literally bulldozed their way into a mill. Four persons were killed in the firing that took place.[37]

As factories in Landhi remained on strike, police forces searched for the 'ring leaders' in the hills behind the industrial area where the workers' colonies are situated much like in the way that they are situated in SITE. A battle was fought when they disrupted workers' meeting in which two more workers were killed and about fifty injured.

Although the government did pay 'compensation' money to the families of workers who had been killed, as it had done in SITE for the June killings, by this stage it was not willing to negotiate on any demands. The chief minister of Sindh gave employers permission to terminate the services of those workers who did not resume work within a period of forty-eight hours.

> The army was called out in Landhi, and another worker was killed. The police escorted workers en masse into factories to resume production."[38] During October, labour leaders of SITE had already been arrested to pre-empt any meaningful sympathy-strike occurring in that industrial area.

The government consolidated its strong position through a presidential ordinance in October 1974 which further amended the existing labour laws.

> "The industrialists immediately acclaimed the ordinance as 'fulfilling a need which was being felt for long, for effectively maintaining industrial peace in the country'."[39]
>
> "In February 1975, the labour minister said that its aim was to check the multiplicity of trade unions which were hampering the growth of a 'healthy' trade union movement."
>
> "(...) the law also aimed at dealing with corrupt labour leaders who created unrest in the industry to serve their own ends. Such leaders were neither friends of the workers nor of the people and hence needed to be punished if they worked for illegal strikes."[40]

Analysis

Proletarian revolutions go through several phases. There are ups and downs, ebbs and flows; there are several basic analogies between revolutions in different periods of history, and different features that influence the process of a revolution. The elements of history, culture, level of socio-economic development and even the terrain of a country where the revolution is taking place all have a certain impact on the revolutionary movement. There is also the question of the timing and the duration of a revolutionary upheaval. Some revolutionary movements can continue for years with small ebbs and flows while others can be in an explosive state for weeks.

The energy unleashed by the 1968-9 revolution in Pakistan was also because of a politically virgin proletariat with no long history of reformist trade unions and parties. But this upsurge also went through a tortuous process, the main reason being the lack of a genuine Marxist leadership and a revolutionary organisation.

Such a party needs a clear programme, perspectives, correct ideas, flexible strategy and tactics and above all a bold, determined and courageous leadership. The most outstanding example of such a party was the Bolshevik party under the leadership of Lenin and Trotsky. In his brilliant work, *State and Revolution,* written during the course of the revolution in 1917, Lenin clearly defined the pre-conditions of a revolutionary situation.

The first condition was that the ruling class should be split and unable to rule as in the past. The second condition is that the middle class should be in ferment and vacillating between the ruling class and the masses. The third condition is that the working class should be prepared to fight and make great sacrifices to win.

Last but not least, what is needed is a revolutionary organization with a revolutionary leadership that is able and willing to put itself at the head of the masses and lead them to victory.

In the light of these postulates developed by Lenin the situation in Pakistan in those days of the 1968-9 revolution was ripe with these conditions. The conflict between the ruling classes had been exacerbated by the crisis in society and the economy. Even the 'invincible' Ayub Khan regime was being torn apart by the conflicts between the stalwarts that had become irreconcilable and led to revolts and betrayals by the most trusted lieutenants of Ayub Khan.

Ayub Khan's governor of West Pakistan, Malik Amir Mohammad Khan, notorious for his tyranny and oppression, who gave Ayub Khan vital support, had been deposed; it was a severe blow to the cohesion of the regime.

Even the split between Ayub Khan and Zulfiqar Ali Bhutto in 1966 was a clear indication of this sharpening of contradictions within the ruling class and its regime. The squabbling amongst the ruling classes was further intensified by the rising tide from below. However, the Americans and other serious strategists of capital were terrified and used all the energy at their disposal to quell the movement.

The crisis had gripped all classes and strata of society. The initial outburst was led by the students and this in itself reflected the deep malaise within the middle classes. Unemployed engineers, doctors and other professionals were in the forefront of this militant resistance to the regime. The high growth rate and industrialization under the Ayub regime was unable to provide jobs and absorb even the professionals and the white collar workers from the lower middle classes. The graduates in different fields of science and the arts burnt their degrees in the demonstrations in the main squares of most main cities and towns of Pakistan. This was an expression of the extreme disenchantment and disillusionment of these middle class youth with the capitalist system. The vacillations amongst the middle classes had reached a stage of explosive convulsions. And as it happens in every revolution the petty bourgeoisie was riding more and more with the proletarian masses as they could see no way out of their woes and deprivations in the existing order. This further galvanized the movement and gave it a greater confidence and encouragement.

But above all, what the workers and the poor peasants indubitably demonstrated was their will, capability and determination to carry out a socialist revolution.

As has been explained in the previous chapter, the revolutionary wave swept the whole country. Even in the remote areas of Pakistan the reverberations of the revolutionary upheaval were palpable. From the remote areas of Sindh to the Pushtoonkhwa (North West Frontier) the peasant revolts were unprecedented in recent history. The landed aristocracy felt besieged and their centuries of rulership was threatened. Their oppression and tyranny was tattered and smashed by the hurricane of the peasant revolts. Such was the character of this epoch that the workers leaders were so emboldened they went to extremes that were unthinkable in ordinary times. They had suddenly felt an instinct of such courage and valour that they did the impossible. The occupations of factories, bringing the whole country to a standstill through a wheel jam, general strike were things that were read in books or known through the narrations of the veterans of the previous revolution.

The role of the strike in general is to make the working class aware of

> itself as a living social force. The general strike is the highest expression of this. Lenin was fond of quoting the words of a German song: "All the wheels stand still if your mighty arms so will!" By participating in the strike movement, especially where this achieves an active form with mass participation, the workers acquire a feeling of their own strength through unity. The strike is a levelling phenomenon, serving to bind together the most advanced, politically conscious workers with the broadest layers of the class, who are aroused in action from the inertia of "normal" times.[41]

Yes there was violence, killings and other adventurous acts; these are part and parcel of every revolution in history. But some of these extreme measures were the result of the absence of a revolutionary party that could have given a greater organization, cohesion and discipline to this mass revolt. The revolution does not unfold in an orderly and pre-determined fashion, like an orchestra responding to the flourishes of a conductor's baton. It is a living play of forces, an equation even more complex than war between nations.

The 1968-9 revolution very graphically demonstrated the strength, consciousness and the capacity of the workers to transform society. They proved on the streets, in the factories, in the villages and landed estates that these wretched of the earth when they move on to a revolutionary plane can work wonders, even in a so-called theocratic state like Pakistan. A revolution in action is the most decisive school for the working classes. In the 1968-9 revolutionary movement the toiling masses, most of them 'illiterate' and 'primitive', learned how to organise, debate and enthuse the struggle at lightening speed.

Within hours they learnt how to man the barricades, organize protests, fight and protect themselves from the repression of state force, and then regroup for a new assault. In the mass demonstrations there was a spirit of class solidarity previously unseen in Pakistan; hand-in-hand they marched forward, very few aware of whose hand they were holding, whether a woman worker clasped the hand of a male worker, Christian or Muslim, etc. The prejudices of religion, sex, ethnicity, race, nationality, clan or tribe evaporated in the red heat of the revolutionary struggle. Red banners, flags and pagaris (head covering) coloured the whole landscape. In the so-called conservative Pakistani society men and women were attired with some symbol of red clothing. The whole atmosphere was filled by a euphoria never experienced by the oppressed masses in Pakistan before these titanic events.

But to gain a proper perspective of this struggle and draw the correct conclusions from the revolution it is important to understand the ideological essence, the destiny envisaged in the psychology of the masses, and above all of what they hoped to achieve in their own way. There was not a trickle of pessimism and the more the attacks of the State intensified, the more the revolution was stimulated and the masses infuriated against the system.

Students and youths refused to pay the fares on trains and buses, and the authorities were impotent to press upon them to pay up. Mainly in the cities, people dwelling in rented houses refused to pay rent. Workers occupied the factories and peasants took over the landed estates.

In reality the masses in this revolution were challenging the existent relations of property; and the ownership of property is not challenged in a 'democratic' revolution. The foremost symptom of a socialist revolution is the challenging by the deprived of the sacred ownership of property in a capitalist/feudal set-up. This revolt against the prevalent property relations was the basic aspect that made the character of the 1968-9 revolution socialist.

As we have seen above all the objective conditions as laid out by Lenin in 1917 were certainly there. But the tragedy of the 1968-9 revolution was the absence of the subjective factor. Revolutions don't occur every day. But the culmination of the objective conditions and the subjective factor is a decisive necessity. The objective conditions are constantly changing. But when the mass consciousness starts to move towards a collective struggle to change society it is vital that the subjective factor has to be in place to accelerate this movement into change, intervene in the objective situation and rapidly ripen it to lead it to the revolutionary overthrow of the existing system. The objective situation and the subjective factor have to go through a dialectical interaction to motivate and invigorate the revolution to achieve a socialist victory. The absence of this interaction cannot bring the outcome of a successful revolution.

Trotsky wrote on this historical process that leads to a qualitative change for a revolutionary conclusion. Trotsky wrote in 1928:

> It is a typical Menshevist dodge to shift responsibility for the mistakes of the leaders on the "masses" or to minimize the importance of leadership in general, in order thus to diminish its guilt. It arises from the total incapacity to arrive at the dialectic understanding of the "superstructure" in general, of the superstructure of the class which is the party, and the superstructure of the party in the shape of its central leadership. There are epochs during which even Marx and Engels could not drive historical development forward a single inch; there are other epochs during which men of much smaller calibre, standing at the helm, can check the development of the international revolution for a number of years ... Among the numerous difficulties in a proletarian revolution, there is a particular, concrete, and specific difficulty. It arises out of the position and tasks of the revolutionary party leadership during a sharp turn of events. Even the most revolutionary parties run the risk of lagging behind and of counter posing the slogans and measures of struggle of yesterday to the new tasks and new exigencies.[42]

Hence the most vital lesson we can learn from the success of the 1917 October revolution in Russia and the derailed revolution of 1968-9 in Pakistan is the lack of this cohesion of the objective and the subjective.

But after the failure of reforms the ruling class went to war, and as is known, revolutions are born from the womb of the war. Although the movement had ebbed to some extent after the abdication of Ayub Khan, still the end of war brought another wave of revolutionary struggles. As there were tremors and revolts in the army after the war, similarly the advanced workers in Karachi and other industrial cities of Pakistan yet again endeavoured to change the system. This was the case in the 1971-2 period when Pakistan was going through the throes of a traumatic defeat. But this time the movement was isolated amongst the advanced layers of the workers.

The processes that unfolded after 25 March 1969 can be observed in every revolution. The fall of the old regime is greeted with enthusiasm by the masses. There is universal rejoicing, as men and women enjoy the new-found freedoms. This is the stage of democratic illusions, a carnival in which people become drunk with the sensation of liberation and hopes that know no bounds. Alas, this beautiful love-feast is not destined to last. The enormity of the illusion rapidly finds its counterpart in the depth of disappointment as expectation cracks its head against reality. "We have scotched the serpent, not killed him," exclaims Shakespeare's Macbeth. Gradually, the idea begins to dawn upon the masses that, beneath the tinsel and the speeches, nothing has really changed. The old order has merely swapped its garb and its mode of address, but the same old masters still remain, and the same old problems too.

This rapid spread of disillusionment does not affect all layers at once. It finds its first expression in the ranks of the most advanced section of the masses. Vaguely realizing that the power won with so much effort and sacrifice is slipping out of their hands, the advanced guard instinctively lashes out. This is a moment of utmost danger for the revolution. The advanced guard understands more than the mass, and impatiently pushes ahead with demands for precipitate action. It is necessary to win over the rest of society, which lags behind and has not yet drawn the necessary conclusions. If the advanced guard breaks away from the mass, it can become isolated and cut down by the reaction.

The new PPP government was carrying through a process of reforms and selective repression. Ultimately, by 1974 the movement had ebbed. Disillusionment was widespread and individuality and selfishness had come back to impose their psychologies on society.

A revolutionary opportunity that had taken decades to come was lost. As a consequence the masses were to pay a heavy price and endure decades of hardship and suffering. In the final analysis the absence of a revolution party and a clear Marxist leadership was the only reason that this great revolution had receded and was derailed. That is the most vital lesson of the 1968-9 revolution.

The whole question of the relationship of the Party and the mass movement can be reduced to the difference between the finished scientific programme of Marxism and the necessarily unfinished, incomplete and contradictory movement of the masses.

The generation of today has to learn and absorb the lesson of the vital importance of building a Marxist revolutionary force. Another 1968-9 impends. It will come sooner rather than later. This time the presence of a subjective factor shall lead to a victorious outcome. After all, this is now the struggle for the survival of civilization and human existence.

NOTES

1. Played the longest role as the country's main economic planner. Joined the Planning Commission of Pakistan in 1957, remained the chief of the commission, finance minister and major economic planner of the country in most regimes for almost forty years in the first fifty years of Pakistan's existence.
   Quoted in Zafar Shaheed, *The Labour Movement in Pakistan*, (Oxford), p. 269.
2. Ayub Khan, *Ayub Khan Diaries 1966-72*, (Oxford), pp. 547-548.
3. *Dawn*, 11 April 1969.
4. Zafar Shaheed, *The Labour Movement in Pakistan*, (Oxford), p. 65.
5. Introduction to Industrial Relations Ordinance (IRO) 1969.
6. Sections 26 to 32, Industrial Relations Ordinance IRO 1969.
7. Zafar Shaheed, *The Labour Movement in Pakistan*, (Oxford), p. 268.
8. *Dawn*, 12 January 1972.
9. *Dawn*, 6 January 1972.
10. *Imroze* (Lahore), 20 September 1969; and *Pakistan Observer*, 21 September 1969.
11. *Musawat*, 22 July 1970.
12. *Combat* (Karachi), 28 March 1970.
13. *The Pakistan Times*, 10 October 1969.
14. General Akbar Khan was also charged for treason in the 1957 'Rawalpindi Conspiracy Case' along with the CPP leaders. Including the Left-wing poet Faiz Ahmed Faiz, they were incarcerated and sentenced to prison for different periods of time.
15. *The Pakistan Times*, 14 November 1969.
16. *Dehqan* (Lahore), Vol. 1, No. 2, 13 September 1971.
17. *The Pakistan Times*, 26 March 1971.
18. Names of two battle grounds where Prophet Mohammad had fought wars with the 'infidels' in the 8th century A.D.
19. Major General Hakeem Arshad Qureshi, *The IndoPak War*, (Oxford 2002), pp. 91, 92.

20. Ibid p. 95.
21. Gavin Young, *Observer* London, 19 December 1971.
22. Lt. Gen. Gul Hasan, *Memoirs of Lt. Gen. Gul Hasan Khan,* (Oxford), pp. 275, 313.
23. Ibid. p. 339-346
24. Leon Trotsky, *Transitional Programme*, p. 17.
25. Henry Kissinger, *White House Years,* p. 907.
26. Ibid., pp. 907-8.
27. Taseer, *Bhutto*, p. 130.
28. Lt. Gen. Gul Hasan, *Memoirs of Lt. Gen. Gul Hasan Khan*, (Oxford), pp. 347–351.
29. Z.A. Bhutto, Addresses to a Nation 20 December 1971, in Z.A. Bhutto, *Speeches and Statements vol. 1,* 20 December 1971–31 March 1972 (Karachi: Government of Pakistan 1972), pp. 1-16, quotation at p.1.
30. Ibid, p. 17.
31. Pakistan Pictorial 1973: 75.
32. *Dawn*, 30 January 1972.
33. *Dawn*, 21 and 25 May 1972.
34. *Dawn*, 30 May 1972.
35. *Dawn*, 9 June 1972.
36. *Dawn*, 13 June 1972.
37. *Dawn*, 19 October 1972.
38. *Dawn*, 2 November 1972.
39. *Dawn*, 15 October 1974.
40. *Dawn*, 3 February 1975.
41. Alan Woods, *Bolshevism: The Road to Revolution,* p. 211.
42. Trotsky, *The Third International after Lenin,* p. 73.

Seven

CRISIS OF THE LEFT LEADERSHIP

Rise of the Pakistan People's Party

Those who make the revolution halfway only dig their own graves.

—Louis de Saint Just (1767–1794)[1]

It seems that the lesson of this coup d'etat is that a via media, a modus vivendi, a compromise, is a Utopian dream. The coup d'etat demonstrates that the class struggle is irreconcilable and that it must result in the victory of one class over the other. Obviously, whatever the temporary setbacks, the struggle can lead only to the victory of one class. This is the writing on the wall.

—Zulfiqar Ali Bhutto (1928–1979)[2]

Stalinism and Maoism

The Left in Pakistan had already faced the severe blow of the role of CPI leadership during the national liberation struggle and the trauma of partition. The new regime in Pakistan had intensified repression against the Left. The Sino–Soviet split further damaged the unity and growth of the Left forces in the country.

In the 1960s the major conflict between the different Left and 'Communist' parties were further complicated by the Sino–Soviet split. Although there were no real ideological or theoretical contradictions and differences, they were blindly following the Moscow and Peking 'lines' which were using such Stalinist groups and even larger 'communist' and 'socialist' parties as pawns in their foreign policy pursuits.

In August 1964, Ted Grant in his document on the Colonial Revolution and the Sino–Soviet split gave a Marxist analysis of this conflict between these bureaucracies. He elaborated on the causes and real 'ideological' basis of this split and its impacts on the colonial revolution. Ted Grant wrote:

> The rationalization of the split by 'ideological' considerations was a means to try and gain support within the Communist Parties on a world scale. The Chinese, for the moment, have used radical slogans as a means of mobilizing support in the Stalinist world movement against the Russians, especially among the colonial peoples. Because of their radical slogans, at this time, the Chinese appealed to the cadre elements in the Stalinist parties looking for a revolutionary road.
>
> "(...) The split between the Stalinist bureaucracies on national lines adds further confusion among the broad masses throughout the world. Even among the advanced workers, while creating certain opportunities for the ideas of Marxism, it further complicates the task of revolutionary Marxism.[3]

As explained in an earlier chapter, the rot in the Left in the subcontinent and internationally started with the degeneration of the Soviet Union, the coming to power and control by the Stalinist bureaucracy in the Kremlin and the beginning of the decline and disintegration of the Third International in the later half of the 1920s. In the Indian subcontinent this degeneration took a bit longer to complete in the period around 1936.

At the time of Partition the Muslim communists of the CPI were also to join the Muslim League, as if the communists were believers in the sectarian divide of the people. It is not accidental that the author of the election manifesto and programme of the Muslim League was a 'communist', Danial Latifi. Stalin's classification, which included religion as a major national trait proved to be an ideological and political disaster for the CPI in the 'practical politics' of the South Asian subcontinent.

The CPI later in its various congresses and CC meetings condemned these mistakes, especially after the death of Stalin in 1953. However the damage was done: in Pakistan, where the communist party of Pakistan never became even a modest mass party, this ideological policy was the fundamental cause. There is no doubt that the successive regimes in Pakistan were intrinsically so weak and the Left movement in the region and specially the colonial world was in such a rapid flow that the ruling elite had a constant mindset of fear of the Left. Hence, throughout the first five decades, every regime was rigorous in its repression and incarceration of left activists; even when they were not a substantial enough force to cause any serious threat to the state and the prevalent system.

This uninterrupted repression by the state was one of the factors which to some extent hindered the growth and attainment of a mass base for the communist parties in Pakistan. But when and where has a communist or a Bolshevik party not been subjected to state repression? Nevertheless, they did gain a mass basis, led socialist revolutions, and transformed societies. The Left historians and intellectuals in Pakistan have attributed the CP's ultimate failure to organizational mistakes and the short comings of the individual leaders; this assumption is not entirely false. Yet from our point of view the main cause of the failure of communists in Pakistan was not religion or the theocratic nature of the state, nor were organizational or individual characteristics and personalities of the leaders to blame.

Our contention is that it was the basic ideological and theoretical foundations which were flawed and historically false. All the tactics, methods and strategies employed to build a mass revolutionary party flow from the ideological foundations of the organization that is trying to build such a party. Most Left activists also came from the parent CPI or other left parties that were based on the ideology that the character of the revolution in these countries of ex-colonialism was not socialist but of a national democratic nature. This gave them a fatalistic excuse to go along with any section of the ruling classes, derive a falsely perceived conception of its progressive traits to support it, and to carry through the 'national democratic revolution'. This meant that they were preparing neither themselves nor the proletarian masses to overthrow the rotten capitalist system embedded within the remnants of feudalism and subservient to imperialism. Hence they had virtually crossed out a socialist revolution from their agenda.

For all their 'practical' and 'grass roots' politics, the problems faced by the oppressed masses were still being aggravated and perpetuated by naked and aggressive capitalist exploitation. Hence, though being 'communists,' they were in no position to persuade the wider masses and the proletariat to support them in their efforts to become a substantial force in the country's politics. This led to the disillusionment of the 'cadres' and gave rise to crisis, conflicts and splits, again not really on genuine ideological and theoretical issues but on individualistic, organizational and tactical matters.

Lenin and Trotsky

The main problem was that there was no genuine Marxist tendency in existence in those times. The only ideological options open to them were different versions of Stalinism. Unfortunately some petty bourgeois student elements who came from Britain or Europe who claimed to be 'Trotskyists' played such opportunist, ultra-Left roles that they further repulsed the Left activists from genuine Marxism and Trotskyism. Marx, Engels and Lenin were universally acceptable to the Left in general, not as theoretical and political ideologues and institutions, but more as charismatic symbols of the Left as interpreted by the Stalinist leaders. In the 1950s and 1960s Stalin was the hero of the Left, but with the rapid and massive gains of the Chinese planned economy under Mao, he too became the hero of the new generation of youth that entered Left politics.

Trotsky was not only ridiculed but was pronounced as a traitor, an imperialist agent, and a Nazi fascist by the intellectuals and leaders of all the Stalinist sects operating in Pakistan. Lenin and Trotsky were posed as two irreconcilable ideas, personalities and schools of thought. Again the theoretical level was quite low. Selected works of Lenin which suited the Stalinist leaders were studied and discussed in the study circles in Pakistan. Lenin's works, such as *Two Tactics of Social Democracy* were used out of context to substantiate and justify the two-stage theory. This in itself was proving to be counter-productive and alienated the Left groups from the proletarian masses and the radical youth who were seething with revolt against the exploitative system.

There is no doubt that there existed important theoretical and tactical differences between Lenin and Trotsky. In fact from the 1903 split in RSDLP till the spring of 1917 there was some heated debate and polemics between Lenin and Trotsky; there are several writings of Lenin where he rebuked Trotsky, especially on the issue of trying to unite the Mensheviks and the Bolsheviks. Trotsky later confessed his mistake in not joining the Bolshevik faction in those crucial times.

But the differences between Lenin and Trotsky were grossly exaggerated by the Stalinist intellectuals in Pakistan. The Stalinist school of falsification was in full spree here, without a profound Marxist tendency to confront it; the Kremlin bureaucracy had expunged Trotsky from all the documents, banners and pictures of the October revolution and his vital role in the first five years of Soviet Government. Similarly, the Stalinist leaders in Pakistan never mentioned the role of Trotsky in the 1915 Zimmerwald conference in founding the left opposition of the Second International and other points of united action between the two leaders of the October revolution. In his brilliant work *Bolshevism—The Road to Revolution*, Alan Woods elaborates on the differences and the later unity of Lenin and Trotsky that led to the victory of the socialist revolution in Russia in 1917:

> The Russian bourgeoisie, like the German bourgeoisie which Marx and Engels had castigated in 1848, had come on the stage of history too late, its social base was too weak, and above all its fear of the proletariat too strong for it to be able to play a progressive role. The fusion of industrial with landed capital, and the dependence of both upon the banks; the dependence on foreign capital was precisely what ruled out the possibility of a successful bourgeois-democratic revolution in Russia.
>
> In all of Lenin's speeches and writings, the counter-revolutionary role of the bourgeois-democratic liberals is stressed time and time again. However, up until 1917, he did not believe that the Russian workers would come to power before the socialist revolution in the West—a perspective that only Trotsky defended before 1917, in his remarkable theory of permanent revolution. This was the most complete answer to the reformist and class collaborationist position of the right wing of the Russian workers' movement, the Mensheviks. The two-stage theory was developed by the Mensheviks as their perspective for the Russian revolution. It basically states that, since the tasks of the revolution are those of the national democratic revolution, the leadership of the revolution must be taken by the national bourgeoisie.

> Trotsky, however, pointed out that by setting itself at the head of the nation, leading the oppressed layers of society (urban and rural petty bourgeoisie), the proletariat could take power and then carry through the tasks of the bourgeois-democratic revolution (mainly the land reform and the unification and liberation of the country from foreign domination). However, once having come to power, the proletariat would not stop there but would start to implement socialist measures of expropriation of the capitalists. And as these tasks cannot be solved in one country alone, especially not in a backward country, this would be the beginning of the world revolution. Thus the revolution is "permanent" in two senses: because it starts with the bourgeois tasks and continues with the socialist ones, and because it starts in one country and continues at an international level.
>
> Lenin agreed with Trotsky that the Russian liberals could not carry out the bourgeois-democratic revolution, and that this task could only be carried out by the proletariat in alliance with the poor peasantry. From 1905 until 1917, on the fundamental question of the attitude to the bourgeoisie, Lenin's position was close to that of Trotsky, and, in fact, identical. This was publicly acknowledged by Lenin at the Fifth (London) Congress, as we have seen, following in the footsteps of Marx, who had described the bourgeois "democratic party" as "far more dangerous to the workers than the previous liberals.[4]

Lenin explained that the Russian bourgeoisie, far from being an ally of the workers, would inevitably side with the counter-revolution. "The bourgeoisie in the mass", he wrote in 1905, "will inevitably turn towards the counter-revolution, and against the people as soon as its narrow, selfish interests are met, as soon as it 'recoils' from consistent democracy (and it is already recoiling from it!)."

What class, in Lenin's view, could lead the bourgeois-democratic revolution? "There remains 'the people', that is, the proletariat and the peasantry. The proletariat alone can be relied on to march on to the end, for it goes far beyond the democratic revolution. That is why the proletariat fights in the forefront for a republic and contemptuously rejects stupid and unworthy advice to take into account the possibility of the bourgeoisie recoiling".[5]

Alan Woods further elaborates on Lenin's position on this vital issue:

> Where Lenin differed from Trotsky was on the issue of the possibility

> of the Russian workers coming to power before the workers of Western Europe. Up to 1917, only Trotsky thought that this would happen. Even Lenin ruled this out, insisting that the Russian revolution would have a bourgeois character. The working class, in alliance with the poor peasants, would overthrow the autocracy and then carry out the most sweeping programme of bourgeois-democratic measures. At the heart of Lenin's programme was a radical solution of the land problem, based on the confiscation of the landlords' estates and land nationalisation. However, as Lenin explained many times, the nationalisation of the land is not a socialist, but a bourgeois demand, aimed at the landed aristocracy. He repeated on dozens of occasions that the Russian revolution would stop short of carrying out the socialist tasks, since, as everyone agreed, the objective conditions for building socialism were absent in Russia. But Lenin's case did not rest there. Lenin was always an uncompromising internationalist. His whole perspective was based on the international revolution, of which the Russian revolution was only a small part.[6]

Despite the hostility and antagonism that the Stalinist intellectuals and historians have tried to fabricate between Lenin and Trotsky, the situation was totally different.

Trotsky always considered Lenin's position to be progressive in relation to that of the two stages theory of the Mensheviks, but also pointed out its shortcomings. In 1909 he wrote:

> It is true that the difference between them in this matter is very considerable: while the anti-revolutionary aspects of Menshevism have already become fully apparent, those of Bolshevism are likely to become a serious threat only in the event of victory.[7]

These prophetic lines have often been taken out of context by Trotsky's Stalinist critics, but in fact they accurately express what occurred in 1917, when Lenin came into conflict with the other Bolshevik leaders precisely over the slogan of the 'Democratic Dictatorship of the Proletariat and Peasantry', which Lenin abandoned in favour of a policy that was identical with that of the permanent revolution. When this book was published after the revolution, Trotsky wrote in a footnote:

> This threat, as we know, never materialized because, under the leadership of comrade Lenin, the Bolsheviks changed their policy line on this most important matter (not without inner struggle) in the spring of 1917, that is, before the seizure of power.[8]

From a materialist point of view, the final test of all theories is found in practice. All the theories, programmes and perspectives that were advanced and passionately defended by the different tendencies in the Russian labour movement concerning the nature and motor-force of the revolution were subjected to the acid test in the events of 1917. At this point, the line separating Trotsky from Lenin dissolves completely. The line of Lenin's *Letters From Afar* and his *April Theses* is indistinguishable from that which we read in Trotsky's articles published in *Novy Mir*, written at the same time, but thousands of miles away in America. And, as Trotsky had warned in 1909, the counter-revolutionary side of the theory of the democratic dictatorship of the proletariat and peasantry only became evident in the course of the revolution itself, when Kamenev, Zinoviev and Stalin used it against Lenin to justify their support for the bourgeois Provisional Government. An open split developed between Lenin and the other leaders of the Bolshevik party who, in effect, accused him of Trotskyism.

In point of fact, the correctness of the theory of the permanent revolution was triumphantly demonstrated by the October revolution itself. The Russian working class as Trotsky had predicted in 1904 came to power before the workers of Western Europe. They carried out all the tasks of the bourgeois-democratic revolution, and immediately set about nationalizing industry and passing over to the tasks of the socialist revolution. The bourgeoisie played an openly counter-revolutionary role, but was defeated by the workers in alliance with the poor peasants. The Bolsheviks then made a revolutionary appeal to the workers of the world to follow their example. Lenin knew very well that without the victory of the revolution in the advanced capitalist countries, especially Germany, the revolution could not survive in isolation, especially in a backward country like Russia. What happened subsequently showed that this was absolutely correct. The setting up of the Third (Communist) International, the world party of socialist revolution, was the concrete manifestation of this perspective.

The Bourgeoisie and the Bureaucracy

The situation is clear still today. The national bourgeoisie in the colonial countries entered into the scene of history too late, when the world had already been divided up between a few imperialist powers. It was not able to play any progressive role and was born completely subordinated to its former colonial masters. The weak and degenerate bourgeoisie in Asia, Latin America and Africa is too dependent on foreign capital and imperialism, to carry society forward. It is tied by a thousand threads, not only to foreign capital, but to the class of landowners with which it forms a reactionary bloc that represents a bulwark against progress. Whatever differences may exist between these elements are insignificant in comparison with the fear that unites them against the masses. Only the proletariat, allied with the poor peasants and urban poor, can solve the problems of society by taking power into its own hands, expropriating the imperialists and the bourgeoisie, and beginning the task of transforming society on socialist lines.

Had the Communist International remained firm on the positions of Lenin and Trotsky, the victory of the world revolution would have been assured. Unfortunately, the Comintern's formative years coincided with the Stalinist counter-revolution in Russia, which had a disastrous effect on the Communist Parties of the entire world. The Stalinist bureaucracy, having acquired control in the Soviet Union, developed a very conservative outlook. The theory that socialism can be built in one country, —an abomination from the standpoint of Marx and Lenin really reflected the mentality of the bureaucracy, which had had enough of the storm and stress of revolution and sought to get on with the task of "building socialism in Russia".

Instead of pursuing a revolutionary policy based on class independence, as Lenin had always advocated, they proposed an alliance of the Communist Parties with the "national progressive bourgeoisie" (and if there was not one easily at hand, they were quite prepared to invent one) to carry through the democratic revolution, and later on, in the far distant future, when the country had developed a full-fledged capitalist economy, for socialism. In reality they had now even abandoned the second stage and capitulated to liberal democracy and a rotten bourgeoisie. This policy represented a complete break with Leninism and a return to the old discredited position of Menshevik theory of the two stages.

In India this Menshevist two-stageism was practised by the pro-Moscow CPI with the so-called progressive Indian bourgeois party, the Congress under the leadership of Nehru. The zigzags and the betrayals and attacks on the workers by the bourgeois congress government created disillusionment and conflicts within the ranks of the CPI. This ultimately led to a split in 1964 with the formation of the CPI (M) which was now taking the pro-Peking line. But as there was no fundamental ideological difference between the Russian and Chinese versions of Stalinism, the CPI (M) (Communist Party of India-Marxist) faced a similar crisis, which led to the 1969 split that gave birth to the CPI (ML) (Marxist Leninist). Yet the ideological foundations of these parties remained the same.

However in the 1950s and 1960s and the 1970s there was some semblance and at least a nominal adherence to 'socialism' and 'communism'. These Left currents at least brought some reforms in the Left front governments in Kerala, West Bengal and Tripura. There were historical and peculiar political reasons for these Left parties having a relatively bigger mass base, to which these reforms gave a certain impetus. But now the CPI (M) in particular has virtually abandoned even the defunct two-stage theory. Now they have ended up in the one-stageism which is the eternal rule of bourgeois democracy under the oligarchy of finance capital. Now they have gone so far that they are forcibly evicting poor peasants from the lands that they had acquired during the land reforms carried out by the CPI (M) led Left-front government in Bengal in the late 1970s and 1980s. In Singur, Nandigram, and other places the violence of the State and CPI (M) 'cadres' were used for the forced eviction of these poor peasants. These evictions were made from the land to be provided to multinational conglomerate investment, mainly India's Tata group and Indonesian Salim group of industries. These policies of neo-liberal Capitalist economy are playing havoc with the peasant base of support for the Left parties in Bengal and else where. There is an increasing ferment within the ranks of Left parties. Apart from a large number of youths going over to various Maoist groups and armed struggle there is the opening up of enormous possibilities for Marxism to attract this Left youth towards the programme of revolutionary socialism.

Students

In Pakistan the parties toeing the Moscow line were mainly mired in the limited democratic causes. They became stale and couldn't put up any significant mass resistance against the Ayub dictatorship. Meanwhile, the growing impact of the developments in China started to influence sections of the students and youth.

During the late 1950s and early 1960s, the NSF had partially rectified the fragmented condition of the student Left by promoting a degree of central direction and national-to-district levels of organization for 'progressive students ... nationalist, socialist, communist'. It is certainly of importance that the period of the NSF's greatest strength coincided with the early years of the Ayub Regime.

This resulted in part from the Regime's attempts to control and manipulate student politics by bureaucratic penetration of the university system. The University Ordinances (1962), imposed during the Martial Law period and continued after it was lifted, were especially despised. They provided for the forfeiture of degrees for untoward political activity and imposed political controls on faculty salaries, promotions, foreign academic contacts and trips abroad. Another repressive act was the 'Student Affairs Department'. This operated at Punjab University as a campus branch of the Criminal Investigation Department (CID), the police intelligence service. For 'politically reliable' students there were scholarships given by the Student Affairs Department, but for the 'politically unreliable' there were the ubiquitous classroom CID informants, the threat of expulsion from the university, expulsion from the city, a visit to the Chuna Mandi Police Station, or perhaps to the dreaded

Lahore Fort. The student communities at Dacca, Karachi and Lahore rioted against these University Ordinances, as well as against events abroad, such as the French role in Algeria and the alleged complicity of the United States in the assassination of Patrice Lumumba. In all of these student actions there were strong anti-regime undercurrents.

The debate on 'Maoism' among Pakistani Leftists was an intense one, but it was not something in which most students involved themselves. If the visible hallmarks of their new political consciousness were anti-Americanism, a Marxist rhetoric and a pro-China tendency, the reality was that the far stronger underlying current was that of Nationalism. Most of the pro-Bhutto student leaders were neither Marxists nor revolutionaries, but different nationalist versions of Stalinist factions. They were more committed to some kind of basic structural change that would set the nation on the road to economic and military self-sufficiency.

China and Pakistan

But here again the irony was that the Chinese bureaucracy under Mao had a close relationship with the regime, and Pak–China friendship associations were sponsored by the Pakistani State. Yet most Left parties and student organizations belonged to the pro-Peking Left. This led to utter confusion. Important sections of the military elite and the state bureaucracy had also a very fraternal relationship with the Chinese bureaucracy (Communist Party of China, CPC). The Chinese and the Russian bureaucracies, pursuing the policies of 'socialism in one country,' degenerated into a socialism embedded in National chauvinism. The comrades were discussing issues in the language of artillery fire and cross-border bloody skirmishes. These antagonisms, which created the Sino-Soviet split, had severe ramifications on the Left movements especially in the neo colonial countries. Against the Leninist method of internationalism they were pursuing narrow nationalist agendas prioritised by the perks and privileges of the bureaucratic castes in both the USSR and China. Had China become a part of the USSR, as Lenin had envisaged the USSR to be the new socialist union of all the countries of the world, history would have been very different.

Because of the antagonisms between the Pakistani elite and the Indian ruling class, and the support of the Soviet Union for the Nehruvian Congress government in India, the Chinese bureaucracy, in retaliation against Russia, gave unconditional and outright support to the military junta in Pakistan.

Ted Grant writes on the role of the Chinese bureaucracy and the ramifications of the Stalinist ideology of "National Socialism":

> The real face of Chinese Stalinism is revealed in the opportunism of the leadership in the colonial world, where they have given support to the rotting, feudal, bourgeois upper strata in many countries: the support of the Imam in the Yemen, the loans to Afghanistan, to Sri Lanka, to Pakistan, support of Soekarno in Indonesia, etc. Without being able to compete in resources, they have used the slender means of the Chinese economy in competition with the Russian bureaucracy and with imperialism. Their ideology, their conceptions, cannot rise above the narrow national interests of the Chinese bureaucracy. Their 'internationalism' consists in trying to build an instrument of support similar to that possessed by the Russian Stalinist bureaucracy. Their ideology, methods and attitudes are a counterfeit of Marxism, as much as that of the Russian bureaucracy, at various stages of its development.[9]

After the rigged election of January 1965 the Chinese Prime Minister Chou en Lai was the first international leader to congratulate Field Marshal Ayub Khan on his "historic" victory. In his message he said that this victory reflected the mass support for Ayub Khan.

After the September 1965 war Marshal Chen Yen, the commander of the Chinese People's Liberation Army, visited Pakistan and compared Ayub Khan's 'basic democracies' with 'people's communes'. In a statement Marshal Chen Yen said: "President General Ayub Khan's great and dynamic leadership had unified the whole Pakistani nation and defending the sovereignty gave a resounding answer to the enemy."[10]

In 1967 the leader of the visiting Chinese trade delegation gave the following statement:

> Under President Gen. Ayub Khan's great leadership Pakistan has

> made enormous progress in both Industrial and agricultural fields. The day is not far off when Pakistan will achieve total economic Independence.[11]

There was a barrage of such statements from Chinese officials and the pro-Peking Left in Pakistan had no option but to somehow support this despotic regime. The main problem with both the pro-Moscow and pro-Peking Left was the lack of Marxist analysis and perspective. They were more involved in activism than in building a solid cadre base with an advanced theoretical and political base. The rapid achievements of the planned economy, both in the Soviet Union and China, had startled them. Basing themselves on the 'practicalities', what they saw or knew about these countries was a far greater rate of growth and progress compared with Pakistan. Hence, that was all the 'socialism' they could follow and accepted the ridicule of Trotsky and other Marxists who had said decades ago what would be the ultimate fate of those 'socialist' countries. It was Lenin in 1921, Trotsky in his graphic work *Revolution Betrayed* in 1936, Ted Grant in his several works in 1943, 1951 and 1959, who predicted the collapse of the Soviet Union, disintegration of Stalinism, and the degeneration of the planned economy in the so-called People's Republic of China.

Left Disarray

The pro-Moscow Communist party spokesman in a statement confessed the class collaborationist policies of two-stageism. He said,

> Our modern rising bourgeoisie will come into conflict with the dominating American and European bourgeoisie in the World Market. Hence, under economic compulsion Habibullah, Valika's and Saigols (Home of the largest Pakistani bourgeois entrepreneurs) will have to turn for trade towards the socialist block. This act will enable us to overcome the domination of Western monopoly. This is that direction towards which we are on the move. If I condemn President Ayub's opening up this avenue towards left, I would be definitely mad.[12]

Such vacillations, ideological confusions and ambiguity towards the class contradictions inevitably lead to the disarray of the Left movement. This was the main obstacle to the formation of a Bolshevik-Leninist Party that could fulfil the revolutionary tasks faced at the time. The class collaborationist ideology led to opportunism, giving rise to tendencies of adventurism and ultra-Leftism. A large number of Left activists, workers and youth made enormous sacrifices and suffered the tortures and brutalities of the bourgeois state. The basic motive of sacrifice and struggle was for them 'socialism' and 'communism', but in reality their leaders espoused the cause of bourgeois democracy. As soon as the activists realized this they left in disgust, some into the political wilderness, and others into crime and corruption. Ultimately they felt betrayed by the 'cause' itself; the tragedy being that the cause of revolutionary socialism was misinterpreted and falsified by the false ideology of two-stageism (Menshevism).

It was in these conditions of political unpreparedness, organizational incapacity, lack of Marxist perspectives and ideological incoherence that the Left leaders and intellectuals were shell shocked by the momentous upheaval of 1968-9; most were bewildered and confused. The role and character of the Stalinists gave rise to the phenomenon of populism yet again in a country like Pakistan.

Populism and Bhutto

Populism was mainly the product of the contradiction between the Stalinist ideology of two-stageism and the socialist aspirations and character of the mass movements that had erupted mainly in ex-colonial countries, particularly in the post-Second World War period. The most significant examples have been Peronism in Argentina, Soekarnoism in Indonesia, Nasserism in Egypt, and similar regimes in other African, Asian and Latin American countries. The phenomenon of modern populism was based on individual leaders who came to the fore through historical accidents and who gained support by revolutionary sloganeering and socialist rhetoric. It also reflected a certain primitive political culture that gave rise to an exaggerated role and dependence on individuals as liberators and heroes for the masses.

This extraordinary reliance and popularity got them

immense political authority. To enhance their support they could only go to the extent of radical reforms. As for overthrow capitalism, they neither had an understanding of revolutionary Marxism nor had they built parties with the revolutionary ideology and organizational structures and ability to overthrow the old order. But, as in the case of the proletarian Bonapartist states, they defied the two-stage theory and in a peculiar manner vindicated the validity and truth of Trotsky's theory of permanent revolution, albeit perversely. However, in absence of traditional workers', socialist or communist parties, they became the new political traditional modes of expression of the masses. However their role and character was and is reflective of the condition and State of the movements of the workers and the oppressed masses in those countries at the time.

The traditional Left started to split more rapidly. Some of the pro-Moscow elements who were working in the 'nationalist', 'democratic', and 'progressive' parties had joined the DAC (Democratic Action Committee). This was a political alliance of diverse bourgeois and Right-wing parties. One of the main Stalwarts of DAC was Nawabzada Nasrullah Khan, a conservative Right-wing politician and a petty landlord from south Punjab. The irony is that this DAC also included extreme Right-wing elements, including the Islamic fundamentalists. The arch Islamic fundamentalist party, the Jamat-i-Islami, at that stage the main agent of US imperialism, was also part of this right wing 'democratic' alliance.

The Santema dictum goes: "Those who don't learn from the mistakes of history are doomed to repeat them." These Left leaders were still struggling in bourgeois alliances for 'Democratic' change.

While these sections of the Left were playing 'party-party' and juggling with democratic change the revolutionary blizzard bypassed them without even noticing their existence.

Zulfiqar Ali Bhutto, being shrewder in sensing the mood of the mass movement, had embarked upon the 'need for socialism' and other radical slogans. This PPP programme clicked with the masses' moods, aspirations and sentiments; the PPP became the largest party of the masses in the history of

Pakistan, almost overnight. The first activists and cadres that gave the PPP a foothold and standing were from the different Maoist groups and other scattered left activists. These groups were disillusioned and frustrated by the traditional Stalinist leadership of the Left.

The founding convention of the Pakistan People's Party was held at Dr. Mubashar Hasan's home on main boulevard Gulberg, Lahore, on 30 November and 1st of December 1967. The founding documents, which were prepared by Bhutto and J.A. Rahim in Paris in 1966, were presented in their final form after long consultations with Dr. Mubashar Hasan, who was also a member of the 'principles committee'. They were very radical and called for a socialist change in the aims and objectives of the new party that was being set up in these two days. Very few of those attending the meeting realized that history was being made at that gathering. The founding document of PPP said:

> The ultimate objective of the party's policy is the attainment of a classless society which is only possible through socialism in our times.[13]

As was expected, Bhutto's speech, the main attraction at the convention, was full of passion and vigour. He concluded by saying, "We have to tackle basic anomalies ... change this system and put an end to exploitation. This can only be done by socialism. That is why our party stands for socialism."[14]

After the founding convention Bhutto went into full political action across the country, sensing only too well that the masses were yearning for a radical change. To galvanize those burning aspirations he went all over the country, presenting himself as the revolutionary socialist who would lead the transformation of society through revolutionary change. In one of those initial speeches in 1968 Bhutto said:

> My dear friends, it is said that I am a wealthy man and a feudal lord. It is said that I have no right to struggle for socialism without distributing my wealth among the people ... socialism can be introduced only when all means of production are brought under state control. But even so I hereby announce that if my wealth can be of any good to the nation I will not hesitate to give it away. But I

> cannot be so foolish as to hand my wealth over to capitalists and feudalists under the capitalistic system, so as to enable the rulers to make more money and spend more on their luxuries ...
>
> (...) But you cannot fool the people by such useless arguments. I believe in socialism; that is why I have left my class and joined the labourers, peasants and poor students. I love them. And what can I get from them except affection and respect? No power on earth can stop socialism—the symbol of justice, equality and the supremacy of man from being introduced in Pakistan. It is the demand of time and history. And you can see me raising this revolutionary banner among the masses. I am a socialist, and an honest socialist, who will continue to fight for the poor till the last moment of his life. Some ridicule me for being socialist. I don't care.[15]

The Founding of the PPP

The men and women who gathered to found the Pakistan People's Party were indeed a diverse group in terms of their social identities, previous political affiliations, ideological proclivities and general characteristics. They held varying notions about the ultimate aims of the PPP, and about the role of Bhutto in it. Some of them, friends from better days and protective of future opportunities, formed the beginnings of an inner circle around Bhutto. Others saw him as the polar opposite to Ayub Khan, and a leader who could unify the political forces against the military-bureaucratic forces and bring parliamentary democracy back to Pakistan. Still others, students and anti-feudalists, regarded Bhutto as a genuine progressive democratic socialist who would, with the aid of a highly organized political party, seek a socialist reconstruction of the economy and society of Pakistan.

Bhutto's concept was not so much of a party as it was of a political movement, where groups and leaders and fragments of groups were held together segmentally, with vertical lines of authority leading to the Chairman. This meant, of course, that neither ideology nor organization could be too rigid or refined. The founding convention dealt substantively with both the ideology and organization of the People's Party, both aspects being greatly influenced by later events.

Bhutto was not a Marxist. He came to ride on the rising tide of the 1968-9 revolution as a result of the tumultuous events that were rapidly unfolding at that time; he happened to be in the right time and place to lead this unprecedented mass uprising. However, he was a widely-read person and had seen movements and societies in restive conditions in many countries of the world. He had studied at some of the most famous institutions in US and Britain. He had a relatively advanced political understanding, and the experience of what had gone on across the world in the 1940s and 1950s had a certain influence on him. He cannot be totally compared to Chou en Lai, but in that period there were several individuals from the privileged classes in the colonial world who were affected by the massive upheavals of the colonial revolutions in the post-war era. In the colonial revolutions we saw quite a number of peculiarities when even individuals from upper classes were radicalized. But Bhutto had not gone that far; on his return from abroad he was inducted into the Cabinet of President Iskander/ Skander Mirza in 1956, and ultimately as a minister of Foreign Affairs in Ayub Khan's cabinet in the early 1960s.

Sobho Gianchandani explained this transition in a recent interview with *Newsline,*

> Bhutto had wanted to join the Awami Party. G.M. Syed told me a joke regarding this: "One day, Bhutto came to my residence and said, "Shah Sahib, I want to join your party." Jokingly, I said to him, "Do you know ours is a party of rebels?" Bhutto replied, "I know." Comrade Hyder Bux Jatoi interrupted us and asked Bhutto, "Have you taken your father's permission? A Khan Bahadur's son cannot become a member of a rebel party." Bhutto shouted back, "Revolution is not the monopoly of Hyder Bux Jatoi! I am also a revolutionary." Hyder Bux Jatoi persisted. Bhutto spoke to Shah Nawaz Bhutto via telephone. Meanwhile, Iskander Mirza contacted Shah Nawaz Bhutto and told him, "I have planned a great career for your son Zulfiqar, tell him not to join the rebels." Consequently, the next day Bhutto came and submitted his resignation, saying he didn't want to be a rebel. "I told you so," shouted Hyder Bux Jatoi."[16]

After the 1965 war with India, Bhutto and Ayub Khan had a split which was inevitable due to the rising tensions and conflicts amongst the ruling elite. This was inevitable in the immediate aftermath of the war, which had aggravated both the economic crisis and the social unrest. These, although not explosive, had an effect on the cohesion and unity of the regime.

After he was deposed by Ayub Khan his ego was damaged and he was seething for revenge against a military dictator whom he regarded, and perhaps rightly so, as a mediocrity in intellect and political strategy. But this whole episode, with its melodramatic publicity, made Bhutto a revered victim of tyranny amongst the masses in general. In the subcontinental culture the victims get extraordinary sympathy and people try to share their own tragedies with those who are hurt by evil. This gave him personal authority and the political leverage to propel himself to leadership of the masses.

But this is only one aspect of the equation. The objective situation was changing rapidly. He had an instinctive understanding of the mass moods and sudden changes in mass psychology. Hence the empathy between Bhutto and the masses was prepared by a string of subjective happenings and the sharp turns in the objective conditions. Bhutto understood the need for radical change and a socialist programme to bring about the changes in their lives that the masses were yearning for. The rising tide of the movement also swung and swayed Bhutto; his speeches, acts, and style all clichéd with the immediate situations and events unfolding with a lightening speed around him. Never before had the masses heard or envisaged on such a mammoth scale the call for a socialist revolution such as Bhutto was spreading across the country.

In April 1968 in a pamphlet titled *Political Situation in Pakistan*, he wrote:

> Out of the welter of confusion a crystallisation is taking place. A growing body of people, with the younger generation at their head, believe that the old ways are no longer sufficient to surmount the problems of Pakistan. Each epoch has its own political significance; its own seismic pattern. This epoch, exciting and full of challenge, requires a fresh approach for building society anew on the finest aspirations of the entire population of Pakistan. We are not prepared to return to the past. Nor are the people willing to tolerate the present conditions much longer. For this reason, the Pakistan People's Party declares: "All power to the people!"[17]

His position on Democracy was quite accurate. In explaining the real nature of bourgeois democracy he was very close to

Lenin's definition in *Proletarian Revolution and the Renegade Kautsky*. Bhutto wrote in the same pamphlet:

> Democracy is essential but is not an end in itself. In the struggle to establish democracy we must never lose sight of the economic objectives, which remain paramount. Without economic progress a nation cannot find satisfaction in democracy alone. Democratic freedom is essential, but economic equality and justice are supremely important. Profound changes in national life cannot come without economic changes. Economic problems remain pivotal. Democracy must go hand-in-hand with enlightened socialism if the servitude of the people is to be ended. The limited resources of this overpopulated country are being wasted and falling commodity prices in the international market diminish its capacity to purchase essentials from industrial countries. In such a situation socialism is the only answer to our economic problems. Socialism offers the only way to end exploitation and to foster unity. Unity will remain a slogan and an illusion until exploitation is ended.
>
> We are on the brink of economic catastrophe. A new class, small in number, of capitalist barons, is unabashedly plundering national wealth. The disparity between the rich and the poor keeps on growing. Here in Pakistan there is only loot. On the pretext of encouraging private initiative, scandalous incentives are given to facilitate massive exploitation.[18]

Again he defines socialism in the following words:

> Only socialism, which creates equal opportunities for all, protects from exploitation, removes the barriers of class distinction, is capable of establishing economic and social justice. Socialism is the highest expression of democracy and its logical fulfilment.
>
> The universality of the precepts of socialism is essentially due to two reasons: first, the basis of modern socialism is objective; second, socialist thinking is relevant to all countries in every part of the world in their actual economic and political condition. Socialism is, therefore, of direct interest to Pakistan, an underdeveloped country marked by internal and external exploitation.
>
> (...) The region of the earth with the highest concentration of poverty is Pakistan. The stigma has to be wiped out by socialism. The immediate task would be to end predatory capitalism and to put socialism into motion. The means of production that are the generators of industrial advance or on which depend other industries must not be allowed to be vested in private hands. All enterprises that constitute the infrastructure of the national economy must be in public ownership.[19]

In a speech at the District Bar Association at Hyderabad on 26 June 1969, Bhutto thundered:

> The Pakistan People's Party is a party of the people of Pakistan. Let me make it quite clear that it is a party of the workers and peasants and the students of Pakistan. It is a revolutionary party.[20]

Ideological Confusion

This was perhaps the most radical definition of the Pakistan People's Party. Yet this was not the full story of the PPP. The other side of the story is that Bhutto and the PPP leadership of the time, although very left and revolutionary in expression, were always burdened by ideological confusion and contradictory ideas and tendencies. Hence they were incapable of laying the basis for a genuine revolutionary party to lead the masses in overthrowing capitalism and carrying through a socialist transformation of Society.

It was not just Bhutto, but also the other main leaders of the PPP with Maoist and other diverse left backgrounds who were pursuing a mixed bag of ideas that were a crude mixture of socialism, nationalism and even with streaks of Pan Islamism that they interpreted in the form of 'Islamic Socialism'.

These ideological deviations resulted in the inevitability of the derailment of this glorious revolution. The ideological confusion and lack of a clear Marxist position are evident in some of the speeches made by Zulfiqar Ali Bhutto at the time. For example, in a speech at a public meeting in Mansehra, Pushtoonkhwa (NWFP) Bhutto even tried to gain the support of the primitive layers of the masses by exploiting Pakistani and Muslim prejudices. He undermined the class basis and socialist ideals of the revolution that was in full swing when he said:

> The conflict between Hindus and Muslims dates back one thousand years into history. Why can't it be carried into the future? If the nation can fight for one thousand years for its survival, it can do so in the future as well.[21]

At the Frontier (Pushtoonkhwa) convention on 3 November 1968 at Sherpao, he once again tried to compromise socialism with Islam (religion), saying:

> Why socialist parties have not succeeded in India is because Hinduism is against socialism, just as it is against Islam. Hinduism can never tolerate socialism, because the Hindu religion provides for various classes. While socialism has not made any headway in India, it can make tremendous progress in Pakistan because there is little difference between Islam and socialism.
>
> I want to say this clearly that in the socio-economic sector there is no difference between Islam and socialism. Had these two systems been in conflict with each other, I would have given up socialism.[22]

This was in contrast to the reality. One economy is based on the charity shown by the rich towards the poor. In other words, the existence of propertied classes and impoverished classes is considered a social norm. Under socialism this class divide is eliminated and it strives for a classless society.

At the same time this notion of pan-Islamism or later third-worldism as propagated and pursued by a certain variety of Stalinist leaders was also part of the strange mix of contradictory ideologies and systems.

Once again in a speech at a mass rally in Peshawar on 5 November 1968, Bhutto said the following:

> Had the Pakistan People's Party been in power at the time of the Arab-Israel war in the Middle East we would have deprived the Israeli Defence Minister of his second eye. But it is regrettable that the largest Islamic State could not play its role which she could and should have played. And the situation is that while Kashmir is with the Indians and Jerusalem with the Israelis we still claim that Pakistan has made big progress. If the Pakistan Peoples Party comes into power, and it will Insha-Allah (God willing), then you will see that not only will the lot of the poor labourers and peasants improve, but also no Indian will be seen in Kashmir and no Israeli in Jerusalem.[23]

In the address to the District Bar Association at Hyderabad on 26 June 1968, Bhutto eulogized the revolutionary ideological basis of Partition:

> Pakistan came into being because we were Muslims. We shall sacrifice everything for Islam. Islam means the strengthening of the Muslim people.[24]

The point is that, within the ideological and institutional confines of the existing state and structure, the tasks of the national democratic revolution cannot be accomplished. This includes the demands for the separation of religion from state, i.e. a secular state. A socialist transformation cannot be accomplished merely by the completion of the national democratic tasks, but these tasks can only be achieved by adopting socialist measures. A socialist revolution doesn't only transform the market economy into a planned economy, but through its revolutionary actions it changes the social, cultural, moral and ethical values of capitalist society. The Liberals in Pakistan hold up Jinnah's speech of 11 August 1947 as proof of Jinnah's determination to see Pakistan as a secular rather than a theocratic state. This speech was delivered without notes, but as he put it: "a few things as they occur to me".

But again this is an exceptional quotation with self-serving attributions to Jinnah by the Liberals. Most other speeches and statements do not subscribe to this perception. For example, on 25 January 1948, Jinnah spoke to the Bar Association of Karachi, and said:

> Why this feeling of nervousness that the future constitution of Pakistan is going to be in conflict with Shariat Laws? Islamic principles today are as applicable to life as they were 1300 years ago.
>
> Islam is not only a set of rituals, traditions and spiritual doctrines. Islam is also the code of every Muslim, which regulates his life and conduct in even politics and economics and the like.[25]

The Pakistanization and Islamization of socialism by the leadership even in those days was typical of populist swings due to the contradictory pressures of various sections of society. This balancing act, a sort of popular Bonapartism, has a fragile basis and is not long lasting. The inevitable results were proved by events that history has witnessed in the four decades after those upheavals.

The most important aspect was the historically exceptional period and a revolution in action that had aroused the masses to an advanced level of consciousness. Hence, if Bhutto had to appease what he thought of as apparently backward layers of society by using nationalist and religious rhetoric, in most other regions and industrial areas it was the revolutionary fervour that was pushing him more and more towards the slogan of radical socialism.

Like Bonapartism of different forms, the balancing between classes through a populist movement is shortlived, hollow, and debilitated in its basic character. In this balancing act there are always pressures from the conflicting interest of irreconciliable class positions in society and in politics. The intrinsic weakness of populism causes it to appease and bend to these contradictory class pressures; consequently such regimes are inherently in crisis and turmoil. The description of PPP as a 'multi class' party reflects this deep conflict of contradictions of populism.

There never has been and there never can be a 'multi-class' party. In the end every political party defends the interest of one class or the other; to fabricate the character of a political party as 'multi-class' is demagogic to say the least. The crux of the matter is that the PPP started as a party but has developed into a tradition, a hope perhaps, a movement or a platform where the masses gather as they move into political activity. But they can only begin here, the struggle can never end, aims cannot be achieved, and the change the masses are yearning for can never be accomplished through such a medium of political activity. When the stranglehold on the PPP by ruling classes and imperialism is broken it will not be the same entity anymore. It will be a totally different culture of political and of revolutionary struggle altogether.

It was the movement, historical mammoth rallies, strikes, barricades, and the valour of the workers that was radicalizing Bhutto further and further towards the Left. Bhutto was not giving the 'voice' to the people. The revolutionary fervour of the masses in reality was giving Bhutto the language and courage to call for a socialist change.

Writing a doctorate thesis on Pakistan People's Party (published in a book) Philip E. Jones analyzed the party's origins and Bhutto's role in the following lines. He wrote:

> Without too much exaggeration, it can be said that the dominance of this one individual is the crucial factor determining the organizational and political directions taken by a populist party. Perhaps it would be worthwhile to distinguish here between an 'organizational-base,' or Bolshevik, type of party that stresses the discipline, ideology, and objectives of organization, and a single leader, or 'furtherist,' type in which organization and ideology are subordinated to the particular

> proclivities and vision of the supreme leader. Though both are mass movement phenomena, the Bolshevik party model is the more thoroughly revolutionary in that it aims to rebuild the state structure from the ground up. The 'furtherist' party model aims to capture the pre-existing state institutions and to bend them to its own ideological and political goals. 'Furtherist' parties thus tend to downgrade their own organization in favour of becoming part of the state apparatus. Clearly, aside from party-state relations, these two models have very different outcomes in terms of leadership styles, organizational strategies, recruitment policies and ideological emphases.
>
> (...) During its early years, the years of the ascendancy of the 'ideological' wing of the party, the PPP adopted the outward symbols of the Bolshevik model in its provision for a Chairman and a Central Committee and in its grass roots organizational strategy. Yet, in the cultural and political conditions prevailing in Pakistan, it was perhaps only a matter of time before the PPP would transform itself visibly into a 'furtherist' party. Though this process was well underway before the 1970 elections, it became more and more obvious during the years of power. The long internal struggle between the 'ideologicals' and the 'politicals' emphasized the nature of the People's Party as a transitional structure that reflected both the passing age of elite politics and the emergent age of mass politics.[26]

Along with J.A. Rahim, Bhutto announced the decision for a new party from the Hyderabad residence of Mir Rasul Bakhsh Talpur on 16 September 1967. It would be a "national progressive organization having its roots deep in the masses equally in East and West Pakistan."

The founding convention of the Pakistan People's Party was not, as Bhutto admitted, a "spectacular success". According to PPP sources, the Ayub Government had gone to considerable lengths to ensure that this would be so. It had bought all the seats on PIA flights from Dacca to Lahore on the day before the convention was held at the home of Dr. Mubashar Hasan out in the elite suburb of Gulberg, some five miles away from the volatile inner city and the complex of educational institutions around Gol Bagh. According to *Dawn*, some 300 delegates attended the convention, while the most optimistic PPP figures put the number at 500, or about half the number expected.[27]

There were no delegates from East Pakistan, a fact which allowed the NPT (National Press Trust) papers to dismiss Bhutto as a 'national leader', but which also ominously presaged future events.

> The Pakistan Times called it a 'faceless gathering of political romantics, runaway students, and ideological oddballs.' Not to mention the 'briefless lawyers and crypto-communists' who were also present.[28]
>
> Dawn thought the 'gathering looked more like a teenagers' jamboree than a solemn political conclave,' and opined that, 'with the country already plagued by innumerable political parties, the addition of still another could hardly be expected to kindle popular enthusiasm.'[29]

The district administration was concerned, if not unduly alarmed, and went so far as to impose Section 144 on the city and to refuse the new party permission to hold its first public meeting, which was scheduled for 3 December at Mochi Darwaza. (Mochi Darwaza) 'Cobbler Gate'—is to Lahore politically, what Lahore is to Punjab. For decades politicians have gone to Mochi Darwaza to prove their popular appeal. Mian Muhammad Shafi, Fazl-i-Hussain, Maulana Zafar Ali Khan, Maulana Ataullah Shah Bukhari, M.A. Jinnah, Liaqat Ali Khan, the Nawab of Mamdot, Mumtaz Daultana, even Ayub Khan, have all had their moments at Mochi Darwaza. The name of a long-vanished gateway into the old city, Mochi Darwaza was an open space along Circular Road, which used to be surrounded by the most densely populated wards of Lahore. To the north and west is the old city, with its veritable warren of alleys, narrow passages and cul-de-sacs, and to the east and south are the teeming wards of Gawalmandi, Ramgali and Qila Gujjar Singh). Movements of even modest appeal have always been able to get good crowds at Mochi Darwaza.

In spite of the smaller than expected turnout the mood at the convention was upbeat. Z.A. Bhutto, who was elected Chairman of the convention on the first day, noted that the "beginnings of great movements were often modest and small".

There were four sessions in two days. The first was mainly a long speech by Bhutto, and the second was presentations by self-appointed 'representatives of the peasantry, lawyers, businessmen, engineers and youth leaders...,'which 'demonstrated how extensive the appeal of the party was to politically conscious people'. In the third session, the delegates debated the 'Foundation Meeting Documents' and the resolutions drawn up overnight by the Convention's

Resolutions Committee. During the fourth session, the new party was founded. The 'Foundation Documents' and convention resolutions were adopted, the party decided to call itself the Pakistan People's Party, and the delegates chose a tricolour party flag, the latter item being the one which caused the most discussion.

Certainly, Bhutto and the party leaders were in the thick of things in the next stormy years. The movement exploded from the very beginning: Bhutto and K.H. Meer consulted with student leaders during the Rawalpindi disturbances of 7 to 9 November 1968; the PPP Chairman led a PPP delegation out to Pindi Gheb to attend the funeral of Abdul Hamid (the polytechnic student whose killing by police firing had sparked off the revolt) on 8 November; while other PPP figures addressed the crowds around the Inter-Continental. On 10 November Bhutto went down to Lahore by train, meeting large crowds along the way, who somehow had heard he would be passing by. At Lahore he was welcomed by a mammoth crowd and an automobile had to be brought directly on to the station platform before Bhutto could make an exit from his railway compartment. The next day, in a highly charged atmosphere, the PPP Chairman addressed the Lahore District Bar Association. He told the assembled lawyers he refused a Government suggestion that he should appeal to the students to stop their demonstrations. He did so "because they are fighting and I am fighting with them".

Bhutto's Arrest and the Left-Right Struggle

On 13 November, he was scheduled to travel down to Multan by train, but was arrested along with his host, Dr. Mubashar Hasan, at 1:30 a.m. under the DPR (Defence of Pakistan Rules). The large crowd waiting at the station for the PPP Chairman erupted, setting off the first disturbances in that city.

The incarceration of Bhutto left the leadership ranks of the People's Party somewhat disorganized and it was only after defeating a sharp internal challenge that J.A. Rahim emerged as acting chairman. This, and the nature of the November Movement, enabled secondary and more ideologically oriented figures to emerge as the active leadership element in the party.

Reappearing after a six month hiatus, *Nusrat* (PPP's weekly journal) began to function as a crucial link, coordinating policy and propaganda for PPP groups all over West Pakistan.

The 25th of November was the beginning of a Left-Right struggle among political parties to gain control over the movement and the political power that lay beyond it. The Left-Right polemic was carried on most vigorously between the PPP and Jamat-i-Islami, JI.

By January *Nusrat* was publishing regular weekly articles on what it called Maududi' or 'Maududism', the philosophy and past political behaviour of the founder of JI. In early January, on his return from medical treatment in Europe, the founder, Sayyid Abu A'la Maududi, violently denounced 'socialism' and said that, "It would come to Pakistan only over the corpses of Pakistan's true Muslims".[30]

In March, the day after the failure of the RTC, in which Maududi represented the JI, the Amir (leader of Islamic parties/states) of the JI asked his party members "to form committees in every mohalla to smother the tongue that utters the word socialism".[31]

On 10 February 1969 the High Court changed the conditions of Bhutto's incarceration from imprisonment to house arrest at Larkana. On 11 February, he refused to fly in the aircraft put at his disposal on the grounds that a bomb had been planted in it, and went down to Larkana by train, meeting huge crowds at Multan, Rahim Yar Khan, Rohri and Sukkur.

On 14 February, along with four companions at Larkana and other groups around West Pakistan, Bhutto began his 'fast unto death' against the Emergency Rule Laws imposed by the Ayub regime.

On the same day, as Bhutto began his fast, the Government announced the Emergency would be lifted on 17 February and privately informed Bhutto that he was no longer under any form of restraint. Unwilling to let the issue be taken from him too easily, Bhutto decided to continue his fast until at least 17 February, and then, after the announcement by the Law Minister of lifting the Emergency, he said "if it was not a trick, he would break his fast".[32]

Bhutto made a triumphant entry into Karachi on 17 February. He intended, as he had told a journalist in Larkana two days earlier, to start the second phase of the struggle from Karachi, Pakistan's most proletarianized city, which was "being punished for voting against Ayub Khan".[33]

On 18 February, after long consultations with his supporters and party, Bhutto told a meeting of the Karachi Press Club that he would not join the Round Table Conference (RTC) all parties' talks. "The people wanted a complete change, not just concessions".[34]

Clearly, the Left wing of the People's party had been able to convince their party Chairman that the Movement had gone too far and penetrated too deeply to accept any compromise with the regime.

There was only one incentive in which Bhutto did not completely rule out his participation, as he shared with his close associates.

It was Bhutto's interest in exploring the possibility of co-operation with Sheikh Mujibur Rahman on a joint PPP-AL (Awami League) compromise at the RTC. From his first post-imprisonment interviews, the PPP Chairman had emphasized that no settlement could be made without his and Sheikh Mujib's participation.

He was aware of the meteoric rise in the latter's' popularity in East Pakistan, and suspected that Mujib might now be in a position to compromise on the 'Six Points'. Bhutto flew to Dacca on 23 February and began to make statements sympathetic to Mujib. "He explained that while he did not agree with all the 'Six Points' he was open to a public debate on them. He would withdraw his presidential candidacy if an agreed candidate should emerge from East Pakistan and he began to demand that the Government withdraw the Agartala Conspiracy Case against Mujib".[35]

Bhutto met Awami League leaders in Dacca and traveled to Lahore in the same aircraft as Mujib on 24 February, while the latter was on his way to the RTC. It became quickly evident that Mujib's position on the 'Six Points' had been stiffened, not softened, by his new popularity, that the RTC would likely be a deadlock, and that there was no likelihood of a joint PPP-AL stand.

At a news conference in Lahore he intimated that he would join the RTC if a consensus on a directly-elected Constituent Assembly could be reached between the opposition parties. This was unlikely, since the Jamat-i-Islami supported the reinstitution of the 1956 Constitution, a position that Bhutto had explicitly rejected.

On 2 March, he clarified his position further when he said he would join the RTC "the moment Ayub resigns." In that event, the Speaker of the Assembly should head a caretaker government until direct elections could be held for a Constituent Assembly.[36]

To opposition charges that his refusal to join the RTC without preconditions was disruptive, Bhutto replied that by staying away he was keeping the opposition leaders at the RTC honest and answerable to the masses. During this period, the PPP Chairman was again on the move around West Pakistan, almost daily addressing vast public rallies, and attempting to consolidate support.

He also began to court the leaders of the Movement, workers leaders, and social groups and even to make specific commitments by a future PPP Government in return for their support.

Bhutto saw 'nothing new' in Ayub's statement to the RTC in which he accepted two of the opposition demands. The PPP Chairman charged that a civilian coup d'etat was brewing between the rightist parties and the regime. The prospect of a Right-wing coup pushed Bhutto and Bhashani into a formal alliance.

Bhutto, who professed to be disappointed at the results of the earlier promise to cooperate, and who was known to feel his brand of socialism was different from that of Bhashani, wanted to come to power through elections. Bhashani wanted to get power through a revolutionary workers and peasants movement preferably through a guerilla struggle. He denounced the idea of elections, telling workers in Karachi that "any one trying to participate in the polls would do so at great risk to his property and we would burn his home and crush him".[37]

When the RTC consensus began to break down over Sheikh Mujib's insistence on the 'Six Points,' and with the disturbances all over the country continuing unabated, it was only a matter of days before Ayub would have to play his last card, the reinstatement of martial law. On 24 March 1969, according to the account given by Piloo Mody, the PIA aircraft Bhutto was taking from Karachi to Larkana was diverted to Rawalpindi 'for mechanical reasons'. On the plane's arrival in Rawalpindi, Bhutto was taken directly to see the Army Commander-in-Chief. Yahya Khan informed Bhutto that the Army saw no recourse but to take over the Government and asked for Bhutto's conditions of support. Bhutto made three conditions: an independent foreign policy, the break-up of One Unit and general elections on an adult suffrage basis within a year. Yahya accepted these conditions on the spot.

On 26 March 1969, Ayub was gone and Bhutto had called off the movement.

The subservience of party organizational matters to the broader strategic objective of winning elections was evident from the earliest days of the People's Party. In marked contrast to its swelling popularity, the spontaneous growth of local party units in many parts of Punjab and Sindh, and the requirements of the Interim Constitution, the work of organizing the formal structures downward from the Chairman was remarkably slow, particularly in Punjab.

> According to PPP notables close to the centre of activity in the People's Party, party organization was not a priority of the Chairman and party organization was kept rudimentary for some time after the founding convention.[38]

The Central Organizing Committee and the Principles Committee were appointed shortly after the convention, but neither acted without specific directions from the Chairman.

The Central Committee was not appointed until 24 January 1971, after the elections. A shadow Central Committee does seem to have existed earlier, made up essentially of the Organizing and Principles Committee members, together with individuals invited by the Chairman. Its most important and only recorded meeting took place on 23 March 1969 at Karachi, "where it committed the PPP to a policy of dismantling the One Unit Scheme".[39]

Thereafter, the Principles Committee, made up of Bhutto, J.A. Rahim, Dr. Mubashar Hasan, Hanif Ramay (appointed in 1968) and Abdul Hafiz Pirzada (appointed in 1969), acted off and on as an ad hoc Central Committee in matters of party discipline and policy enunciation. "J.A. Rahim was made Secretary General of the party in early 1970".[40]

None of the other national party officers appointed later in 1970 were founder-members of the party, but were figures of note and influence who joined the party during the election campaign. They were: Makhdum Talib ul Maula (Pir Jhandewaro of Hala Sharif), named a Vice Chairman, Mian Mahmud Ali Kasuri, also made a Vice Chairman and Maulana Kausar Niazi appointed Propaganda Secretary.

On 4 March 1969, the East Pakistan People's Party (PPP/EP) was dissolved. A. Kassim Choudhury and others attempted to reorganize a fragmented PPP/EP, but the party in the Eastern wing never recovered. So weak was it that, unlike other major parties with their main bases of support in West Pakistan, the PPP failed to run a single candidate in East Pakistan for the National Assembly in the 1970 elections.

The 23 March 1969 edition of *Nusrat* announced that "the first National Conference of the Pakistan People's Party would be held from 4 to 6 April 1969 at Lahore".[41] This was clearly an attempt to consolidate the gains made by the PPP during the November movement. Delegations were invited from among students, women, lawyers, intellectuals, journalists, peasants and workers, as well as from established PPP committees.

The imposition of Martial Law on 25 March 1969 included a prohibition on political activity and the PPP conference at Lahore had to be called off. The first National Conference was held from 1 to 3 July 1970 at Hala Sharif in Sindh, the second, and perhaps the last, at Rawalpindi on 30 November and 1 December 1972. At this stage the PPP was in power.

Attempts at Grass Roots Organization

The People's Party in Punjab expanded more rapidly at the bottom than at the top. Several periods of rapid organization are apparent. The first occurred immediately after the founding convention of 1 December 1967, when delegates returning home organized the first primary units and set off a wave of 'spontaneous' party organizations. These units were organized by local groups on their own volition, without reference to higher units, which, in most cases, did not yet exist. Most of these original units would later seek accreditation or be discovered by district organizations, though a few of them would fall foul of local rivalries. Approximately eight to ten per cent of all primary units organized between December 1967 and December 1970 were set up in the first three months after the founding convention.

The second surge of primary unit organization came in the urban areas in late 1969 and early 1970 and was related both to the approach of the election campaign and to urban unrest among workers, students and journalists. During this period many of the local units based on special interests were formed, including women's units. It also brought the high tide of Left influence in the PPP. The third period of rapid expansions was less viable, but it began after the Conference of Students, Workers and Peasants at Toba Tek Singh on 22-23 March 1970.

There was another mass influx into the party organization at the primary unit level between July and mid-December 1970. It was occasioned by the proximity of the elections, the efforts of the People's Party candidates, and the bandwagon effect of the PPP's high pitch radical campaign that brought a wave of the older type of political figures into the party.

At its upper levels the Pakistan People's Party remained, from the beginning, very much a party of personal loyalty to Chairman Bhutto.

> On the whole, Bhutto's personality worked well for him. His incisive brilliance and worldly wisdom were impressive to intellectuals, the educated classes and to foreign diplomats, journalists and research scholars. With the common people and the party faithful, his dynamism, passion and humour aroused a strong response. He had

> an excellent memory for names, faces and children and many party workers recounted to us the warm encounters they had had with their Chairman. Yet, Bhutto was a difficult, even dangerous, man to cross. He demanded unquestioning obedience from his social equals and subservience from below. When angered he could act in a highly arbitrary and often arrogant manner.[42]

Jones further elaborates on Bhutto's personality in his book.

> It is not surprising that Bhutto used highly personal forms of leadership in the party, which operated through an informal hierarchy of access to the Chairman. The inner circle which had formed around Bhutto even before the founding of the party, and which came to be known among the party faithful as the 'central cell,' was made up of the few who had direct personal access to Bhutto.[43]

Only J.A. Rahim was able to confront Bhutto directly on issues he felt deeply about. His seniority, his role in the conception and founding of the People's Party, and his evident integrity, gave him an authority that Bhutto could ignore only at the peril of damaging his own, and his party's credibility. Rahim was increasingly concerned about entry into the party in 1970 of dubious elements, big landlords and maulanas, whose commitment to socialist principles was highly suspect and who might constitute an alternative cell that would compete for the favour of the Chairman.

The existence of an informal network of authority that only partially coincided with the formal structures encouraged a tendency to 'empire building' within the party on the part of those closest to the Chairman.

The Left wing of the PPP was itself a collection of groups of varying size, organizational integrity, ideological emphasis, and proximity to the 'party cell'. Apart from the larger constellation around Sheikh Rashid, which would include the Pakistan Kisan Committee, most of these groups had their origins in the radical union politics of the latter part of the November Movement. These included the Mazdur Majlis-i-Amal ('Worker's Action Committee') of Multan, the Taraqqipasand Mazdur Mahaz ('Progressive Worker's Front') of Lyallpur, the People's Labour Front (Rifat Hussain) of Rawalpindi, and the Muttahida Mazdur Mahaz ('United Worker's Front') of Lahore. The Thal Mehnat

Kash Mahaz ('The Labourer's Front') and the Chingari group of intellectuals and worker cadres around Dr. Aziz ul Haq and 'Ladu Sahib' had somewhat different origins. The former was a worker peasant alliance formed by NAP-B (National Awami Party-Bhashani) cadres in parts of Mianwali and Muzaffargarh Districts. It allied with the People's Party in March 1969, organized much of the PPP infrastructure in Leiah and Bhakkar Tehsils, but broke with the party when, under the influence of G.M. Khar, when PPP tickets were given to 'feudal and other class enemies'. The Chingari Group, which later called itself the Young People's Front, took its inspiration from the Naxalite magazine, Chingari, published in Canada, and had links, albeit tenuous, with the Communist Party of East Pakistan (Marxist-Leninist).

These groups on the far Left maintained their own organizational boundaries and tended to see their links with the PPP as a form of 'association'. Socialists around Sheikh Rashid had their primary political identity with the People's Party but were mainly from a Maoist background.

The issues of industrial and student politics were part of the background of discord percolating inside the PPP in 1969 and 1970, but these would not become divisive issues until 1971 and 1972, when they became central to the disputes that started the exodus of the Left cadres from the party.

On 1 August 1969, Sheikh Muhammad Rashid (alias Baba-e-Socialism [father of socialism] in later days) presided over the first recorded meeting of the Punjab and Bahawalpur Council of the PPP, at which resolutions on these problems were passed with large majorities.

The party councillors were also critical of the recent entry of several noted Convention Muslim Leaguers into the People's Party and expressed the concern that discretion ought to be exercised in the enrolment of new members; otherwise the PPP would be 'flooded with undesirable elements.' Finally, the Council called for an early party convention, so that the organizational structure of the party could be streamlined and democratized. These resolutions were an indication that the party members were pressing for a greater voice in the party, that they distrusted Bhutto's efforts at elite recruitment, and that they wanted a speeding up of the development of party structures to strengthen their positions and to balance the highly personalized leadership at the top.

They were not unrelated issues, since the elite within which Bhutto was looking for support was that of mainly large land holders.

Bhutto's pre-election attitude to the land question displayed the same kind of unwillingness to become tied to specific positions that is evident in his public approach to other major issues.

Together, the Mochi Darwaza and Toba Tek Singh meetings confirmed to the Punjab Left that the ground swell of popular acclaim for the PPP was genuine and that the party likely would win a large number of seats in the elections.

The danger they foresaw was that professional politicians, capitalists and landed aristocracy would enter the PPP to get candidacy tickets and the 'socialist character' of the party would thereby become seriously compromised, if not destroyed.

At the 29 March 1970 meeting of the Punjab-Bahawalpur Council (Provincial Organizing Committee and District/City officers) at 4-A Mozang Road, Lahore, the Council was provided with resolutions for debate, which, if passed, would be recommended to the larger party.

- Individuals with class interests contradictory to the party manifesto should not normally be given party membership.
- In no case should party membership, office or ticket be given without the agreement of the relevant local party committee. Opportunists, i.e. professional politicians, landlords and capitalists with 'family boroughs' should be kept out of the party.
- All party offices, including the Central Committee, should be filled through election.
- The party should control the sale and distribution of party literature.
- A party financial wing should be set up to administer party funds.

- The PPP should adopt a land ceiling of fifty acres of irrigated land.
- All the principal means of production and all major industries, including jute and textiles, should be nationalized without compensation.
- Finally, the progressive foreign policy envisioned by the party must not be compromised by U.S. interests or pressure.[44]

Philip Jones explains the rising ideological and class conflicts due to such resolutions from below in the PPP even before the 1970 elections.

> These resolutions angered the Khar-Ramay groups (central cell). They infuriated the PPP Chairman, since they struck directly at his broad election strategy.
>
> (...) Sensitive enough not to hold this confrontation at Mubashar's house, the PPP Chairman chose the Lahore Inter-Continental Hotel. The meeting mainly consisted of a long, furious harangue by the Chairman directed at the left socialists, mixed with frequent insult and bitter ridicule.[45]

The incident took its toll: Amanullah Khan was suspended from party membership; the Punjab Left would never again press its case so openly in the party, nor would the Punjab-Bahawalpur Council meet again.

The Chairman may well have wanted to press his 'disciplinary measures' further, but he recognized both the importance and the strength of the Punjab Left.

> The suspension of Amanullah Khan brought on a chain reaction of open protests, student resignations and resolutions from various groups in the Punjab PPP denouncing the 'undemocratic attitude of the central leadership.' Amanullah Khan was reinstated on 25 August.[46]

Suppression of the Left

Looking back, it does seem that the 29 March meeting was the high watermark of the Punjab Left in the People's Party. Though their decline after it was not precipitous, it was visible. As the PPP election campaign gained momentum after the party's Hala Conference, much of what the PPP left had sought to guard against began to happen.

Bhutto refused to discuss motions from the Left on party organization, threatening to resign the PPP chairmanship if the Left continued to demand that parliamentary and party offices be separated.

The Left had its own internal weaknesses. The 'old Left' leadership, a collection of labour organizers and 'drawing room socialists' beset with doctrinal and personal conflicts, had largely stayed out of the PPP and remained potent, but primarily urban centred. Its rural support base, while real enough, was only fitfully organized. Where it was organized, it's Kissan Committees and Kissan Forces proved unable to stem the quiet 'counter revolution' pursued after the elections by the rural elite, district bureaucrats and thanedars (officer in charge of a police station).

After the transfer of power, the Left was unable to press Bhutto to go beyond a minimal enactment of the PPP land reform proposals. In the cities, the social base of the Left was largely confined to the transient student community, the new labour organizations, whose leaders were harshly treated by the PPP regime. They wanted the implementation of the PPP programme and voted for socialist change, in the sense that the PPP promised to end the elite monopoly of the levers of political power and economic repression. At the same time, however, for many pro-PPP masses it was the image of Bhutto, not ideological justification that carried the PPP programme. Hence, even the far Left in the PPP spectrum never directed its criticisms at Bhutto, only at those around him.

It is also clear that the Left, for all its inherent shortcomings, was further weakened by actions and policies supported by Bhutto from his singular position as PPP Chairman. Time after time Bhutto refused to implement schemes to strengthen party organization. Possibly it was simply not perceived in the pre-power years as being crucial. These were heady times for Bhutto. His charisma was in full flower in Punjab, and it may well be that he thought it always would be, that he could always 'go back to the people', and that this was sufficient leverage with which to bargain with the established power groups and to pursue his 'internal united front strategy' of party organization.

Scope for manoeuvre was something Bhutto has always felt he needed because:

(a) Prior to the elections he was sceptical of a PPP victory.
(b) After the elections he knew he would receive power only at the hands of the military oligarchs.
(c) After gaining power there would be the political and military consequences of the civil war, and his unwillingness to be pushed too far to the Left by the forces he had helped to arouse.

The Elite Bourgeoisie take Control

The discomfiture of the party Left was anything but assuaged by the new wave of elite entrants into the PPP. This trend was strongest in the rural areas, where landed aristocracy comprising of zamindars continued to join the PPP. By the end of 1974, the post-transfer of power entrants in Punjab included the Legharis and Khosas of Dera Ghazi Khan; the Pirachas, Tiwanas, Bandials and Qureshis of Sargodha; various of the Bukhari Sayyid lineages (Pir Mahal, Kuranga and Shah Jiwana); the Daultanas, Khakwanis and Gilanis of Multan; the Kharrals of the Ravi riverine in Lyallpur (now Faisalabad); the Pirs of Makhad, Manki Sharif and Taunsa Sharif; the Korejas of Liaqatpur (Rahim Yar Khan); the Tammans and Jodhras of Campbellpur (now Attock); as well as civil service moguls like Aziz Ahmed and Malik Khuda Bakhsh Bucha.

The entry of the elitist class representatives, upper middle class, traders and even leaders of criminal gangs and rassagir (police pimps) elements, was undoubtedly a protective reaction, for access to the power system has always been crucial to the gaining and holding of land and wealth. For the most part, in return for lip service to the PPP Manifesto and an expression of loyalty to Bhutto, they found easy entry into the PPP. Though their traditional authority had been challenged, often successfully, in the 1970 elections, these elitist groups soon proved their residual authority to be remarkably resilient. They still had the best access to the district and provincial bureaucracies, often through personal connections with relatives and school chums in the upper bureaucracy, and could play the game of 'brokerage' far more effectively than the PPP officeholders or activists who had no social access to elite circles.

They used these contacts to rebuild their influence, getting local petitioner jobs, transfers, promotions, more canal water, agricultural loans, fertilizer, tube well connections, etc. Moreover, biraderi (clan) and other parochial influences had begun to re-emerge as factors in party and cabinet making politics, as well as in by-election strategies.

Once this began to happen, the landed classes, their skills honed by long experience in parochial politics, proved adept at expanding influence. By 1974, the names of the old local feudalists had begun to emerge in the lists of district PPP officeholders, as weil as on the District Councils of the People's Works Programme (PWP), the successor to the Rural Works Programme and the major channel of development funds to the local level. By mid-1975, members of aristocratic families held the Secretary-Generalship of the Punjab PPP (Syed Nasir Ali Shah), the Punjab Chief Ministership (Nawab Sadiq Hussain Qureshi) and the Punjab governorship (Sadiq Muhammad Khan, Amir of Bahawalpur). Finally, in late 1976, these politicians of the ruling classes virtually controlled the ticketing politics for the 1977 elections. The list of PPP candidates reads like a 'who's who' of the families that dominated electoral politics in Punjab from 1920 to 1958.

These acts, together with a raging inflation, in part the result of the PPP Government's attempts to satisfy its numerous constituencies and the general decline in moral, education, familial, institutional standards and law and order, apparently ate away at the PPP's popularity in the urban areas, to some extent.

Baluchistan

Bhutto had revived the army as an institution mainly for the perpetuation of his own role. As we have seen earlier on, that even in the aftermath of the 1971 defeat the state could have been overthrown and replaced by a workers' state. But as there was neither the intention nor the preparation, so the old order began to revive and reassert itself. But after the revival and restoration of its social credibility Bhutto began to feel that the establishment had its own agenda, compulsions and priorities. He could not do much about it. Now the army was going to reassert itself by military action.

In a country like Pakistan there is never a dearth of opportunities for military action. Mostly there are too many for the army to handle. This time the old insurgency had arisen again in Baluchistan, where the National Question was a burning issue. There had been an established tradition of guerrilla struggle in Baluchistan. The Baluch youth took inspiration from the struggles in China, Cuba and Che Guevera's armed struggle in Bolivia and Latin America.

The PPP could not form governments in Baluchistan and the Pushtoonkhwa (NWFP) in 1971-72 because NAP and JUI had majorities in the provincial assemblies of NWFP and Baluchistan; hence they formed provincial coalition governments in these two provinces. The revival of the central state and its assertion soon created tensions. These erupted and the centre acted against the provinces of oppressed nationalities. The alibi to opt for the military action was soon manufactured.

The capture of arms in a diplomatic shipment to the Iraqi embassy on 10 February 1973, alleged by the Pakistan government to be destined for Baluchistan, and the subsequent death of Hayat Mohammad Khan Sherpao, Bhutto's right-hand man in the NWFP, in an explosion in Peshawar in February 1975, gave Bhutto his excuse. He dismissed the NAP-JUI provincial government in the NWFP, and banned the NAP the day after Sherpao's assassination. The Baluchistan government resigned in protest.

In pursuit of political supremacy in all provinces, Bhutto had to constantly challenge the NAP and specifically the Baluch leadership. He saw in the efforts of the NAP a repeat of the Bangladesh issue, a fear heightened by his knowledge that the NAP had supported the Awami League in East Pakistan and that NAP supporters in Baluchistan were fighting the Pakistan Army in the Pat Feeder area (south of Sibi) for the control of agricultural lands. This led Bhutto to declare that the provincial leadership of the Baluch sardars had failed "to take effective measures to check large-scale disturbances in different parts of the province ... causing a growing sense of insecurity among the inhabitants and grave menace to the peace and tranquillity of the Province".[47]

He thus managed to displace the NAP leadership from Baluchistan and sent the Pakistan army into the province, ostensibly with the aim of constructing roads and providing electricity and water to the poor Baluchis.

The Pakistan army was back into the political process, a move that was later to haunt Bhutto. The minor Baluch leaders, those who could, took to the hills with their followers. The major sardars (tribal chiefs) and other NAP leaders, including Khair Baksh Marri, were taken into custody by the government, charged with treason and subsequently brought to trial in Hyderabad.

> Mir Hazar Khan, a lieutenant of Khair Baksh Marri, who led the insurgency in the Marri area until 1976, when he left for Afghanistan but continued to direct actions from there.
>
> The Pakistan Army had meanwhile profited from the gift of thirty Huey Cobra helicopter gunships from Iran, which was fearful of the potential spill over of the uprising in Pakistani Baluchistan into Iranian Baluchistan. The army used these gunships against the people of the Marri tribe (including women and children) who had taken refuge in the Chamalang Valley on 3 September 1974. This action drew the Marri fighters down from their hideouts in the hills and a three day battle ensued in which the heavily out gunned Marris suffered grievously.[48]

Fighting continued in the barren wastes of Baluchistan, with the tribesmen giving battle continuously despite the numerical and weapons superiority of the Pakistan army. Finally, the Bhutto government issued a White Paper on Baluchistan in December 1974, claiming victory, and stating that the army would withdraw. However, this withdrawal did not take place until well after the end of the Bhutto government.

There were heavy casualities on both sides. The Baluch youth had put up a fierce resistance and at that stage the armed struggle had a Left-wing inclination, although the methods, tactics and ideological basis was not classical Marxist-Leninist revolutionary strategy. The Pakistan army had played a brutal role and to some extent repeated the role it played in East Bengal in 1971. The Baluch struggle did not end as proclaimed by the government in 1974. It continued sporadically, but did not surrender. The irony is that after Bhutto's fall through the military coup a sort of truce came about under the dictatorship of General Zia, who was one of the main instigators of this cruel military action. In an act of extreme hypocrisy he withdrew the so-called 'Hyderabad conspiracy case' and freed the Baluch leaders. Even some of those leaders who were in exile in Afghanistan were brought back on Military C-130 planes and Zia met them at Rawalpindi with his satiric grin. The main cause of the exhaustion of this armed struggle against the Pakistani State was its prolongation with little result, and its isolation from any active mass support in other areas of Pakistan and the region.

But this conflict re-inflamed the national question in Baluchistan for several years to come. It is not a question that has been resolved, nor can it be solved within the confines of capitalism. With the worsening crisis in Pakistan the national question has become more complex and even more violent. Without a Leninist methodology the problems of nationalities will continue to fester, creating diversions for the class movement. National liberation can only be achieved by the overthrow of a system that, along with class exploitation, is exploiting on the basis of nationality, gender, religion, etc. Only the replacement of the bourgeoisie with a workers' revolutionary state can guarantee all the democratic rights, including national and lingual independence. That is only possible through a socialist revolution.

There were, during the middle Bhutto years, many indications of the revival of bureaucratic authority. These included the bureaucracy's dominance of the PWP (People's Works Programme), where district and tensile level bureaucrats soon combined with PPP, MNAs, and MPAs to exclude party office holders from any role in the programme. But, more than this, the bureaucracy penetrated the party itself. They took over the responsibility for organizing Bhutto's district tours and audiences (katcheries), leaving the party leaders responsible only for amassing large crowds, a function performed through a process resembling subinfeudation.

Two other developments during 1974 require at least some mention. One of these was the removal of Dr. Mubashar Hasan from the powerful Central Ministry of Finance. This was seen as a gesture to the industrialists and an indication that even the 'Third Worlders' in the PPP were coming under pressure from the old establishment. The other development was the removal of J.A. Rahim from both his cabinet and party positions in July.

The removal of Rahim marked a watershed for the PPP. He was one of the few men around Bhutto who was neither dazzled by the PPP leader nor corrupted by power. Anything but a sycophant, he had been a constant spokesman in the PPP for maintaining the socialist ideological and organizational integrity of the party, hoping that it could oversee the major policy functions of government.

Conclusion

The vast numbers of Left activists, intellectuals, and trade unionists who had joined the PPP made some profound mistakes which not only led to the demise of the PPP itself, and imposition of Martial Law by Zia-ul-Haq, but also led to a decline of the Left movement in the society and its various institutions long before the collapse of the Soviet Union and the fall of the Berlin Wall.

The reality is that the Left which entered the PPP was neither theoretically developed enough, nor was it organizationally prepared to play a revolutionary role in this transitional movement of the Pakistan People's Party.

To talk about socialism is one thing, to have a clear Marxist understanding and ideological clarity for a revolutionary change is another. Bhutto often used to relate to all sorts of varieties of socialism, even the most reformist types. He often mentioned Sweden and Scandinavia in his remarks. Some still do. From the reactionary role of the 'Socialist Second International' that even continues today there are so many varieties including centrism, Left reformism and innumerable varieties of Stalinism that proclaim to be socialist, but in reality are reformist tendencies that strictly adhere to Capitalism and in the last analysis play a counter revolutionary role.

Firstly, they were an amalgamation of diverse ideological backgrounds which never had and never could develop a genuine Marxist theoretical foundation to face the challenges and execute the tasks that loomed large on the horizon. Secondly, they themselves were swayed and influenced by the massive popularity of Zulfiqar Ali Bhutto.

The Left leaders in the PPP were so naive, to say the least, that they attributed the rise in mass consciousness to his personality, rather than the social upheaval that had galvanized the people to seek a revolutionary change in their lives, their society, and the system that oppressed them. Bhutto had merely been the focus of their desire for change.

This popularity reached its zenith when he was going more and more radical in his revolutionary and socialist rhetoric. The enormous response he got further moved him to the Left. But when the ruling classes counter-attacked the movement with war and reforms the left leadership didn't have a clue how to mobilize the working masses to combat and defeat the attacks of the state. With the PPP in power in a bourgeois state the subsequent reformist policies were inevitable. To expect to achieve revolutionary aims through exercising power in a bourgeois state structure was and is a Utopia which the great teachers of scientific socialism had fought against at every historical juncture since 1848.

Above all what this Left leadership lacked was the concept of internationalism. Marxism is internationalism or it is nothing. From the First to the Fourth Internationals all theoretical and organizational premises begin from Marxist Internationalism. The Stalinist concept of 'National Socialism' laid the basis of patriotism and Pakistani and other forms of national chauvinism. This was perhaps the weakest aspect of the theoretical basis of the left in the PPP. Thus they could be easily manipulated by notions of national sovereignty, national interests and national defence, etc. Such petty bourgeois concepts, and the apologetic attitude of the Left towards them, gave leverage to the Rightists and the state to stem the growth of a revolutionary force within and outside the PPP. The 1971 war was also able to distract the Left-wing elements because of their confusion on the principle of Marxist Internationalism.

Again, due to its contradictory ideological foundations, the Left in the PPP could never organize itself as an independent revolutionary entity, either inside or outside the PPP. They were practising a sort of a deep entryism, and a very clumsy one at that. The Left did not try to forge a loose united front against the Right-wing, so once in power the PPP leadership could easily manipulate, sow discord and out-manoeuvre the Left leaders. Some left the Party while others had to capitulate to a large extent on all their real policies while verbally chanting 'socialism'.

If we examine the origins, structures and the growth of the PPP it wasn't even up to the organizational standards of the traditional working class parties of the Second (socialist) International. However, the PPP became part of this International (which Rosa Luxemburg used to call a stinking corpse); it was rapidly moving towards the right. In this process of transformation it has come to a pass that the policies of social democracy are indistinguishable from those of the conservative parties of Europe.

However, the PPP, being the product of the 1968-9 revolution which the Stalinists had betrayed, gave space and opportunity to Bhutto to take the initiative. He used revolutionary language and socialist slogans to take up the reins of the great revolutionary movement. The PPP has become the traditional political expression of the working class and oppressed masses and there is no mass alternative to the PPP to this day. The problem is that the national leadership comes under immense pressure to carry out the policies of the ruling class, in direct contradiction to what the masses desire. This will inevitably lead to a Left opposition emerging, whereby the working masses attempt to push the party in the direction of class struggle. The Marxists base themselves on this perspective and work to build up a Marxist tendency within the party that can offer leadership to this instinctive movement of the toiling masses.

If Bhutto can be accused of using socialist rhetoric for his rise to power, then neither can most of the PPP Left be absolved from such rhetorical masquerading. If Bhutto perverted socialism with a nationalist and religious admixture, then most of the Left leaders from Maoist and Stalinist backgrounds were definitely indoctrinated, if not with religion, with nationalist and patriotic diversions from the class struggle. In fact it was in perfect harmony with their own 'Left' ideological and political training, education, and understanding. It fitted with their prophecies of what they considered socialism. Such a discourse and the psychology of two-stageism also gave them the pretext of attributing to Bhutto the role of a progressive bourgeois, a beacon of hope that could carry through the national democratic stage of the revolution to lay the basis of a socialist revolution in some far-off future.

Most were ardent adherents to the ideology of partition and strong advocates of Pakistani nationalism. Again, on the question of 'leadership', with the despotic examples of Stalin and Mao, the Left leaders had the non-Bolshevik approach of an individual guide, a great messiah and leader of the masses in Bhutto. Instead of a collectivist approach towards creating a leadership on the basis of polemics, discussion and debate they felt intimidated by Bhutto's personality.

This rise of the individual was due to his role as a leading minister in the past, propped up by the media of the ruling classes and later on by the masses. The trust and confidence the masses had placed in him in the absence of a collective Bolshevik leadership and a democratic centralist party was because of the absence of a revolutionary alternative. Although the role of the individual in history cannot be totally denied, the fate and destiny of a revolution can neither be restricted by, nor can it be dependent on, one single individual. Marx could not have been Marx if there was no Communist League or the First International. Lenin could not have been Lenin had there been no Bolshevik party. The Left leaders out in the wilderness were desperate to find a short cut to the helm of mainstream politics. They used Bhutto's bandwagon to get there. And they got there, but at the cost of eulogizing Bhutto as the 'Quaid-e-Awam' (Leader of the people) and abandoned the idea of building a revolutionary communist party that was indispensable in carrying through the revolutionary movement towards a socialist victory. Lenin used to say quite often, that there was no short cut to revolution. And, as Ted Grant said, most short cuts always lead to an abyss.

In the PPP's transition from 1967 till today the 'Left' of the party has had many opportunities to take the lead and push for a genuine socialist programme. But so far it has failed to do so. That is why the role of the Marxists in the party is so important. Life teaches and the toiling masses that follow the PPP will learn from events. If the Marxists are present patiently explaining their programme they can play a key role in building a mass revolutionary Left tendency within the party. With irreconciliable ideological and theoretical positions and principles, combined with flexibility in tactics, the Marxist tendency can first become a mass opposition within the party and later lead a socialist victory in the next period. The lessons of 1968-9 and the experiences and mistakes of the PPP Left can serve as an important factor in the theoretical and organizational development of this subjective factor in Pakistan.

Wars and revolutions are exceptional periods of history. These don't occur frequently and do not last for a very long time, because in a revolutionary situation the social order and the routine and normal life of the prevalent system are in disarray. This creates such a volatile situation that society can't exist in it indefinitely. In such a situation the state's power comes into open conflict with the working classes. Either a revolutionary party takes over this power and forms a workers' state or the ruling classes prevail through civil wars and other violent means. In the aftermath of a revolutionary defeat the exploitation is carried out on a bigger scale. The revolutionary situation of 1968-9 carried on for 138 days in its first major upheaval.

A revolutionary party must take over the political and organizational structure. This party, after capturing the state power, forms a workers state and sets up the order of a new social system. However, if a revolutionary party is not prepared for the revolution, and does not fulfil the task of building a new system, it is forced to use the old structure of the state's apparatus and is unable to complete the revolution, despite its radical programme and policies. In the end, it can't use the old structures of state; rather the state uses it and throws it out after diffusing the mass pressure from below. PPP has gone through this process many times.

In his last book written from the death cell in Rawalpindi jail, Bhutto wrote:

> It seems that the lesson of this coup d'etat is that a via media, a modus vivendi, a compromise, is a Utopian dream. The coup d'etat demonstrates that the class struggle is irreconcilable and that it must result in the victory of one class over the other. Obviously, whatever the temporary setbacks, the struggle can lead only to the victory of one class. This is the writing on the wall.[2]

This last historic confession of Zulfiqar Ali Bhutto was perhaps honest and genuine, but the subsequent leaderships of the PPP have abandoned it to the dustbin of history. They seem incapable of learning from Bhutto's historical message written in his death cell as they seem incapable of seeing beyond capitalism. The masses, however, still cling to the PPP; whenever they enter the political arena, whether in elections or in a movement, they cling to the PPP precisely because of the programme and the revolution of 1968-9 that gave the party its historical role as a mass traditional party.

The problem is that the masses do not have the leadership they deserve. In almost three decades the party has been in power three times, each time disappointing the aspirations of the masses. Every experience of the masses with the PPP in government has confirmed this, the present experience being no exception. But nothing in history is wasted. This experience will lead millions of workers and peasants to conclude that there must be a serious change. The present coalition government is doomed to failure. Zardari is throwing away the gains the party made in the elections. The Marxists have warned consistently over and over again that unless the party leaders adopt a genuine revolutionary programme to expropriate the landlords and capitalists, they will create the conditions in which reaction can raise its ugly head once more. Events may unfortunately confirm this prognosis, but that will not be the end of the story. As the teeming ranks of the party, as the toiling masses draw conclusions from their own experience they will see that the

Marxists were the only ones who warned them. In those conditions a mass Marxist Left of the PPP can be formed. The growing class polarization and revolutionary movement of the masses will put huge pressures on the party, separating the proletarian wing from the reformist.

The same conditions that created the PPP in 1968-9 will create the conditions for the transformation of the Marxist tendency within the PPP into a mass force. If a substantial Bolshevik force is developed and plays a decisive role in the historical events that are approaching, then the victory of revolutionary socialism in Pakistan shall be guaranteed.

NOTES

1. French revolutionary leader, became President of National convention and was guillotined when Robespierre fell.
2. Z.A. Bhutto, *If I am Assassinated,* (Vikas Publishing House, Delhi 1979), p. 55.
3. Ted Grant, *The Colonial Revolution and the Sino-Soviet Split,* August 1964, The Unbroken Thread, pp. 308, 309, 310.
4. Alan Woods, *Bolshevism—The Road to Revolution,* p. 310.
5. Lenin Collected Works, vol. 9, *Two Tactics of SD in the Democratic Revolution,* p. 98.
6. Alan Woods, *Bolshevism The Road to Revolution,* pp. 311-312.
7. Trotsky, *Our Differences, in 1905,* p. 332 and footnote of same page.
8. Ibid.
9. Ted Grant, *The Colonial Revolution and The Sino-Soviet Dispute,* August 1964, The Unbroken Thread, p. 309.
10. *Pakistan Times* (Lahore) 30 March 1966.
11. Ibid, 29 October 1967.
12. *Outlook,* 25 April 1964.
13. Pakistan People's Party Founding Documents, p. 5.
14. Bhutto, *Starting With a Clean Slate,* p. 45.
15. Stanley Wolpert, *Zulfi Bhutto of Pakistan,* (Oxford) p. 124.
16. Sobho Gianchandani, Interview in *Newsline,* October 2008.
17. Bhutto, *Awakening of the People,* statements, articles, speeches of Z.A. Bhutto, p. 90.
18. Ibid p. 93.
19. Ibid, pp. 94, 95.
20. Ibid, p. 233.
21. Ibid, p. 169.
22. Ibid, p. 179.

23. Ibid, p. 197.
24. Ibid, p. 240.
25. Quote from, *The News* Islamabad, 28 September 2008.
26. Philip E. Jones, *PPP Rise to Power*, pp. 98, 99.
27. *Dawn*, 1 December 1967.
28. Political Correspondent, *Ideological Oddballs Get Together*, *The Pakistan Times*, 2 December 1967.
29. 'A Damp Squib', *Dawn*, Editorial, 4 December 1967.
30. *Nusrat*, No. 16. 12 January 1968, p. 15.
31. *The Pakistan Times*, 15 March 1969.
32. *The Pakistan Times*, 18 February 1969.
33. *Dawn*, 16 February 1969.
34. *Pakistan Observer*, Dacca, 19 February 1969.
35. *Dawn*, 24 February 1969.
36. *Morning News*, 3 March 1969.
37. *The Pakistan Times*, 02 August 1969.
38. J.A. Rahim, interview, *View Point*, 12 October 1973.
39. *Nusrat*, No. 27 (30 March 1969), p. 7-8.
40. *Morning News*, 17 January 1970.
41. *Nusrat*, No. 26 (23 March 1969), p. 4.
42. Philip E. Jones, *PPP Rise to Power*, p. 217.
43. Ibid, p. 217.
44. *The Pakistan Times*, 31 March 1970.
45. Philip E. Jones, *PPP Rise to Power*, p. 245.
46. *Musawat*, 31 August 1970.
47. Shuja Nawaz, *Crossed Swords*, (Oxford), p. 333.
48. Ibid, pp. 334-335.

Eight

DICTATORSHIP AND DEMOCRACY

Regimes Changed, the Masses Continue to Suffer

In the history of society there have been many methods of class rule. This is especially true of capitalist society, with many peculiar and variegated forms: republic, monarchy, fascism, democracy, dictatorship, Bonapartist, centralised and federal, to give some examples. —Ted Grant (1913–2006)[1]

If we are not to mock at common sense and history, it is obvious that we cannot speak of pure democracy" as long as different classes exist; we can only speak of class democracy ... Pure democracy" is the mendacious phrase of a liberal who wants to fool the workers ... Bourgeois democracy, although a great historical advance in comparison with medievalism, always remains, and under capitalism is bound to remain, restricted, truncated, false and hypocritical, a paradise for the rich and a snare and deception for the exploited, for the poor. —V.I. Lenin (1870–1924)[2]

After sixty-one years of its existence, Pakistan has gone from a 'nation' searching for a country to a country searching for a nation. Forty years after the 1968-9 revolution, the masses are still yearning for emancipation, perhaps more desperately than ever before. The agony has intensified, the social and economic wounds are festering and lives of the working classes and the dispossessed are nothing but torment; anguish and anxiety have become the social norm. It is not surprising that *The Economist* in January 2008 wrote of Pakistan as "The most dangerous place on Earth".

In her 1991 book, *Waiting for Allah*, the correspondent of the *Financial Times*, Christina Lamb, described the conditions in Pakistan in the following lines:

> Twelve thousand more people will be born in Pakistan this day. Two

> thousand will be dead within a year. More of them will learn to use a gun than to speak the national language. Only a third will have access to clean drinking water and only 15 per cent will have sewerage. A quarter will go to school. Many will become heroin addicts. This is a country killing its own future.
>
> It is in this moment, in which the day has not quite decided how it will treat mankind, that Pakistan is trapped. 'Islam in danger' was the cry raised to justify the necessity of dividing India and inventing a country for Indian Muslims. Today in their very own homeland Muslims need safeguarding from each other.
>
> (...) the needs of the masses will remain ignored because the gulf between the two groups is too wide. It would take a revolutionary to challenge the entrenched power structures. The only other way for these to be dismantled now would be for the country to break up.[3]

Since these words were written the conditions in Pakistan have greatly deteriorated; wars and insurgencies are raging in several areas. US imperialism's 'war on terror' has become a curse for this country. After devastating Iraq and Afghanistan, the imperialists are now bombing and killing in the North West and other regions of Pakistan. Suicide bombings, fundamentalist frenzy, bloodshed and destruction have made Pakistan a scary land for people around the world. There is no respite for the masses. In the first six months of this democratic government led by the Pakistan People's Party there has been an avalanche of attacks on the living standards of the already impoverished masses. The cost of basic needs has sky-rocketed. There has been a more rapid price hike of basic commodities in this period than any other period in the country's troubled history. Unemployment and poverty have surpassed all records. Health, education, water, infrastructure, transport and other basic facilities are in a despicable state. The life of common people is but an agonized existence. And still these miserable conditions continue to deteriorate.

After the 1968-9 revolution, the 1971 war with India, and the break-up of the country, the PPP government under Zulfiqar Ali Bhutto ushered in a number of reforms. These reforms, introduced in various fields such as labour laws, land, education, health, etc., were the most radical reforms in the history of Pakistan. On the one hand these reforms were the by-product of the 1968-9 revolution, while on the other hand they created a certain social base and support for the PPP and Z.A. Bhutto. However, in the conditions of Pakistan's capitalism their implementation and benefits to the masses remained very limited. The large-scale nationalizations under the first PPP regime were also limited, as multinational corporations were exempted from these takeovers by the State. Secondly, they were not given over to workers' collective democratic control. It was the civilian bureaucracy that took over the running of these industrial units. Although sections of the Pakistani capitalist class were hurt by these nationalizations, which included some Pakistani banks, insurance companies and other sectors, capitalism as a socio-economic system remained intact.

The radical land reforms introduced by the new government were also only partially effective. The landlords collaborated with the state bureaucracy and got away with large portions of their estates by cooking the books and other corrupt methods. In any case, the structures of the capitalist state and armed forces remained intact. To have their revenge on the PPP government, the capitalist infused inflationary trends in the economy that further minimized the benefits of these reforms for the downtrodden masses. The Oil shock of 1974 and the recession in the world economy further aggravated the crisis of the Pakistan economy. The failure of the reforms to deliver, the rising inflation, and increasing crisis, started a process of disillusionment and lull amongst the masses that were supporting the PPP government. The army, as soon as it came back into its standing, launched its adventurist aggression in Baluchistan in 1973-4, which exacerbated the national question and gave rise to instability and intensified the political crisis.

The Americans were also unhappy with Bhutto: to ascertain his mass support he had taken steps that had annoyed Washington. A Right-wing alliance, the Pakistan National Alliance (PNA), was forged with the backing of the CIA. On the charge of rigging the March 1977 elections an agitation group named Nizam-e-Mustafa (System of Prophet) was launched, again with the connivance of the CIA. Finally the PPP government was overthrown and Bhutto was deposed by the military coup of 5 July 1977. This coup was led by the COAS

(Chief of the Army Staff) General Zia-ul-Haq. Bhutto's popularity again began to surge throughout the country. The dictatorship was threatened, so Bhutto was arrested and after a shadowy trial he was executed on the gallows. This judicial murder by the brutal Zia dictatorship was in reality the revenge of the Pakistani ruling class as Bhutto had given them some scratches with his nationalizations in the 1972-4 period.

General Zia's Dictatorship

General Zia-ul-Haq's eleven-year despotic rule was perhaps the most dreadful period for the masses of Pakistan. He used Islam as a battering ram to crush the Left wing, PPP workers, trade union and student activists, and the poor peasants trying to struggle for a change.

One of the most brutal, murderous acts of the Zia dictatorship was the massacre of the workers of the Colony Textile Mills in Multan in January 1978. The author was a participant in this struggle. A close friend and one of the most militant leaders of the workers in Multan, Mohammad Shafi was martyred in this bestiality. There were thirteen thousand workers in the colony textile mills. It was perhaps the largest and most profitable textile factory in Pakistan. After the reforms of 1969 and 1972 the workers used to get annual bonuses in November or December every year, equal to about three months of their salary. The workers knew that in the year 1977 the production and profits on the mill were much higher than in the previous years, so they were expecting a higher bonus. But in July 1977, now that Bhutto had been overthrown and a military dictatorship imposed, the bosses used the Martial Law regime to deprive the workers of their rights.

Due to the terror of the military regime several traditional trade unionists and the CBA (Collective Bargaining Agent) union had capitulated to the owners. They were even negotiating with the textile mill bosses for a far smaller bonus that year. November 1977 passed by, and December was coming to an end, but still no sign of any bonus! Anxiety amongst the workers began to rise; they had waited all year for this bonus to help make ends meet. The bosses were showing an attitude of contemptuous indifference while the discontent amongst the workers was turning into a wave of frustration and anger. Talk of taking some action was going round on the factory floors.

On the morning of 29 December 1977 the workers arriving for the first shift went to their machines but refused to work. The workers who had done the night shift refused to leave the premises and sat down in the compound of the mill. A 'tools-down' strike had commenced. There was no violence yet the strike was complete. The bosses sent in their goons and police to threaten the workers and break the strike. The workers refused. The persuasion of the trade union leaders also failed to get the workers to start work. These parleys continued for the next three days. On 2 January 1978 the daughter of the owner of Colony Textile Mills, Mughees A. Sheikh was getting married. The mill owner was a very close friend of General Zia, who had flown in from Rawalpindi to attend the ceremony. This further aggravated the already tense situation. The news spread among the workers that the dowry being given to the daughter by the owner was worth at least ten times the bonus that was due for the 13,000 workers of the Colony Textile Mills.

At almost midday the workers who were on a tools-down strike were moving towards the factory's main gate for their daily midday gate meeting. A rumour reached the ear of Zia-ul-Haq that the workers were coming to attack the wedding ceremony. Shaking with hatred and rage, the general stood up and contemptuously ordered the workers to be crushed, which was exactly what the agent provocateur and the bosses' goons had wanted. The police, who had cordoned off the mills for three days, and the paramilitary forces of the state, took up their positions then all hell broke loose!

The paramilitaries started firing directly at the workers who were gathering for a peaceful gate meeting. In a scene of indescribable horror workers screamed and stampeded over the bloodstained corpses of their workmates, crushing many others as they desperately tried to evade the carnage. Blood was everywhere, streaming from the bodies of the workers whose only crime was to ask for their basic rights.

The firing continued uninterrupted for three hours. By six

o'clock in the evening, when darkness had set in, the state forces had 'conquered' the textile mill workers.

In the factory compound and lawns the state forces had prevented the bodies of the injured from being taken to hospital. Those who tried to pick them up were hampered by the police. Dozens had died on the spot. Several injured had died due to excessive loss of blood because they were prevented from being rushed for medical treatment.

In the darkness of the night the state forces, without differentiating between the dead and the injured, brought up trucks and threw the bodies into them. Some were thrown in the huge factory gutter, while others were buried without coffins in the nearby village of BagaSher.

In spite of the terror of this ruthless state, hundreds of workers and students (including the author) kept on taking the injured to the hospitals and tried to save the lives of as many workers as possible.

Later on an effort was made to remove the bodies of the workers from the gutter and place them elsewhere, in order to arrange for their proper burial with their comrades and relatives present.

There are varying estimates of the casualties that occurred during this massacre. There were eighty bicycles standing in the factory stand, the workers who once rode them to work had gone for ever, never to ride back to their homes in the shanty towns. The press, under Martial Law, reported 18 deaths and 25 injured. Most workers thought that more than two hundred were killed. The Workers' Action Committee that had emerged during this struggle estimated that 133 were killed and more than 400 injured in this brutal, wanton slaughter by the military dictatorship. Instead of arresting the goons of the bosses, who had, along with the state forces, fired on the workers, along with the manager and the owner, Mughees A. Sheikh, who instigated this massacre, the regime didn't even allow a case to be made against them. In its callousness the state arrested and charged with murder the members of the Workers' Action Committee, some of whom had been killed in the massacre. Those who escaped it were prosecuted by the state. Those arrested included Amir Ali, Nur Din, Mukhtar Shah, Mohammad Yousaf, Mohammad Sharif and Mohammad Ramzan.

But, even after this bloody massacre, the workers still had the courage to come out in protests and demonstrations, after which the administration had to release most of the arrested members of the Committee. Due to these protests, on 4 January 1978 the Martial Law administrator of Multan said that an inquiry would be held. The workers' leaders refused to join the inquiry in the local Martial Law headquarters, and demanded that if any genuine inquiry was to be held it should not involve Martial Law authorities; the workers steadfastly refused to recognize the legality of the regime. They demanded that an inquiry should be held at the factory gates, conducted only by lawyers and judges who would be nominated by the workers of the factory.

The other industries that faced similar repressive acts in these months were: Premier Textile Mills, Lyallpur (now Faislabad); Sutlej Cotton Mills, Okara; Rustum Sohrab Factory, Shahdra (Lahore); and the ADC Workshop at Quetta. But, if we take into account the eleven long brutal years of this dictatorship, the acts of tyranny and repression of the workers continued throughout the whole period.

The nightmare of Zia-ul-Haq's dictatorship produced more martyrs, and even more zealous fighters, than perhaps any other period of the country's history. The most formidable challenge of a mass uprising that the Zia dictatorship faced was the historic movement of 1983, mainly centred in Sindh.

The MRD and Sindh

The main opposition parties had formed an alliance named the Movement for the Restoration of Democracy (MRD). It included several small Left parties, Right-wing parties, nationalists, and even some smaller Islamist parties. The Pakistan People's Party was the main party in this alliance. This alliance was formed on 6 February 1981. Its programme was limited mainly to the restoration of civilian rule and constitution. However, the MRD movement could not take off due to the hijacking of a PIA plane by AZO (Al Zulfiqar), an organization that based itself on armed struggle to overthrow the military dictatorship (although it was a successful operation, and was able to acquire the freedom of 40 mainly PPP and Left-wing activists from the Pakistani prisons). At Kabul airport they had to shoot a military officer to press for their demands. Led by Mir Murtaza Bhutto, a PPP Left wing leader and elder son of Zulfiqar Ali Bhutto, they wanted to use the armed struggle to stimulate and inspire a mass movement against the Zia dictatorship. However, in the immediate aftermath of the successful hijacking bid the movement didn't erupt.

Zia further intensified his repression. But the movement did erupt in 1983. It was a widespread movement, but the betrayal by the Right-wing leaders in the MRD restricted it mainly to the interior Sindh. Had the main urban centres joined in with the same zeal, the Zia regime could have been overthrown, perhaps with revolutionary consequences. This isolation of the movement in Sindh made it easier for the state to increase the repression to crush the movement. But there was heroic resistance by the workers, poor peasants and the youth of Sindh against the dictatorship. In spite of the genocide carried out by the Pakistan army in Sindh, this uprising was the toughest threat Zia-ul-Haq had to face during his eleven years of despotic rule. In this movement more than 1,200 people were killed and thousands injured by the army in Sindh. They used military gunship helicopters, even in the smallest villages, to crush the resilience of the masses in the most backward areas of the country. More than 20,000 people were arrested and a large number of them were still languishing in jails when Benaizr came to power. Although this movement in the cities, towns, and villages of Sindh was unable to overthrow the Zia dictatorship, it had jolted the State apparatus. It had an enormous impact internationally and exposed the brutalities of the Zia despotism to the whole world. It was in reality this movement of 1983 in Sindh that had forced General Zia to non-party parliamentary elections in 1985. This movement was the main revolt from below that had opened up cracks within the regime.

This brutal dictatorship introduced draconian medieval Islamic laws to carry out a general repression and intrude into the very personal and private matters of individuals' lives. Public flogging was carried out on more than 80,000 people, inflicting an atmosphere of fear and terror upon society. Atrocious laws were introduced against women, which included the infamous Hudood ordinance that deprived women of the right to testify against rapists. According to these laws the testament of a woman witness was considered to be only half that of man. Even laws for stoning women to death for adultery were promulgated by this despotic obscurantist regime.

Student and labour unions were banned, and any political dissent was crushed with the brutal might of the State. One of the first acts of this dictatorship was to restore to the capitalists those industries that Bhutto had expropriated in the 1972-3 period. Through martial law the capitalists and landlords were back at the helm of society with a vengeance. It was basically the counter-revolution to crush the gains made by the toiling masses of Pakistan through the 1968-9 revolution.

But the main sponsor that propped up and perpetuated this draconian regime was US imperialism. Zia-ul-Haq was the main beneficiary of the geo-political situation that arose in this region after the Soviet invasion of Afghanistan in December 1979.

Zia-ul-Haq was an officer in the armoured corps, who had been trained in the highest American military training centre at Fort Bragg. He said his prayers to God, but his actions were subordinate to his real master, the United States of America. For example, in 1970 he headed a military operation in Amman in which 18,000 Palestinians were massacred. This operation, planned by bloodthirsty Israeli and US experts, was undertaken to save the US and Israeli agent, King Hussein of Jordan, from the revolutionary uprising of Palestinians in Amman. But it was Zia, then a Brigadier, who executed this brutal massacre. It did not run counter to his Islamic ideals and he did not hesitate to slaughter the Muslims 'over there'. In that period, the various Islamic revivalist movements were deeply connected to US imperialism.

The dynamics of governance under a dictatorship led Zia

to rely in a cohort of like-minded and liable officers whom he would rotate out of office periodically, before they struck roots or gained too much influence. He plied these officers with gifts and favours, producing a new crop of millionaire generals who became part of the vested interest group that ran the country for over a decade.

> Zia used Islam with a cynical disregard, using state collected wealth taxes, (known as zakat), as largesse for political purposes. The immediate beneficiaries of these actions were the mullahs and the religious parties, specifically the Jamat-i-Islami.[4]

Zia ordered his military commanders to select and appoint Nazim-us-Salat or prayer leaders in their areas of control, who would ensure that people performed their daily prayers according to the prescribed ritual.

Afghanistan

The active involvement of the army high command and intelligence services, particularly the ISI, in the conduct of the Afghan war, the ISI's direct and unfettered access to overseas financing from the CIA and private and official Saudi sources, and involvement in the making and breaking of domestic political parties and alliances gave the ISI a permanent role in foreign policy.

> Inflow of arms and drug money to finance the Afghan jihad produced its own blowback effects. Drug use skyrocketed in Pakistan. Drug smuggling became a major activity, drawing into its trap even the military, whose National Logistics Cell (NLC) trucks carried arms from the port of Karachi to the north and eventually to the Afghan frontier and sometimes commandeered by corrupt officials to carry heroin down to the airports and the seaport.[5]

As the fighting against the Soviets escalated and arms supplies began arriving from the West, the Middle East and even China, a new 'Kalashnikov Culture' was born in Pakistan. Even the ISI was not immune to the temptations of making money from the misuse of the arms supplies for the Afghan jihad.

Once the financial and supply networks had been set up, the ISI, and not the Pakistan Army, took on the principal role for the execution of the covert war in Afghanistan.

Direct collaboration between the CIA and the ISI also increased, particularly between the CIA Director William Casey and General Akhtar Abdur Rahman, the ISI boss.

The CIA also succeeded over time in making some direct contributions to their own favourite commanders, including Abdul Haq, as did the Saudis. Among the conduits were Saudi charities, including those run by a young Osama Bin Laden. The CIA did not shrink from direct bribery also, either directly or through go-betweens.

The British and French were also entering the bribery game by getting into the good books of Ahmed Shah Masoud, the Tajik commander, who reported to Rabbani in Peshawar.

Soon after President Ronald Reagan took office in January 1981, the US opened up the taps for aid to Pakistan, crafting a $3.2 billion plan for the next five years.

> Zia was now suddenly in the catbird seat, calling the shots on other issues too, such as the return to democracy.[6]

The covert aid via the CIA continued to flow at speed. Zia favoured the idea of a referendum that would give a semblance of legality to his rule and perpetuate power.

> Zia met a stream of objections to this idea from his own military commanders. At one formation commanders' meeting, various officers conveyed to him the 'shame that many officers feel in wearing their uniforms in public, since the masses had come to associate the army with dictatorship and harsh Islamic justice. Many of these officers were sub-martial administrators, who had to deal with summary punishments meted out by military courts, which included public floggings and lashings.[7]

In a speech to the nation on 1 December 1984, Zia spelled out the referendum plan and said that a 'Yes' vote would mean that the people had confidence in him and he would stand elected as president for another five years. But the question that was put to the people was not so direct. Rather, on 19 December, the people of Pakistan were asked to respond to a question that was carefully crafted to ensure victory for the only person whose name was on that referendum:

> Do you endorse the process initiated by the President of Pakistan,

> General Mohammad Ziaul Haq, for bringing the laws of Pakistan in conformity with the injunctions of Islam as laid down in the Holy Koran and Sunnah.[8]

Estimates of the turnout were a fraction of the official numbers. Zia thus became a civilian president but retained his uniform at the same time.

Benazir Bhutto had been released from prison and had left the country in 1983 to seek medical treatment abroad for an ear infection.

Zia had tried to change the ethos of the army, making Islamic ritual and teachings part of the army's day-to-day activities. He had changed the motto of the army from Jinnah's 'Unity, Faith, and Discipline' to 'Iman, Taqwa, Jihad fi sabeelillah' (Faith, Obedience to God, and War in the path of Allah) soon after taking over as COAS in 1976.

> Apart from elevating the status of the regimental maulvis or religious teachers, he allowed members of the fundamentalist Tablighi Jamaat (preachers) to preach at the PMA (Pakistan Military Academy). It was routine for Tablighi Jamaat representatives to deliver the khutba (sermon) after Friday prayers at the PMA in Kakul till 1984. In 1985, the new commandant, Major General Asif Nawaz, forbade the Tablighis' entry, stating: 'This is a military academy, not a seminary!' I was visiting PMA, Kakul when this occurred.[9]

Jamat-i-Islami took advantage of the changing demographics and nature of the army by sending out directives to its members to try to sign up for the army by taking the Inter Services Selection Board examination.

Benazir Bhutto

On 17 August 1988, General Zia was killed in a plane crash near Bahawalpur in his special security C-130 air force plane. He was accompanied by a host of senior officers of the Pakistan army, including the Committee of Joint Chiefs of Staff (CJCS) General Akhtar Abdur Rahman, as well as the US ambassador to Pakistan Arnold Raphel and the US defence attache Brigadier General Herbert M. Warson. None of the 32 people on board the C-130 survived.

There was rejoicing in the streets of Pakistan. It was a jubilant mood across the country. The oppressed masses felt relief and freedom from the longest and the most vicious dictatorship in the history of Pakistan.

At the height of his power and tyranny Zia had perhaps entered into the domain of insanity. He was so far away from the realities on the ground that he started considering himself as a demigod. He was becoming too expensive even for his masters in Washington. Moreover he was defying them on certain important policy matters such as the Geneva Agreement on the Afghan conflict and Pakistan's nuclear enrichment program. He had become a liability for the Americans that they had wanted to shed.

The masses detested him. He relied on the backward sections of society to gain a social base and that was crumbling. The economy was in a mess and the country was paralyzed by sectarian warfare, drugs and social unrest. A million people thronged the streets of Lahore to welcome Benazir, daughter of the leader that had emerged from the 1968-9 revolution, Zulfiqar Ali Bhutto. After his assassination through the gallows he had become a traditional legend for the struggle of the toiling masses against oppression. The Pakistan State and army could not have stood up to the rising tide of the masses from below. They had no choice but to bring Benazir into the government to help quell the unrest.

The Americans and their 'desi' (local) strategists in Islamabad had already done their homework. Benazir had been released by Zia and allowed to go abroad in 1984 by individuals and forces sharing mutual contacts. There is little doubt that London and Washington were involved. Within a couple pf days she had flown from London to the USA. There she met with US congressmen, senators and officials of the State department. Michael Galbrith, Benazir's close friend at Harvard was the main arbiter between her and an imperialist power which was involved in the assassination of Bhutto, and whose daughter was now being groomed to replace him, when the masses rose again to overthrow this exploitative system.

The PPP leadership had gone to the extent of calling those party activists burning US flags at the mammoth rally of

10 April 1986 in Lahore as agents of the dictator Zia-ul-Haq.

It was no secret under whose influence Zia had been persuaded to allow her back to Pakistan in 1986, even permitting her to hold large rallies. But it also exposed the internal decay of his regime. Ever since Benazir's return to Pakistan in 1986 the General had felt the Americans were trying to oust him.

Benazir had been lobbying in Washington, where she had developed powerful backers and was getting herself prime coverage in the Western press.

The plane crash in which Zia and the army top brass were killed had a shattering effect on the confidence of the army and the State. After the somewhat tailored elections Benazir Bhutto took oath as the first woman Prime Minister of Pakistan. Her supporters let off fireworks and danced on the streets. Most did not know that their expressions would contort from jubilation to sullen anger in the short span of twenty months.

At the historic oath-taking ceremony the tall, cold-eyed American ambassador stood aloof in the mirrored and wood-panelled room, carefully watching proceedings in which he had had a not unsubtle hand. Already starting to acquire his nickname as Viceroy of Pakistan, it was only when Ambassador Robert Oakley had called on Benazir for tea that the decision was made public that she might become Prime Minister.

Could Bhutto trust the superpower whose aid was so essential but whom she believed to be behind the removal and by implication the death, of her father? After all, she'd had a hard time stopping her supporters burning US flags in the election run-up.

ISI chief General Hamid Gul had been behind the propaganda campaign of the Right-wing opposition, creating the IDA (Islamic Democratic Alliance) which, in an attempt to denounce her Western background, air-dropped leaflets showing her dancing in a Paris nightclub and her mother clad in sequined Western evening dress waltzing with President Ford as evidence of their 'anti-Islamic' behaviour.

Benazir claimed there would be no vengeance, but not all her party felt the same. Some of them there had suffered indescribable tortures, and many had endured lashings and electric shocks while forced to exist in the midst of disease and their own excreta in beetle and rat-infested, suffocating cells in the notorious Lahore Fort and other torture centres of the state.

Only six months earlier a group of army officers had been beaten up in broad daylight in the garrison town of Rawalpindi, showing just how discredited the army uniform had become.

Benazir was reluctant to accept power-sharing in the broad-based government of national consensus that General Aslam Beg (the army chief) and the president Ghulam Ishaq recommended. Some PPP leaders advised sitting in opposition, but given Pakistan's coup-ridden history, she did not believe they could rely on the prospect of a future election.

She had dinner with Beg, a meeting with Gul, and tea with the US ambassador, saying the right thing each time. The West stepped up its pressure, she made the front cover of *Time magazine*, and editorials of leading international bourgeois papers warned that she must be allowed to take over. Ultimately, perhaps, it was the fear of the volatile province of Sindh erupting and leading to the further break-up of the country which was crucial in persuading the army to accept her. But above all it was the fear of the mass movement of the working class.

The delay before she was given office, and the promises she had had to make, had only served to confirm the public perception that their rulers in Pakistan did not come to power through popular will but because powerful institutions decide that they should.

But she was to have less of a free hand than her father. She reassured the US that foreign policy would not change. She had agreed to keep on General Beg as the army chief for three years, General Hamid Gul as the ISI boss and Sahbzada Yaqub Khan, Zia's Foreign Minister to continue.

The army was to have a say in the choice of Defence Minister, a portfolio she ended up nominally retaining, and the large chunk of budget given to defence would be maintained. Contrary to all her rhetoric, the lucrative land and scholarships given to army personnel and their offspring, as well as plum jobs heading public sector corporations on their retirements, continued.

Everyone wanted something. She was already receiving 60,000 applications a day for jobs. Political exiles were returning; her mother wanted her brother Murtaza back from his exile in Syria, but he was wanted in Pakistan for a hijacking.

The provincial election results had been disastrous, leaving Bhutto with no government in the largest province. Punjab, home to 60 per cent of the population, was to be governed by Nawaz Sharif, the protégé of Zia, who had never had to struggle for his position.

> The ambiguous results of the 1988 elections, in which neither of the main parties had won a majority, had meant that independent MPs had become a very highly priced commodity, well worth the £100,000 investment it had generally cost them to get elected.[10]

Benazir had no qualms about adopting the class collaborationist policies that she had learned in the school of Right-wing social democracy, mainly through David Owen, etc. in Britain and the US democratic senators, during her exile. She also had discussions at the state department and offices of White Hall in London.

> We need winners", Benazir told a crucial meeting of the party hierarchy. "We have to be sure of victory." Party workers who had struggled and suffered for the fight to restore democracy over the last eleven and a half years would be denied tickets in favour of big names who were prepared to join the party even if they had formerly allied with Zia.
>
> Yusuf Raza Gilani, a minister under Zia, now the Prime Minister was one of those welcomed in, the past apparently forgotten in the rush for power. At one point the committee set up had even approached Jamat-i-Islami, the right wing religious party which had long been the PPP's most vicious enemy and had distributed sweets on the announcement of Bhutto's hanging.[11]

Senior PPP members were unhappy albeit temporarily. "I'm not sure if power is worth it on this basis," confided Jehangir Badr one night in Lahore. "We don't know what we represent any more." How could they convince the electorate of Bhutto's assertion that 'the PPP is the only party of the poor and downtrodden'?

> (...) It was not just the old faithfuls who were being forgotten; policies

> were going by the board too. The party founded on Marxist principles had dropped its street socialism in favour of advocating free market economics and Thatcherite privatization. Ali Bhutto would not have recognized his party.[12]

PPP workers who not long before had burned American flags at rallies were forced to listen to praise for the country's main benefactor. Bhutto was to present the illusion of change to the people while reassuring the army, civil service, business community and important Western allies that if the party were to win power it would not upset the status quo. The US ambassador had already been quoted in the press, warning against radical economic policies.

Exit Benazir

When Bhutto became Prime Minister she found that everywhere she went she was mobbed by supporters waving petitions, demanding recompense for their sacrifices during martial law. Ministries in Islamabad would be under daily siege by people waving green, red and black party cards and demanding entry to see their 'People's Minister'.

Committed to cutting development expenditure but the victim of promises made to lure people into the party, Bhutto appointed the biggest cabinet in Pakistan's history and an entire battalion of advisers, more than seventy in all.

On 6 August 1990 Benazir's government was abruptly dismissed by President Ishaq, accused of corruption and maladministration. The State had been able to quash the hopes, derail the movement, and stem the tide of the people through a 'people's' government. Now it ditched Benazir.

Once more the men in khaki had created a living victim, the role Benazir Bhutto played best.

Pakistan's US backers were starting to get edgy. The plot was never meant to be so messy. Benazir was prevailed upon to back down, and made to notice increasing meetings between US diplomats and the opposition. On a trip to Delhi in autumn 1989, the US ambassador Oakley warned the then Prime Minister, Rajiv Gandhi, to expect a change of government next door.

In Pakistan the exuberance which had greeted Bhutto's

assumption of office had rapidly dissipated. On few occasions in history has a ruler squandered so much goodwill so quickly. Like her predecessors, Benazir had quickly become obsessed with Machiavelli's axiom that 'the first rule of politics is to stay in power'.

Corruption, always a deeply-rooted feature in Pakistani politics, was rife with the return of democracy and more blatant than ever before. Having been on the outside for so long, many of Bhutto's colleagues felt it was their turn to make money, receiving pay-offs for passing on lucrative contracts.

Not a move was made to repeal Zia's repressive Hudood ordinance, under which women could be jailed for being raped, even though 3,000 women along with their children were languishing in Pakistani jails for 'crimes' against Hudood. The government had shrunk too from endorsing draft legislation to end the medieval practice of bonded labour.

Time and again the interests of masses who had voted Bhutto in were ignored, even insulted, in order to appease her own Parliamentarians and the mullahs, landlords, imperialist interest and capitalists.

The Oligarchy

Nawaz Sharif was selected by Zia's Punjab governor and former ISI chief Lieutenant General Ghulam Jilani Khan. First he was installed as the Finance Minister in Punjab and later as the Chief Minister. Nawaz Sharif's father Mian Mohammad Sharif was from a small trading background and he had built an industrial enterprise and other financial assets in the typical style that upstart businessmen in Pakistan have been practising since its inception, in connivance and bribery with the civilian and later on the military bureaucracy.

After Zia had ousted Bhutto in a coup in 1977 he had based himself on these obscurantist small businessmen and industrialists by returning their nationalized factories and small businesses. This strategy to build a social base mainly on the petty bourgeoisie went well with Zia's ruthless Islamization process and attaining a support base for capitalism. Mian Mohammad Sharif, Nawaz Sharif's father was one of the first industrialists who got his assets back after the imposition of Martial Law. He was obviously a diehard supporter of Zia and tried to involve the new military rulers to push his business further.

He offered generous shares and partnerships in his business enterprises to the new Punjab Governor, General Jilani. Like most senior officers, Jilani was also very much interested in this. Under Zia's dictatorship the influx of capital into the army and the involvement of the officers of the armed forces in finance became rampant. Mian Mohammad Sharif's offers were so generous that they surpassed even General Jilani's highest expectations. He felt an obligation towards the older Mian and wanted to repay him for his generosity by inducting one of his sons into politics under the canopy of Martial Law. As the story goes, of the many sons of Mian Sharif the one not involved in any worthwhile business, and who could be spared for politics, was Nawaz Sharif.

Supposedly Jilani liked the choice. Nawaz Sharif was mediocre, raw, and could be indoctrinated into any political ideology to give credibility to the military regime; that didn't need much calibre, sharpness and creativity anyway. Nawaz fitted the bill almost perfectly. The money, the media, and the State were always there to project him as Zia's protégé. The military minds of those officers of the army running the Intelligence and other departments are, through design, not likely to have a consciousness or creative instincts beyond a certain constructed thought and imagination. Their policies are formulated by intellectuals and experts who themselves are based at the most on the philosophy of logical positivism and empirical outlook. The military mindset is made to be subservient. Control by discipline, fear and subservience is inculcated into their psychology; the whole chain of command is based on these lines.

In any case, the army is not a democracy of any sort; even the level of Athenian democracy cannot be allowed within the structures of the bourgeois army. The senior commander doesn't have to consult with his junior colleagues. Command is final and unquestionable in military operations. All the military institutions, even the likes of Sandhurst in Britain and Fort Bragg in the USA, indoctrinate such ideas and training in the courses they run for officers from different countries of the world. Thus, as a result of their basic training, they also get along better with politicians of similar mindsets.

Sensing the potential of the hitherto controlled PPP government of Benazir Bhutto, the army high command and the ISI under Lieutenant General Hamid Gul found it necessary to shore up the Right-wing opposition and especially the Muslim League in the key province of Punjab, the largest and economically most prosperous province of the country.

Gul travelled to Lahore, the capital of the Punjab, to help cobble together a coalition under the umbrella of the Islamic Jamhoori Ittehad (IJI, or the Islamic Democratic Alliance), led, among others, by Zia's chosen young Punjabi politician, the affable Nawaz Sharif. Among the techniques reportedly used by Gul and Sharif to keep these meetings hidden was the designation of the encounters as meetings between Hamid Gul and Hussain Haqqani, a former *Far Eastern Economic Review* correspondent, who had signed up to be an advisor to Sharif and later became his official media advisor. He had orchestrated a filthy smear campaign of character assassination against Benazir Bhutto at the time.

Haqqani later was to switch over to Benazir Bhutto, who made him ambassador to Sri Lanka. Some observers of the scene accord Haqqani a prominent role in the formation of the IJI and in the Sharif government's operations. He is now the PPP government's ambassador to the United States.

The titular head of the IJI was a PPP turncoat, Ghulam Mustafa Jatoi, one of the famous 'uncles' (or veteran colleagues of her father) that Benazir Bhutto had let go from her party on her return to Pakistan from exile. The aim of the ISI was to present a counter-weight to the PPP in the Punjab, its traditional stronghold.

> The ISI chief and his deputy, Brigadier Imtiaz Ahmed, reportedly geared up the IJI with threats that Bhutto would roll back the nuclear programme and damage the planned jihad against Indian occupation of Kashmir.[13]

Haqqani cites how Gul persuaded the Jamat-i-Islami head Qazi

Hussain Ahmed, to join the coalition against the PPP (He does not mention his own role in this period).

In the elections of 16 November 1988, due to these intrigues and her own political/ideological retreat, Benazir had a victory of sorts but not a real mandate. But in the 1990 elections, with Benazir now discredited, the establishment and the ruling classes had developed a Right-wing alternative, the IJI, led now by the State and Nawaz Sharif.

Not surprisingly, the IJI, with an IJI caretaker prime minister and pro-IJI ministers in power, was swept into power in November 1990, capturing 105 out of 216 seats in the National Assembly and control of all four provincial governments. The Pakistan Democratic Alliance (PDA), headed by the PPP, won 45 seats, the second largest bloc in the assembly. Thus, Bhutto was elected leader of the opposition. Despite loud complaints by Bhutto and others about irregularities, the election observers from the National Democratic Institute for International Affairs, funded by the US Congress, gave the results its seal of approval.

The caretaker Prime Minister, Jatoi, having done his duty, was dispensed with in the National Assembly as he vainly tried to become the regular Prime Minister. Nawaz Sharif had been pre-ordained for that role. As Admiral Sirohey notes:

> As far as the JCSC was concerned, Mr Nawaz Sharif was the next Prime Minister ... There was a very fortunate situation for the country when there was harmony between the President, the Prime Minister and the armed forces.[14]

The following two and a half years would prove how poor Sirohey's judgement was on political matters.

Sharif swept into the capital, flush with his success at the polls and having secured his base in the Punjab, where his brother Shahbaz Sharif was an activist chief minister. The PPP had been sidelined for the time being. He was the first businessman-cum-chief executive with a platform that was pro-business. He also believed that he had a mandate from the people that allowed him to reshape the economy and Pakistani politics. Very quickly, he brought into play a series of privatizing moves that garnered the support of the business community and began opening up Pakistan's highly controlled bureaucracy-run economy. His own family assets had been taken over in nationalizations by Z.A. Bhutto. He was determined to recreate his business empire again and also to empower the new rapidly rising urban petty-bourgeoisie that had brought him to power in the 1990 elections.

In power Sharif knew that he could not do much for the general uplift of the oppressed toiling masses of Pakistan. Poverty alleviation and socio-economic reforms that could bring prosperity for the downtrodden of the country had no room in the capitalist economy; the fiscal crisis and economic crunch did not allow for that. Instead he embarked upon grandiose projects, more in comparison with the Mughal emperors', especially Shah Jahan, rather than the present-day social democratic and liberal leaders who ape Western methodology and end up in further deterioration of the conditions of the masses.

He announced the building of the Lahore–Islamabad highway, majestic airports at Karachi and Lahore, and several other such imperial projects for a country where the vast majority of the people were deprived of food, health care, education, tapped water and sanitation facilities. He idealized the economic miracles of the Asian Tigers and often boasted of turning Pakistan into a Singapore, a Taiwan or a South Korea.

However, he signed agreements with Daewoo and other East Asian multinationals, along with multinational firms from the Sheikhdoms in the Gulf, giving them contracts to build these projects. But one thing he never forgot: these contracts must include financial kickbacks that would bolster his family fortunes and businesses. One of his close associates disclosed to the author in citing anonymity, an incident that showed the real lust for profit and plunder Nawaz Sharif had to boost his financial assets. The motorway project was started in his first stint of office in 1992. But he was deposed in July 1993.

On 26 November 1997 Nawaz Sharif inaugurated the Lahore–Islamabad Motorway, which is perhaps technologically one of the most advanced in South Asia with its spacious lanes and modernity. After inauguration he travelled from Islamabad to Lahore in a grandiose cavalcade with his coteries on this motorway. At the end the leading coteries were invited to a lavish dinner bash at the palatial farm estate of the Sharifs at Raiwind in the suburbs of Lahore. During this celebration one of the PML leaders after gulping a few doubles had developed some courage and told Nawaz Sharif that he had only built a road just 300 miles long, but a thousand years ago Sher Shah Suri had built 2000 miles long Grand Trunk Road from Calcutta to Peshawar. So what was there to boast about?

Sharif seemed to be taken aback and said: "Oh! He had made such a long road, then he must have made a lot of money out of it also!"

This anecdote somehow expresses the corrupt psychology of the Pakistani bourgeoisie and its new-found political representative.

Nevertheless, corruption soared during Sharif's stint in power to even higher proportions than in the previous regime. The economy was again in a crisis and the social turmoil was rapidly exacerbating the tensions between the ruling elite and their representatives in the presidency, the army, and the Prime Minister's office. Ultimately Sharif was sacked by President Ishaq Khan, a Right-wing bureaucrat who served most military dictators and civilian autocrats in power. But then Sharif used his father's motto, to never say goodbye to a bureaucrat or a judge before he had pocketed the bribe given to him. Nawaz Sharif used this trick on the judiciary and was reinstated by a panel of senior judges of the Supreme Court of Pakistan on 26 May 1993. But the conflict between the 'pillars' of the State continued and finally the Army Chief General Waheed Kakar got Sharif and Ishaq Khan both to resign on 18 July 1993.

The Return of Benazir

An interim government was set up and fresh elections were held on 24 and 27 October. The final results were a narrow win for the PPP with Sharif blaming the caretakers for tilting in Benazir's favour by publicizing the list of defaulters on governmental loans. The disarray within the State had once again forced the elites in Washington and Pakistan to bring her back to pre-empt the danger of another mass upsurge that could have gone out of control and threaten the system.

Benazir in her second term as Prime Minister had her own party stalwart, Farooq Ahmed Leghari, as the President. He was a vicious feudal lord and had his private prisons where the poor peasants and youth who dared to question the tyranny in his estates in South Punjab were incarcerated and tortured. Several were killed, but the state could not impose its writ in his region due to his connections in the bureaucracy and the armed forces. Leghari had also been a minister in Zulfiqar Ali Bhutto's cabinet. After Bhutto was deposed in a coup in 1977 Leghari was the first feudal lord who lodged a case against the PPP government's (1971-7) land reforms and got some of his land which was distributed to the tenants back through a judicial order under the rule of Zia.

Benazir was over the moon on his election as president. At the time the Marxists had written in Jeddojehad (The Struggle) that he will be the person to depose her again in a much more vicious manner. That happened soon. The only person who had faced Leghari in the region both in the elections and in the unrelenting struggle against his atrocious subjugation of the oppressed of that region was Comrade Rauf Khan Lund. He stood on a PPP ticket against Leghari's when the rest of the PPP stalwarts had beaten a retreat in fear of the wrath of Leghari and the state power he controlled.

Apart from contesting elections against the Leghari, Comrade Rauf has been organizing rallies, leading agitations and revolutionizing youth and workers against the feudal aristocracy and their client state in this vast hinterland that borders with Baluchistan and Sindh.

This time round Benazir tried to be more compromising with the army, the ISI and the ruling elite. She overstretched her policies to foment a closer relationship with the USA. On the economic front she continued with the pro-capitalist neo-liberal policies that Nawaz Sharif was pursuing. During her 1995 visit to Washington she tried to appease both the Americans and the army. The already exorbitant expenditure on 'defence' was further enhanced. The armed forces added Orion anti-submarine aircraft, air-to-air and surface-to-surface missiles, radar equipment and parts of the cobra helicopters to their arsenal as a result of this visit. But the working classes continued to suffer. Conditions of the masses continued to deteriorate. Another social turmoil was brewing.

The privatization process had begun during Benazir's first government of 1988, starting with the MCB (Muslim Commercial Bank). Now the agenda of the imperialist institutions was being pursued even more thoroughly to appease the ruling classes and the establishment. Nawaz Sharif's government had taken the privatization and other anti-working class measures quite far. There were several struggles in that period.

There was student unrest and strikes in several sectors of the economy. The bosses, with the backing of the state, also intensified their attacks in this 'democratic' dispensation. One of the most cruel and mean attacks was the assassination of Comrade Arif Shah, the leader of the Punjab Labour Federation with a membership of 65,000 workers. This attack was planned and executed by the capitalists owning the industries on Sheikupura road in the suburbs of Lahore. Comrade Arif Shah's body was pierced with 33 bullets from the Kalashnikov rifles of the hired goons of these pious businessmen. There was a widespread grief that engulfed the whole region. There was an outburst of protest demonstrations and road blockages. Arif Shah was brutally murdered on 20 January 1995, and the PPPs democratic government couldn't even arrest the perpetuators of this heinous crime. The PPP never again won elections from Arif Shah's constituency. But this murder also destroyed the Punjab Labour Federation, one of the largest and most militant trade union organizations in Punjab. It was also a big blow to the development of the forces of revolutionary Marxism. But again the revenge of this murder was to destroy the system of the bosses who had engineered Arif Shah's murder.

The Assassination of Murtaza Bhutto

Meanwhile Murtaza Bhutto, Benazir's estranged brother, had returned to Pakistan. He was more radical and tried to push the PPP towards its original Left path, but the media tried to make this a soap opera, a rift within the Bhutto clan, personal rivalries in the family, etc. The main reason for the state's fear of Murtaza was the radical impact his presence was having on the PPP. Frustrated by the betrayal of the PPP's then leadership he formed a separate faction of PPP and an alternative party, and a great many youths were being attracted towards him because of his Left radical stance; in the past he had waged an armed struggle against the State. On 20 September 1996 when Murtaza was returning to his Clifton home in Karachi, his caravan of vehicles was stopped and directly fired upon by the police.

He was mortally wounded and lay dying on the street for quite sometime. He breathed his last on way to the hospital. Various conspiracy theories have been circulating ever since. The inquiry commission has yet to finalize its report. With the changes in the corridors of power the inquiry has been delayed and diverted.

It was in reality a revenge killing of a revolutionary who had taken up arms against the state. The connivance of other individuals in this brutal assassination is very much possible; perhaps the truth will never come out before a revolution in Pakistan. Several of his close friends and comrades were also assassinated in this atrocious target killing. The whole country was shocked by his sudden death; there was palpable grief and sorrow amongst the masses everywhere. People were wailing on the streets, in the city squares, in shanty towns, and in the villages.

Mir Murtaza was a friend and comrade of the author. We had wide-ranging discussions on Marxist theory, political strategy and organizational methodology for a socialist revolution in Pakistan. Most of these discussions took place in Karachi and Lahore. There was agreement on most theoretical and political issues. Mir had a firm belief that a social revolution was the only way out of the agonizing problems the masses were suffering from.

The tragedy for the masses was all the more painful and melodramatic because he was assassinated by the state forces while his sister was the chief executive—the Prime Minister of

Pakistan. Apart from the grief of her murdered brother she had to face deposition from power by Farooq Leghari, her most admired and trusted party stalwart, who had become the President of the Islamic Republic.

The crisis in economy, the rampant corruption and social tumult aggravated the contradictions between the ruling troika the President, Prime Minister and the chiefs of the Army Staff. Farooq Leghari finally dissolved Benazir's government on 5 November 1996.

This orgy of democracy continued. The musical chairs being played by different sections of the ruling class would have been amusing had the plight of the masses been not so grim.

Nawaz Sharif

The elections of 3 February 1997 brought Nawaz Sharif to power. The conservative State had once again rejected the appeasement of Benazir and brought their favoured representative of capital, back into the corridors of power, this time with a heavy mandate of 137 seats for the PML out of a total of 217. The PPP got only 18 national assembly seats, none from Punjab. But this mandate proved to be too heavy for Sharif's political acumen.

Using this mandate Sharif tried to enhance his powers. He had the support of the Islamic fundamentalists, good working relations through shadowy deals with the generals, and he was at least superficially subservient to the Americans. Benazir's PPP had badly discredited itself by going too far in class collaborationist policies and the masses were restive and put in despair by the role of the PPP government. Nawaz Sharif thought he held all the cards; but he couldn't handle them when the crunch came.

On 11 May 1998, India tested three nuclear weapons at Pokhran, following it on 13 May with another two tests. This was greeted with great public acclaim at home and was presented overseas as India's attempt to counter China and Pakistan's aggressive designs. US intelligence had failed yet again to predict the test. Now it was time for the Pakistani rulers to decide whether or not to follow suit. The Indian gambit was to force Pakistan either to acknowledge that it had been unable to weaponize its nuclear programme, or to go for a test and suffer the consequences of its action. Either way, relative to India, Pakistan stood to lose.

The Secretary General of Finance, Mueen Afzal, reportedly opposed Sharif's desire to proceed with the test, regardless of the economic consequences. Sharif must have known that Pakistan was facing a severe financial crisis, with dwindling reserves and a potential default against its obligations to foreign debtors should it face sanctions after going openly nuclear.

Publicly, Pakistan played coy during this period, leading many to speculate that the Prime Minister, who was not known for making tough decisions rapidly, had managed to avoid this one too and thus saved Pakistan from the aftershocks of testing.

Then on 28 May 1998 Pakistan responded to the Indian tests with five tests at Chagai.

Within thirty seconds the black granite of the Ras Koh Hills at Chagai turned white as a result of the tremendous heat of the explosion. Pakistan had matched the Indians five to five. "Today we have settled a score!"[15]

Prime Minister Sharif now thought he was a national hero. As he attempted to establish total control over the government and the country, he found Army Chief Karamat lacking the desirable enthusiasm for his various ideas. Among the many steps that Sharif took was the 15th Amendment, which would enforce Islamic Law throughout Pakistan and raise the government's actions in that regard beyond the reach of the courts. Hassan Abbas, author and former police officer, refers to this as Sharif's dream of a 'caliphate', he wanted to use the army to run the civil administration also, drawing it closer into his embrace, but failed to get the amendment through. Karamat recalls being bombarded with new ideas of army involvement in civilian administration at almost every meeting he held with Sharif.

Among the suggestions that came from Sharif was to use the army to patrol the GT (Grand Trunk) road, conduct surveys of schools to determine how many were actually operating with staff, and helping the Water and Power Development Authority (WAPDA) monitor its customers' meters to ensure there was no pilferage.

Sharif, after removing the Chief Justice and the President Farooq Leghari, went on to remove the Army Chief General Jehangir Karamat. General Pervez Musharraf was made the new chief due to the tribal and ethnic squabbling between the other senior generals.

But the crisis-ridden Pakistani capitalism was jolted with the severe blow of sanctions after the nuclear tests. Sharif played the role of nationalist in the audience of the bourgeoisie, land lords and the petty bourgeoisie. He further consolidated his support of the Islamic fundamentalists and the Right-wing. He was being praised by the intelligentsia, and sections of the military elite and civilian bureaucracy. Even the ex-Stalinist Left was praising him as the progressive bourgeois leader the country had been needing for almost half a century. Some of these left intellectuals got posts as his advisors, to help him complete the 'national democratic revolution'. Other ex-Left leaders compared him to Sun Yat-sen the leader of the 1911 bourgeois revolution in China.

The Kargill War

But the economic and social crisis that flared up created instability and chaos. Foreign currency accounts were ceased and other drastic measures were taken. The masses had again to bear the burnt of the nationalist adventure Sharif had undertaken. Living standards fell sharply and the economic chaos created even greater social convulsions. On a macro-economic level the country was on the verge of default and the international financial and economic rating corporations were listing Pakistan as a proverbial failed state. This economic meltdown clearly shows how and why, in this epoch of globalization and the crushing domination of imperialist monopolies, the nascent bourgeois cannot carry out or complete the national democratic revolution on a capitalist basis.

As if Sharif's nuclear blunder was not bad enough, the army generals launched another terrible misadventure at Kargill in Kashmir. This was the Kargill war provoked by the Pakistani generals to straighten the line of control and to have a strategic superiority in the area by capturing some hilltops higher than the Indian positions.

This also meant that by capturing these Kargill heights the main Indian highway to Dras, Srinagar and Leh would be threatened. The Kargill operation was started in February 1999 and although Sharif was briefed, it was decided and conducted under the army chief Pervez Musharraf. Not only did the Indians gave them a bleeding nose, they also prepared for a major retaliation of the other fronts. The so-called peace process initiated by the Americans was seriously threatened.

Facing defeat and further escalation of the war, Sharif was sent to plead for Clinton's help to resolve the crisis. The Americans, already annoyed by the nuclear explosions, further humiliated the Pakistani rulers. This war created greater contradictions once again between the army and civilian rulers. The basic factor of the continual recurrence of conflicts between different sections of the state and the ruling classes was the incapacity of the capitalist system to stabilize the economy, political superstructure and society. And all the rulers wanted to govern through this historically obsolete system. Hence all of them were shortlived and had to be deposed in disgrace for corruption and other charges. Crimes like corruption are inevitable in a system that is not in a crisis because of corruption but its organic and intrinsic crisis breeds corruption.

The social status and existence of these rulers inevitably forces them to indulge in corrupt practices, which further aggravates the crisis and ends up in their own overthrow.

At the helm of power Nawaz Sharif, with his limited intellectual capabilities, could understand none of this. Even more he had become a megalomaniac, having artificially unchallenged authority in the corridors of power. In this state of mind he now decided to remove Musharraf. He was in for a shock.

Musharraf

Shahbaz Sharif, the prime minister's brother, arrived in Washington in September 1999. On behalf of Nawaz Sharif, Shahbaz wanted a public statement from the US against a coup, something that the US found hard to construct in the abstract.

But they did provide a tepid statement from the State department.

That statement did not do the trick; especially when things within Pakistan had taken a turn for the worse between Sharif and Musharraf. As reported in *Dawn*:

> Chief of Army Staff General Pervez Musharraf on Thursday dismissed reports of differences with the government as disinformation ... Mr. Musharraf was speaking after chairing a meeting of top military commanders.[16]

Musharraf conveyed through Shahbaz that he did not want to become chairman if it meant giving up his job as army chief.

The next day, Musharraf had lunch with Sharif, at the Sharif's Raiwind estate. Musharraf recalls a tableau that had been repeated earlier with previous chiefs, including Asif Nawaz:

"It was very pleasant. Here, Abba Ji (Nawaz Sharif's father) is telling me, that 'You are like a son to me. These two don't dare say anything against you. If they do, tell me.' So Nawaz Sharif says, 'Why should we do this? He is like a brother to us'".[17]

Then there was an exchange of gifts and the two families went to Makkah to get their sins absolved at official expense.

Within a month or so, however, Nawaz Sharif was to make his move against his 'brother' while Musharraf was out of the country in Sri Lanka on an official trip. Musharraf was due to arrive back on 12 October. His flight was delayed, but when they came close to Pakistan, the captain of the aircraft was informed that they could not enter Pakistani airspace and needed to go to a neighbouring country, with the exception of Dubai.

Short of fuel, the plane was diverted eventually to Nawabshah. But then events on the ground overtook this saga in the air and Musharraf's generals acted in his absence; they took Sharif into their control and got the plane to land at Karachi.

The Hollywood-style drama in the air ended in the middle of the evening and a visibly rattled Musharraf took charge of the country, going on the air in his military uniform to announce that he was taking over the government. Moving with deliberate speed, Musharraf took on the relatively neutral title of Chief Executive, and explained the 'rationale' behind the coup in words only too familiar to those Pakistanis who had survived previous martial law regimes.

Musharraf took power through the fourth 'bloodless' coup of the army in about half a century of Pakistan's existence. He called himself as a "reluctant coup maker". Musharraf may or may not be a reluctant coup maker, but the army and the State were certainly reluctant to execute this coup, at least this time. Not that the generals had developed any democratic credentials, nor had the lust for direct power and plunder diminished amongst the military's top brass. Their assets and share in the country's economy under the so-called civilian rulers of the previous regimes had continued to expand. They controlled the foreign affairs and other vital policy making during these regimes; the weak bourgeois governments of Benazir and Nawaz Sharif had gone all the way to appease the military high command.

In reality, it was because of the intrinsic weakness, lagging cohesion, and internal contradictions of the government that the army had become so reluctant to come to the forefront and face the masses. Musharraf declared himself as a chief executive, rather than a chief Martial Law Administrator as was the tradition of the dictators of the past.

The Musharraf regime was a debilitated dictatorship from the beginning. Hence the repression was selective and controlled. This regime had started to induct 'civilians' much more rapidly in the government, and at the same time imposed military officers into the civilian departments to filch their share of the loot that they would have plundered in martial law administrations. This was aimed on one hand to bribe the army in dubious ways and then use the civilian politicians to give the regime a democratic image. Like every dictator in the past he praised the democratic form of government and innovated his own hilarious interpretations and definitions of democracy. Most chattering classes (intellectual petty bourgeoisie) were cautiously welcoming the reluctant coup maker and his new regime with a liberal cosmetic make-up.

Most anti-Nawaz Sharif politicians were jubilant at the opening of this opportunity for them to be the perpetrators of more plunder. Even Benazir welcomed the change, although not with much enthusiasm from her exile in Dubai. But the workers and the toiling masses were mostly indifferent. They had enough of the decades of bourgeois democracy, in which they only experienced their living standards fall, the pain of poverty and unemployment increase, and the miseries of life aggravated. Hence this 'reluctance' didn't have to face much resistance.

The traders, shopkeepers, and other middle layers of the society who were the main support base of Sharif perhaps had drawn faces but didn't dare to come out. The main businessmen, the bourgeoisie upon whom Sharif relied and represented were searching for backdoor deals with the new regime. Their assets and bank accounts were more important than any one section of the Right-wing replacing the other. The Islamic fundamentalists, in liaison both with the army and Sharif, obviously chose the greater benefactor, the army, to sponsor them and continue the protection they needed for their money making through drug trade and other criminal means. They in turn were facilitating, the 'hawks' in the army to pursue the policy of 'strategic depth' in Afghanistan and Kashmir. This policy of 'strategic depth' was initiated by the ISI and it has continued under every civilian and military regime without any hindrance or interference from any democratically elected rulers.

These people's rulers never depended on the people, nor ever pursued a path to ameliorate the grievances and miseries of the impoverished masses. The class interest of these 'people's representatives' conjoined them with the army and America, who were their demigods due to their belief that US imperialism and the army were the real arbiters of power. The policy of 'strategic depth' was designed to orchestrate a semi insurgency in Kashmir to substantiate the expansionist designs of the Pakistani ruling classes whose main stalwart was the army itself. In Afghanistan it was to make this relatively weak country into a satellite of the Pakistani state.

But the Indians, being a larger 'imperial' power, retaliated with counter-aggression and the overt and covert conflicts continued to destabilize the whole region. This policy continued after the advent of Musharraf. The warlords, drug barons, Taliban and other warring fundamentalist factions were another factor that further aggravated this orgy. Now the dominant US imperialism was intruding with its own interests of oil and strategical needs. Musharraf tried to portray himself as a liberal, a radical bourgeois reformer on the lines of Turkey's Mustafa Kamal Ataturk. His first pictures sent out to the media were holding two white terriers and his daughter wearing a sleeveless shirt. But his 'modernism' was as artificial as Zia-ul-Haq's 'fundamentalism'. The deals and agreements between the US multinationals (particularly UNOCAL) and the warring warlords and Taliban were breached and betrayed several times. There was a history of such deals for more than two centuries. US imperialism had abandoned the Islamic fundamentalists after the Soviets pulled out of Afghanistan. They had deserted a country which was in a conflagration of bloody strife between different warring Islamic factions, instigated by the imperialists themselves and fuelled by the local and financial interests of regional powers and the black economy in the garb of Islamic obscurantism. Those reactionary outfits, whose aid and sponsorship was cut by the Americans, instilled a poisonous hatred among the fanatic recruits from the Madrassahs. They created a new 'Satan' after 'communism' in the form of US imperialism as a target to whip up frenzy amongst the beastly fanatics.

All this was to further the economic gains of the Islamic bosses and their local sponsors through the nefarious means of drug and arms smuggling. US imperialists reciprocated with almost exactly the same response, as they also needed to externalize their own exploitation of the US and European workers by fabricating a myth of another evil, Islamic fundamentalism, after the fall of Stalinism.

Even if 9/11 would not have happened some other similar disaster was bound to take place in one form or the other. The theory of the 'Clash of civilizations' needed such human destruction with the traumatic effects around the world to promote its ideology and evil designs. The inferno ignited by the Americans in Afghanistan was bound to spread and the strategists of imperialism were hell-bent on utilizing it to impose US hegemony and the cruel exploitation of cancerous capitalism. It is entirely false that the main centres of power in the Pakistani State were supporting the Taliban against US dictates. It is true that there were short interludes in which, in the absence of the US, the ISI went ahead more than designated, but that was when the attention of Pentagon and the CIA was diverted elsewhere. It is also true that after the departure of US from the scene the ISI and the so-called rogue elements of the state built up their own networks and infrastructure in this internecine war of constantly changing loyalties, deceit and treachery.

Musharraf's 'U turn' on the threat of being 'bombed into the stone age' by Richard Armitage, the US under secretary of state, was a fallacy. It was no surprise for anyone knowing the history and nature of the Pakistani state and capitalism that it was utterly incapable of standing up to US imperialism. Only during Z.A. Bhutto's initial period of governance, and when the US had engineered his demise, did the government gave some occasional outbursts of anti-imperialist sentiment. Musharraf made a big thing out of this in order to somewhat improve his credibility, with a strange, rather contradictory message of being a saviour and subservient imperialist ally. In his memoirs Musharraf quotes General Aziz Ahmed, on a visit to Washington at the time of 9/11 saying that Armitage had said that, "not only that we had to decide whether we were with the America or with the terrorists, but that if we chose the terrorists then we should be prepared to be bombed back into Stone Age".[18]

During Musharraf's last US visit Armitage denied it in the American media in his usual bullying manner. The truth probably was closer to the report on terror attacks by the Kean/Hamilton commission.

US Ambassador Wendy Chamberlain brought him a copy of the official list of seven demands. The US asked Pakistan to:

- Stop al Qaeda operatives at its borders and end all logistical support to Bin Laden;

- Give the United States blanket over flight and landing rights for all necessary military and intelligence operations;
- Provide territorial access to US and allied military intelligence and other personnel to conduct operations against al Qaeda;
- Provide the United States with intelligence information;
- Continue to publicly condemn the terrorists' acts;
- Cut off all shipments of fuel to the Taliban and stop recruits from going to Afghanistan; and,
- If the evidence implicated Bin Laden and al Qaeda and the Taliban continued to harbour them, to break relations with the Taliban government.[19]

In effect, the United States wanted carte blanche to proceed against whomever they thought had attacked it by establishing extra-territorial rights in Pakistan, among other things.

On Kashmir, Musharraf was churning out one solution after another. Even by bourgeois standards they seemed ridiculous. Most were just extravagant flights of thought, especially those in the late hours of the night when he hit the bottle. The peace process with India was the victim of a similar discourse. The Indian counterparts were no less absurd. The 'cunning fox' of Indian politics Atal Behari Vajpayee, who seemed to be all over the place, turned every issue into a romantic saga. His hypocrisy was evident, but neither he nor Musharraf could control the main bastions of state power, either in India or Pakistan.

The conflict and contradiction between the two countries was and is the pivotal base for the existence of some of the largest armies and arms spending in the world. From the kickbacks to the involvement in the economic and financial structures of these countries, very strong vested interests have developed in the evolution of the two states. Hence every initiative of Musharraf was torpedoed by sections of the same forces that he was supposed to be commanding. The story was not much different on the other side. The problem that had now emerged was that both were nuclear armed states and a war would always bring the danger of a nuclear conflict. That would mean the mutual annihilation of both countries, along with the assets of the ruling classes, and possibly the elite itself would have perished in the ensuing Armageddon. The imperialists had two contradictory interests in this game of war and peace: on one hand their relatively heavy investments in India; they wanted to preserve these from any turmoil and war that could damage their assets. Hence they did their utmost to prevent the rulers of India and Pakistan from engaging in total war. This was shown in the aftermath of the so-called terrorist attack on the Indian parliament building on 13 December 2001.

As Steve Coll reported in *The New Yorker*:

> Little was known about the attackers, but India suspected the Pakistan government and its Inter Services Intelligence (ISI) agency was behind the attack. Since the late 1980s, ISI has covertly funded and armed violent Islamist groups in Kashmir. By 2001, two of the larger jihadi groups—Lashkar-e-Tayyaba and Jaish-e-Mohammad—had developed ties to Al Qaeda. After the December 2001 attack, Indian Prime Minister Atal Bihari Vajpayee ordered the Indian military to mobilize for war. India and Pakistan's looming confrontation became the first nuclear crisis of the 21st century and it posed a very modern problem the impact of stateless religious networks with millenarian ideas.[20]

On the other hand they were against a durable peace or a permanent settlement of Kashmir and other issues. They want the antagonism to prevail as it provided profitable markets for their Military Industrial Complex. After all India and Pakistan are some of the largest buyers of Imperialist sophisticated weaponary.

Indian military officials sought to respond, on the assumption that the militants had Pakistani backing. Some 700,000 Indian troops were placed in Kashmir and the Indian Air Force was poised on Pakistan's borders. The Indian Navy moved into battle positions in the Arabian Sea.

There was a sudden outburst of war hysteria in India. Sabre rattling began. Troops were put on high alert on both sides. The poison of Hindu chauvinism and Indian nationalism was churned out by the press and television and had engulfed large sections of the Indian society, especially the petty bourgeois. The Pakistani ruling classes and the state were forced to respond, although much weaker, and besmirched in its own scandals and quagmire of crisis, they had no other option. Pakistan's modest forces and weaponry were rushed to the borders. The war hysteria had now gripped the South Asian subcontinent.

War seemed imminent. The Pakistani media, intelligentsia, and media's response was no less pernicious. A wave of Pakistani chauvinism and Islamic fundamentalism was unleashed. They were seething for revenge. The diplomatic efforts to resolve this stand-off failed miserably. White Hall in London and state department in Washington intervened forcefully but to no avail. Even the imperialists were now jittery over the rapidly deteriorating situation. But then at last the saviour from an ultimate destruction intervened. He was one of the main bosses of IBM, a multinational with substantial investments, mainly in India. Atal Behari Vajpayee, the Prime Minister of India from the Hindu obscurantist party BJP (Bhartiya Janata Party) ultimately caved into his threat of immediate removal of investment and flight of capital from India.

At the same time the imperialists had vested interests in the continuation of antagonisms and hostility between the two major powers of the subcontinent, albeit in a controlled scenario. The British had already left behind the thorny issues of Kashmir, water distribution, boundary disputes, etc. when they departed. They wanted to continue the policy of divide-and-rule from afar. This discord gave them an important leverage to maintain their economic exploitation and further their imperialist interests. The United States, apart from its strategic interests in the region, wanted to exploit the labour, mineral resources, and the direct financial plunder of both countries. But another aspect is that one of the main sources of the looting of the wealth of these countries is the exorbitant profits from the sales of armaments and weapons of mass destruction to them. The ruling classes, the Sate, and other local brokers have their own fortunes tied up with this extortion through the sale of arms. The cost of these devices of devastation has increased several times more than the cost of most commodities extracted, grown and produced in India and Pakistan. Therefore the enmity must continue, but in a controlled fashion; it must not be allowed to escalate into a full-scale war. Thus there is a very clear common denominator between the interests of imperialism and the national bourgeoisies of the subcontinent. The policy they have to maintain can be summed up as: they cannot afford to start an all-out war, and they can't sustain a durable peace. This pendulum-like swing between war and peace goes on and on, while more than 1.5 billion inhabitants continue to suffer the agonies of hunger, poverty and disease that makes life a continual misery for succeeding generations; it is not an accident that the South Asian subcontinent, with 22 per cent of the world's population, endures 40 per cent of the world's poverty. Meanwhile, the delicate balances and equations that are set in societies in such intense turmoil and turbulence are so tense and acute that any major crisis can escalate into a full-scale war. Such a scenario in two nuclear states with jittery rulers can bring about death and destruction on a scale more horrific than anything ever experienced in human history.

On the domestic front, in spite of the celebrated macro-economic figures, the conditions of the masses under Musharraf continued to deteriorate. The regime got a lot of laurels from the World Bank and other imperialist institutions. These institutions have had a tradition of sending their employees or chosen representatives to become finance ministers of Pakistan. Apart from Dr. Mubashar Hasan, every finance minister of Pakistan was either an employee, or was selected and sent by the IMF and the World Bank. This started right from the very inception of the country; after Musharraf's takeover, Shaukat Aziz was brought over for the job. He was a banker at Citi Corp. and was selected by the IMF. He was even elevated to the post of Prime Minister while retaining the portfolio of finance. Consequently, the masses were even further subjected to poverty, unemployment, disease and worsened infrastructural conditions of life. The chorus of praise from the offices of IMF and the World Bank in Washington was echoed by most of the bourgeois economic experts of Pakistan. The development and growth of economy under this regime has been expressed by another Pakistani expert, Shuja Nawaz, who is the editor of *Financial Development*, the multilingual quarterly of the IMF and the World Bank. In his recent book *Crossed Swords* he wrote the following:

> Musharraf could point to the economic progress under his regime. Earlier, Sharif had introduced privatization and the ascendancy of the business class a good start for the hitherto moribund government-controlled economy, but he had allowed it to be tainted by corruption. Musharraf's regime continued the pro-business trend, under his finance minister and then Prime Minister, Shaukat Aziz. Its economy began growing at a rapid pace, hitting 7 per cent average GDP growth. Pakistan managed to escape the strictures of the IMF and began attracting investment flows from expatriate Pakistanis and the Middle East. It benefited enormously from the flow of US aid following the global 'War on Terror' launched by the United States following attacks on its soil by Osama Bin Laden's Al Qaeda from bases in Afghanistan.[21]

Although he rightly attributes corruption to Sharif, under Musharraf the corruption and plunder perpetrated by the ruling classes continued unabated. In an article in *Dawn*, some of the figures of bad loans and bank write-offs emerged:

> Pakistan borrowed from external sources $15 billion during last four years and the government banks and financial agencies wrote off loans worth Rs 33 billion in three years ...These figures were placed before the Senate by the minister of state for finance Omer Ayub. The massive write-offs on an ascending scale began with Rs. 5.6 billion in 2003, and went on with Rs 10.42 billion in 2004, Rs 9.908 billion in 2005 and Rs 19.338 billion 2006 (...)
>
> The industrial sector was the major beneficiary with Rs 25.82 billion. The trade sector's write-off was Rs 3.21 billion and the agricultural sector got away with Rs 2.83 billion. The total number of borrowers who got such write-offs, he said, was 11, 220 in 2003, 17, 869 in 2004, 45,249 in 2005 and 19,378 in 2006. Eleven investors from the industrial sector got away with a write-off of Rs 12.37 billion in 2003 (...)
>
> In addition to the Rs 33 billion loan write-off, they also got subsidies totalling Rs 24 billion, which makes a total of Rs 57 billion.
>
> Trading in Pakistan is said to be substantially profitable, particularly in imported goods. That is why most industrial houses have opened their own trading houses for foreign goods and services. Yet they got a loan write-off of Rs 21 billion ...
>
> Many farm lords obtain loans with no intent to repay and eventually get it written off. What is striking is that along with a loan default of Rs 33 billion which was written off in three years, they also got subsidies of Rs 24 billion to make it doubly profitable. Clearly, the outflow of public funds is a continuous process under any 'system' of government. Such loans were given by government banks and financial institutions, often under political pressure or to reward some

> politicians, and often written off following the same kind of political bargaining. Many of the sitting members of parliament are beneficiaries of such write-offs. They include Chaudhary Shujaat Hussain and his family members. The loans were also given to the friends and relatives of senior officials in Islamabad who controlled the banks, and later written off under their influence (...)
>
> At its peak, the non-performing loans were around Rs 250 billion. Some of the borrowers had no intention to repay, or planned to repay one or two instalments and then default, as they were a large company.
>
> (...) Industrialists prefer to borrow money from banks while keeping their own money in banks on a long-term basis and earning large profits.
>
> The country's foreign debt, which had gone down to $35.47 billion in the year 2004, has risen again to $40.172 billion which includes some foreign liabilities. In the year 2006 Pakistan borrowed $3.014 billion. This has happened in spite of the record home remittances of overseas Pakistanis of $6.5 billion and the record overseas direct investment of $6.4 billion. In addition, Pakistan borrowed $ 3.64 billion last year.[22]

As we have seen in this work, even during the period of a relatively healthy boom in the world capitalist economy in the 1960s, the high growth rates under Ayub failed to raise the general social conditions and develop society in relation to the economic growth. How then could Pakistani capitalism have developed society under the high economic growth rated under Musharraf/Aziz regime, when the world economy was itself in crisis and booms were only artificially propped up by heavy credit financing and a series of bubbles that were going to pop? In March 2001 the US economy, the largest in the world, was facing a virtual negative growth rate scenario. The sickness of Pakistani capitalism had worsened in spite of the fact that a rosy picture of the macro-economic statistics was being presented. Shuja Nawaz again praises the Musharraf/Shaukat Aziz economic management:

> One of the biggest challenges faced by Musharraf when he took over was the sorry state of the economy. Pakistan's foreign exchange reserves at the time were around $300 million, with foreign direct investment (FDI) around the same figure. Relative political stability, the inflow of remittances from expatriates after 9/11, the opening up of the economy to private foreign investment, all contributed to a healthier economy, with foreign exchange reserves rising to around

> $13 billion. Workers' remittance rose from $1.1 billion in 2000 to $4.3 billion in 2005. FDI meanwhile rose to $2.2 billion, according to the World Bank.
>
> A key role in this was played by the steady management of money supply and interest rates by the State Bank, giving businessmen some sense of stability. According to the government, the GDP rose from around 4.1 per cent in 2000 to 7.8 per cent in 2005. Military spending, though, showed a decline from 4.1 to 3.4 per cent of GDP. But the US and other financial assistance following Pakistan's alliance with the United States in the 'War on Terror' yielded immediate gains; between 2001 and 2006, some $10 billion had come in through open channels to Pakistan.[23]

US aid was mainly spent on the so-called 'war on terror'. Rather than dousing the flames of this insurgency it further fanned them. The destabilization and turmoil resulting from this horrendous misadventure has resulted in unimaginable suffering for the poor masses, especially in the FATA region. And yet this aid gave a glossy shine to the macro-economic statistics. Similarly, the reliance on FDI (Foreign Direct Investment), that is the worldwide cornerstone of neo-liberal economic development, hardly brings any respite to the plight of the workers and the downtrodden masses. Not surprisingly, the policies initiated by this monetarism or Reaganomics has brought disastrous consequences for the working classes.

These policies of privatization, down-sizing, deregulation and liberalization enforced by most post-1980 regimes at the behest of capitalism, have resulted in further impoverishment of the masses. And the main aim of these policies was to create a more 'feasible' climate in which to attract the FDI.

Shaukat Aziz and Musharraf were always bragging about these rapacious economic policies. They were perhaps more aggressive in this crusade than their predecessors. They used massive credit financing to bloat the economy and boost the growth rate. But as elsewhere, this resulted in rather debilitating the economy and the piling up of public and state debt. This led to a consumer boom in property and certain other sectors, although this consumerism was confined mainly to Pakistan's relatively small middle class. The vast population was almost excluded from this cycle and there was a negligible 'trickle down' effect. But expansion of these selective sectors had a negative impact on infrastructure. The already weak infrastructure was creaking under the burden of this consumerism. This gave rise to contradictions between commodity consumption and the infrastructural facilities. Poverty intensified and the gap between 'haves' and 'have-nots' further widened, while the banks accumulated massive profits and the corporate sector rejoiced at these 'reforms'. Speculators had a heyday. The Index soared and the stock exchange casino became the most profitable venue of investment.

This socio-economic malaise expressed itself in sporadic strikes, a rise in terrorism and crime, and increasing chaos and anarchy. The middle classes were in desperation and vacillating vigorously. Musharraf's pro-imperialist stance and the absence of a Left resistance on a class basis gave room for the Islamic fundamentalists. In the 2002 elections the Islamist alliance MMA (Muttaheda Majlis-e-Amal) got more seats in the parliament than in any other election. Although their votes were less than the number of seats they got, in Pakistan's history they had never managed to get as many before. This reflected a degree of stagnation in society.

The Islamists had demagogically started to champion the anti-imperialist cause. With the US aggression raging in Iraq and Afghanistan there was very strong anti-US sentiment in Pakistan. The PPP and other 'secular' and nationalist parties failed to come out in a clear confrontation with imperialist aggression; hence the field was left open for the Mullahs. But even then they could not muster the support that was potentially there. The masses had perhaps seen through the hypocrisy of the religious–imperialist conflict; the million man marches called by the MMA attracted not more than a few thousand. There was no apparent threat to Musharraf. The state agencies had been in action and kept on manipulating and manoeuvring the willing politicians into various agreements, deals and alliances. So pathetic were the dominant political leaders that they had lost the will to struggle and build up mass resistance to a much weaker dictatorship compared to those in the past.

Even negotiations between Sharif and the regime were going

on through the back door.

Firstly, their economic policies hardly differed from those being pursued by the Musharraf regime. Secondly, they were looking for short cuts. The PPP had been out of power for some years now and the Right-wing leaders wanted to jostle back into power to resume their plunder. Most political parties participated in all the electoral and political facades that the regime had set up to proclaim its democratic legality. From the local bodies to the parliamentary elections of 2002 almost all the mainstream parties participated and Musharraf used this for the perpetuation of his own rule.

It was not just American support that kept Musharraf in power; that could have been turned into its opposite as soon as a mass movement erupted. It was the compromising attitude of the bourgeois-dominated opposition that gave him the greatest leverage. But the rise in social contradictions, aggravating economic crisis below, and pressures of the 'war on terror', started to have their impacts.

The regime was now suffering from intense decay and was in constant decline. This increased pressure on Musharraf and his Western backers. The 2005 communications strike, the PIA engineers and several other strikes in vital sectors of the economy further alarmed the ruling classes.

London and Washington started efforts to broker a deal between Musharraf and Benazir in the autumn of 2006. Instead of going to the masses to build up a movement to overthrow the regime, the PPP leadership was busy in various manoeuvres and deals with the dictator. The so-called 'charter of democracy' was signed between Sharif and Benazir in London. But its fate was sealed at its inception. Both were trying to outplay each other and calling for democratic politics, while totally side-lining the real issues and the economic woes of the people. The larger imperialist brokers now came into play and a grand coalition between Musharraf was being manufactured to stave off the impending threat from below.

The Lawyers' Movement

Most movements were mainly on petty issues, problems of

political super structures, gender questions and similar trends which were more related to the middle classes. These movements were mainly inspired by the mushrooming television channels and the media. They were organized by smaller and medium parties with an important role within the NGOs (Non Governmental Organizations). These were correctly dubbed by the media as 'civil society' activities, as the Left–Right divide had been abandoned and this petty bourgeois class collaborationism cliché became fashionable amongst the middle class activists; the huge deprived and downtrodden majority of the population, the 'uncivil' society, was quite indifferent to these mobilizations.

One of the largest and more significant of these 'movements' was the lawyers' movement for the restoration of the Chief Justice and 60 other judges sacked by Musharraf. This was a movement with demands that suited the media barons and the civil society. They were asking for the independence of a judiciary in a society where the overwhelming majority of the population was deprived of the right to have food, and who could never afford the astronomical amounts of money in fees needed just to enter the corridors of the palatial Supreme Court building.

Musharraf was more perturbed about the media rather than these movements, but such was his crises-ridden regime that he was jolted by the coverage they received. The caravans and rallies had the attendance of a few thousands, but nevertheless the ideological and political Left–Right divide was obliterated by the all important 'civil society.' At the same time, some of the PPP lawyers were the main leaders of the movements, the whole emphasis was on their 'non-political' character.

This in itself was absurd: a non political movement was trying to fill a political vacuum against a dictatorship.

A number of Left groups, NGOs and sects also entered the fray, putting in all their efforts for meek bourgeois demands.

Musharraf's main political support came from the ethnic neo-fascists, the MQM (Muttaheda Qaumi Movement). They used violence and terrorism against the lawyers' movement.

The conflict between the judiciary and the army was after

all a clash between two vital pillars of the state. The basic task of the creation and existence of both these institutions was the preservation and protection of the rule of capital from the wrath of the masses. As the crisis worsened the Musharraf regime panicked and aggressively tried to suppress acts that could have been detrimental to the integrity of the whole system. At the same time the judiciary, through suo-moto actions and other decisions, was only trying to vent the steam rising from below. This conflict clearly reflected the crisis within and between the different institutions of the state.

There was very little room for a revolutionary programme in such movements. However, the Right-wing and liberal forces, including a section of the PPP leadership, were justifying the dictatorial acts of Musharraf by giving him tacit support. They were all guilty of supporting a dictatorship, however weak it might have been. After this capitulation they didn't have the nerve to stand up against him and call for a successful mass movement. However, the lawyers' movement was a big fish in a small pond; in a political vacuum it seemed larger than life in spite of its modest size.

The masses had yet to enter the arena of politics in their millions. When at last they did, they came out in a numerical strength and force that cut across all the other prevailing political and social movements and trends.

In the midst of the raging crisis and increasing instability the imperialists speeded up their efforts to craft a set-up that could serve their aims in a more subtle manner. These efforts of Washington and London ultimately led to the clandestine one-to-one meeting between Benazir and Musharraf in July-August at one of the palaces of the ruler of Abu Dhabi. Both sides publicly kept on denying the 'deal'. The main crux of the deal was that Musharraf, being rapidly discredited amongst the masses and his edifice of power in jeopardy due to his support for American capitalist-imperialism, needed a coalition partner who had the confidence, and could contain, the hopes and aspirations of the masses.

The Assassination of Benazir

Benazir was the most obvious person to play that role. They

were trying to do the impossible. The return of Benazir, the elections, and the transition of power were meticulously planned. The PPP leadership's handpicked subservient party apparatus, at different levels, was given instructions to organize a big but controlled welcome rally. The ethnic MQM (Muthaheda Qaumi Movement), an ardent ally of Musharraf that controversially had mass support in Karachi, was roped in by the regime to facilitate the process. The civilian bureaucracy was also mobilized. All was set and the Americans thought that their plan would work.

Then came the 18th of October 2007, the day of Benazir's return to Karachi after yet another exile. The PPP leaders were taking bus loads of people for the reception at Karachi. They had been assigned this task and its results would have been an important factor for getting party tickets in the forthcoming elections. A substantial crowd was needed to prove the popularity that the party had claimed to the Americans. Most political pundits, TV commentators, intellectuals and newspaper columnists had written off a mass movement and the possibility of the resilience of working classes to rise and struggle for the real issues. The 'uncivil society' was now in the arena. According to some estimates between two and two and a half million wretched souls had converged upon Karachi Airport from across the country. The downtrodden, the dispossessed, the deprived, the exploited; all those suffering the miseries of this system came.

They came with their dirty and torn clothes, wearing broken plastic slippers, sweating, tired, faces drawn—yet there was a gleam in their eyes that exuded both anger and revolt towards the system that had made their lives so dreadful. They had perhaps come for a glimpse of Benazir—the daughter of Zulfiqar Bhutto, who had called for a transformation of life and society a socialist revolution! The hope and tradition of almost four decades had passed to the new generation.

Benazir, when she came out of the airport was flabbergasted by the mammoth crowd. The sheer size of the welcoming rally had torn the deal to shreds and the designs of the imperialists were shattered. In reality these teeming millions had come to show her a glimpse of themselves, their poverty, misery, tragedies and deprivation.

The state, whose warring factions had been drawn into a fragile compromise to abide by this deal, was baffled.

One of the significant aspects of this welcoming rally was the burning of US flags in front of Benazir's truck as it came on to the main Shara-e-Faisal road. It was the Marxists in the PPP, activists of the PTUDC (Pakistan Trade Union Defence Campaign) and other revolutionary youth organizations orientating towards the traditions of the masses, who were torching the imperialist symbol. These incidents of the burning of US flags about every half a kilometre were shown on some major TV networks, but most preferred to ignore them. Perhaps they didn't want to disturb the 'deal' and the 'plan'. But the rogue elements in the state wanted to do just that. Their first act was a huge explosion near the Karsaz crossing on the Shara-e-Faisal. More than two hundred perished in the blast, and thousands were hurt. Benazir escaped the explosion and was whisked away to her residence in state protection.

The masses were still not deterred. The election campaign began and it took the shape of a militant movement. The zeal of the masses was turning her towards some radicalism at least. She was bound by the deal and the connection with the Americans. Yet the masses turned out to her rallies with a vigour that instigated her into more and more radicalism. This was too much at stake for the conservative sections of the Pakistani state. It was not, what she was saying in her speeches. It was what she had come to symbolize for the masses.

Twenty-one years previously, on 10 April 1986, on her first main return to Pakistan from exile, more than a million had turned out at the Lahore airport. She had two stints of power. She had failed to satisfy the aspirations of the masses. Yet the tradition of the 1968-9 revolution was alive once again. Reaction had to act more decisively. The friction within the factions of the state had turned red hot. As a result, on 27 December 2007, Benazir was killed in the crossfire of the war between these factions of the state. This time the mass upsurge was not of hope and aspirations. It was a burning vengeance. Government offices, businesses, banks, police stations and other symbols of capitalism and the state were burnt down within hours of the news of her assassination. This happened in most cities and towns across Pakistan. The country came to a standstill. Not a wheel turned.

The fury of the masses had forced the state to retreat. How could they have faced the molten lava from the volcanic eruptions of the wrath of the masses? The Musharraf regime declared three days' mourning; it couldn't do much else anyway. The mobs roamed the cities, towns and villages in several parts of the country, but the neo-fascist goons of the Islamic Fundamentalists and the mafia thugs of the MQM were no-where to be seen. They had just disappeared as if they had never existed. The Army, Rangers and police patrols rolled in much later. Even then they were terrified of the people. The mass reaction had struck like lightning.

The PPP/Right-wing Coalition

But the movement was rudderless. Had the PPP leadership called for a General Strike and demanded elections on the scheduled date of 8 January 2008 the subsequent history would have been different. But the PPP leadership was abiding by the 'deal'. They turned the grief and anger into sorrow and despair. Zardari became the functional co-chairman. The party activists and mass support was articulated into praying for the emancipation of her soul, rather than to guide them to the path of struggle. The imperialists were in close contact with the PPP leaders during these events. They were the real decision makers at such a crucial juncture. The leadership compromised with the regime at every step; both were being directed by the Americans. The PPP leadership once again dumped even the slogan of socialism in the garbage of bourgeois democracy. Democracy was posed to be the best revenge. Yet the aspirations and needs of the masses yearned for the revolution to be the only revenge. The elections were postponed till the 18th of February. The PPP leaders abandoned even the rhetoric of 'Food, Shelter and Clothing' and other issues of class struggle that the movement had thrown up. They embarked upon the Utopia of national reconciliation. The section of Islamic fundamentalists, the nationalists, the ethnic fascists, the Right-wing bourgeois parties and the PPP populists were to be united into a great national reconciliation. How else to diffuse and dissipate the class struggle?

Meanwhile the Americans and the state machinery went into full action to prepare the most meticulous rigging in the history of Pakistan. If the elections were held on 08 January after those traumatic events, the PPP would have won a two-thirds majority. But the elections of February 18 were a different story. The mass upsurge had been pushed back into pacification and demoralization by the democratic counter-revolution led by Right-wing PPP leaders. The movement had ebbed, and once again the field was open for the bourgeois politicians who resumed the orgy of money-laundering and corrupt politics. The most profitable business was now in full swing.

The election results were tailor-made for the needs of US imperialism. Nawaz Sharif's younger brother Shahbaz had come back from a visit to Washington a few days before the elections. Even the fundamentalists through the Sharifs PML(N) (Pakistan Muslim League [Nawaz]) had conveyed their cooperation with the new set-up. The Nawaz league were given an extra quota of about fifty seats in these fabricated results. It is not accidental that the 'international community', imperialist media, the national media, the EU and other Western observers, the NGOs and above all the civil society hailed these elections as free and fair.

The correctness of the results was given 'universal' acclaim. But even if one has a slight understanding of the election process, the rotten infrastructure of the electoral machine, the voting lists and the whole mechanism in Pakistan, free and fair elections can never be conceived in the present set-up.

The end result was that the PPP was proclaimed as the victor and the largest party in the parliament. Yet the truth is that the PPP's Pyrrhic victory was a defeat for the masses which supported it, both in terms of the actual results and the ramifications of these elections on the policies of the new PPP government.

The PPP Right-wing leaders had given up the two-thirds majority results in favour of a coalition government because the policies necessary to sustain the existence of the decadent capitalist system would have invited the wrath of the masses. The PPP leaders were too terrified to confront the masses and take the responsibility of government on its own in such a situation, so they opted for a coalition government even before the elections were actually held. But the Right-wing parties let the PPP lead the coalition government and face the music; they were only too happy to wait in the wings for the PPP to meet the fate of a disgraceful deposition once again, and let the power fall into their laps at a time when the masses might be pushed into greater demoralization and become too apathetic to fight the attacks of the ruling class.

The magnificent movement of the masses that took place in the autumn and winter of 2007 had shocked and jolted the ruling classes so vigorously that the PPPs nominee for Prime Minister, Yousaf Gillani, was elected unanimously. That was perhaps the first and last display of this hypocritical and treacherous unity of the Pakistani ruling classes against the proletariat and the toiling masses.

The fissures in the Pakistani state had not coalesced after the assassination of Benazir, rather the cracks had widened and the contradictions further sharpened. The warring factions of the state had not given in but had just lain low, waiting for the storm of the mass upheaval to pass over. After the formation of the coalition government the major partner, the PML(N), withdrew its fifteen ministers just 41 days after the start of the new government.

Of course, this new government proved to be another disaster for the masses right from the start. The coalition government included the Islamic fundamentalists JUI (Jamiatul Ulema e Islam), the Pashtoon nationalists ANP (Awami National Party), tacitly to begin with the ethnic neo-fascist MQM, Independents and others. When the PML(N) left the government, the *Economist* of 10 May 2008 gave a rather pessimistic picture of the situation:

> Pakistan is in a mess again. It is teetering on the brink of food riots,

> industrial lay-offs and strikes against the daily 12 hour nation-wide power cuts. The economy is slipping. Capital flight has taken nearly 5 per cent off the value of the rupee against the dollar in the past few weeks. The war against extremists in the tribal badlands is going nowhere. Instability has returned to haunt politics.[24]

The attacks upon the masses which the Musharraf regime had shrunk from implementing, due to their fear of an upsurge from below, were now unleashed by the new 'people's' government. In the first six months of the regime it managed to accumulate the highest ever inflation, trade deficit, current account deficit and payments on interests of foreign and domestic loans. All those macro-economic figures that the Right-wing Musharraf regime had been able to contain, mainly by fudging statistics and other manoeuvres of economic trickery exploded to expose the real face of the Pakistani economy. Of course this could have only been done by a government with a democratic people's mandate that everybody on the top in every field had hailed. The rupee had plummeted in the exchange rate market and this greatly inflated the amounts of balance of payments and the import bill. Nawaz Sharif's economic guru, Ishaq Dar, upon whom the PPP leadership was relying for an economic miracle, had been pulled out just in time to expose the 'economic managerial capabilities' of the 'mixed' economists of the PPP. But what happened below was atrocious. There was an unprecedented price hike, rise in unemployment and poverty, power cuts and prolonged load-shedding of electricity, and a rapid decline in the already adverse conditions of life. The toiling masses were bewildered and in an agony of shock. The despair worsened. Not only did the policies of the previous government continue unabated, but they were now being executed much more aggressively and with cruel indifference to the suffering and deprivation of millions. After a brief interregnum the suicide bombings and terrorist attacks came back with a vengeance. There were now more suicide attacks and bomb blasts in Pakistan than in Iraq. According to a column in the daily *The News*:

> On an average terrorist violence is killing 10 Pakistanis a day. Imagine 11,129 innocent Pakistanis have already lost their lives. Over the past

> 9 months 4,141 innocent Pakistanis have been killed. Last year Maulana Fazlullah of Tehrik-e-Nifaz-e-Shariah-e-Mohammadi (TNSM) actually seized 59 villages in Swat and established a parallel government ... In the NWFP at least 20 of the 24 districts have strong militant presence ... The government pays Rs. 300,000 to who dies in a suicide attack while death worshippers among us pay Rs. 1,500,000 to who ever is willing to wear a suicide jacket. Guess who has more recruits![25]

The Americans, frustrated by their failures in the Afghan insurgency, had been making incursions into Pakistan's tribal areas, using drones, fighter aircraft, and heavy bombing, resulting in huge 'civilian' casualties, mainly women and children. As the demise of the Musharraf regime was approaching, the Americans intruded with land forces to attack the tribal hamlets, killing many innocent civilians. This was a provocation to demonstrate that the Pakistani rulers had been pushed into submission. The rising casualties of the army in this insurgency in Pakistan's northern areas have overtaken those inflicted in the1965 war with India.

These catastrophic events have had petrifying impacts on the morale and composure of the army. The dissenters, especially in the middle and lower ranks, were running high and the number of deserters was growing. Yet the Americans wanted even more action from the army. But Musharraf was trying to restore morale and control the fractious tendency in his army, so he wasn't going to push it as hard as the Americans would have liked. In their frustrations the neo-cons in the United States were getting annoyed with him. He refused to cooperate or accept on equal terms their stooge in Afghanistan, Hamid Karazai. Their plan to bring Benazir as a balancing force against Musharraf had backfired. But the imperialist hardliners had little choice; they had to continue. This new democratic façade and the rapid decline of Musharraf provided them with a new opportunity. Zalme Khalizad, the extreme Right-wing neo-con and close friend and partner of both Zardari and Karzai, started to egg Zardari on for the presidency of Pakistan. Musharraf resigned and in another relatively quiet and hustle-free affair Zardari became the civilian President of Pakistan.

Political and Economic Corruption

The result of the so-called elections, already fixed in advance with bribes and blackmail to the electoral college of corrupt politicians, was a foregone conclusion. It was decided in Washington and executed in Pakistan. In Pakistan the presidential election is the only electoral procedure in the constitution where the candidates don't have to declare their assets. The neo-con's victory was exhibited by Karzai being the guest of honour at the oath-taking ceremony of the new President!

Zardari today is the second richest man in Pakistan.[26]

Nawaz Sharif is not far behind. The Sharif family is the fourth richest.[27]

Perhaps he needs just one more stint as the head of state to make it to number one. And these are the people proclaimed to be the victims of incarcerations, repression, imprisonment, etc. What victims?

The Presidency of Zardari is not a solution or an end to the turmoil afflicting the Pakistani society. It is the beginning of yet another period of conflagration and social convulsions.

Such reliance of imperialism and the degree of slavishness the present rulers have undergone is unprecedented, even in Pakistan; subservience to imperialism has been the common characteristic of almost every regime in its history. Above all, this shows the immense crisis of Pakistani capitalism. One of the major reasons for this crisis is rabid imperialist exploitation, and to survive Pakistani capitalism needs even more assistance from imperialist institutions. As long as capitalism remains the economic and social system in Pakistan the stranglehold of imperialism will be tight and secure. This is tolerable and even profitable for the ruling classes, but it is playing havoc with the lives of the masses of the country. Without the overthrow of capitalism in Pakistan the yoke of imperialism can never be broken.

According to the standards of bourgeois economics Pakistan was facing a default on its balance of payments in September 2008. That meant it could be declared once again, after the 1998 nuclear explosions backlog, a failed state, at least in economic terms. It was once again one of the few clients of the IMF pleading for a bail-out. The Americans, with their own economic problems, couldn't pump in any more cash. The ADB (Asian Development Bank) did give a paltry $500 million, barely enough to keep it breathing; the regime needed at least $15 billion to stabilize the financial crisis. The PPP-led government, perhaps for the first time, decided to end subsidies on fuel, electricity, food, fertilizer and other basic necessities by December 2008. Thus the IMF demands were fully met for the first time by any regime in Pakistan. It also announced the privatization of the remaining assets.

The first resistance began in the Oil and Gas sector with a strike in the Qadirpur gas field in Sindh. The Forex reserves were falling at about $800 million a month, mainly being sucked up by the trade deficit. The record remittances of $6.5 billion sent by Pakistani workers abroad were taken up by the debt and interest payments on foreign loans. On the other hand the foreign investments in different basic sectors are fleecing the economy.

According to the *Dawn Economic Review*, 22–28 September 2008:

Pakistan's GDP growth: Past and Future [30]

	2004-05	2005-06	2006-07	2007-08	2008-09	% of GDP
GDP	9.0	5.8	6.8	5.8	4.2	100.0
Commodity Producing Sector	9.5	5.1	6.0	3.2	4.2	44.9
♦ Agriculture	6.5	6.3	3.7	1.5	4.0	21.0
♦ Manufacturing	15.5	8.7	8.2	5.4	4.2	18.8
♦ Construction	18.6	10.2	17.9	15.2	10.0	3.6
♦ Electricity and Gas	-5.7	-26.6	2.5	-14.7	-8.0	1.5
Services Sector	8.5	6.5	7.6	8.2	8.0	55.1

Sources:
Pakistan Economic Survey, 2007-08
Dawn estimates for 2008-09

(*Dawn Economic Review*, 29 Sept. – 05 Oct. 2008, Shahid Javed Burki)

> Recent large payments of arrears of some Rs. 100 billion by the federal government to oil companies explicit liabilities cash flow streams from the federal budget have gone up from Rs. 16.2 billion in FY06 to Rs. 63.10 billion. Contingent liabilities of the federal government have meanwhile gone up from Rs. 69.9 billion to Rs. 156.2 billion. The budget has become more of an exercise in public relations ... The assessment of the State Bank is that the budget overstates revenue and understates expenditure ... Total expenditure was budgeted at Rs. 1,555 billion, but according to the revised estimates, it turned out to be Rs. 1,948 billion, an excess of 25.3 per cent. Current expenditure was budgeted at Rs. 1,056 billion, but this was Rs 1,516 billion, as per revised estimate, an excess of 43. 6 per cent.[28]

The IPPs (Independent Power Producing Plants) installed by multinational corporations after agreements with the previous PPP government in 1995, have been sending back to their headquarters an average profit of $1billion per year. If the amount of about $15 billion would have been invested by a workers' state in a planned economy, Pakistan would be having a large capacity of electricity to export. Now the government has paid these IPPs the sum of $33 million just in dues for them to restart producing electricity. The price was raised by 31 per cent plus 15 per cent GST on the night Zardari was sworn in as President. Eiteslat, the Arab multinational that bought the PTCL during the Musharraf regime, obviously with huge kickbacks, has been able to earn profits equal to the equity raised to buy Pakistan's telecommunication sector. After the privatization of the remaining assets, how could the economy function and be sustained in the long run? The bourgeois economists have just no real answer.

Such is the doom and gloom of the capitalist strategists in Pakistan that they have lost confidence in their own system as the economy takes an uncontrollable downward spiral. Even if we look at the official figures of Pakistan's economic growth indicators it gives a depressing picture, and in Pakistan official figures are not even believed by the serious economists of the bourgeois itself. The estimates for the fiscal year 2008-09 have been made by Shahid Javed Burki who is one of the World Bank directors and former finance minister of Pakistan.

Although these figures show a gradual decline their impact,

along with the fiscal crisis and balance of payment, is much larger. Even Burki's estimates, especially in agriculture, are more wishful thinking rather than an economic perspective. All sectors of the economy are in crisis and agriculture is probably the worst effected.

According to the year 2000 Agricultural Census, only 37 per cent of rural households own land, and 61 per cent of these land owners had less than five acres. Much of the direct gains in income from crop production, particularly irrigated agriculture, go to higher income farmers. Hence the growth in agricultural sector further widens the rich–poor divide in the rural areas. The increase in growth rate of the agriculture is negated in another report in *Dawn* that deals with Pakistan's main cash crop—cotton.

> The news is that we are going to miss the cotton production target of 14.11 million bales for the year 2008-09, for the fourth year in a row, in spite of a better plant plantation and the growth of greater number of bolls. 'The general crop condition is much better than last year. Yet we will not achieve the output target for the year'. Dr. Qadir Bux Baloch, Agriculture Development Commissioner (ADC) at the Ministry of Food Agriculture and Live Stock told Dawn ....

The report continues,

> The smaller domestic crop than expected means that the textile industry's dependence on imported fibre will rise. This short crop size last year compelled the industry ... to spend $1.291 billion to import 4.6 million bales during August 07–July 08 to meet the requirements. This year more foreign exchange will be needed to import the fibre.
>
> The main reason is the sudden increase in fertilizer prices that has spiked from Rs. 600 per bag to Rs. 3100 within six months. The prices of other infra structural facilities like electricity, water, and transport have also rocketed. This will be a disaster especially for farmers with small land holdings.[30]

In most rural areas markets are asymmetric with respect to the rich and poor farmers. UNDP (United Nations Development Programme) report shows that the poor farmers pay a higher price on their input and get a lower price on their output compared to the large farmers. Consequently the poor peasants are losing as much as one-third of their income due to such asymmetric markets. The UNDP report shows that 51 per cent of the tenants get locked into debt dependence on the landlord, and out of these 57 per cent are obliged to work as labourers on the landlord's farm without any wages, while 14 per cent work for a wage below the market rate. This report also indicates that due to inadequate diet and lack of access to safe drinking water and sanitation facilities, 65 per cent of the poor in the sample survey were suffering from ill health. Disease emerged as a major factor that pushes people into poverty, due to high medical costs combined with income loss due to absence from work. This constitutes a major structural factor that accentuates poverty, inequality and constrains GDP growth by constraining the productivity of the poor.

The condition of the production and targets of crops other than cotton have a similar fate in this fiscal year 2008-09.

The GDP growth rate of 4.2 per cent by Burki's estimate may actually be even worse. The meltdown in financial and investment banking in USA can move towards a world slow-down or recession. This will have even further damaging effects on Pakistan's economy. The GDP growth rate might be halved to 2.1 per cent in 2008-09 by this aggravation of world wide economic downturn.

Lenin once said that politics is but precipitated economics. With such an economic rot the politics must reflect that. If we look at the coalitions, the leaders, the intrigues, betrayals, political and ideological treachery has become the norm in Pakistani politics. In the recent times it has even worsened. The callous indifference of the ruling classes and the generals, bureaucrats and political representatives towards the plight of the masses is horrendous. The conditions to which the masses of this society have been subjected by this system are deplorable and intolerable.

According to the WHO (World Health Organization) report of 1981, "For the masses living in this region the health conditions in 1857 were better than today".[31]

In 2005, ten thousand people in Pakistan were falling below the poverty line every week. Now the figure has crossed 15,000. These are varying figures, but the ADB figures show 47 per cent living below absolute poverty and 78 per cent living on under two dollars a day. Eighty per cent of the population is forced into non-scientific medication due to their financial situation. The WHO report, according to *News Line* September 2008, says that "50 per cent of the medicines in the market in Pakistan are counterfeit".[32]

According to officials of the World Food Programme more than half of Pakistan's 173 million people are now short of food due to the surge in prices. The WFP survey says: "The 'food insecure' had risen from 60 million to 79 million from March to September 2008."[33]

The WFP report says: "There is a very big gap between the increase in prices and the increase in wages... the purchasing power of the poor has gone down by almost 50 per cent." And that was in March. UNICEF says that 200,000 Pakistani children die annually because of unsafe drinking water, dysentery, diarrhoea, typhoid and gastro-enteritis. Out of the 137 poorest countries Pakistan's GDP percentage spending on education stands at number 134 and health at 137! Yet Pakistan is the 11th largest importer of arms and weapons of mass destruction.[34]

Human Development in South Asia 2007, a ten-year review published by the Mahbub ul Haq Development centre, states the following on the conditions of human life in Pakistan:

Progress in life-expectancy during ten years is the slowest in the region.

Percentage of malnourished children under 5 years of age remains more or less stagnant at 38 per cent compared to 40 per cent in 1994.

* Maternal mortality rate per 100,000 live births has increased significantly from 340 deaths in 1993 to 500 deaths in 2000.
* Incidence of tuberculosis per 100,000 population has increased from 150 in 1995 to 181 in 2004.
* Public spending on health as percentage of GDP has gone down from 0.8 per cent in 1995 to 0.4 per cent in 2004.
* Half of the adult population is still illiterate.
* Presently, 6.5 million children are out of school; second highest rank in the world.

* Pupil–teacher ratio at primary level has increased from 32 in 1998 to 37 in 2004.
* Percentage of trained teachers has declined from 82 per cent in 1995 to 78 per cent in 2004.
* Public expenditure on education has declined from 2.7 per cent of GDP in 1992 to 2 per cent of GDP during 2002-04.
* 73.6 per cent of population still lives below US $2, a day classification.
* Percentage of rural poor has increased from 31 per cent in 1990 to 35.9 per cent in 2004.
* Share of females in labour force has declined from 27 per cent in 1994 to 26.5 per cent in 2004.
* Unpaid female family workers are 46.9 per cent of female employment as compared to male unpaid workers which are 16.4 per cent of male employment.
* This report although composed mainly from the analysis of bourgeois experts still paints a dismal picture of the education sector in Pakistan.

The review continues:

> The recent Education for All (EFA) Report reveals that Pakistan has the highest number of out of school children in the world after Nigeria. Currently, there are 6.5 million children in Pakistan that are out of school. Of the total children who are not enrolled in schools, 80 per cent are not expected to enrol, about 10 per cent have dropped out, and the rest are expected to enrol later.
>
> Several factors explain the high number of children who are not expected to enrol. In a survey, factors that were identified by parents were: children with no interest in getting education (74%); education is too expensive (73%); school distance a hindrance (70%); children working as household help (69%); children needed to earn for family (67%); non availability of school (66%); lack of opportunities for future education; and discouraging behaviour of teachers (64%).
>
> Poor access to school is a major factor for out of school children. According to another survey conducted by the government in 14 districts of Pakistan, it was identified that only 54 per cent of children have access to primary schools.[35]

Sixty-eight per cent of diseases in Pakistan are poverty related. Most deaths are through curable diseases. Annually 165,000 women die in Pakistan due to lack of obstetric facilities during childbirth. The infant mortality rate is 137 deaths out of over 1,000 live births. The conditions of physical infrastructure are in a rotten state and further deteriorating. The electricity shortages are rising. There is a dearth of around 6,000 megawatt of just the present needs. Thirty-five per cent of all electricity generated is wasted through bad transmission lines and open wiring. A large, unspecified amount of electricity is stolen through bribery and corruption. The railways, built by the British, are in a poor state. Far more railway tracks and stations have been dismantled than the number of miles of the track laid since the so-called independence in 1947. The canal system of irrigation, also developed under the Raj, has deteriorated. About 30 per cent of canal water seeps due to the conditions of the canal beds. This on one hand deprives water for farming and also destroys vast tracts of fertile land through water-logging and salinity. Some huge, expensive and modern highways have been built, but in the vast countryside and inner cities the roads are muddy, pot-holed, and broken down.

The state has failed to build a proper social and physical infrastructure. Rather, as the years pass by, it has become more and more fractured by the continuing economic crisis, corruption and plunder of the ruling classes. The present PPP government has cut another 70 billion rupees from the budgetary allocation for developmental projects. In any case the funds allocated and those from World Bank project are usurped by all levels of the bureaucracy. The contractors here pay out to everyone, from the top minister of a department to the official at the lowest rung of the bureaucracy; very little is left for real development. Due to this corruption the quality of construction of most developmental projects is very bad. Hence, even those projects that are completed decay rapidly and are out of use in a very short span of time.

But government contractors have still amassed billions despite all the expenditures through state corruption on construction projects, etc. This contractual system has played havoc with the development of the country. Most political representatives from a local union council in a village or neighbourhood to the parliament are funded in their election campaigns by these contractors, or in several cases the contractors themselves are the elected representatives of the people. Elections in Pakistan at all levels today are based on money and financial resources.

Ahmed Rashid exposed the drug connection and Pakistan's democracy. In his book published in the year 2000, he wrote:

> Western anti-narcotics agencies in Islamabad kept track of drugs lords, who became Members of the National Assembly during the first government of Prime Minister Benazir Bhutto (1988-90) and Nawaz Sharif (1990-93). Drugs lords funded candidates to high office in both Bhutto's Pakistan People's Party and Sharif's Pakistan Muslim League. Industry and trade became increasingly financed by laundered drugs money and the black economy, which accounted for between 30 and 50 percent of the total Pakistan economy, was heavily subsidised by drugs money.[36]

Most ministries and posts are traded on the political black market of Pakistan. This is the real character of the democracy in Pakistan which asks for innumerable sacrifices by the poor at the behest of the bourgeois democratic leaders of the country. Pakistan has failed to develop its infrastructure and society under the methods of state capitalism. But what the strategists of the ruling classes concluded from this was that the solution was to privatize the infrastructure and the state-controlled service sector. It was an international phenomenon after the 1980s when Reaganomics and Thatcherism became the economic mantra of the strategists the world over. How could Pakistani economic experts desist from that? They ape every move of the bourgeois economists from the Western universities with big names. Their colonial mentality and slavish attitude towards the Raj has persisted from generation to generation.

But the privatization of the infrastructure and basic services has thrown the Pakistani society from frying pan into fire. This means above all an actual denial of proper health and education facilities to about 80 per cent of the population; the privatized health and education, with relatively bearable standards, can only cope with about 15–25 per cent of the middle class with some buying capacity for these services.

The privatization and related policies have ravaged the vast majority of the people. Old people and children die outside hospital gates, in front of pharmaceutical stores full of medicines, because they just don't have the money to buy the medicines which could cure them. The privatization of assets has brought some foreign investment. But this is more capital intensive than labour intensive. Hence the takeover of any institution or industry by the multinationals doesn't generate jobs, but makes thousands of workers redundant. This has happened in Telecommunications and several other privatized state enterprises. The notion that through privatization corruption can be abolished is deceptive, false and absurd. Since 1977 every regime and political leader or military dictator has pursued the same fundamental economic policies. The fourth PPP government, now incumbent, is the most Right-wing and carries out most aggressive anti-working class policies than any other PPP government before. All the political parties and leaders dominating the country, media, and political horizon also have the same economic programmes. Sixty-one years after the partition, this false dawn has brought only destitution to the vast majority of the populace for more than three generations.

Winston Churchill was a conservative British politician of the 'old type', from the generations that still believed in and represented the classical British aristocracy. He still harboured the delusion of the grandeur and glory of the British Imperial Raj, even at the end of the Second World War when it was crumbling. During the process of transfer of power to India, Winston Churchill said:

> Power will go in to the hands of rascals, rogues and freebooters. Not a bottle of water, not a loaf of bread shall escape taxation. Only air will be free and the blood of these hungry millions will be on the head of Mr. Attlee (then Prime Minister). These are men of straw of whom no trace will be found after a few years.[37]

He was talking about Jinnah, Nehru, Gandhi and other leaders of India. The nascent bourgeois and feudal aristocrats who had supported Jinnah for the creation of Pakistan as a separate entity at least had a dream. In the 19th century the strategists of British imperialists drew plans for decades not years. Churchill had a nostalgic yearning for those days; he knew their dream of a prosperous, progressive and modern Pakistan would be shattered sooner rather than later. That is what has happened.

But what should the workers and the toiling masses do to end this nightmare of capitalist drudgery? They did in 1968-9 what was their task in history. The revolution could not and cannot wait for a Leninist party to be formed and a revolutionary Marxist leadership to emerge. In such times the masses don't have time for that. Through the 1968-9 revolution they had at least created a mass tradition—the PPP. The main target and slogan was the overthrow of the twenty-two families who represented capitalism in Pakistan. They had demanded food, clothing and shelter. In today's twenty-two families the second richest is the co-chairman of the PPP and the President of Pakistan. The masses are today deprived of 'Roti, Kapra aur Makan' (Food, Clothing and Shelter), even more than they were in 1968-9.

The tradition of political expression of the masses in Pakistan since the revolutionary events of 1968 has been the PPP. The irony is that the leadership of this party has abandoned the founding programme upon which the party was built. 'Socialism' today is a forbidden word in the leading 'bodies' of the PPP. They have used and abused the tradition of 1968. In that sense this leadership has become an obstacle in the path of the toiling masses. The PPP was founded on the socialist legacy and struggle for the emancipation of the working classes, but the present leadership has adopted a programme and policy that meets the requirements of the ruling class, not the working people. This cannot go on for ever. A new wave of struggle will cut across the doom and gloom of reaction in society and it will have a massive impact on the PPP itself. The pressures of opposing classes will separate the bourgeois from the proletarian elements within the party and create the basis for the emergence of a mass revolutionary tendency which will be the first step in the task of providing the leadership the workers require.

NOTES

1. *The Unbroken Thread*, (Fortress), p. 306.
2. 'Proletarian Revolution and the Renegade Kautsky", (Progressive Publishers, Moscow, 1934), pp. 18-19.
3. Christina Lamb, *Waiting for Allah*, (Viking), pp. 19, 20, 21, 295.
4. *Asian Survey*, Vol. XXVIII, No.10, October 1988.
5. Lawrence Lifschultz, *'Bush, Pakistan and Drugs: The Kingdom of*

Heroin', The Nation, 14 November 1988.

6. Kux, *The United States and Pakistan*, (The Adst-Dacor Diplomats and Diplomacy Series), p. 257.
7. Shuja Nawaz, *Crossed Swords*, (Oxford), p. 379.
8. Ibid, p. 281.
9. Ibid, p. 385.
10. Christina Lamb, *Waiting for Allah*, (Viking), p. 49.
11. Benazir admitted that a committee had been set up for negotiation with Jamat-i-Islami during an interview with author, 10 June 1988, Christina Lamb, (Viking), *Waiting for Allah*, p. 52.
12. Christina Lamb, *Waiting for Allah*, (Viking), p. 56).
13. Hussain Haqqani, *Pakistan: Between Mosque and Military*, p. 202.
14. Iftikhar Ahmed Sirohey, *Truth Never Retires*, (Jang, 1996), p. 445.
15. John Ward Anderson and Kamran Khan, 'Pakistan Sets Off Nuclear Blasts,' *Washington Post*, 29 May 1998.
16. Dawn news wire service, 23 September 1999.
17. Shuja Nawaz, *Crossed Swords*, (Oxford), p. 525.
18. Musharraf, *In the Line of Fire*, (Free Press, 2006), p. 201.
19. Thomas H. Kean, Chair and Lee H. Hamilton, Vice Chair, *The 9/11 Report: The National Commisssion on Terrorist Attacks Upon the United States*, (New York: St. Martin's Press, 2004) pp. 473-74.
20. Adrian and Clark, Deception: *Pakistan, the United States, the Secret Trade in Nuclear Weapons.* (Walker and Company, New York), 2007.
21. Shuja Nawaz, *Crossed Swords*, (Oxford), p. 533.
22. *Dawn*, 25 August 2007.
23. Ibid op .cit. p. 547.
24. *Economist*, 10 May 2008.
25. *The News on Sunday*, 28 September 2008, p. 9.
26. List of 22 richest families, Appendix II of this book.
27. Ibid.
28. *Dawn, Business and Economic Review*, 22–28 September 2008.
29. *Dawn Business and Economic Review*, 29 Sept.–05 Oct. 2008, Shahid Javed Burki.
30. *Dawn* 28 Sept. 2008.
31. Quoted in Lal Khan, *Socialist Revolution and Pakistan*, Amsterdam 1983, p. 79.
32. *News Line*, September 2008, p. 45
33. *The News on Sunday*, September 2008.
34. *Jedddojuhd*, issue 1–15 February 2008, p. 12.
35. *Human Development in South Asia, 2007*, Mahbub ul Haq Development Centre, p. 147.
36. Ahmed Rashid, *Taliban: Islam, Oil and the New Great Game*, (I.B. Tauris 2000), p. 121.
37. *Dawn*, 4 October 2008.

Nine

REDEEMING THE 1968-9 UPRISING

Perspectives of Revolutionary Socialism

Man's own social organization, which has hitherto confronted him as a process dictated by nature and history, now becomes a process resulting from his own voluntary action. The objective extraneous forces, which have hitherto dominated history, are now under the control of man himself. It is only from this point that man will himself make his own history fully consciously, it is only from this point that the social causes he sets in motion will preponderantly and ever increasingly have the effects he wills. It is humanity's leap from the realm of necessity into the realm of freedom.

—Frederick Engels (1820–1895)[1]

The problem of how to cultivate and adjust, how to improve and 'finish' the physical and spiritual nature of man, is a colossal one, serious work which is conceivable only under conditions of Socialism.

—Leon Trotsky (1879–1940)[2]

Forty years after the 1968-9 revolution, the social fabric of the country is in tatters. The movement that had erupted on 18th October, against all assumptions and odds was thrust back into a temporary lull and despair for a period. The state, due to its internal contradictions and decay, couldn't have crushed the upsurge. The state is not just the army, judiciary, legislative bodies, executive and institutions. The Pakistani state and its agencies today have deep involvement in the hierarchies of political parties, the clergy, and its institutions such as the media and other influential groups in society. It has wrapped its tentacles so tightly that it seems impossible to rebel against it. The state may be monarchical, dictatorial or democratic, these are the basic tasks assigned to it by the ruling classes.

But the state and society that exists in Pakistan is the product of a certain type of socio-economic development, not only after the Partition but long before that. Hence it is vital to understand the patterns of this development, and the processes through which the state and society have evolved to reach this situation of crisis and turmoil. From the point of view of political economy Pakistan can be described as a semi-capitalist, semi-feudal society under the domination of capitalist means of production and exchange. On one hand the Pakistani bourgeoisie is forced to rely on imperialism due to its weak economic foundations, while at the same time its historical belatedness forces it to retain, co-opt and align with the remnants of feudalism. And overall this is the stranglehold of capitalist imperialism, both political and economic, with its crushing domination of the world market. This domination is sustained and superimposed in an institutional form by the IMF (International Monetary Fund), the World Bank, the WTO and other institutions and agreements. It would be beyond the scope of this work to discuss the Asiatic mode of production, but it suffices to say that classical feudalism never existed in this region as was the case in European history.

Feudalism, the remnants of which are very much there, was introduced or rather imposed upon the subcontinent by the British. It was the 'Permanent Settlements Act' introduced in the Bengal Assembly by Lord Palmerston in 1793 that laid the basis of 'modern' feudalism in South Asia. The designs of the Raj were to create a class of local loyalists who would act as stooges of British imperialism and betray the masses of the subcontinent. The whole history of the existence of feudalism in Pakistan is closely intertwined with the colonial rule.

But in present-day Pakistan there is a nexus between the capitalists, landlords, generals, top bureaucrats, judges and top politicians. It is hardly possible to separate them into specific categories of the different backgrounds of the ruling elite. Sometimes members of the same family are part of various designations of the elite of different departments. They are interrelated through marriage, business and other partnerships in agriculture and financial enterprises.

Combined and Uneven Development

This admixture of the Pakistani ruling class is in itself proof of their reactionary character and historical ineptness to carry through the basic tasks of the national democratic revolution. Due to the failure of Pakistan's nascent bourgeoisie to complete the tasks of converting Pakistan into a modern capitalist democracy, its social and economic evolution has been of a very complex and convoluted character. This complexity is basically due to the uneven and combined nature of development. To develop political perspectives and, above all, to have a Marxist analysis of Pakistan, it is vital to investigate the political, cultural, social and moral implications of this evolution upon Pakistani society.

The so-called national bourgeoisie of Pakistan failed to build the infrastructure upon which a modern industrial nation would have been built. The reactionary ruling classes, incapable of gaining sufficient profit to develop society, indulged in all sorts of exploitation. The national question in Pakistan has not been solved, and was in fact aggravated by the exploitation of the oppressed nationalities. Hence it failed to create a unified nation state.

As we have explained earlier, instead of abolishing feudalism through an agrarian revolution, the intrinsic economic weakness forced it to patch up and include the landed aristocracy into its ranks. Similarly the bourgeoisie, being historically an atheist class, in Pakistan had to use religion to lay the foundations of a separate state from which to carve out its independent market. But to stave off the crisis, and to divert movements from below, it used religion to gain the support of the backward layers of society and break the unity of the class struggle. Hence secularism remains a mere verbosity for the elite.

The bourgeoisie played a relatively enlightened role in the advanced countries of Europe during the revolutions of 17th, 18th and 19th centuries, but the parliamentary democracy in Pakistan (the most efficient form of rule by the bourgeoisie in advanced capitalist countries) always remained debilitated, farcical and fragile. It never took roots, and the country's relative and incomplete industrial and economic development, in an epoch of imperialist domination, made Pakistan even more vulnerable to exploitation by imperialism as monopoly finance capital intervened aggressively. Capitalist investment in Pakistan required the use of the most advanced industrial technologies, in order to extract maximum profit for the multinationals. This intrusion of modern and advanced technology in a primitive country created islands of development which were contradictory in many ways. This seems to be the peculiar pattern of socio-economic evolution that was taking place in Pakistan and other 'developing' countries.

The law of combined and uneven development worked out by Marx, Lenin, and Trotsky explains this complex and contradictory pattern of socio-economic development.

The law of uneven development governs the entire history of mankind. Capitalism finds various sections of mankind at different stages of development, each with its profound internal contradictions. The extreme diversity in the levels attained, and the extraordinary unevenness in the rate of development of different sections of mankind during various epochs, serves as the starting points of capitalism. Capitalism gains mastery only gradually over this inherited unevenness, breaking and altering it with its own means and methods.

In contrast to the economic system that preceded it, capitalism consistently aims to expand economically by expanding into new territories, surmounting economic differences and converting self-sufficient provincial and national economies into a system of financially independent relations, as Marx wrote in *The Communist Manifesto:*

> The need of a constantly expanding market for its products chases the bourgeoisie over the entire surface of the globe. It must nestle everywhere, settle everywhere, establish connections everywhere.
>
> The bourgeoisie has through its exploitation of the world market given a cosmopolitan character to production and consumption in every country. To the great chagrin of Reactionists, it has drawn from under the feet of industry the national ground on which it stood. All old-established national industries have been destroyed or are daily being destroyed. They are dislodged by new industries, whose

> introduction becomes a life and death question for all civilised nations, by industries that no longer work up indigenous raw material, but raw material drawn from the remotest zones; industries whose products are consumed, not only at home, but in every quarter of the globe. In place of the old wants, satisfied by the production of the country, we find new wants, requiring for their satisfaction the products of distant lands and climes. In place of the old local and national seclusion and self-sufficiency, we have intercourse in every direction, universal inter-dependence of nations. And as in material, so also in intellectual production. The intellectual creations of individual nations become common property. National one-sidedness and narrow-mindedness become more and more impossible, and from the numerous national and local literatures, there arises a world literature.

By drawing the countries economically closer to one another and levelling out their stages of development, capitalism operates by methods of its own, that is to say, by anarchic methods which constantly undermine its own work, set one country against another, and one branch of industry against another, developing some parts of the world economy while hampering and throwing back the development of others. Only the correlation of these two fundamental tendencies both of which arise from the nature of capitalism—explains to us the living texture of the historical process.

Imperialism, thanks to its universal penetrability and mobility, and the break-neck speed of the formation of finance capital as its driving force, lends vigour to both these tendencies. Imperialism links up incomparably more rapidly and more deeply the individual national and continental units into a single entity, bringing them into the closest and most vital dependence upon each other and rendering their economic methods, social forms, and levels of development more identical. At the same time, it attains this 'goal' by inflicting such antagonistic, aggressive methods against backward countries that the unification and levelling of world economy which it has achieved is upset by it even more violently and convulsively than in the preceding epochs.

In his epic work *The History of the Russian Revolution,* Trotsky explains:

> The European colonists in America did not begin history all over again from the beginning. The fact that Germany and the United States have now economically outstripped England was made possible by the very backwardness of their capitalist development. On the other hand, the conservative anarchy in the British coal industry as also in the heads of McDonald and his friends is a paying-up for the past when England played too long the role of capitalist pathfinder. The development of historically backward nations leads necessarily to a peculiar combination of different stages in the historic process. Their development as a whole acquires an unplanned, complex, combined character.
>
> (...) The laws of history have nothing in common with a pedantic schematism. Unevenness, the most general law of the historic process, reveals itself most sharply and complexly in the destiny of the backward countries. Under the whip of external necessity their backward culture is compelled to make leaps. From the universal law of unevenness thus derives another law which, for the lack of a better name, we may call the law of combined development by which we mean a drawing together of the different stages of the journey, a combining of the separate steps, an amalgam of archaic with more contemporary forms. Without this law, to be taken of course, in its whole material content, it is impossible to understand the history.[3]

If we examine the social relations in Pakistan, this law has deep and evident impacts on the daily lives of the masses. As the new generations develop they go through a stage of utilizing the instruments their ancestors and even people of their own generation used in the social and economic routine of daily life.

> The Marxist theory of combined and uneven development found its most perfect expression in the extremely complex social relations in Russia at the turn of the century. Side by side with feudal, semi-feudal and even pre-feudal modes of existence there sprang up the most modern, up-to-date factories, built with French and British capital. This is precisely the phenomenon we now see in the whole of the so-called Third World, and was most strikingly revealed by the development of South-East Asia in the first half of the 1990s. This provides a most remarkable parallel with the development of Russia exactly a hundred years earlier. And it is entirely possible that the political outcome could be similar. The development of industry in such a context acts as a spur to revolution. Russia shows just how quickly that can occur. Out of the stormy development of Russian capitalism in the 'eighties' and 'nineties' came the equally stormy awakening of the proletariat. The wave of strikes in the 1890s was the preparatory school for the revolution of 1905.[4]

In Pakistan there are hundreds of thousands of people today who use mobile phones but have never used a 'normal' land line phone. They have skipped a stage of technological evolution without even realizing it. The other aspect of the Law of Uneven and Combined Development is that a child can stand in a dirty street and think that his country has an atom bomb but he has no shoes. Most people who use modern mobile phones often don't have proper electricity supply, piped water and taps, metalled roads, sewerage and sanitation facilities, the basic needs in their homes and neighbourhoods.

There are some of the best hospitals and 'state of art' cosmetic and health fitness clinics. Yet the vast majority of the population is denied treatment for simple curable diseases such as malaria. They take their children and the sick to 'pirs' (Sufi masters) who mumble a few words and then blow their breath on to the patients as a cure; in their state of helplessness and poverty they do not have much choice. There are hospitals with modern equipment but the patients are too many to be treated and very few can pay the bills. In most public hospitals there are two or more serious patients sharing one bed. Pakistan is perhaps one of the few countries that has more doctors than nurses.

Modern locomotives and carriages are manufactured and imported. But the railway track is more than a hundred years old, so the trains cannot run at the stipulated speed; they are always late and there are frequent railway accidents.

There are the most advanced and expensive cars travelling on pot-holed roads alongside the traffic of bullock-carts, donkey-carts, and other means of transport representing the pre-medieval periods. There is a contradiction between the vehicles and the roads. There are too many vehicles and too little room for driving and parking.

In some of the most remote villages where water supply and sanitation are almost non-existent, there are cables of TV networks that show programmes from London, New York, Beijing, Moscow and Tokyo. In the most modern neighbourhoods with posh mansions and skyscrapers there are people living in straw huts with no basic facilities available.

These dirty spots in these posh neighbourhoods are explicit of the patterns of combined and uneven development that the elite have ruled over for generations in this society's evolution under crony-capitalism.

In most cities and industrial towns there are multinational factories with advanced computerized technology. Close by are the brick kilns still based on the technology of the period of the Indus valley civilization of 7,000 years ago. Similarly, the motorway that plies between Lahore and Islamabad is one of the most advanced highways in Asia. Some metres away from this exhibition of advanced technology are hamlets consisting of mud-built houses depicting another era of history.

But even in the countryside the aggressive and blatant intrusion of modern capitalism has had a devastating impact on the lifestyle of the villagers. Although they were isolated and primitive, social and economic relations still prevailed. But the intrusion of capitalism, with its truncated forms of brutal exploitation, has not transformed those pre-medieval forms of life. Rather it has distorted them with its unevenness, imprinting the ugly face of capitalism upon the relatively calm life and landscape, with plastic bags choking the village drains, polluting the clean forests and fields.

The incomplete brick and concrete lining of the streets, dangerously dangling electrical wires and the never ending construction works on 'development projects' have become a permanent feature of rural life. Instead of bringing prosperity it has created such misery that village life has become worse for the rural masses in the 21st century than it ever was a hundred years ago.

The Changing Role of the Mullahs

These socio-economic semi-capitalist relations have also worsened the so-called feudal set-ups and relations within the communities. The British had tried to impose feudalism but that process was far from complete and many areas in Pakistan kept on living in some form of Asiatic despotism even till the 1960s. There is a long list of impacts this distorted capitalist development has inflicted upon society. But one of the important changes that it has brought to the rural and suburban life is the rise of Islamic fundamentalism. Through the influx of monetary capital the mullahs, who were one of the several departments in the village socio-economic life, like farmers, cobblers, iron smiths, barbers, etc., became rich, and their rates changed. In the past, under this division of labour, the role of mullahs was to perform rituals at marriages, death and other similar functions. Some were peasants themselves and had a humble existence and attitude.

This was the situation more or less till the 1970s. Since the 1980s, with Zia's Islamization, the mullahs got a boost: the landed aristocracy, rapidly investing in industrial enterprises by mortgaging their land estates to the banks, started to use the preachers more viciously for the subjugation of the masses by spreading obscurantism. At the same time the black money generated in the Afghan jihad was used to build up a reactionary religious network as a bulwark against the revolutionary movements. The spread of the1968-9 revolution into the remote villages, with their own perceptions about Bhutto being a symbol of change, had threatened vested interests even in the country side.

The whole character of the village preacher and the mosque changed with the intrusion of these paralytic capitalist relations. Loudspeakers blaring from village mosque pierce the calm of village life without a trickle of prosperity coming to social life: medium-sized villages have several mosques and no proper hospital or school; where there is some sort of hospital there is seldom a doctor and the necessary paramedical staff; thousands of ghost schools are without teachers. With the failure of the state to provide these basic amenities, 'private' schools and clinics have mushroomed in most urban and rural localities. They are influenced by the Islamists in a society where the traditional leadership of the toiling masses betrays the movements again and again. The black economy's role has also increased in these sectors. The 'Madrassahs' are flourishing and they are a sort of relief for the poor peasants who, unable to afford to feed and educate their children, thrust them in these fanatic faculties, knowing how badly they would be treated by the mullahs. Some of the children would become suicide bombers, blowing themselves and innocent people to shreds.

There are also tragic cases of parents who are forced by poverty to sell their children, or commit collective family suicides. The ebbing of the movements, the lull in the society, the lack of a revolutionary alternative on the political horizon, adds to the frustration of the suburban and urban petty bourgeoisie.

These vacillating and convoluted psychologies are the product of the contradictions of the modernism and primitiveness of society, a salient feature of the combined and uneven development in Pakistan; hence they try to find solace in religion by growing beards and putting on 'Zia' caps. The only thing they find here is the justification of being absolved of their crooked dealings and all sorts of sins of petty deceit, counterfeiting, and other business crimes. The social and cultural impact of these patterns of growth is nauseating. In the urban and even rural areas more girls and women wear a veil or 'purdah' in the 21st century than in the last century. Hypocrisy has become the norm in social relations. Underlying vulgarity, lumpenism, prostitution and gang rape has been the result of this social and cultural suffocation, along with a rapidly rising rate of poverty.

The present situation, with its patterns of social distortion, demonstrates the capacity and extent to which crony-capitalism in Pakistan can develop society.

The Role of Parliament

The evolution in Pakistan cannot go through the same stages by which the bourgeoisie evolved in the past three centuries in the advanced capitalist countries. Today the role of capital is grossly retrogressive, and actually pushes society backwards. This is more than evident in the rise of fundamentalism, ethnicity, parochialism, narrow nationalism, gender and religious discrimination and other prejudices of the past. The conflicts arising from these prejudices result in the breaking-up of the class unity of the oppressed, and bleed the social life of the country. But this whole situation doesn't mean that society is dominated and overwhelmed by dark reaction. This reaction is but a temporary, fragile and superficial manifestation of the current despair that presently prevails.

However, the empirical analysts and ideologues of the ruling classes are in a state of doom and gloom, and to combat the exaggerated role and power of 'reaction' they offer 'liberal democracy', a 'sovereign' parliament, a liberal, enlightened and progressive bourgeoisie.' Their strategy is to create a political system aping British and Western parliamentarianism.

Alan Woods analyzes the role of the parliament in countries like Pakistan.

> The laws governing parliamentary activity can be observed in the parliamentary fractions of reformist workers' parties at all times. The pressure of the ruling class, its ideology and institutions, is nowhere so intense as in the parliamentary hothouse. The bourgeoisie has perfected over a long period the necessary mechanisms for bribing, pressurizing and corrupting the parliamentary representatives of the proletariat. Unless the latter are thoroughly imbued with class consciousness and the necessary theoretical understanding to enable them to see through the tricks and manoeuvres of the enemy, they will inevitably tend to succumb to pressure and get sucked into the parliamentary morass of committees, procedure, points of order and worse. It is not necessarily a question of direct personal corruption, careerism, bribes, etc., although all these weapons are actively employed to buy off the workers' leaders. In the case of right-wing reformists, many are themselves middle class lawyers, doctors and economists standing far closer in their lifestyle and psychology to the bourgeoisie than to the workers they profess to represent. Even the most honest left reformists, even devoted workers from the factory floor steeled in years of struggle, can rapidly fall under the spell of the rarefied atmosphere of this artificial world, far removed from the reality of the class struggle.
>
> For a reformist party, which in any case subordinates everything to the question of electing members of parliament, the independence of the parliamentary faction from the party, the sacred right of each individual deputy to 'follow his or her conscience' is accepted as normal. This is just another way of expressing the independence of the reformist leaders from the working class, and their absolute and total dependence on the bourgeoisie. But for a revolutionary party, for which the parliamentary struggle is only one element in the general struggle of the working class to change society, this is unthinkable. The party, as the organized expression of the most conscious elements

> of the proletariat can and must exercise control over its elected representatives at all levels, above all its members of parliament.[5]

These bourgeois reformists also want the Pakistan's social and economic evolution to grow and develop on the lines by which it evolved in the advanced capitalist countries. They want a 'free' and 'impartial' judiciary, although the law can never be higher than the economic structure of society and its cultural development conditioned thereby. They use clichés, quotes and philosophies from the period of the dawn of capitalism. This only breeds greater inequality and vulgarity of the social and cultural level in Pakistan. Here the most significant aspect of the Law of Combined and Uneven Development comes into play. The other side of this equation means that backwardness at a certain stage of the development of the economy on a world scale becomes a sort of privilege. These societies cannot go through the phases of development the advanced countries went through. Hence they have to leap over those so-called historically 'necessary' stages. This means that where capitalist modernity fails to overcome the primitiveness of a society, a leap in the process of evolution, i.e. a revolution, becomes a historical and socio-economic necessity.

In spite of the exploitation of modern investment, one positive feature is that it creates an advanced proletariat; it is the advent of the proletariat that creates the force and the vanguard that would lead the peasantry and other oppressed classes to make that historical leap to revolution. This was proved most glaringly by the 1968-9 revolution itself. The advent of the fresh, virgin proletariat, developed mainly during the industrialization process of the late 1950s and 1960s on to the arena of history, created a revolutionary situation and uprising of a clearly socialist character. We have explained this phenomenon earlier on in this work.

But forty years on, the democratic intelligentsia have learnt nothing from the revolutionary storm that lashed through Pakistan in that period. This revolution was itself a reaffirmation of the Law of Combined and Uneven development. It was a socialist revolution in a so-called theocratic state. The democratic intelligentsia of all shades is doomed to repeat their ideological follies because they have failed to comprehend the character and nature of those historical events.

The sort of social and economic ramifications that come from the capitalist policies of the liberal democracy only strengthen reaction rather than combating it. Hence the rise of fundamentalism and other reactionary tendencies gives them justification for not only propping up the corrupt Pakistani bourgeoisie, but also an excuse to cosy up with the West.

The imperialists need this instability and 'ideological' conflict in a relatively controlled form for its own strategic and policy interests. This support of the ex-Left for these liberal democrats is in reality a justification for their defeat in their cause and commitment to the socialist transformation of society. Under capitalism liberal democracy had no option but to become a lap-dog of imperialism.

A bourgeois democracy is really the disguised dictatorship of the banks and monopolies. In the modern epoch, where the concentration of capital has assumed unheard-of proportions, the power of the big monopolies has been absolute. Normally, the capitalist class prefers a democratic regime, which is the most economical form of government. They can permit the illusion of democracy, while, in practice, all the levers and controls remain firmly in their hands. They control the parliamentary representatives by a thousand invisible threads. They own the banks and monopolies and therefore can exert colossal pressure on any government. They own the mass media and can mould public opinion. Finally, they can rule by resting on the leaders of the labour movement who have no intention of going beyond the limits of the system.

Bourgeois democracy is a very fragile plant, which usually only exists when the ruling class does not feel directly threatened by revolution. Under conditions of economic upswing, the bourgeois can afford to give certain reforms and concessions in order to blunt class antagonisms. When the class struggle passes these limits the bourgeoisie casts away the smiling mask of democracy and begins to organize coups and dictatorships. As we saw once again in April 2002 in Venezuela, the bourgeoisie can shift from democracy to dictatorship with the ease of a man passing from a smoking to a non-smoking compartment of a train.

Aims of Socialism

If forty years ago the character of the Pakistani revolution was socialist, it is more so today. The unaccomplished tasks of the democratic revolution are festering wounds on the body of Pakistan. They cannot be completed, as has been proved for more than six decades, by the decadent bourgeoisie. These tasks need enormous resources to be fulfilled. That is why without a socialist revolution even the democratic revolution cannot be completed.

Trotsky wrote in the 'Draft Programme of the Communist International':

> From the uneven sporadic development of capitalism flows the non-simultaneous, uneven, and sporadic character of the socialist revolution.
>
> (...) From Marx on, we have been constantly repeating that capitalism cannot cope with the spirit of new technology to which it has given rise and which tears asunder not only the integument of bourgeois private property rights, but also the national hoops of the bourgeois state. Socialism, however, must not only take over from capitalism the most highly developed productive forces but must immediately carry them onward, raise them to a higher level and give them a state of development such as has been unknown under capitalism.[6]

In its advance of the economic and social levels to new heights above the level of capitalism, a socialist revolution also takes measures in completing the national democratic tasks. These socialist measures of expropriating the imperialist's assets, finance capital; refusing to pay back the already paid loans with interest; taking over the commanding heights of the economy and landed estates, will put an end to the horrendous drain of national resources by imperialist and capitalist exploitation. These expropriations rapidly develop society and the means of production to sustain a socialist economy in a short period of time.

The agrarian revolution, the solution of the national question, the building up of the social and physical infrastructure and other tasks can be completed at a rapid pace with the transformation of the market economy to a planned socialist economy. Here the fundamental reason for production would be transformed from the incentive of profit to the incentive of the fulfilment of the human need. The national question can only be solved through the acceptance of the rights of self-determination of the toiling masses of the oppressed nationalities. With the advent of a socialist system, the rapid rise in the prosperity, and unprecedented social and economic progress, it is more likely that the working classes of the oppressed nationalities would opt for a voluntary unity with the socialist federation that will begin to emerge and expand, transcending the geographic demarcations of bourgeois states. Lenin was very pertinent on the national question and its relation with the socialist revolution.

Lenin wrote in 1922:

> The aim of socialism is not only to end the division of mankind into tiny states and the isolation of nations in any form, it is not only to bring the nations closer together but to integrate them.[7]

Stalinism

In the uninterrupted process of completing the tasks of the democratic revolution, in continuity with the building of socialism, the revolution in Pakistan will attain the character of permanent revolution. It is also true that the revolutionary overthrow and replacement of the bourgeois state with a proletarian state will pose a daunting task. The propagandists of the ruling classes have been viciously hurling accusations for more than a hundred years that socialism or communism is a dictatorship. First they compared the democratic centralism of Bolshevism with military dictatorships in capitalist countries. Then they got the alibi of Stalinism in Russia, which they exploited to the extreme. Stalinism was not Marxism, but a totalitarian caricature of socialism which was the result of the bureaucratic degeneration of the Soviet Union. It was not the product of the revolution but the political counter-revolution of the bureaucracy led by Stalin. This occurred mainly due to the defeat of the revolutions in advanced countries—Germany

(1918-19), Britain (1926), France (1924), Austro Hungarian Empire (1920), China (1924-25) and several other countries.

The isolated backwardness and the extermination of the Bolshevik cadres in the imperialist drive to crush the revolution were some of the factors that led to the rise of Stalinism. Above all it was predicted by Lenin in July 1921 that if the revolution doesn't expand into the advanced countries then the 'Russian Revolution was doomed. Leon Trotsky, Ted Grant and other revolutionary teachers had predicted the collapse of the Soviet Union due to this Stalinist totalitarianism, decades in advance.

The main purpose of this barrage of propaganda was that, 'Socialism has failed', 'Marxism is finished', 'End of history', 'Clash of civilization', 'Communistic dictatorship', 'Command economy', etc. is a colossal deception devised to divert the attention of the masses from the stark reality of the dictatorship of finance capital, which exercises its economic and social repression through military dictatorships and bourgeois democracy with equal ferocity. This whole propaganda campaign of bourgeois intellectuals and imperialist media is to conceal the crisis and doom of their own system. Alan Woods sums up the present state of mind of bourgeois ideologues and their gloom behind the ruthless attacks on Marxist philosophy and ideology, in his brilliant work *Reformism and Revolution*. Alan writes:

> The crisis of the capitalist system is reflected in a crisis of bourgeois values, morality, religion, politics and philosophy. The mood of pessimism that afflicts the bourgeoisie and its ideologues in this period is manifested in the poverty of its thought, the triviality of its art and the emptiness of its spiritual values. It is expressed in the wretched philosophy of post-modernism, which imagines itself to be superior to all previous philosophy, when in reality it is vastly inferior.
>
> In its youth the bourgeoisie was capable of producing great thinkers: Locke, Hobbes, Kant, Hegel, Adam Smith and Ricardo. In the period of its decline, it is only capable of producing intellectual pygmies. They talk of the end of ideology and the end of history in the same breath. They do not believe in progress because the bourgeoisie has long since ceased to be progressive. When they talk of the end of history it is because they have ended in an historical dead-end and can see no way out. When they talk of the end of ideology, it is because they are no longer capable of producing one.[8]

It is true that democracy under revolutionary socialism is neither parliamentary democracy nor is it the same as the Athenian democracy or other 'democratic' methods of various types of parliamentary systems in history. Never has a revolution been won through a parliamentary struggle, nor can it ever be achieved through this institution of the bourgeois state. Lenin wrote a Marxist classic *The State and Revolution* during the gigantic events of the 1917 revolution. This showed the importance of theory and political education that the great teachers of Marxism always attached to the struggle for a victorious revolution. Lenin wrote in 1917:

> The exploiting classes need political rule to maintain exploitation, i.e., in the selfish interests of an insignificant minority against the vast majority of all people. The exploited classes need political rule in order to completely abolish all exploitation, i.e., in the interests of the vast majority of the people, and against the insignificant minority consisting of the modern slave-owners the landowners and capitalists.
>
> (...) We cannot imagine democracy, even proletarian democracy, without representative institutions, but we can and must imagine democracy without parliamentarianism, if criticism of bourgeois society is not mere words for us, if the desire to overthrow the rule of the bourgeoisie is our earnest and sincere desire, and not a mere "election" cry for catching workers' votes.
>
> (...) But it is clear that the old executive apparatus, the bureaucracy, which is connected with the bourgeoisie, would simply be unfit to carry out the orders of the proletarian state.
>
> (...) Democracy is a form of the state; it represents, on the one hand, the organized, systematic use of force against persons; but, on the other hand, it signifies the formal recognition of equality of citizens, the equal right of all to determine the structure of, and to administer, the state.[9]

In the same work Lenin also describes and elaborates democracy under socialism. The class nature of its content and the highest form of democracy mankind had ever experienced in its history.

Lenin continues:

> In a socialist society, the 'sort of parliament', consisting of workers deputies will, of course, establish the working regulations and supervise the management of the 'apparatus', but this apparatus will not be bureaucratic. The workers, after winning political power, will smash the old bureaucratic apparatus, shatter it to its very

foundations, and raze it to the ground; they will replace it by a new one, consisting of the very same workers and other employees, against whose transformation into bureaucrats the measures will at once be taken which were specified in detail by Marx and Engels: (1) not only election, but also recall at any time; (2) pay not to exceed that of a workman; (3) immediate introduction of control and supervision by all, so that all may become 'bureaucrats' for a time and that, therefore, nobody may be able to become a bureaucrat.

(...) The proletariat is oppressed, the working people are enslaved by capitalism. Under capitalism, democracy is restricted, cramped, curtailed, mutilated by all the conditions of wage slavery, and the poverty and misery of the people. This and this alone is the reason why the functionaries of our political organizations and trade unions are corrupted or rather tend to be corrupted by the conditions of capitalism and betray a tendency to become bureaucrats, i.e., privileged persons divorced from the people and standing above the people.

(...) That is the essence of bureaucracy; and until the capitalists have been expropriated and the bourgeoisie overthrown, even proletarian functionaries will inevitably be 'bureaucratized' to a certain extent.

(...) For the first time in the history of civilized society the mass of population will rise to taking an independent part, not only in voting and elections, but also in the everyday administration of the state. Under socialism all will govern in turn and will soon become accustomed to no one governing.[10]

The State

Similar is the question of the state and its institutions. The present state is structured, indoctrinated and trained to protect the bourgeoisie and its system. A totally different and transformed social and economic system cannot be run by the same state. In reality the present state structure in its present character shall and always has, tried to crush the revolutionary movement of the workers and the toiling masses. A revolution should have no misunderstanding about this. It has to smash the present state structure to put upon new form and structure of the state. In his epic work *The Origins of the Family, Private Property and the State*, the great Marxist teacher Frederick Engels summed up the historical analysis of the state:

The state is, therefore, by no means a power forced on society from

> without; just as little is it 'the reality of the ethical idea', 'the image and reality of reason', as Hegel maintains. Rather, it is a product of society at a certain stage of development; it is the admission that this society has become entangled in an insoluble contradiction with itself, that it has split into irreconcilable antagonisms which it is powerless to dispel. But in order that these antagonisms, these classes with conflicting economic interests, might not consume themselves and society in fruitless struggle, it became necessary to have a power, seemingly standing above society, that would alleviate the conflict and keep it within the bounds of 'order'; and this power, arisen out of society but placing itself above it, and alienating itself more and more from it, is the state.[11]

This expresses with perfect clarity the basic idea of Marxism with regard to the historical role and the meaning of the state. The state is a product and a manifestation of the irreconcilability of class antagonisms. The state arises where, when and insofar as class antagonism objectively cannot be reconciled. And, conversely, the existence of the state proves that the class antagonisms are irreconcilable.

In his early writing Marx gave a profound analysis of the state.

> These actual relations [the economic structure of society] are in no way created by the State power, on the contrary they are the power creating it. The individuals who rule in these conditions, besides having to constitute their power in the form of the State, have to give their will, which is determined by these definite conditions, a universal expression as the will of the State, as law—an expression whose content is always determined by the relations of this class, as civil and criminal law demonstrate in the clearest possible way...[12]

After the collapse of the Soviet Union and the fall of the Berlin Wall it became fashionable amongst the urban petty bourgeois (as was 'socialism' fashionable in 1960s) to call the overthrow of the bourgeois state and revolution a utopian dream. The formation of a Bolshevik-Leninist party, a democratic proletarian state and the possibility of the alternative of a socialist revolution as a way out, are dismissed with contemptuous scorn by the 'ex-communists' and 'Left' leaders of the PPP. This is not the first time it has happened in history. Every revolutionary party had to go through such insults and scorn in its period of struggle for revolutionary socialism. Lenin sharply retorted to these 'reformist' intellectuals:

> But there are none so deaf as those who will not hear. And the very thing the opportunists of present-day Social-Democracy do not want to hear about is the destruction of state power, the amputation of this parasitic excrescence."
>
> (...) The course of events compels the revolution 'to concentrate all its forces of destruction' against the state power, and to set itself the aim, not of improving the state machine, but of smashing and destroying it.
>
> (...) We are not Utopians, we do not 'dream' of dispensing at once with all administration, with all subordination. These anarchist dreams, based upon incomprehension of the tasks of the proletarian dictatorship, are totally alien to Marxism, and, as a matter of fact, serve only to postpone the socialist revolution until people are different. No, we want the socialist revolution with people as they are now, with people who cannot dispense with subordination, control, and 'foremen and accountants'.
>
> (...) The subordination, however, must be to the armed vanguard of all the exploited and working people, i.e., to the proletariat. A beginning can and must be made at once, overnight, to replace the specific 'bossing' of state officials by the simple functions of 'foremen and accountants', functions which are already fully within the ability of the average town dweller and can well be performed for 'workmen's wages.
>
> We, the workers, shall organize large-scale production on the basis of what capitalism has already created, relying on our own experience as workers, establishing strict, iron discipline backed up by the state power of the armed workers. We shall reduce the role of state officials to that of simply carrying out our instructions as responsible, revocable, modestly paid 'foremen and accountants' (of course, with the aid of technicians of all sorts, types and degrees). This is our proletarian task, this is what we can and must start with in accomplishing the proletarian revolution. Such a beginning, on the basis of large-scale production, will of itself lead to the gradual 'withering away' of all bureaucracy, to the gradual creation of an order an order without inverted commas, an order bearing no similarity to wage slavery an order under which the functions of control and accounting, becoming more and more simple, will be performed by each in turn, will then become a habit and will finally die out as the special functions of a special section of the population.[13]

At the peak of the 1968-9 revolution we saw at least the beginnings of this process. As the revolution fought the state, those areas where the state forces were routed were in fact liberated and an alternative order was needed. We saw the factory, neighbourhood and even village committees created. There was a collective and fraternal control by the workers and the property-less masses. This restored an order which was voluntarily accepted and supported by the oppressed masses. The 'common people' participated in their functioning for the period when situations of dual power remained.

The vote of the army in the 1970 elections clearly indicated the revolutionary impacts the soldiers and lower ranks had during the period of 1968-9. The whole situation was crying out for a revolutionary party, that is, in some ways a state within a state. Had there been a cadre organization in Pakistan like the Bolsheviks in 1917 in Russia, the alternative revolutionary state could have rapidly emerged to replace the state apparatus that had been cracked by the revolutionary assault of the mass movement.

Foreign Aggression

The other important aspect in such a revolutionary situation in Pakistan would be a factor of foreign aggression. There is no doubt that imperialism would not tolerate such a change. But these days there are many things that are intolerable for imperialism, from Venezuela to Iran, from Iraq to Afghanistan and of course regions of Pakistan. How far can it go? With the economic crunch and a virtual meltdown of the financial systems of imperialism, it only displays its impotent rage. The first point is what capacity does imperialism retain, and even in its madness how much longer can it go on ravaging countries and devastating civilizations?

Trotsky once termed US imperialism as a monster with feet of clay. This seems quite apt if we look at the present-day wrangling of imperialism. It is through their military and civilian stooges, who have stacked their plunder in imperialist banks that the imperialist used to control Pakistan. The revolution shall overthrow these stooges, along with their state apparatus, and forcibly retrieve the billions they have plundered by the blood, sweat and tears of the Pakistani working class.

Secondly, from the Bolshevik revolution of 1917, the Chinese revolution of 1949, to the Cuban revolution of 1959 and the various revolutions in several countries, especially in Asia, Africa and Latin Amercia, they have been able to crush very few. Why are the imperialists so nervous and hesitant in the case of the Venezuelan revolution? They've blown hot and cold, but they haven't done much to Chavez's challenges to their hegemony and authority. They might assassinate Chavez but even that cannot stop the rising tide of revolution in Latin America, where one president after another, when elected, at least presents himself as 'Left'.

The experience of 1968-9 shows that the ruling classes of the subcontinent went to war to stop the spread of the revolution. The Indian ruling classes intervened with all their military might not only to defeat the Pakistan army but more so to crush the revolutionary soviets that had developed in the liberated areas of East Bengal. A mass revolutionary party in India could have turned the whole scenario into its opposite with relative case. The communist parties in India had a certain mass base but their leadership was Stalinist and not Leninist. Labels are not the test of a product.

The most important precedent in defiance of imperialist military aggression is the revolutionary war launched by the Bolsheviks in the period 1918–1921. When twenty-one imperialist armies attacked the nascent Soviet Union, apart from the rapid rearmament and preparation of the Red Army by the military genius of Trotsky, the Bolsheviks issued an appeal to the soldiers of the attacking armies that the revolution was that of a class and not a nation. It was their class that was in power. Hence it was their duty to defend the revolution rather than attacking it. There were rebellions in the imperialist armies which was a major factor in salvaging the socialist revolution in Russia.

Internationalism

But socialism cannot be built and a planned socialist economy cannot be sustained for a very long time in a single country, whatever the size and indigenous resources of that country might be. If a country as huge as USSR, with one-fifth of the world's surface, could not be sustained on a national basis, how can any other country do it?

The question arises: how can socialism drive the productive forces, which have tried to violently break through under socialism, back into the boundaries of a national state? Hence, for the building of socialism itself, arises the inevitable necessity of expanding the revolution beyond the borders of the nation state where it has been successfully carried out.

Lenin made it very clear before the revolution in Russia. In 1915 he said:

> The Marxian doctrine, which postulates that the socialist revolution can only begin on a national basis... that is, the building of socialism in one country is impossible ... has been rendered doubly accurate today. In the modern epoch, imperialism has developed, deepened and sharpened both of these antagonistic tendencies.
>
> (...) uneven economic and political development is an unconditional law of capitalism. Hence it follows that the triumph of socialism is, to begin with, possible in a few, or even in a single, capitalist country. The victorious proletariat of that country, having expropriated the capitalists and having organised socialist production at home, would be up in arms against the rest of the capitalist world, attracting oppressed classes of other countries to its side, causing insurrections in those countries against the capitalists, and acting, in case of need, even with military power against the exploiting classes and their governments.[14]

Trotsky explains the process further:

> Imperialism ... aggravates to an exceptional degree the contradiction between the growth of the national productive forces of world economy and national state barriers. The productive forces are incompatible with national boundaries. Hence the flow of foreign trade, the export of men and capital, the seizure of territories, the colonial policy, and the last imperialist war, but also the economic possibility of a self-sufficient socialist society. The productive forces of capitalist countries have long since broken through the national boundaries. Socialist society, however, can be built only on the most advance productive forces, on the application of electricity and chemistry to the processes of production including agriculture; on combining, generalising, and bringing to maximum development the highest elements of modern technology.[15]

Marxism is internationalism or it is nothing. From the task of defending the revolution against imperialist aggression to the building of socialism, the expansion of revolution is a prerequisite. The revolution of 1968-9 had already stirred up the masses in South Asia. A socialist victory in Pakistan could have resulted in revolutionary upheavals from Afghanistan to the Far eastern borders of India and even beyond. Hence the creation of a revolutionary subjective factor is linked to the building of the Marxist International in all the countries of the region; it is vital for the success of revolution in Pakistan.

At the same time a revolutionary international is duty bound to build up active support and campaigns to defend the revolution in Pakistan or in any other country. This support on a world scale, especially amongst the workers and youth of the advanced capitalist countries, would play a decisive role in the defence of revolution.

In any case there are long cultural, economic and social relations with Iran and Afghanistan , stretching back thousands of years. India and Pakistan were an entity as a civilization as old as seven thousand years, till just 61 years ago. Even the relatively small political upheaval reciprocates in the two countries. The masses in India are suffering from capitalist exploitation as never before. It is the same situation in Afghanistan, Iran, Bangladesh and other countries of the region.

The masses are seething with revolt everywhere, looking and yearning for a way out. In this closely interconnected world, with Internet, satellite television and other modes of communications, a revolution in Pakistan would be such an inspiration that it would trigger mass revolutionary uprisings, especially in the countries of South Asia. Such a transformation would spread the revolution with a swiftness unimaginable in the present milieu. This will be the beginning of the task of moving towards a socialist voluntary federation of the peoples of South Asia. In other words it would be another USSR in the making. And this time over, it will fulfil Lenin's intention of the creation of the USSR. It will spread far beyond the frontiers of South Asia. That would be a decisive defeat of imperialism and capitalist exploitation on a world scale.

Pakistan has been nowhere near any really stable situation

throughout its tumultuous history, but the present instability is unprecedented even by Pakistani standards. The imperialists made strenuous efforts to carry through this transition from Musharraf to Zardari. Even the bourgeoisie admits the loosening and the process of the disintegration of the cohesion of the state. *Dawn* described the condition of the Pakistani state in a recent article:

> The violent extremists in our midst are not aberrations. They are the products of a generation of softening-up the state and Islamising society. They are the most virulent and aggressive strain of obscurantism, and benefit daily from the role that their ostensibly non-militant counterparts, such as Al Huda, the Tableeghi Jamaat and the thousands of unregulated and illegal mosques and madressahs, have played in propagating a neo-conservative Bedouin worldview in Pakistan.
>
> (...) For decades such elements enjoyed state patronage and were used by the state as 'strategic' instruments which greatly augmented their strength and appeal. Now those instruments have spun out of control and the state itself has become their target.
>
> The terrorists are widely believed to have the support of renegade elements within the security apparatus.
>
> Finally, the terrorists seem to have an accurate measure of the administrative capabilities of the Pakistani state. The professional competence and integrity of Pakistan's security apparatus is so low, and its internal indiscipline so high, that the state is incapable of anything more than a few weeks of extra vigilance after each major attack.[16]

The Situation Today

The Americans want the new 'democratic' dispensation to perform and will try to prolong its rule. However, the imperialists have big problems with money themselves; they can't be very generous to Zardari or prop up a crumbling Pakistani economy. But still they have embroiled themselves in a messy situation where a lot is at stake for them, resting on the fate of the Pakistani State.

If we analyze the above quoted article in the *Dawn*, it seems to be a near impossible task. With the exacerbation of this 'war against terror' the internal indiscipline and the dissensions within the state would further increase. The strain on the army high command will be tremendous. It is already facing a lot of criticism and bickering among the middle ranking officers about the 'abuse' of the army by the US and its toady politicians. Events are exploding at a rapid pace in Pakistan, with some really major shocks whose frequency has increased in the last period.

Any major event can force the army to intervene again. The obscurantist elements in the security forces and state have not weakened and the PPP government is still trying to appease them. The Islamists don't have many votes in the parliament; the pressure probably came from within the state apparatus and Zardari succumbed to it. Apart from terrorist acts and major accidental events, the further aggravation of the economic crisis, price hikes and the social anger against them could lead the army to move in to stave off a bigger mass outburst.

These social convulsions can also effect the psychology of the Pakistan army which has a tradition of making such interventions. A military coup or martial law would be much more brutal than the rule of tin-pot dictators like Musharraf. At the same time it would be quite shortlived, as the army would not be able to resolve any of the problems faced by society.

The Americans are exerting their pressure on the military high command (which was very much of their own choice) to refrain from making such a move. The generals probably don't want to move in yet. The strategists of the ruling classes might try to go for an in-between strategy. 'Elections' could be held and Nawaz Sharif or some other Right-wing politician might be brought in to make a change for a temporary respite. But a Right-wing alliance would be in crisis even sooner and an even greater turmoil would again be confronted by the dithering state. Nawaz Sharif is waiting in the wings for such an opportunity, and has the support of the Right-wing. But how far can he solve the greater convulsions that impend?

If there is a coup from the middle ranks of the army then it will be a bloody affair. The imposition of Islamic fundamentalism is not ruled out, but it is not very likely. Even if some of the Right-wing obscurantist generals take the power structure of the state the economy is such that they will not be able to alter anything radically. The Islamists cannot win this insurgency mainly because there are various groups fighting different insurgencies in different areas.

There is no cohesion or coordination between them in different areas. They belong to diverse religious sects that are often at odds with each other and settle their scores through bloody gun battles. If there is any coordination it can probably be through some rogue state agency. But the possibility of such a coordinated effort by the fundamentalists is remote. Their social base is mainly urban and suburban petty bourgeois in the tribal waste lands, and amongst primitive sections of the society. Amongst the workers and the masses in general their support is very limited. If the Islamist fanatics cannot win this war, the Americans and the regular army can't defeat them either.

The reality is that sections of the Pakistan army are actually involved on both sides. The imperialists know this and say it, but cannot do much about it. If we analyze the insurgency and war, for example in Swat, the collusion and collision between the warring sides is quite evident. With the army being involved with the fundamentalists for decades, it is hardly surprising that the material and financial interest of sections of the army are linked with the Taliban financing system.

But in the face of defeat the imperialists could easily change the goal posts: if you can't fight them, join them. The Americans had supported and done deals with the Taliban when they were in power in Afghanistan, they can do another grand deal with the Islamic fundamentalists again. After all, modern Islamic fundamentalism was the brain child of John Foster Dulles, the secretary of state to Eisenhower, the US president in the 1950s. In 1956 after the defeat of Zionist, French and British imperialism by Egypt under Gamal Abdel Nasser the CIA decided on a plan with heavy funding to create Islamic fundamentalist reactionary forces to kill and attack the Left forces and progressive elements in the 'Islamic world'. The Afghan Jihad against the Left-wing government in Kabul in the 1980s was after all sponsored and supported by the CIA through the auspices of Pakistani and Saudi Arabian intelligence agencies.

Eric S. Margolis, a former high-ranking official in the US establishment and now a veteran American journalist, in an article in the *Khaleej Times,* wrote the following:

> Taliban was founded as an Islamic movement dedicated to fighting Communism and the drug trade. It received US funding until May, 2001. In fact, the CIA maintained close contacts with the Taliban, many of whose members were Mujahideen from the anti-Soviet war of the 1980's, for possible future use against the Communist regimes of Central Asia and against China.
>
> The 9/11 attacks made the CIA immediately cut its links with Taliban and burn its associated files.
>
> (...) The Karzai government cannot extend its authority beyond Kabul because that would mean overthrowing the very same drug-dealing warlords that are its allies. There is no real Afghan national army, just a bunch of unenthusiastic mercenaries who pretend to fight while playing footsy with Taliban.
>
> Contrary to Western propaganda, Taliban are not 'terrorists'. The movement had nothing to do with 9/11 though it did shelter Osama Bin Laden, a national hero of the war against the Soviets. The 9/11 attacks were plotted in Germany and Spain, not Afghanistan. Only a handful of Al Qaeda members are left in Afghanistan. The current war is not really about Al Qaeda and 'terrorism', but about opening a secure corridor through Pashtoon tribal territory to export the oil and gas riches of the Caspian Basin of Central Asia to the West.
>
> The US and NATO forces in Afghanistan are essentially pipeline protection troops. As that great American founding father Benjamin Franklin said, 'there is no good war, and no bad peace.' It's time for the West to face reality in Afghanistan.[17]

It will be a bloody and protracted crisis in which the oppressed will be the biggest sufferers.

As we have explained earlier, with the continuation of capitalism prosperity under the incumbent or any other regime is ruled out. The conditions of the masses can only worsen. The national question could come to the fore again, but the possibility of the nationalists gaining a mass base in the oppressed nationalities and opting for secession is very limited. Nevertheless, the insurgency in Baluchistan can still flare up to a higher intensity. The break-up of Pakistan, though not ruled out in extraordinary situations, is not the most likely perspective. At the same time, the national contradictions will keep on exploding into conflicts and will be a source of violent clashes, intensifying the instability already prevalent in the country.

This can give rise to chaos and anarchy. Yet there is another perspective that is the victim of a conspiracy of silence by the mainstream journalists and analysts: it is the perspective of a class struggle and the eruption of another mass movement. The movement after 18 October 2007 was not of the calibre of the1968-9 upsurge. Hence, it was diffused with relative ease by the PPP leadership. It seems that the immediate eruption of a mass revolt is not the most likely possibility. The present turbulent situation has two sides to it. This period is punctuated with frequent strikes and sporadic uprisings of the workers, some of which are quite fierce. A slight pause in the economic decline that is going on in Pakistan at the moment can give rise to a potentially revolutionary situation with at least the beginnings of a mass movement. Events and accidents can occur that could convert it into a more militant mass movement. Such a perspective is possible in the next period. The events taking place in Latin America and elsewhere can accentuate such a movement. Another main obstacle for the mass movement is the political tradition of the toilers in Pakistan. Alan Woods explains the role of such traditions:

> In order for the heavy, multi-millioned masses to draw all the necessary conclusions, a further experience was necessary. It is natural for people to take the line of least resistance, even in a revolution. For this very reason the masses always cling obstinately to their traditional mass organisations. The thinking of the masses is very economical: why discard an old tool before trying to make it work?[18]

In the wake of a revolutionary movement the monolith of the PPP leadership will begin to crack. There will be a number of splits in the party. There will be a number of 'Left- wing' leaders emerging when presently there is none in the PPP. If the movement sustains itself for sometime it will gain more strength day by day. This at a certain stage shall lead to a call for a general strike, which can come from the trade union or political leadership that emerges from this movement, as happened in the movement of 1968-9. The role of the Marxist tendency will become crucial at this stage.

Riaz Lund

There have been several recent events that graphically illustrate that the revolutionary potential of the workers and youth can be aroused and support for revolutionary socialism can be galvanized by the bold intervention of the Marxist organization. The most significant exhibition of this prospect came to the fore during the elections of February 2008. Comrade Riaz Lund, a steel worker, was sacked due to his militant role in the struggles of the steel mills. Comrade Riaz was contesting against the neo-fascist MQM on a PPP ticket. Being a long-standing revolutionary Marxist, Riaz Lund's campaign was launched on a socialist programme; the main slogan of his campaign was, "irreconcilable struggle till the victory of socialist revolution".

The election posters, the red banners, flags, slogans and speeches in his campaign were full of revolutionary fervour. Marxists from all over the country had come down to Karachi's industrial district of Malir, the constituency from where he was contesting this election. The MQM goons tried to attack and intimidate the comrade, as was their usual practice of using neo-fascist tactics to win elections. But this time, as some of their leaders confessed, there was a different sort of resistance and campaign. The Marxists struck back and repulsed the attacks of the MQM. As the trains used to enter Karachi, Malir, being one of the first stations of the metropolis, had all the walls covered with posters and banners calling for a socialist revolution. Millions of passengers coming and going out of Pakistan's Petrograd, Karachi got a revolutionary message. Socialist ideas and slogans were echoing on the streets of Karachi after about four decades. On Election Day it looked more of a revolutionary carnival than an electoral activity. The state was worried, as Comrade Erik de Bruyn from Belgium had come as an election observer. The MQM failed to rig the votes at the polling stations as their terror tactics were repulsed by the Marxists. Results started to come from some of the most remote areas of Pakistan, but the state refused to declare the result of NA-257, a constituency in the industrial heartland of Pakistan. In the late hours of the night, as rallies of supporters of Comrade Riaz Lund gathered outside the main election offices, the MQM thugs and the police hijacked the ballot boxes and polling officers from the basement backdoors and took them in police vans to the Governor's house, where an MQM activist was the Governor of Sindh.

The wrath of the workers was rising as the night was passing by. The authorities could not dare to declare the fabricated result throughout the night. Only the next day in the afternoon they released the result on television. In the 'official' rigged result Riaz got 46,800 votes, which was one of the highest ever against MQM in that constituency in Karachi. In the evening Riaz spoke at the rally in which he said:

> The whole of Karachi knows, the whole of Pakistan knows, and the world will know that we won the elections. Our victory is the message of revolutionary socialism as the only way out of this horror of capitalism, which reached millions of workers and youth through this campaign. Till a victorious socialist revolution, our struggle shall never waver or stop. Go forward! Victory shall be the destiny of the proletariat.[19]

The Struggle for a Socialist Future

The whole art of building the revolutionary party and cementing it with the masses consists precisely on knowing how to connect the finished scientific programme of Marxism with the unfinished, confused and contradictory consciousness of the masses.

If a revolutionary organization with a substantial quantitative and qualitative force is there, then it can start radicalizing the objective situation in a decisive way. A new 1968-9 on a much higher historical plane can emerge.

The spectre of another 1968-9 will haunt the ruling classes and the imperialists. The working class in Pakistan has gone through traumatic experiences and despairing betrayals by leaders for almost three generations. The new generation of the proletariat, working on technologically more advanced instruments and modes of production, has emerged. There may be other superficial changes in society and the classes, but historically, socially, and economically their character and role has not altered fundamentally. The proletariat and youth of today's Pakistan might have to make a greater effort to come to the fore and play their historical role than their predecessors did in 1968-9. There have been many events, many betrayals and many mixings of banners. Yet it is a role that they have to play. With the intensity of crisis today, and capitalism dooming this society to death and destruction, it is a question of survival of the working classes and the toiling masses. That is what this struggle is all about.

Through a general strike the proletariat can make the country come to a standstill. The electric supply would be in the hands of the workers. Not a phone will ring, not a plane would fly, not a train will run, not a factory will function and not a wheel shall turn. That is the real meaning of a general strike. The labour which runs society can stop its functioning and take it into its own hands. We saw that happen in the wheel jam strike of 17 and 18 February 1969. It can happen again. A successful general strike will shake the already crumbling confidence of the ruling classes and the state. It will send tremors through the echelons of power. But at the same time it will give the workers a realization of their enormous strength as a class. Hence the confidence and courage to move the class struggle forward. The urban poor, the peasants, and other oppressed sections of society will develop a new confidence in the proletariat. They will follow the proletarian leadership. The youth would be in the forefront of the struggle inspiring the proletariat right from the start. In such conditions the non-issues will be wiped out from the political horizon of society; the religious fundamentalists, the ethnic neo-fascists and other reactionary forces that come to the fore in conditions of lull shall vanish into oblivion. A new dawn will be in the offing.

Such a pre-revolutionary or a revolutionary situation will have a deep impact on the soldiers who, after all, are workers in uniforms. It will also strongly influence young officers and other ranks in the armed forces to side with the proletariat. This will be a decisive stage for the revolution.

But even more decisive will be the presence of a revolutionary party armed with ideological clarity and a correct theoretical perspective.

Only a superficial mind seeks to interpret major political events in terms of personalities. This is a trivial approach to history and politics. It is on the level of sentimental novels and gossip journalism.

Theory occupies a place in revolutions that military strategy occupies in war. A mistaken strategy in war will lead inevitably to mistakes in tactics and practical operations. It will undermine the morale of the troops and lead to all kinds of blunders, defeats and unnecessary loss of life. It is the same in a revolution. Mistakes in theory will sooner or later be reflected in mistakes in practice. A mistake in everyday life can often be rectified. Everyday mistakes are not usually matters of life and death. But revolutions are life and death struggles and mistakes in them have to be paid for very dearly. Consequently, serious revolutionaries must pay serious attention to theory.

If it is politically, organizationally and morally prepared, then it can become a mass force in a very short span of time. Such a force will be able to direct and organize a revolution.

No ruling class in history has ever given up its power and privileges without inflicting violence, mayhem and bloodshed to preserve its system of exploitation. Hence a revolution is not a peaceful affair. This doesn't mean that revolutions come through the barrel of the gun. The decisive force behind a revolutionary victory in the class war is the unity of the class, its will, determination, and valour. The proletariat doesn't wish or want to use violent means to achieve its revolutionary goal. But the Marxists and the revolutionary proletariat are not pacifists. The answer to the violence is not non-violence. The violent attacks perpetuated by the bourgeoisie have to be answered with a ruthless fight against the ruling classes, along with their state forces and gangs of thugs.

After all, this is a class war. But the armed struggle of the proletariat is not about using terrorism, nor is the guerrilla war a classical method of revolutionary Marxism. The defence of the revolution begins with the armed defence committee of the workers on strike at the factory gates, and goes to the extent of the fight of the soldiers and lower ranks of the armed forces against the violent and terrorist forces of the ruling elite. But the organic force behind the revolution is the General Strike, which brings all of society to a halt and gives the masses confidence in the success of the revolution.

The Pakistani ruling classes and their state, being weak and immersed in a crisis, are extremely nervous. This makes them more viciously cruel, short-tempered, and merciless. Hence they have a tendency to resort to violent means abruptly and viciously. They lack confidence in themselves. This means that a revolution in Pakistan would have to go through turbulent and even bloody episodes. The better the preparation of the revolution by the Marxists, the more the proletariat are steeled and tempered, the more shortlived and futile will be the attacks and violence inflicted upon the revolution by the bourgeois state. An awakened and risen people cannot be defeated by the mightiest armies in the world.

Hence nine-tenths of the task of the revolution is the winning of the masses to its side. As Marx said, that when an idea is taken up by the masses it becomes an invincible force. That is the real power of the revolutionary insurrection and its victory. After the overthrow of capitalism and its state the creation of a socialist republic will open up a new era for the oppressed. When their chains are broken after centuries of slavery, the feeling of elation will give such courage and strength that it will electrify the masses and work wonders. In Pakistan a victorious socialist revolution will open up opportunities and bring changes to the social life of the country that could not have been imaginable for past generations. Some of them could be implemented with immediate effect.

In *Revolution Betrayed*, Trotsky explains:

> The transitional epoch between capitalism and socialism taken as a whole does not mean a cutting down of trade but, on the contrary, its extraordinary extension. All branches of industry transform themselves and grow. New ones continually arise, and all are compelled to define their relations to one another both quantitatively and qualitatively. The liquidation of the consummatory peasant economy, and at the same time of the shut-in family life, means a transfer to the sphere of social interchange, and ipso facto money circulation, of all the labour energy which was formerly expended within the limits of the peasant's yard, or within the walls of his private

> dwelling. All products and services begin for the first time in history to be exchanged for one another.[20]

The nationalization of the means of production and the introduction of a planned economy marks a big step forward as opposed to the anarchy of the market and private ownership. The state can now regulate and plan the economy, but only within the confines of the law of value. In the transitional period the law of value is not abolished, but is modified. Trotsky points out:

> The nationalisation of the means of production and credit, the co-operativizing or statizing of internal trade, the monopoly of foreign trade, the collectivization of agriculture, the law of inheritance—set strict limits upon the personal accumulation of money and hinder its conversion into private capital (usurious, commercial and industrial). These functions of money, however, bound up as they are with exploitation, are not liquidated at the beginning of a proletarian revolution, but in a modified form are transferred to the state, the universal merchant, creditor and industrialist. At the same time the more elementary functions of money as measure of value, means of exchange and medium of payment, are not only preserved, but acquire a broader field of action than they had under capitalism.[21]

With the further development of the productive forces, the reduction of the working day and the raising of productivity to undreamed-of heights, the raising of living standards and the cultural level of the whole population, the conditions will be prepared for a further development of the socialist element and the progressive elimination of the remnants from the past. The speed and the ease with which this transition is made depend above all upon the material conditions of society.

A nationalized planned economy, of course, gives us a huge advantage over capitalism. The workers' state can consciously regulate and plan production (though within limits determined by the general level of economic and social development). It can determine the rate of investment, the proportions between means of production and means of consumption, the price of articles of consumption, etc.

Alan Woods in his epic work *Reformism or Revolution* elucidates the real future under socialism. He writes:

> A planned economy would enable humanity to exploit natural resources in a rational and scientific way, balancing the needs of human consumption with the need to preserve and cherish our beautiful world and pass on our natural heritage intact to future generations. Socialism in our time will not signify a regime of austerity. On the contrary, a genuine socialist society will begin at the highest point achieved by capitalism. It will signify, not a reduction in living standards, but an all-round increase in the standard of living, together with a general reduction of working hours. This is the prior condition for a real participative democracy—that is, a workers' democracy. Without it, all talk of socialism will be mere empty demagogy.
>
> Socialism, as understood by Marx and Lenin, presupposes that the development of the productive forces has reached a sufficient level that it would eliminate all material inequality. The abolition of classes cannot be established by decree. It must arise from a superabundance of things that would universally raise the quality of life to unheard-of levels.
>
> All the basic human needs would be satisfied, and therefore the humiliating struggle for existence would cease. A general reduction in working hours would provide the conditions for an unparalleled development of culture. It would enable men and women to participate in the administration of industry, the state and society. From the very beginning the workers' state would be characterised by a level of democratic participation far superior to the most democratic bourgeois republic. As a consequence, classes would dissolve into society, together with the last vestiges of class society—money and the state.[22]

A socialist revolution doesn't change only the economics and the state. It casts aside the rotten cultural, moral, ethical and social values imposed upon society by the ruling class. It instils a new enthusiasm in the human spirit, elevates social and moral values and pulls the oppressed masses out of the abyss of despair and depression in which the capitalist system has kept them for generations.

The new enriched and enlightened spirit and feeling of the revolution gives the masses the courage and the will to live life with a new vigour and optimism, and break the shackles of their physical and psychological bondage.

Capitalism has scarred the face of Pakistan, which has been spattered with dirt and garbage. The streets, shanty towns and villages where the bulk of the population lives have been turned literally into reeking, stinking garbage dumps.

There are heaps of 'solid waste', hospital residue, and rubbish lying in hospital premises close to the patients' wards, spreading more disease than the hospitals are able to cure. Streets are polluted with water from the blocked sewage pipes and bubbling gutters.

The exploited toilers, in despair at the hopelessness of the situation, become accustomed and adapted to this filth and stink. They lose the energy to clean up the heaps of rubbish in front of their poor dwellings. But the energy unleashed by the revolution will galvanize the masses to move into taking action to cleanse their society of all the dirt, along with the exploiting classes and their institutions that have turned Pakistan into a huge dumping ground for all kinds of garbage.

In December 1917 Lenin wrote:

> One of the most important tasks of today, if not the most important, is to develop [the] independent initiative of the workers, and of all the working and exploited people generally, develop it as widely as possible in creative organizational work. At all costs we must break the old, absurd, savage, despicable and disgusting prejudice that only the so-called upper classes, only the rich, and those who have gone through the school of the rich, are capable of administering the state and directing the organizational development of socialist society.[23]

But such shall be the mass inspiration of the revolution that the youth and the working classes will be endowed with a confidence and courage such as they have never felt or experienced all their lives. With this consciousness of their social and economic force in society they will rise and advance to fulfil the historical tasks posed by the revolution:

- Health and education would be declared totally free of cost at all levels and for every kind of treatment. Private profit on health care and education would be considered a crime under a socialist system.
- Unemployment can be quickly abolished. The main revolutionary act would be to cut the working week to 20 hours and this alone could throw up jobs for millions of the unemployed.

  Vocational training schools, polytechnics and other similar institutions would be set up. The adult and youth would be given crash training programmes in different fields, with benefits for living to rapidly create a workforce to boost the production and growth for the fulfilment of human needs.

- Most managerial skills and degrees like MBA, etc. in a capitalist society are actually to train individuals to exploit, control and get the maximum out of labour in the minimum time. With the workers themselves controlling the industry and the economy through a socialist plan of production huge sums of money spent on managers and astronomical amounts given to experts and CEOs would be rolled back into the economy and invested in the advancement of technology.
- All the landed estates would be expropriated; there will be distribution of land amongst those landed peasants who wish to own small holdings to do their farming. The main emphasis of the socialist state would be to transform agriculture into industry, mechanize agriculture with the most advanced techniques and develop larger agriculture units with all the facilities that would be owned by society and democratically run by the agricultural workers of those collective farms.
- Part of the surplus produced would be used for reinvestment in more advanced technology, but the major amount would be dedicated to the economy of collective ownership and a rapid five-year plan for the rapid uplift of the masses. The living standards created by these measures would rise at a tremendous speed.
- With the wealth expropriated from the multinationals, big banks, national capitalists, landlords and other swindlers from the ruling classes, audacious plans for housing, high quality underground electric, water, gas supply and proper electrification, advanced irrigation systems, sanitation and water supply projects, advanced railway system, roads and other basic needs of the common people would be launched. The production and supply of needs and basic utilities of the people as a whole would be given top preference.

All the surplus profit from the production and supply of petroleum products, gas supplies, electricity and water would be gathered by the State and used to cut the costs of international trade and imported products, and the masses, through their soviets or councils of democratic control, would themselves decide their basic needs and their collective distribution.

- A political system where all parties will abandon capitalism and will not have political structures based on funds from renegade capitalists or imperialist channels. They would be allowed to function in the political structures of councils of workers, soldiers, peasants and students, etc. These new revolutionary organs of the toilers would actually run society. The method and mechanism of their functioning would be on the basis of democratic centralism. A party that has no support of the masses has no right to be in power. We have already quoted Lenin in this work where he gives details of how the highest form of democracy in history would be practised in the socialist system of society.
- The elections in a system of planned economy would be independent of the vicious role of finance capital, monetary and social inequality. Those contesting candidates would not have any advantage because of their financial and social status in society. The free will of choice would be exercised for the first time in Pakistan.
- The revolution will abolish the difference between the minimum and maximum programme of the revolutionary party. On foreign policy a socialist government will actively support the class struggle everywhere in the world, with a special emphasis on the struggle developing in neighbourhood countries. It will carry out an outright anti-imperialist policy and would support every struggle of the oppressed nationalities, minorities, races and others on a class basis, against imperialism and capitalist exploitation. The support of class struggle in the external policy would be the best safeguard for the socialist revolution itself.

- The class basis of the psychology of the needs and the necessities would be abolished. A revolution above all will abolish the alienation of society of which almost every individual is a victim in one form or another. This alienation creates fear from people themselves which is mostly unreal. This creates isolationism whose needs are dictated by this social fear. The revolution would create an atmosphere of brotherhood and fraternity. This will enhance the socialization of people and for the first time as equal human beings in real life. This will have a sea change effect on the needs in housing, transport and other fields. The whole pattern of such needs would be transformed with the systematically abolished alienation in society. With the resources expropriated from the filthy rich capitalists and imperialist monopolies, advanced and modern collective road and rail transport would be introduced. In such an atmosphere people will prefer to travel by buses and trains rather than in the isolation of cars and private vehicles.
- Gender discrimination would be abolished. This sham representation of women in parliament, comprising rich women from bourgeois aristocratic families who humiliate the very housemaids who are raising their children and doing domestic labour for them, is an insult to the millions of women working hard in the fields and factories. They are being doubly and triply exploited. These are the women who need to, and shall, be liberated by the revolution. Special kindergartens would be set up at village, neighbourhood and factory levels that would generate for women greater security, comfort in work, and relaxation time at home. The exploitation of the domestic labour, mainly done by women, would be abolished. Those who can work in their factories and fields and want to do that job would be freed from these shackles of domestic and family subservience. Women workers in every department would be granted benefit and subsistence allowances during the period of childbirth and other periods of obstetric inactivity.

Every individual shall have the right to believe in whatever faith he or she wishes to believe, and practise it in his or her private life. There shall be no intrusion of any kind by the state into the private lives of individuals. Spreading hatred and using religion for exploitation, violence and intimidation cannot be allowed in a socialist society. The state will be truly secular in character and religion would be the private affair of the individual. Nobody has any rights to question or enforce or remove any belief of the individual.

- The toiling masses of the oppressed nationalities will have the right of self-determination, including secession if the majority wishes that. The socialist state would offer them a union of socialist republics. The revolution will not only change the geography but abolish all the material, ethnic, linguastic, racial, religious, sectarian and other reactionary prejudices of the past. This will end a lot of the nationalist and religious animosities created by the ruling classes to subvert the class struggle of different countries, nationalities, etc. The socialist revolution would unite the toilers against oppression of all sorts and forms.
- Art, literature, culture, film, sports, theatre, music and other creative activities of society shall be liberated from the clutches of finance capital. For the first time this society as a whole shall have full access to the world of art. And art will flourish with so many people playing a role in its creativity on a massive scale. Music composition rhythms and symphonies of a liberated people will give the whole society a bliss and a joy yet unforeseen.

Other similar revolutionary measures would be immediately introduced by the Revolutionary Proletarian state based on the genuine democracy of the working class, in every field and department of society. The production for needs and quality of life will achieve unprecedented prosperity, never seen in history before. That will bring mankind to its ultimate destiny of a communist society where want and need shall be abolished and contradiction between man and man shall be abolished. The culture and civilization shall gain such heights that human beings will be free from all exploitation, prejudices and superstitions for the first time ever. The process of the conquest of nature and the universe by mankind shall begin. This will be the only real redemption of 1968-9 revolution.

NOTES

1. Frederick Engels, 'Anti-Duhring', (Progress Publishers, Moscow 1956), p. 142.
2. Leon Trotsky, *Problems of Everyday life,* (Pathfinder), p. 67.
3. Leon Trotsky, *The History of the Russian Revolution*, pp. 27, 28.
4. Alan Woods, *Bolshevism; The Road to Revolution,* p. 63.
5. Ibid, pp. 383-384.
6. Leon Trotsky, *The Third International after Lenin*, pp. 40, 41.
7. V.I. Lenin, *Collected Works,* Vol. 22.
8. Alan Woods, *Reformism and Revolution*, p. 37.
9. V.I. Lenin, *The State and Revolution*, pp. 27, 48, 57, 95.
10. Ibid, pp. 103,104, 109, 110.
11. Karl Marx and Frederick Engels, *Selected Works*, Vol. 3, (Moscow, 1973), pp. 326-27.
12. Marx, *German Ideology*, p. 184.
13. V.I. Lenin, *The State and Revolution,* pp. 53, 32, 49.
14. V. I. Lenin, *Collected Works,* Vol. 13, (Progress Publishers, Moscow), p. 133.
15. Leon Trotsky, *The Third International after Lenin,* p. 206.
16. *Dawn,* 04 October 2008.
17. Eric S Margolis, *Khaleej Times,* 06 October 2008.
18. Alan Woods, *Bolshevism; The Road to Revolution*, p. 516.
19. Riaz Lund narrated to the author on phone after his speech, 19 February 2008.
20. Trotsky, *Revolution Betrayed,* 1972, p. 67.
21. Ibid, p. 66.
22. Alan Woods, *Reformism or Revolution,* (Wellred), pp. 266-67.
23. Lenin, *Collected Works,* Vol. 26, p. 409.

APPENDICES

Appendix I

THE ROLE OF THE PAKISTAN ARMY

The army in Pakistan has played more of an overt than a covert role as a state institution in ruling the country. And the most organized and powerful institution of a state, like all capitalist states, has the fundamental role of preserving and protecting the assets, social status, privileges and economic exploitation of the local ruling classes and imperialism.

It plays a similar role as in India and other states—albeit more covertly in these countries—in crushing the toiling millions to perpetuate the rule of finance capital and a constantly increasing exploitation of labour. This prominence of the army in Pakistan, however, has been subject to widespread criticism and several books have been written on the role of the army.

But even the most Left-wing of the intellectuals have only looked at the army institution as one single bloc and have not bothered to delve into the nature of its structures and the mutual relationships, contradictions and conflicts between the different layers and sections of the army. This way of looking at the issue has been mainly the product of a mindset that is imbued with the theory of the "national democratic stage" of development as the solution to the impending crisis. With their preconceived prejudice of evolution they have limited their approach to a reformist outlook, i.e. to the idea of improving and reforming the army as an institution in order for it to play its 'proper' defensive, supportive and assistive role for the "democratic, liberal and progressive bourgeoisie" to fulfill the tasks of the industrial revolution imposed traditionally by history on the capitalist class.

This whole notion and ideological outlook is flawed from beginning to the end. The army could only fulfill its role as an institution of a bourgeois state, as it did in the advanced capitalist countries in the past when the ruling classes, other institutions of the state and the economic system itself could play their progressive role in carrying out the national bourgeois revolutions. This is definitely not the case today in Pakistan.

The Pakistan ruling class, due to its late arrival on the scene of history, had to usurp the available resources and the surplus rather than create them. The nascent Pakistani bourgeoisie proved to be incapable of building up the necessary social and physical infrastructure and carrying out the tasks posed by history. It was this parasitic nature of plundering the state and society to maintain its rates of profit that created such a crisis that rocked the country right from its birth. It was to try to control the instability that flowed from all this that the army was forced to step in to halt the rapid deterioration, although it simply ended up by further aggravating this mess. The situation was moving towards such anarchic conditions that it could have fatally endangered the rule of capital itself.

To infer that such arguments are supportive of the military actions and the brutalities of Martial Law in Pakistan is not only absurd but expresses a preconceived idea that is shackled within the cage of the theory of two stages. It was and is the fundamental task of the army to preserve capitalist rule and when this becomes impossible through the 'normal' bourgeois legal procedures, it tries to play out the same role with extraordinary methods, however brutal and vicious they may be. That is the function of the state and the army in bourgeois society.

Therefore, the notion of restricting the army to its 'constitutional' role within a crisis-ridden capitalist system is nothing but sheer utopia. The 'rule of Law', 'independence of the judiciary', 'good governance', 'reforming the institutions' and 'smoothly functioning democracy' are all the products of wishful thinking that totally ignores the socio-economic realities and the horrendous crisis which Pakistani society is going through at this moment in time.

Lenin said long ago "Politics is concentrated economics". In these conditions we have to see the social and economic factors that are the real cause of the military coups. But in Pakistan's history we also see how short the actual periods of direct military rule and repressive Martial Law have been. If we look more closely at the actual periods of direct and open repression through Martial Law, they are short stints within the longer periods of covert military rule in Pakistan. It appears clearly that the weapon of direct military repression gets blunted very rapidly once it is used on society in general. Hence there is a precarious haste of all military dictators to revert to civil administration, civil politicians and civil society representatives within the regime to perpetuate their rule.

The judiciary in normal circumstances is subservient to the army as an institution pertaining to the needs of the vested interests of the ruling classes. Hence these military dictators can easily manipulate the judiciary, constitutional experts, billionaire lawyers and the prevalent intelligentsia to become 'civilian' presidents and heads of state themselves. Field Marshal Ayub Khan was only able to force the military to impose its direct despotic rule for less than two years. By 1960 he had fabricated a new constitution and became a civilian president. Even after the coup of 27 October 1958 he continued with the civilian cabinet that had been working under President Sikander Mirza whom he had deposed in a gentlemanly affair. Yahya Khan had a civilian cabinet throughout. Even Zia-ul-Haq, whose monstrous Martial Law was the most brutal and repressive, used civilian ministers, albeit all of them from the Right-wing parties, especially the neo-fascist Jamat-i-Islami.

These Right-wing parties can never be absolved from the heinous crimes committed by the Zia dictatorship against the radical Left-wing youth and the toiling masses of Pakistan, especially the genocide carried out in Sindh during the 1983 uprising against the despotism of Zia-ul-Haq. He used 'respected' and highly acknowledged legal experts like A.K. Brohi and Sharifud din Peerzada to manipulate the law according to the needs of his dictatorial rule. Zulfiqar Ali Bhutto, who was elected on a socialist programme, was assassinated on the gallows by the civilian courts, not through a military tribunal.

Musharraf the dictator went farther than all his predecessors. He introduced firstly the basic, municipal democracies in 2000 on a non-party basis, as had Ayub Khan and Zia-ul-Haq. This was the first part, and all the political parties joined in the sham electoral process that gave a certain basic legal justification and certain credibility to the Musharraf Regime.

Then he went ahead and held party elections in 2002. Most parties participated in those elections and that was the first parliament to complete its term in the history of Pakistan. In this period his carrot and stick tactics played a certain role, but the inability of the political parties, mainly the PPP (which is perhaps the only party that came from the masses during the 1968-9 revolution) was more due to ideological betrayal and the adoption of so-called pragmatism.

However, Musharraf's policies also aggravated another process that had been taking place within the institutions over the last five decades. The army's involvement in politics and society is a much-talked about and discussed phenomenon. This, however, was the reflection of a rapidly increasing involvement of the officer caste in the economy and finance capital.

During British rule it was mainly a question of allocation of agricultural land to the army personnel, the size depending upon rank. This sense of superiority even amongst the JCOs (Junior Commissioned Officers) and NCOs (Non Commissioned Officers) was palpable as they had greater tracts of land as compared to their fellow peasants, the class they had come from. Hence there was also a material aspect to the loyalty during military service. And this was not of secondary importance. The officer caste during British rule, almost all came from the families of the landed aristocracy. Hence the larger tracts of land awarded to the officer caste added to the already large estates of the rural gentry.

In fact feudalism on the Indian subcontinent was itself introduced by the British Raj to accentuate its hold and perpetuate its rule. It began in Bengal when Lord Palmerston presented the 'Permanent Settlements Act' in the Bengal Assembly in 1793. This was to create a new class of landlords which would be obliged, and hence subservient, to the Raj. Bengal being the vanguard of the resistance against the Raj, had to be tackled first. This class of new feudal lords was used to exploit, contain and repress the peasantry that rose in several revolts against the British. A religious content was also intermingled in creating this aristocracy and it, to some extent, coincided with the class interests created by this policy.

After the creation of Pakistan, the structures of the armed forces continued to exist and function as before. Even before the 1958 coup, the army elite continued to get these land allocations under each and every civilian government. After the beginning of direct military rule under Ayub Khan, apart from the intervention in the ownership of land in the agrarian rural sector, the army officers were inducted into state institutions running industry, finance, commerce, construction and other sectors. Military officers started buying stocks and shares and a few became industrial entrepreneurs. But these were the exception rather than the norm. The majority of the retired middle and high-ranking officers were given high salaried jobs in running state enterprises and other civilian institutions. Although the army treaded to some extent into the economy and finance capital, this was quite limited. Still the main discipline and cohesion of the army as a fighting force was there with certain levels of nationalist fervour remaining. The chain of command inherited from the British was still very much functioning.

British imperialism had developed its military tactics during its long experience of colonial and intra-imperialist wars. The British sergeants and drillmasters had terrible reputations. They were abusive, insulting, arrogant and ruthless towards the soldiers and even the newly commissioned officers who were supposed to be commanding them after graduating from the military academies. Those sergeants that had the worst reputation for their ruthlessness were considered the best. This was essential from the point of view of the British masters to build a strong disciplined army.

In all the old cities of the subcontinent there are two parts and two railway stations. One is the city and the other is the cantonment. The military barracks, exercises and installations were in the cantonment areas, totally cordoned off and secluded from the city populations. Most soldiers and young officers were strictly banned from leaving their quarters and going out of the cantonment perimeter. They needed a special night pass from the sergeants to go out and come in. There was very severe punishment for breaking this code of discipline. The punishment ranged from quarter guards, the lightest, to a court martial which was for acts like murder and treason. The disgrace was such that its scars stayed for life. These practices continued in the Indian and Pakistan armies as the law and structures remained the same as practised and devised by the British.

During wartime these acts and punishment were enhanced and magnified. However, with the semi-Americanization and Islamization of the Pakistan army, and the rapidly increasing involvement of the army in businesses, private enterprise encroached on the cantonments. Real estate business has flourished here because the cantonments were built in the best areas of the cities, with better approaches, better roads and infrastructure, etc. This has been an important factor in the erosion of the discipline of the bourgeois army in Pakistan. But war also had the effect of breaking these codes and disciplines. Especially in defeat, revolts were imminent. After the defeat of the Pakistan army in the 1971 war, there was a big revolt against the red tape and the officer estate. Bhutto could easily remove the top 13 generals that would not have been possible in any other period. But that is all that he did. If he had implemented the clause of the 1970 PPP manifesto of dissolving the standing army and building a "people's militia" as an alternative for defence he could have done it. It was the preservation of the structures of the bourgeois state that ultimately led to his own demise.

This was in spite of the fact that from the 1950s advanced military training had started to shift from the British to the institutions in the United States like Fort Brag, Detroit, etc. During the 17-day 1965 war with India, the defeat was not so heavy and the state media was able to portray it as a victory. The other conflicts and the chronic issue of Kashmir left behind by British imperialism were continuously exploited and abused by the establishment and the official media. These conflicts were used to justify the hefty defence budgets and continuous rise in military spending. The main reason for the military spending advocated and propagated by the imperialists, ruling classes, the establishment and the chauvinist intelligentsia and media, was to prepare the armed forces more to curb internal dissent rather than to fight external wars. The performance of the Pakistani army in the two major wars of 1967 and 1971 speaks volumes about its combat capabilities on the foreign fronts.

But it was under Zia's despotic regime that the character and role of the Pakistan army went through a drastic change. US imperialism, being the biggest sponsor of Islamic fundamentalism and religious terrorism, at that time fully backed the Islamization of the Pakistan army by Zia-ul-Haq. Although it was hypocritical and contradictory, with the help of forces like the Israeli Mossad intelligence agency and other Western institutions involved in changing the ideological cause and basis of the Pakistan army, it could not have been otherwise.

The main venture in which the Pakistan army was involved was the largest ever covert operation unleashed against the Left-wing government in Afghanistan. This jihad which carried out some of the most brutal acts of terrorism, also involved huge amounts of dollars in aid. Initially this money came in from the generous coffers of the Saudi monarchy and American right wing, the Jewish lobby and the US Treasury itself. But soon the CIA set up advanced laboratories and techniques for refining high quality heroine from the poppy grown in the wastelands of war in Afghanistan and the areas along the 1,500 km-long Pak–Afghan border that had no or nominal state control over the tribes and the mountainous terrain.

High-ranking officers of the Pakistan army and intelligence agencies were involved in this CIA-sponsored operation but were actually carrying out most of its practical execution on the ground. They entered into this fray of squandering huge amounts of money generated from this drug trade set up by the CIA to finance the Afghan Jihad. Zia-ul-Haq's overtures to the Indians in the east and his bending over backwards to maintain peace with the traditional Hindu 'enemy' were designed only to continue the Jihad and plunder in Afghanistan. In his book on Taliban, Ahmed Rashid gives a detailed account of this crime-infested jihad and involvement of Pakistan army officers in the drug trade.

> An immense narcotics trade had developed under the legitimizing umbrella of the CIA-ISI covert supply line to the Afghan *Mujaheddin.* 'During the 1980s corruption, covert operations and narcotics became intertwined in a manner which makes it difficult to separate Pakistan's narcotics traffic from more complex questions of regional security and insurgent warfare,' said a landmark 1992 study on the failure of US narcotics policy. As in Vietnam where the CIA chose to ignore the trade in drugs by anti-communist guerrillas whom the CIA was financing, so in Afghanistan the US chose to ignore the growing collusion between the Mujaheddin, Pakistani drugs traffickers and elements in the military.
>
> Instances of this collusion that did come to light in the 1980s were only the tip of the iceberg. In 1983 the ISI chief, General Akhtar Abdur Rehman had to remove the entire ISI staff in Quetta, because of their involvement with the drugs trade and sale of CIA supplied weapons that were meant for the *Mujaheddin*. In 1986, Major Zahooruddin Afridi was caught while driving to Karachi from Peshawar with 220 kilograms of high grade heroin—the largest drugs interception in Pakistan's history. Two months later an air force officer Flight Lieutenant Khalilur Rehman was caught on the same route with another 220 kilograms of heroin. He calmly confessed that it was his fifth mission. The US street value of just these two caches was US $600 million, equivalent to the total amount of US aid to Pakistan that year. Both officers were held in Karachi until they mysteriously escaped from jail. 'The Afridi-Rehman cases pointed to a heroin syndicate within the army and the ISI linked to Afghanistan,' wrote Lawrence Lifschultz.
>
> The US Drugs Enforcement Administration (DEA) had 17 full time officers in Pakistan during the 1980s, who identified 40 major heroin syndicates, including some headed by top government officials. Not a single syndicate was broken up during that decade. There was clearly a conflict of interest between the CIA which wanted no embarrassing disclosures about drug links between the 'heroic' Mujaheddin and Pakistan officials and traffickers and the DEA. Several DEA officials asked to be relocated and at least one resigned, because the CIA refused to allow them to carry out their duties (...)

> (...) The CIA-ISI bribes that were paid off to the Pashtun chiefs to allow weapons convoys through their tribal areas, soon involved the same tribal chiefs allowing heroin runs along the same routes back to Pakistan. The National Logistics Cell, an army run trucking company which transported CIA weapons from Karachi port to Peshawar and Quetta was frequently used by well connected dealers to transport heroin back to Karachi for export. The heroin pipeline in the 1980s could not have operated without the knowledge, if not connivance, of officials at the highest level of the army, the government and the CIA. Everyone chose to ignore it for the larger task that was to defeat the Soviet Union. Drugs control was on nobody's agenda.[1]

In this orgy of destruction and loot Zia and his coterie of generals amassed huge amounts of black money. But the military generals under Zia, in spite of the army being put on the ideological foundations of radical Islam with US patronage, were not content with the black capital coming from the drugs trade. They had to share this drug money with the different warlords, constantly changing loyalties, and the leaders of different Islamic fundamentalist parties and Islamic mercenary outfits involved in this reactionary insurgency. Hence, they also started smuggling the most advanced US weaponry for the jihad through the Pakistani supply lines under the auspices of the sections of the Pakistan army involved in this CIA-planned operation.

They stored and smuggled large stockpiles of this ammunition and weaponry to the various jihad groups in other regions. These Islamists smuggled them onwards with even greater profit margins. The Americans were shocked to discover this corruption when US helicopters were fired upon by US-made advanced sophisticated Stinger missiles by the Iranian Islamic Revolutionary Guards in the Persian Gulf in the mid-1980s. When the plane carrying a US investigation team entered Pakistani air space in 1988, the largest ammunition dump in Pakistan, Ojri camp near Rawalpindi, where most of the US weaponry for the Afghan Jihad had been stored, was ignited. Thousands of rockets exploded and went in different directions. Hundreds were killed, thousands injured and hundreds of dwellings, mostly in Rawalpindi but some also in Islamabad, were destroyed. Those who were responsible for this 'accident' have never been apprehended, not even by the Americans. How could they have been?

This massive influx of black capital plundered from the Afghan Jihad meteorically raised the stakes of the top military brass in the economy, industry and the services sector. The old officers, who had been allocated land holdings in the past, became financial pygmies in comparison with the officer caste that had filled their coffers with the black money from the Afghan Jihad. They became senior partners with the civilian entrepreneurs in the various business enterprises in Pakistan. Their ownership and stakes in the country's overall economy grew rapidly.

Apart from the Afghan Jihad, the other main military enterprise, through which the officials involved made huge fortunes, was Pakistan's nuclear programme. Although the Americans knew the details all along it is only now, mainly due to their growing conflict with Iran, that they are making a fuss about proliferation. Massive monetary gains were made by Pakistani military and semi-military elite officers through the proliferation of this programme. But even before that, successive civilian and military regimes spent astronomical amounts from the treasury of a country with an impoverished and destitute population. It is really a tragedy for these teeming millions forced to live in terrible conditions, while their so-called political leaders and dominant political parties all have been fully protecting and supporting this madness of trying to be a nuclear power.

In the past it was the State, chauvinist leaders and the media that propagated the idea that the atom bomb would be a source of "formidable defence" of the "nation", and that this would drastically reduce the spending on the army and conventional military hardware. However, after the detonation of the nuclear devices in May 1998 at Chagai, Baluchistan, the expenditure on conventional weaponry and the armed forces has risen astronomically. Not just the military regimes but the civilian 'democratic' governments have also upped even more, this wasteful expenditure on this scrap for human destruction. In the last couple of years it seems that instead of the atom bombs defending them the whole nation is being asked to protect the atom bombs! Thousands of troops have been deployed and most advanced anti-war missiles have been installed around the nuclear installations to protect them being attacked from US or Indian or Israeli forces, or their being stolen by the fundamentalist *Jihadis* or other terrorist outfits.

The initial money-laundering of black capital amassed mainly by the military elite, was carried out by the notorious BCCI (Bank of Credit and Commerce International). There was even a shady CIA involvement in setting up this bank. Some of the most notorious swindlers involved in various bank scandals were involved in organizing this money-laundering racket. However, it was the criminal charges levelled against most of its high officials that exposed the whole fraudulent process and led to the winding up of this bank. But ever since there have been several other individuals and companies involved in this sinister game, mainly diverting this capital into real estate, construction, manufacturing, stock exchange, services, electronic and print media and several other sectors of the economy. A huge portion of this black economy exists in Pakistan and the Gulf cities, mainly Dubai. This is the financial basis of the Taliban and other fundamentalist organizations.

The most important aspect of this financial involvement of the top military brass, over some decades now, has been the formation and consolidation of an 'evil nexus' of military generals, Supreme and High Court judges, top lawyers, senior civilian bureaucrats, rich mullahs, senior former diplomats, top businessmen, entrepreneurs, the landed aristocracy and of course the media tycoons.

There are several layers of this nexus which externally can be seen in the form of top players of the so-called 'civil society'. And this evil nexus rules over Pakistan whatever the political structure of the regime in power. It is this nexus that controls the military, the state and all major political parties of the country. During the Musharraf period this nexus further consolidated itself and expanded its wealth. But all this has also given rise to greater contradictions within this nexus and they are now exploding in different forms and they are at each others' throats in their lust for plunder.

But, as we saw in the last months of 2007, whenever there is a threat from the masses the nexus rapidly reconciles. This nexus is all about loot and money. It is dominated by the army and America. They need the army to protect their loot and exploitation and US imperialism to allow them to be their commission agents in the much wider range of capital generation through the exploitation of labour and speculation of finance capital.

However, very frequently the contradictions within this nexus erupt into open conflicts. Sometimes they take the form of conflicts between different institutions of the state itself. In other cases their conflicts take the form of issues related only to their vested interests that clash due to the worsening crisis of Pakistani capitalism.

Hence, without understanding the complexities of this ruling nexus it is very difficult to define real issues, genuine movements with honest motives behind political manoeuvrings. However, this massive influx of finance capital into the upper structures of the armed forces has had the effect of aggravating the contradictions within these institutions.

To understand the real role of the army and to develop its perspectives it is necessary to understand the character of the period in which we are attempting to analyze the phenomenon. Secondly, it is also important to understand the class content within the army itself. The character of the army changes in the different conditions through which society is moving at any particular moment in time.

In normal conditions the army acts as a cohesive institution to carry out the dictates of the ruling class and protects their interests with all forms of brutality inflicted upon the working classes. This cohesion of the army, apart from other factors, is maintained through tradition, routine and involuntary enforced discipline. However, these factors only play a role in normal conditions, which are often prolonged in history.

In the last analysis the army comes from society itself and is the reflection of society. In these conditions it is not just the army but society as a whole that remains dormant, subdued and in a state of relative lull. The burden of tradition, the force of religion, the manipulation of the media, the school system, the syllabus, the dominating philosophies, intelligentsia, politics, etc., all impose the culture, habits, consciousness, and psychology of the ruling class upon society and with it the reluctant acceptance of class oppression and subordination.

It is not just through the state, the army and the police that the ruling classes maintain their domination. Repression is only used by the ruling class when other methods of mass subjugation fail to keep their control over society. History is witness to the fact that these 'normal' conditions don't prevail forever. Often historical events shake mass consciousness so suddenly, that they dramatically change the whole situation. This gives rise to movements and mass uprisings that can often attain revolutionary proportions.

Such pre-revolutionary and revolutionary situations in society do infect the armed forces. Although the army is the last institution to join the revolution, when the class contradictions within the army sharpen and explode, the soldiers, lower ranks and young junior officers enter the revolutionary fray of the mass movement. This is a decisive phase in any revolution. From here onwards, in the presence of a Marxist party and a genuine revolutionary leadership, the task of socialist revolution races towards a victory.

In Pakistan we have striking examples of the revolutionary impact of the 1968-9 movement within the army. There was enormous ferment in the barracks. The restive mood amongst the soldiers was beginning to affect the officers. As the main target of the movement was made to be Field Marshal Ayub Khan, even his loyal generals were showing open dissent. In early 1969 the British and American diplomats sent messages to Washington and London that young officers could carry out a military coup with a socialist doctrine if the situation were not retrieved. The army had refused to impose Martial Law if Ayub retained the presidency. General Yahya Khan, the commander-in-chief, Ayub's close buddy, explained this reality to him in so many words.

Since 1958 the social background of the younger officers had changed. Industrial growth under Ayub had had a big social impact. Not only a large virgin proletariat had developed, but young people from a lower middle class background had joined the officer ranks of the army. The soldiers and these young officers were radicalized by the revolutionary mood of the workers and students in the cities. In the 1970 elections, which the PPP was contesting on a socialist programme, the vast majority of the electoral ballots from the barracks were cast for the PPP candidates. Such was the intensity of the threat of revolt from within the army and its cleavage along class lines that it became an important factor in the decision to wage the 1971 war with India. Thus, they opened up the Western front to stave off this revolutionary wave that was threatening to overthrow capitalism through a socialist revolution.

However, due to the ebbing of the revolution, the failure of reformism under Bhutto again strengthened the control of the generals over the army. In the 1980s, with the collapse of the Soviet Union, the betrayal of the Chinese Stalinists and the disastrous decline of the Pakistani Left, reaction started to dominate society. Religion and fundamentalism filled the vacuum of the Left in decline. Zia-ul-Haq prolonged his treachery and tyranny through them.

However, once the movement erupts in the coming period it is bound to affect the consciousness within the army once more. There are reports that there is a burning hatred amongst the ranks of the army against the top brass amassing this mammoth wealth. Their perks, their privileges and their plunder have rekindled class hatred amongst the soldiers towards the officer caste.

The lower ranking officers are also in a desperate psychological state. The war being fought for US imperialism has led to a rapid rise in the number of desertions within the army. Morale is very low and it is not an accident that the Pakistani military outfits are losing their battles in the tribal areas. It is for these reasons that General Kayani has given wage rises and other privileges to the lower ranks and soldiers. They are rapidly withdrawing army officers from civilian posts where a lot of them had been deployed during the Musharraf regime.

The present set-up is unraveling at a rapid pace. The

Musharraf regime has been replaced by a civil-military hybrid which lacks the willingness and/or the ability to take on the threat posed by extremism and militancy. The fact is that the civilian government and the country's military establishment appear to be losing control of the situation.

By opting to negotiate with the *jihadis* from a position of weakness, the Pakistani authorities are inadvertently sending a message to every armed non-state actor of any worth in the country that all the *jihadis* have to do to make the government more pliable is use their weapons. This signal has led to the spread of the Taliban in Pakistan. Any pause in militancy is not because the state has succeeded in containing the insurgency; rather, it is because the *jihadis* have made a tactical decision to pause in keeping with their strategy. While the *jihadis* are brimming with confidence, judging from the way Islamabad is randomly oscillating between negotiations and military operations, the government does not appear to have a discernable policy for dealing with this situation.

The problem is actually far larger than an intelligence failure. There are different bases of contradictions within the Pakistan army. They are between the nationalist and religious sections, fundamentalist and liberal elements and pro-China and pro-American officers. But the fundamental and the most decisive contradiction is the class contradiction. The poor soldiers and ranks have a seething hatred towards the top brass who have become billionaires as their women flaunt and exhibit this wealth with a repugnant vulgarity.

There always is a revolutionary side to the army. In the Bolshevik Revolution of 1917, led by Lenin and Trotsky, the soldiers' soviets in the regiments and barracks played a decisive role in the revolutionary insurrection that led to its victory. There has never been a revolution in which the soldiers and ranks did not play an important role. Even in the subcontinent the first introduction to Bolshevism and communism was brought by the soldiers of the British Indian Army who were sent to annihilate the October revolution. Paradoxically they were the ones who brought the message of revolutionary Marxism on their return home to their native towns and villages in the Indian subcontinent. This was an important factor that laid the foundations of the communist movement in the South Asian Subcontinent.

In the coming revolutionary epoch, a mass movement will surpass the scale and intensity of that of 1968-9 in Pakistan, and so will the response from within the army itself. In the last 40 years the class contradictions have sharpened rather than diminished, and they will explode with a greater resonance and force. However, this time there should be and there shall be a Marxist organization and leadership to organize the workers, youth, poor peasants, other oppressed sections of society, and of course the soldiers and young officers, into a revolutionary movement and party to carry out the tasks of the socialist transformation of society. In such a situation no force on the planet will be able to hinder or stop the overthrow of this rotten capitalist system through the victory of a revolutionary insurrection.

NOTES

1. Ahmed Rashid, *Taliban, Islam, Oil and The New Great Game in Central Asia,* 2000, I.B Tauris, pp. 120, 121.

Appendix II

PAKISTAN'S RICHEST LIST OF 2007

Short-listing Pakistan's most influential business magnates or groups has never been an easy task because there are the people who have been very powerful in nearly every regime that has held this country's reins since the last 60 years and then we have had those seasonal species that manoeuvred their voice to be heard better than most within the power corridors, but later vanished into the oblivion for one reason or the other. We have selected only those tycoons who have made their presence felt for a better part of country's history, have earned consistently, have been setting up units at regular intervals or have been legends in stocks, currency or real estate business.

The list excludes many names that have previously qualified and all of Pakistan's most prominent feudal landlords who would definitely make it to the top 10, except the few land owners which have declared their assets and workforce and registered with the CBR Islamabad. In order to promote the new and 'unknown' Pakistani magnates we have excluded previous entities.

Unfortunately, our extensive research does not currently include the names of a few stars that shone brightly amidst the galaxy of the influential creed of yesteryear like C.M. Latif of BECO—the Steel Man of Pakistan—who did make a name once, but then got gifted with contentment somehow, although the late business wizard got very badly hit by Bhutto's nationalization of 1970 which had inflicted an astounding thud to everybody in business then. Had it not been the case, many of our tycoons may well have managed to gain the kind of status greeting the likes of Birlas and Tatas in India today, if not the one saluting Bill Gates or Warren Buffet. Among these gifted individuals, you will find politicians-turned-businessmen, businessmen-turned-politicians or even the businessmen-cum-politicians. With malice towards none and with no intention to decorate somebody, we thus take the pride of announcing these names. We hope this document will go a long way in serving as the most authentic endeavour of its kind for a very long time to come. It has been prepared very carefully in consultation with leading real estate barons, stock moguls, business leaders of virtue and senior bureaucrats at the Central Board of Revenue.

1. Mian Muhammad Mansha Yaha, Pakistan

Ranking: 1 Worth: £1.25b ($2.5 billion) Industry: Businessman

Mansha has around 40 companies on board. Mansha, who owns the Muslim Commercial Bank is also setting up a $17m paper mill. He is one of the richest Pakistanis around. Nishat Group was the country's 15th richest family in 1970, 6th in 1990 and Number 1 in 1997. Mansha is on the board of nearly 50 companies. He is deemed to have made investments in many bourses, currency and metal exchanges both within and outside Pakistan. He could have bought the United Bank too, but then who doesn't have adversaries. Nishat Group comprises textiles, cement, leasing, insurance and management companies. If Mansha was bitten by Bhutto's nationalization stint of 1970, his friends think he was compensated by Nawaz Sharif's denationalization programme to a very good effect. There is no stopping Mansha and he is still on the move.

Nishat Group assets are $4.4 billion. He is sometimes regarded as the richest Pakistani around by his friends claiming he does not "show it off".

2. Asif Ali Zardari, Pakistan

Ranking: 2 Worth: £900 m ($1.8 billion) Industry: Politics

Asif Zardari dubbed 'Mr. 10%' an unknown happy-go-lucky son of a small-time businessman who struck gold by marrying one of the world's most glamorous women, former Prime Minister of Pakistan Benzair Bhutto. Taking advantage of his wife's authority he is known to have taken kickbacks from many deals inside and outside of Pakistan. The most famous was a $4 billion deal to buy 32 Mirage jets from the French company Dassault. Documents, which include letters from Dassault executives, indicate an agreement was reached to pay a 5 per cent 'remuneration'—about $200 m to Marleton Business, a BVI company controlled by Zardari. Besides these many more kickback deals were taken with companies such as ARY Gold, Société Général de Surveillance (SGS), Cotecna, and ZPC Ursus, a Polish tractor company.

Zardari's assets holding amounts to hundreds of millions of dollars easily, having eight prime properties in the UK, of which one is the famous Rockwood Estate, 365 acres in Surrey, worth £4.35 m has now been sold and money sent back to the Govt. of Pakistan. Also 14 multi-million dollar mansions in the USA, including owning Holiday Inn hotel Houston, Texas owned by 'Mr. 10%' and Iqbal Memon and Sadar-ud-Din Hashwani.

He also has huge business ventures in the Middle East running into hundreds of millions if not billions. Mr Zardari also has huge stakes in sugar mills all over Pakistan, which include: Sakrand Sugar Mills, Nawabshah, Ansari Sugar Mills, Hyderabad, Mirza Sugar Mills, Badin, Pangrio Sugar Mills, Thatta and Bachani Sugar Mills, Sanghar.

3. Sir Anwar Pervaiz, UK

Ranking: 3 Worth: £750 m ($1.5 billion) Industry: Businessman

Chairman of Bestway Group. The Bestway Group started in 1976 when its first Bestway cash and carry warehouse opened in London. Today they have in total around 50 Cash and Carrys' including their recent takeover of rival group Batleys for around £100 m. Bestway Group ventured into Pakistan's huge cement business in 1995 and set up a cement manufacturing plant in Pakistan at a cost of $120 million.

Taking advantage of Pakistan's growing economy they also acquired a 25.5 per cent stake in United Bank Limited in 2002. Today, the Bestway Group has interests in cash and carry wholesale, property investments, retail outlets, milling of rice, lentils and pulses, cement production and more recently into banking. The group's total sales amounted to in excess of £2 billion.

4. Nawaz Sharif and Shahbaz Sharif family, Saudi Arabia/ Pakistan

Ranking: 4 Worth: £700 m ($1.4 billion) Industry: Politics/ Business

Mr Sharif, businessman-turned-politician, the former Prime Minister of Pakistan. He was ousted in a military coup in 1999 and was forced to forfeit $9 million and some of his assets including his $5 m mansion in Raiwind near Lahore. Before becoming PM he was a major shareholder along with his brother and cousins of Ittefaq Group, having assets well in excess of £50m in the 1990s. However he got richer when he took commissions from foreign companies for construction in Pakistan. He built the first motorway and many new roads and took heavy kickbacks. He then also stole $100 m from the Iqra funds, he started a new scheme 'Ghar Apna' in which he again looted around $40 m, the 'Mulk sawaaro' scheme involving public and government money collections to help pay off Pakistan's debts also was pocketed. Today he lives in exile in Saudi Arabia where it is known he has a new huge business empire in various sectors.

5. Saddaruddin Hashwani, Pakistan

Ranking: 5 Worth: £550 m ($1.1 billion) Industry: Businessman

Saddaruddin Hashwani, Chairman Hashoo Group is known for his dominance in Pakistan's hotel industry, though Hashwanis have huge strength in real estate business too. Hashwanis are involved in trading of cotton, grain and steel and till the nationalization of cotton export in 1974, they were widely being dubbed as the Cotton Kings of Pakistan. Today, this group has excelled in export of rice, wheat, cotton and barley. It owns textile units, besides having invested billions in mines, minerals, hotels, insurance, batteries, tobacco, residential properties, construction, engineering and information technology. In 1984, Hashwani defeated the Lakhanis in the bid for Premier Tobacco but was arrested along with his brother

Akbar in 1986 for allegedly evading customs duty on cigarettes. Sadarduddin's brother Akbar and the children of another late brother Hassan Ali Hashwani together manage around 45 companies. Akbar runs the second Hashwani Group. He is one of the most well-known magnates in Pakistan who is a regular invitee at the Diplomatic Enclave. The list of local and international bigwigs known personally to Hashwani is unending.

6. Nasir Schon and family, U.A.E/Pakistan

Ranking: 6 (tied at 6) Worth: £500 m ($1 billion) Industry: Businessman

Nasir Schon is a prominent business leader of Pakistan and the CEO of Schon Group. Nasir Schon is the son of Captain Ather Schon Hussain, an ex-pilot of PIA. The Schon family is one of the few striving Muhajir Urdu business families in Pakistan. Starting off in Singapore in 1982, the peak of Schon group was in 1995 when they owned National Fibres, Schon Bank, Schon Textiles and Pak-China Fertizilers. Famous for the trend-setting roundabout, Schon Circle, Nasir Schon is also known to be one of the first people to have a Rolls-Royce in Pakistan. Directors of Schon group flew to Dubai in 1997 in exile after the dismissal of ex-Prime Minister Benazir Bhutto. The directors of Schon group were known to have close contacts with the husband of the former Prime Minister, Asif Zardari. Many assets of the Schon group were auctioned by the Nawaz Sharif government. Schon Group is the only group in Pakistan who has paid the government over 3 billion rupees ($65 m) in order to return from exile. Living in Dubai gave Nasir Schon an opportunity to start businesses there. Currently working on an $830 million real estate project known as Dubai Lagoon, Schon group is also fighting to get back the assets they once lost. Currently, the Schon group operates a pilot training centre in Pakistan known as Schon Air.

7. Abdul Razzaq Yakoub and family, U.A.E

Ranking: 6 (tied at 6) Worth: £500 m ($1 billion) Industry: Businessman

Mr Yakoub is a prominent Pakistani expatriate businessman based in Dubai. He is the president of ARY group ($1.5 billion turnover) and World Memon Organization (WMO). He is one of Pakistan's biggest media barons controlling around 7 channels. Besides this he has a huge property holdings in Karachi, Islamabad and Dubai amounting to over $200 m. He is a major player in the gold market also having around 20 outlets in Asia. He has also been involved in paying Asif Zardari $5 m in the 1990s for allowing him to import/export gold, which he denies and claims is government forgeries.

8. Rafiq Habib and Rasheed Habib, Pakistan

Ranking: 7 Worth: £450 m ($900 m) Industry: Businessman

Legend has it that the Goddess of Wealth has been in love with the seasoned Habibs more than anybody else in Pakistan. Most pundits believe that Habibs own at least 100 companies throughout the world, but these content mega-tycoons never boast, something which has made it an uphill task for most to asses their financial standing. This industrial group was founded by Seth Habib Mitha, born in 1878 to Esmail Ali—a factory owner in Bombay. The financial strength of the Habibs can be gauged from the fact that Muhammad Ali Habib gave a cheque of Rs. 80 million to Quaid-e-Azam in 1948 at a time when Pakistan government was penniless owing to delay in transfer of Pakistan's share of Rs. 750 million by the Reserve Bank of India. They had offices in Europe in 1912. They incorporated the Habib Bank in 1941. They own the Habib Bank A.G Zurich, Bank Al-Habib, Indus Motors assembling Corolla cars and many dozens of units in sectors such as jute, paper sack, minerals, steel, tiles, synthetics sugar, glass, construction, concrete, farm autos, banking, oil, computers, music, paper, packages, leasing and capital management. Habibs today are headed by Rafiq Habib and Rashid Habib in two distinct groups. What makes them extremely influential players of all time is the fact that for dozens of top businessmen today, Habibs were a legend once.

9. Tariq Saigol and Nasim Saigol, Pakistan

Ranking: 8 Worth: £425 m ($850 m) Industry: Businessman

Hailing from Jhelum. The pioneer of the Saigol dynasty in 1890 was Amin Saigol who established a shoe shop that eventually transformed into Kohinoor Rubber Works. And then times saw them shining literally like the Kohinoor until their progress was halted by Nationalization in which they lost two-thirds of their wealth. Saigols got trifurcated in 1976 and 15 descendants of Amin Saigol's four sons got a share. The name of the Saigols has been used in this part of the world as similes describing quantum of wealth. Yousaf Saigol, along with his brothers Sayeed Saigol, Bashir Saigol and Gul Saigol then nourished an excellent crop. In 1948, Saigols established the Kohinoor Textile Mills at a cost of Rs. 8 million and this group happens to be the first to open an LC with the State Bank of Pakistan. They bought the United Bank in 1959 and then saw five of their units nationalized. They lived in Saudi Arabia during the Bhutto regime. Today, cousins Tariq and Nasim hold the family's fort together and have risen to unprecedented heights in individual capacities. The NAB did haunt Nasim but Tariq spent more time either accepting or refusing prized slots everywhere. Tariq is the one of the finest business brains around.

10. Dewan Yousaf Farooqui, Pakistan

Ranking: 9 (tied at 9) Worth: £400m ($800 m) Industry: Businessman

Mr Farooqui, the mentor of this group has been the Sindh Minister for Local Bodies and Industries, Labour, Transport, Mines & Minerals. The Dewan Mushtaq Group is one of the Pakistan's largest industrial conglomerates in sectors like polyester acrylic fibre, manufacturing and automotives. Six of their companies are listed at the Karachi Stock Exchange and one at the Luxembourg bourse. Dewan Farooqui Motors assembles around 10,0000 cars annually under technical licence agreement with Hyundai and Kia Motors of Korea. The Dewan Salman Fiber is the pride of this empire as it ranks 11th in the world in total production capacity. The group owns three textile units, a motorcycle manufacturing concern and the largest sugar unit in the country. Dewans also have business interests in India. They possess dozens of millions of shares of Saudi Cement and

Pak land Cement. They also have the franchise licence for BMW in Pakistan and now Rolls Royce showrooms.

11. Sultan Ali Lakhani and family, Pakistan

Ranking: 9 (tied at 9) Worth: £400 m ($800 m) Industry: Businessman

The Lakhanis are currently having a hard time at the hands of NAB. Sultan Lakhani and his three brothers run this prestigious group and the chain of McDonald's restaurants in Pakistan. The NAB has accused the Lakhanis of having created phoney companies through worthless directors and raised massive loans from various banks and financial institutions. Sultan is currently abroad after having served a jail term with younger sibling Amin, though the latter was released much earlier. The NAB had reportedly demanded Rs. 7 billion from Lakhanis, but later agreed they pay only Rs. 1.5 billion over a 10-year period. Lakhanis, like their arch-rivals Hashwanis, are the most well-known of all Ismaili tycoons. Their stakes range from media, tobacco, paper, chemicals and surgical equipments to cotton, packaging, insurance, detergents and other household items, many of which are joint ventures with leading international conglomerates. Though Lakhanis are in turbulent waters currently, their success during the last 25 years especially has been tremendous. They have rifts with large business empires despite being known for their genteel nature. Whichever the government in Sindh or at the Federal level, Lakhanis have had trusted friends everywhere, though the present era has proved a painful exception.

12. Malik Riaz Hussain, Pakistan

Ranking: 9 (tied at 9) Worth: £400 m ($800 m) Industry: Businessman

Malik Riaz Hussain heads the massive project which is currently developing state-of-the-art schemes in Lahore, Karachi and Rawalpindi/Islamabad. Emerging out of the blue, this developer has reportedly developed tremendous connections where it matters in Pakistan—one of the few reasons why his constructed projects get completed in time without hindrance.

Whether he has gifted bungalows free of cost to the country's bigwigs or offered them at highly concessional rates, the reality on the ground is that Malik has managed to mesmerize most through his generous wallet. His land-holding both within and outside Pakistan amount to nearly a billion dollar. He is the man behind the Bahria Town. Irrespective of who is in power, he continues to build house after house swelling his wealth. He is also the first man to drive a Bentley car on Pakistani soil.

13. Sheikh Abid Hussain alias Seth Abid, Pakistan

Ranking: 10 Worth: £390 m ($780 m) Industry: Businessman

Sheikh Abid Hussain alias Seth Abid is one of the most resourceful developers/builders in the country owning vast stretches of land in major cities. On this land worth many billion of rupees, Seth has constructed residential schemes under the brand name of 'Green Fort'. Seth came into this business after decades of notoriety as being one of the spearheads in cross-border smuggling. While many remember Seth for his allegedly illegal trading stints, a lot of informed circles still say with conviction that he, along with Dr. Qadeer and former Premier Bhutto, was the brain behind the success of Pakistan's nuclear programme. About three dozen of Seth's very close relatives, friends and nephews are members of the country's bourses and for many years now, the Seth Abid group assumes the role of king-makers during the annual polls of these stock exchanges. He is a leading investor in stocks, metals and currency but what gives him immense pleasure is his philanthropic institution Hamza Foundation that he sponsors for the welfare of deaf and dumb children. Pakistan has not had a single ruler, politician, bureaucrat or army general who doesn't know the Seth who is a legend. Seth, throughout his life, has avoided publicity—a fact known to most journalists.

14. Mian Mohammad Latif, Pakistan

Ranking: 11 Worth: £350 m ($700 m) Industry: Businessman

Mian Muhammad Latif supervises the Chenab Group along with his brother Mian Ashfaque—a legislator in the National Assembly of Pakistan. Founded in 1975, Chenab Limited set up its first fashion outlet 'Chen One'. Chen One has seven outlets throughout Pakistan. After establishing its retail chain stores in various cities of Saudi Arabia, the group is now planning to establish its new retail chains in Bahrain, UA.E, Qatar, Kuwait and Central Asian Republics. While Chenab Group is an eight-time Export Trophy winner, its Chief Mian Latif has won the 'Businessman of the Year award' on four different occasions from various business bodies. Chenab is principally engaged in manufacture and distribution of clothing, furniture goods, including non-iron suit, quilt cover and curtains, etc. Chenab processes 50 million square metres fabric weaving and 75 million square metres fabric dyeing every year and has established a global sales network spanning five continents. Chenab is licensed to Swedish Texcote Technology in the manufacturing and sale of textile materials, garments and textile house-hold goods. The group's textile products have been awarded the Oekotex 100 accreditation.

15. Haji Abdul Ghafoor and Haji Bashir Ahmed, Pakistan

Ranking: 12 Worth: £330 m ($660 m) Industry: Businessman

The Sitara Group started its activity with textile weaving as early as 1956, under brothers Haji Abdul Ghafoor and Haji Bashir Ahmed. It is now in textile cloth finishing and processing, textile spinning, chlor-alkali sector and in power generation. The units owned by this establishment include Sitara Chemicals, Sitara Chemicals (Textile Division 1) and Sitara Chemicals (Textile Division 11), Sitara Textiles, Sitara Energy and Yasir Spinning. The charities being managed under the aegis of Sitara group are Aziz Fatima Hospital, Ghafoor Bashir Children's Hospital and Aziz Fatima Girls School. Sitara's name with the industrial city of Faisalabad is synonymous. They are the decades-old veterans in business, who have excelled by leaps and bounds. At their units, the owners of Sitara use technology imported from Japan, the UK and Germany and are export leaders in bedding and fabric collection to South America, the USA, Canada, New Zealand and Europe. Their textile divisions together operate at the strength of 33,984 spindles. The Sitara Group, to a common man, is more famous for its lawn brands like Sitara Sapna and Mughal-e-Azam. The men at the helm of affairs in Sitara hardly believe in setting up dozens of units, of which they are otherwise very much capable.

16. Sheikhani Family, Pakistan

Ranking: 13 Worth: £300 m ($600 m) Industry: Businessman

They are one of the most reputed land developers in the country. The Sheikhanis are led by Abu Bakar Sheikhani. The Sheikhanis are famous for their construction and land development. Abu Bakar is deemed to be one of the largest investors in real estate trade at Gwadar Port. He has all the right connections that are required to be in such business. Despite being well known to the national political circles, the man in the street came to know more of him during March/April 1991 when he surfaced as the single largest contributor to then Premier Nawaz Sharif's Debt Retirement Fund with a donation of $8 million. Today, his adversaries dub him a land mafia man, accusing him of selling his Gwadar land at only $4000 per acre only to senior army officials while the same was being sold at $2,50,000 per acre to ordinary investors. But that is the way Sheikhani runs his vast land/construction empire. Accusations don't disturb Sheikhani, who according to many large developers is a man who has managed to create tremendous impact in the land business. The rumours of his landing in any Pakistani city for land acquisition purposes, helps the price of real estate surge unprecedented overnight.

17. Razzaq Dawood, Pakistan/UAE

Ranking: 14 (tied at 14) Worth: £250 m ($500 m) Industry: Businessman

Razzaq presently heads one of Pakistan's biggest construction and engineering conglomerates known as Dawood group/Descon group. With a roster of impressive clients, his group has won many contracts in Dubai, Saudi Arabia and Iraq and employs over 1,000 people directly. His name was more prominent among the top 22 richest families in 1970 until the Bhutto nationalization which then made him set up abroad. He returned to Pakistan in the early 1990s and started from scratch and today makes it to the top easily. The group also has investments of $300 m in Bangladesh in the fertilizer, energy and infrastructure and development sectors.

18. Byram Dinshawji Avari, Pakistan

Ranking: 14 (tied at 14) Worth: £250 m ($500 m) Industry: Businessman

Byram Dinshawji Avari is a prominent Pakistani Parsi tycoon in Karachi, Pakistan. Together with his sons Dinshaw and Xerxes and their direct families, he owns and operates the Avari Group of companies, of which he is the chairman. Hotel management is the Avari Group's core business. In Pakistan, the group owns and operates Avari Hotels which include 5-star deluxe hotel in Lahore, the 5-star Avari Towers and the seafront Beach Luxury Hotel in Karachi. The group is also actively pursuing opportunities for owning and/or managing 3 and 4-star properties elsewhere in Pakistan. The Avari Group is the first Pakistani company to have obtained international hotel management contracts: they operate the 200-room 4-star hotel in Dubai in United Arab Emirates and manage the 200-room Ramada Inn in Toronto at Pearson Airport in Canada.

19. Rafiq Rangoonwala, Pakistan

Ranking: 15 (tied at 14) Worth: £240 m ($480 m) Industry: Businessman

Mr. Rafiq Rangoonwala, Chief Executive Officer Cupola Group of Companies, was born in Karachi, did BA (Hons.) from the University of Karachi, went to the United States of America in 1979, and did the Executive Development Course from Whittemore School of Business, University of New Hampshire along with several management courses from the UK, US, Canada, Australia and Singapore. In 1980, he started his career in Fast Food restaurants from KFC in Houston. Since then he has managed several other brands alongside KFC like Pizza Hut, Harry Ramsden's, TGI Fridays, Pizza Express, etc. He joined Artal Restaurants International as CEO in October 1999 and is currently heading Cupola Group of Companies which has franchise rights in Pakistan for KFC, Indulge, Freshens and

Casa. The associate Investment Company of Cupola is AL ABRAJ, with approximately $400 million under management.

20. Shimmy Qureshi, USA

Ranking: 15 (tied at 15) Worth: £240 m ($480 m) Industry: Businessman

A jet-setting international businessman who flies by jet and swings a polo mallet with some of the world's top players, Qureshi seems a model of successful enterprise. Shimmy's business interests are mainly property, which with the boom and his holdings has taken his wealth to a new level. Although people may remember him for his stunt in the early 1990s with George Lindemann, the billionaire founder of Cellular One, when Lindemann took him to court claiming he cheated them into a deal to buy their home on Hurlingham Drive in Wellington for $3.5 million. A year before the Lindemanns filed their suit, Qureshi bartered with another wealthy family—the al-Thanis, who rule the Arab country of Qatar—to buy Gulf Union Bank in the Cayman Islands.

In May 1997, the al-Thanis agreed to sell Gulf Union to International Business Holdings—a Cayman Islands company owned by Qureshi—for $4.5 million, according to court records.

While Cayman Islands officials were reviewing the deal, Qureshi named an associate, Kazmi, to run Gulf Union and a subsidiary, First Cayman Bank. Within three months, Kazmi, acting on Qureshi's direction, had moved more than $5 million from First Cayman into his own account and into accounts held by Qureshi and the al-Thanis. Shimmy Qureshi also manages all the properties in the USA owned by Asif Zardari.

21. Faruque Khan, Pakistan

Ranking:15 (tied at 15) Worth: £240 m ($480 m) Industry: Businessman

The late Khan Bahadur Ghulam Faruque Khan (1899—1992) was a politician and industrialist of Pakistan. He belonged to the village Shaidu in Nowshera District. Nowshera is the home of the famous Pashtun Tribe, the Khattaks of the NWFP Province in Pakistan. Because of his contribution to Pakistan's Industrial development he is sometimes described as 'The Goliath who Industrialized Pakistan'. Today his family owns Cherat Cement Company Ltd., Cherat Papersack Ltd., Cherat Electric Ltd., Mirpurkhas Sugar Mills Ltd., Faruque (Pvt) Ltd., Greaves Air-Conditioning (Pvt) Ltd., Greaves Engineering Services (Pvt) Ltd., Unicol Ltd., A JV Company Madian Hydro Power Ltd., A JV Company Zensoft (Pvt) Ltd. and prime properties around Pakistan.

22. Shahid Luqman, UK

Ranking: 16 (tied at 16) Worth: £230 m ($460 m) Industry: Businessman

Shahid Luqman, born in Gujrat, is a financier from Manchester and has founded 'Pearl Holdings' for the property finance market. He is a prominent property developer in the UK and in Pakistan his projects run into multi-million pounds. He also runs a loan facility. Although in the past he has filed for bankruptcy, pocketing huge unpaid loans.

23. Mukhtar Ahmed, Pakistan

Ranking: 16 (tied at 16) Worth: £230 m ($460 m) Industry: Businessman

Late Haji Sheikh Mohammad Ibrahim, founder of the Ibrahim Group, settled in Faisalabad after partition of India in 1947 and re-established his ancestral business of cloth trading by the name of 'Ibrahim Agencies'. What is known in business today as the Ibrahim Group with diversified business interests from Spinning to PSF, Financial Institutions to Banking and Energy, started off as a mere cloth trading agency just half a century ago. Recently Mr Ahmed bought a stake in the Allied Bank at $300 m.

24. Aqeel Karim Dhedhi, Pakistan

Ranking: 16 (tied at 16) Worth: £230 m ($460 m) Industry: Businessman

Starting from interests in real estate and stock-brokering in the year 1947, the late Haji Abdul Karim Dhedhi laid the foundation of what today is the AKD group of companies, one of the largest domestic business enterprises in Pakistan with a combined net worth of over $1 billion, of which Mr Karim's share is at $400 m. Mr. Aqeel Karim Dhedhi, son of the (late) Haji Abdul Karim Dhedhi, is Chairman of the AKD Group. He has built the AKD Group as a leading and vibrant set of business enterprises operating in key sectors of Pakistan's economy, ranging from stocks and shares, media, textile, real estate and oil and gas exploration. Yet AKD is still on the move!

25. Syed Family, Pakistan

Ranking: 17 (tied at 17) Worth: £220 m ($440 m) Industry: Businessman

Listed on all three stock exchanges in Pakistan, Packages Limited has maintained a long-time credit rating of AA. The joint ventures and business alliances with some of the world's biggest names reflect their forward-looking strategy of continuously improving customer value through improvements in productivity. The group also acquired a good number of Coca Cola plants in Pakistan. Its famous brands include Nestle Milk Pak, Treet, Mitchells and Tri Pack Films. It has stakes in the textile, dairy, agriculture and rice sectors too. The group's contributions towards the cause of an independent Pakistan are unprecedented. They are the only packaging facility in Pakistan offering a complete range of packaging solutions including offset printed cartons, shipping containers and flexible packaging materials to individuals and businesses worldwide. They employ over 4,000 people.

26. Saif Family, Pakistan

Ranking: 17 (tied at 17) Worth: £220 m ($440) Industry: Businessman

It is owned and operated by the sons of famous NWFP lady politician Begum Kulsum Saifullah. Her eldest son Javid Saifullah heads this very powerful business group. Javid obtained his Master's degree in Business Administration from the University of Pittsburgh, USA in 1973, followed by diversified experience of over 30 years in textiles, telecommunication, cement and Information Technology. He also remained the Chairman of All Pakistan Textile Mills Association (APTMA) for two years and NWFP for seven years. He has also been a member of the Task Force on IT and of Telecommunications Advisory Board, Ministry of Science and Technology, Member of Task Force (Liberalization & Privatization of Pakistan Telecommunication Company Limited), Ministry of Science & Technology. Javid Saifullah Khan looks after the group businesses for the past 20 years. Saifullahs have been power always, in one form or the other. Javid's brothers are Anwar Saifullah Khan (former Federal Minister), Salim Saifullah Khan (king-maker in NWFP politics) and Osman Saifullah (another APTMA).

8 Dec, 2007

Source:
http://www.teeth.com.pk/blog/2007/12/08/pakistans-rich-list-of-2008

Appendix III

PPP MANIFESTO 1970 SALIENT FEATURES

Introduction

This Manifesto of the Pakistan People's Party is not of the old type of other political parties. It is a solemn pledge to the people that the Party will endeavour by all means, with or without elections, to fulfill in practice the programme contained herein.

I. THE CRISIS

Those classes who know themselves guilty of wrongs done to the nation and the reactionary political parties whose eyes are forever turned backwards, attempt now to divert attention by proclaiming themselves champions of fanciful ideologies which they ascribe to the original purpose of Pakistan.

We, on the other hand, appeal to reason, to the accumulated wealth of human knowledge, to the methods and techniques devised by human ingenuity through the centuries, to show the way out of our national misery towards life worthy of a great people. The real problems that confront the nation are political and economic, not religious, since both exploiters and exploited profess the same faith—both are Muslims.

Many governments have come and gone, but the trend towards the relative impoverishment of the people, the enrichment of privileged classes and the growth of parasitic vested interests, has proceeded unabated. All the past governments are certainly to blame for their wrong policies; but they could not act otherwise, being representatives of class and vested interests. They could not be expected to change the system, when their vocation lay in developing it for the profit of the classes on whose behalf they were in power.

Direct colonial rule left behind as its legacy a social and economic order in Pakistan which could be defined as feudal-military-bureaucratic. All the progress since has been its transformation into a dependent capitalist system typical of underdeveloped countries within the imperialist neo-colonialist power sphere.

At the end of the Second World War, the Western colonial powers proceeded, under American guidance, to adapt their methods of exploitation to new conditions. Direct rule over subject peoples was given up, but the former possessions remained bound by economic, political and military compulsion to the former rulers.

As a consequence of the misdeeds of our rulers, subservience to neo-colonialist powers, the adoption of an economic system permitting outright plunder of the people, the concentration of wealth in a few hands, the sharing of power, employment and sources of wealth between businessmen, big landlords and the classes that comprise the civil and military hierarchy of government—all these have brought the country to a crisis, another word for general ruin. It should be noted that the corruption of government and other public servants is only a symptom and not the cause of the disease; for the thread of corruption runs right through the social strata.

The ruling clique supporting the vested interests of banking industry and commerce, have nothing to offer to save the situation except the same old magical incantations of budgetary formulas and development plans. With rising prices, the working class, the lower middle class, and all sorts of employees with fixed incomes are being rapidly impoverished.

In a desperate attempt to save the capitalist system the government is permitting the wholesale expropriation of the unprivileged people of Pakistan.

The crisis is in the bones of our rotten system. The Pakistan People's Party programme will abolish the system itself, seizing the means of production which in the hands of the privileged few are the means of exploitation.

A constitution of merely democratic form will not meet the needs of this country unless it is so framed as to allow and, indeed, initiate changes in the economic and social system. It is unlikely that so long as the vested interests of capitalists and propertied classes remain unchecked anything but a constitution tailored to suit them will be the outcome.

The true solution lies in adopting a socialist programme, such as outlined in this Manifesto, to transform the economy of the whole of Pakistan, stopping exploitation and utilizing available means to develop the country without capitalist intervention.

At the Convention in December 1967 in Lahore, the Pakistan People's Party announced the principles for the practical realization for which it was founded. The ultimate objective of the Party's policy is the attainment of a classless society, which is possible only through socialism in our time.

Since its principal aims are unattainable by petty adjustments and so long as the unjust order of society prevails, the Party considers that indulgence in reformist slogans deceives the people with false hopes, while the country sinks deeper into the morass, until finally, in a situation of despair, explosive violence will take the upper hand.

II. FOREIGN POLICY

The first step must be to get out of entanglements with imperialist-neocolonialist powers.

Pakistan will support the cause of all oppressed peoples in their struggle against imperialist and neo-colonialist powers, in particular the cause of the heroic people of Vietnam who have for long years held the imperialist aggressors at bay. We shall join hands with other nations in an effort to bring about the evacuation of Asian soil occupied by the military forces of the United States and other Western colonialist powers.

III. INDUSTRIAL MEASURES

All production of wealth is the result of human labour. Exploitation in capitalist society depends on the possession of the means of production by the capitalist. In big industries the capitalist plays no nationally useful role, but collects his profit and exploits the labour of others, for his factories are run by technicians, his goods are produced by the labour of the wage-earners, and even the direction of an enterprise need not be the factory owner's.

The necessary services of education and health, housing and public amenities, are being neglected because the surplus value of production is going into the pockets of the exploiters or spent for administration and defence, and therefore little is available for the general welfare of the nation. The evil is inherent in the system. Taxation tricks, petty reforms, moral exhortation, are subterfuges to deceive the people for preserving the system intact.

(b) Nationalization of Industries

In the public sector will be all basic and key industries.

All major industries will be nationalized. This will mean taking over into the public sector textile and jute mills over a certain production capacity. In private ownership these have been the sources of excessive profits, inefficient production, wastage of resources and unhindered exploitation of workers.

In the public sector will be not only the large-scale production of electrical power but also all other sources of energy supply, namely, material, gas, oil and coal.

The public sector will completely contain the following major means of public transport, railways, shipping and airways. It will also take over public road transport, whether of passengers or goods, when it is necessary to run it on a large scale. A special concern will be the conveyance of workers and employees between their homes and their places of work.

IV. FINANCIAL MEASURES

The possession of money institutions in the hands of private parties is the source of exploitation which uses national wealth and private deposits to create money for the financing of monopoly capitalists. All big industries have been set up entirely on bank loans, which means, on the money of the depositors.

Unless the State takes hold of all the banks by making them national property, it will not be able to check inflation.

All banks and insurance companies will be forthwith nationalized.

The establishment of a socialist order will, naturally, change the present basis of taxation, which being designed for a capitalistic society favours the accretion of wealth with the privileged classes. It must be understood that taxation is merely a way of providing public finances, but the money has to come from the surplus value created in industry, agriculture and the rest of the activities that employ human labour and effort.

V. AGRARIAN MEASURES

Apart from the physical, natural side of the problems-such as aridity and flooding—property relations such as landlordism, tenancy, fragmentation, subsistence holdings,—have to be tackled.

The breaking up of the large estates to destroy the power of the feudal landowners is a national necessity that will have to be carried through by practical measures, of which a ceiling is only a part.

The Party's policy for dealing with agricultural problems was laid down in the Programmatic Principles accepted in 1967. Article 6 of the Programmatic Principles states that:

"The Party stands for elimination of feudalism and will take concrete steps in accordance with the established principles of socialism to protect and advance the interests of the peasantry."

VI. PEOPLE'S RIGHTS

Since all the important large-scale industries will be nationalized, it will be possible to offer the workers genuine participation in enjoying the fruits of industrial production. Participation of workers and technicians in factory management will be progressively introduced.

As a necessary part of their employment in factories, the workers must be provided with housing and adequate means of transportation to their places of work. They will be entitled to paid holidays, and recreation camps will be opened where they can spend their holidays in healthy surroundings. They will have the right to training facilities for improving their skills. Hospitals and free medical attention will be incorporated in the system of works welfare. The education facilities for working class children will include a system of scholarships for higher education in technical colleges and universities. Provisions will be made for old-age pensions and homes for disabled and retired workers.

Local bodies under the socialist regime will comprise urban municipalities and agglomeration, in convenient sizes of rural areas corresponding somewhat to district councils.

The present system of administration is a legacy of colonial rule, to which it was, in its time, well adapted. Even in respect of honesty the administration was found to function well when it was watched and controlled from outside. Whatever modifications have been introduced have been done to meet the needs of the rising indigenous capitalist class and to promote the interests of groups that were acquiring wealth by holding the levers of power within government and administration. The administration then became its own master. But this could happen only by forming alliance with the capitalists who were eager to obtain privileges for exploitation.

The socialist regime will need a different structure of administration, and the socialist society, when it comes into being, will itself create the necessary structure.

All citizens of Pakistan, irrespective of religious belief, race or colour, shall enjoy equal political rights, protection before the law, access to occupation of public office, and shall not be discriminated against in any manner in respect of employment.

VII. EDUCATION AND CULTURE

The basic problem of education is that younger generations have to be prepared not merely to understand the universe around them but to alter it. They must acquire a deep comprehension of the nature of social change and of inexorable process of history.

In order to create a truly classless society it is imperative that the horizons of the seekers of knowledge should encompass society as a whole. We must reject the conception fostered by the capitalist system that higher education must confine itself to narrow specialization. The capitalistic system has an interest in this sort of fragmentation of learning because it is able thereby to prevent the intellectuals from questioning the validity of the prevailing system of political and economic values.

The curricula of the university and college courses will have to be thoroughly revised and the divorce between the universities and the life of the people ended. Apart from compulsory military training, which will begin already at the secondary school stage, the student will have to spend a specified period doing national service in labour corps, in fields and towns.

Education will be free up to matriculation and primary education will be compulsory and free. A 5-year programme will be formulated by the end of which all the necessary schools must be built and the primary school teachers trained.

The imperialist, colonialist and neo-colonialist influences must be wiped out from our institutions.

The nation has been intellectually blindfolded by class interests which do not want our people to think for themselves.

VIII. NATIONAL HEALTH

The following objectives will be aimed at:

1. Increasing life expectancy in Pakistan from the present 33 to 60 years within a generation.
2. Reducing within ten years child mortality between the ages of 1 and 5 from 35 per cent to 7.5 per cent.
3. Complete eradication within ten years of microbial diseases such as TB, cholera, small-pox, typhoid, malaria, typhus, rabies, leprosy.

The health programme will include the provision and improvement of hospitals, the enforcement of measures to improve sanitation in towns and villages, the local manufacture of as many essential drugs as possible, health care of school children and, where malnutrition is present, the supply of balanced diets in the schools.

IX. NATIONAL DEFENCE

A 'People's Army' will be created in all regions of the country. This will offer the substitute for the defence in depth which is geographically lacking. The existence of a people's army is the best deterrent to foreign aggression.

X. THE CONSTITUTION

The legal framework of a constitution can guarantee no progress if it is made in the interest of the ruling classes. A constitution, even if democratic in form, will remain ineffective unless it promotes the conditions for progress and creates the institutions necessary for the purpose.

The existing electoral system is a most efficient mechanism for giving preponderance to the propertied classes in parliament. The cost of fighting an election is high which in no case can be afforded by a poor candidate unless he is supported by rich patrons with ample private means.

The electoral system will be so reformed as to give primacy to political programmes. This will be done by introducing the system of voting for party lists and not for individual candidates.

In this system it will depend upon the political party concerned how its candidates are placed in respect of priority in its list. If only rich men are at the head, or only men from a certain class, the voters will know at once what class interests that party actually represents, whatever be its published programme.

CONCLUSION

The Party proposes radical change of the social economic and political structure. The people of Pakistan will themselves bring this revolution to pass. Hence the Party says.

All Power to the People

BIBLIOGRAPHY

Marx, Karl & Engels, Frederick
The Communist Manifesto
The First Indian War of Independence
The Eighteenth Brumaire of Louis Bonaparte
Origin of Family, Private Property and State
Poverty of Philosophy
Anti-Dühring
The German Ideology
The Capital Vol. 2
Selected Works Vol. 3

Lenin, V.I.
The State and Revolution
Left wing Communism 'an infantile disorder'
Proletarian Revolution and Renegade Kautsky
Collected Works Vols. 13, 22, 26

Trotsky, Leon
Revolution Betrayed
Problems of Everyday Life
The Third International after Lenin
History of the Russian Revolution
In Defence of Marxism
Our Differences in 1905
Trotsky Writings 1939
Transitional Programme

Grant, Ted
The Unbroken Thread
Russia: From Revolution to Counter-revolution

The Iberian Revolution—Marxism and the Historical Development of the International Situation

Woods, Alan
Bolshevism: The Road to Revolution
Reformism or Revolution
Marxism and the USA
The Revolutionary Dialectic of Republicanism
Czechoslovakia (1968): Stalinism Rocked by Crisis

Khan, Lal
Partition, Can it be Undone?
Socialist Revolution and Pakistan
Kashmir's Ordeal—A Revolutionary Way Out

Jones, Philip E.
The Pakistan People's Party Rise to Power

Hasan, Mubashar, Dr.
Crises of Pakistan and Their Solution

Bhutto, Z.A.
If I am Assassinated
Speeches and Statements of Z.A. Bhutto Vol.1
Starting with a Clean Slate

Singh, Khushwant
Train to Pakistan

Ali, Tariq
Can Pakistan Survive?

Azad, Maulana Abul Kalam
India Wins Freedom

Collins, Larry and Lapierre, Dominique
Freedom at Midnight

Wolpert, Stanley
Zulfi Bhutto of Pakistan

Shaheed, Zafar
The Labour Movement in Pakistan

Khan, Field Marshal M. Ayub
Diaries of Ayub Khan 1966–72
Friends not Masters

Khan, Roedad
The British Papers 1958–69
Pakistan: A Dream Gone Sour

Lamb, Christina
Waiting for Allah

Khan, Lt. Gen. Gul Hasan
Memoirs of Lt. Gen. Gul Hasan Khan

Qureshi, Major Gen. Hakeem Arshad
The 1971 Indo-Pak War: A Soldier's Narrative

Rashid, Ahmad
Taliban: Islam, Oil and the New Great Game in Central Asia

Nawaz, Shuja
Crossed Swords, Pakistan its Army and the Wars Within

Cumming, Sir John
Political India

Damodaran, K.
Memoirs of Indian Communism; New Left Review no. 93 London

Churchill, Winston
Triumph and Tragedy

Papanek, Gustav F.
Pakistan's Development, (Harvard) 1967

Kissinger, Henry
White House Years

Musharaf, Pervez
In the Line of Fire

Archives
Dawn
Pakistan Times
Business Recorder
The Nation
Pakistan Observer, Dacca, Karachi
Morning News
Combat Karachi
Weekly Lail-o-Nihar Karachi
Nusrat
Musawat
Dehqan Lahore
Imroze Lahore
Mazdoor Morcha, Faridabad (India)
Times of India
Economist
London Times issues May 1968
Khaleej Times

Others
Dual Power in France: A Militant Leaflet
Revolutionary Rehearsal
www.marxist.com
Newsline Karachi October 2008
Letter of Iqbal to Jinnah, Lahore 1942
Human Development in South Asia 2007, Mahboob-ul-Haq Centre